ON THE OTHER HAND

Canadian Multiculturalism and Its Progressive Critics

For many, Canadian multiculturalism represents the hope that we can build a society in which people who have come from all corners of the world can fully participate without first subverting or erasing their unique identities. Many progressive critics, however, dismiss this hope as an illusion that serves to mask ongoing racism and inequality. Foregrounding the capitalist nature of the Canadian state and society, *On the Other Hand* examines the arguments of a range of progressive critics of Canadian multiculturalism.

An exercise in "critical listening," the book aims to both communicate and assess these progressive critiques. It proposes conditions for the intelligibility of social science analysis in general and reflects on the requirements for effective progressive thought and writing. Grounded in a political economy approach, the book argues that capitalism and the capitalist nature of the state must be integrated into our analysis of multiculturalism, immigration policy, and persistent racism.

On the Other Hand reveals how progressive critiques can identify real limits of multiculturalism: limits of which we must be aware if we are either to endorse them or to seek to transcend them.

PHIL RYAN is an associate professor in the School of Public Policy and Administration at Carleton University.

On the Other Hand

*Canadian Multiculturalism and
Its Progressive Critics*

PHIL RYAN

UNIVERSITY OF TORONTO PRESS
Toronto Buffalo London

© University of Toronto Press 2024
Toronto Buffalo London
utorontopress.com

ISBN 978-1-4875-5272-5 (cloth) ISBN 978-1-4875-5275-6 (EPUB)
ISBN 978-1-4875-5273-2 (paper) ISBN 978-1-4875-5277-0 (PDF)

Library and Archives Canada Cataloguing in Publication

Title: On the other hand : Canadian multiculturalism and its progressive critics / Phil Ryan.
Names: Ryan, Phil, 1957– author.
Description: Includes bibliographical references and index.
Identifiers: Canadiana (print) 20240300173 | Canadiana (ebook) 20240300254 | ISBN 9781487552725 (cloth) | ISBN 9781487552732 (paper) | ISBN 9781487552770 (PDF) | ISBN 9781487552756 (EPUB)
Subjects: LCSH: Multiculturalism – Canada. | LCSH: Progressivism (Canadian politics)
Classification: LCC FC105.M8 R935 2024 | DDC 320.56/10971 – dc23

Cover design: John Beadle

We wish to acknowledge the land on which the University of Toronto Press operates. This land is the traditional territory of the Wendat, the Anishnaabeg, the Haudenosaunee, the Métis, and the Mississaugas of the Credit First Nation.

University of Toronto Press acknowledges the financial support of the Government of Canada, the Canada Council for the Arts, and the Ontario Arts Council, an agency of the Government of Ontario, for its publishing activities.

   Canada Council   Conseil des Arts
for the Arts   du Canada

Funded by the   Financé par le
Government   gouvernement
of Canada   du Canada

Contents

Acknowledgments vii

1 Introduction 3

Part I: Setting the Stage

2 Signs of the Times: A Very Brief Overview 17
    2.1 Age of Anger? 17
    2.2 A Canadian Exception? 20
    2.3 Persistent Challenges: Racism and Discrimination in Canada 26
    2.4 Conclusion 33
3 Four Concepts 35
    3.1 The State 36
    3.2 Policy 52
    3.3 Culture 62
    3.4 Multiculturalism 71
    3.5 Summary: Concepts and the Traps of Language 74

Part II: On the Writing of the Progressive Critics

4 Some Mysterious Claims in the Writing of Progressive Critics 79
5 Other Features in the Writing of Progressive Critics 92
    5.1 The Homogenous Ethnic Majority 92
    5.2 Policy and Society 97
    5.3 Dialectical and Undialectical Analysis 98
    5.4 Alternatives? 108
    5.5 Reflections on Possible Political Effects 113

Part III: Past and Present

6 Why Multiculturalism? 119
    6.1 Multiculturalism: A "Simple Story" 120
    6.2 A Critical Progressive Story 124
    6.3 Assessing the Critical Progressive Story 129
    6.4 A White Supremacy State? 134
    6.5 Multiculturalism and the Capitalist State: An Alternative Story 151
    6.6 Just-So Stories? 161

7 Multiculturalism within a Bilingual Framework? 164
    7.1 Contemporary Arguments and Debates 165
    7.2 The B&B Commission Response, and Its Contradictions 167
    7.3 Justifications 170
    7.4 Conclusion 176

Part IV: Yes, but ...

8 On Tolerance (and Other "Gross Concepts") 179
    8.1 Critiques of Tolerance 180
    8.2 The Concept of Tolerance 183
    8.3 Response to Critiques 186
    8.4 Conclusion 193

9 Multiculturalism as Psychic Prop 195
    9.1 Introduction: Material and Ideal Interests 195
    9.2 An Assortment of Claims 197
    9.3 Us, Them, and Others 198
    9.4 Parliamentary Multiculturalism Discourse 201
    9.5 Conclusion 212

10 Of Masks, Nations, and Nationalism 214
    10.1 On Masks, and Ideology 215
    10.2 Of Nations and National Pride 217
    10.3 Concluding Thoughts 228

11 Conclusion 229
    11.1 Society and Our Attempts to Understand It 229
    11.2 On Progressive Thought and Writing 232
    11.3 Multiculturalism: Concluding Thoughts 242

Notes 245

Works Cited 271

Index 297

Acknowledgments

Yasmeen Abu-Laban, Elke Winter, and Will Kymlicka pointed me towards progressive critics of multiculturalism that I should consider for this study. My colleague Jennifer Stewart provided feedback on the brief discussion of statistical controls in chapter two. Andrew Griffith offered invaluable help in my search for information on the demographics of the public Canadian public service, and in my hunt for immigration statistics from the 1950s and 60s.

Daniel Quinlan went the extra mile in his firm support for this project, and the UTP's Press Manuscript Review Committee offered valuable editorial advice. Matthew Kudelka copyedited the work with a wonderful combination of a sharp eye and a light touch.

Carleton University's Faculty of Public Affairs supported the work with a much-appreciated Research Completion Grant.

Finally, I dedicate this book to the person without whom I could not have survived the pandemic.

To Beth
El amor de mi vida

ON THE OTHER HAND

Chapter One

Introduction

In 1914, Henry Ford's company created the Ford English School to teach its immigrant workers not just English but the whole "American way of life." In his 1922 classic, *Public Opinion*, Walter Lippmann describes a graduation ceremony for the school, held at a baseball field on 4 July 1917:

> In the center of the baseball park at second base stood a huge wooden and canvas pot. There were flights of steps up to the rim on two sides. After the audience had settled itself, and the band had played, a procession came through an opening at one side of the field. It was made up of men of all the foreign nationalities employed in the factories. They wore their native costumes, they were singing their national songs; they danced their folk dances, and carried the banners of all Europe. The master of ceremonies was the principal of the grade school dressed as Uncle Sam. He led them to the pot. He directed them up the steps to the rim, and inside. He called them out again on the other side. They came, dressed in derby hats, coats, pants, vest, stiff collar and polka-dot tie, undoubtedly, said my friend, each with an Eversharp pencil in his pocket, and all singing the Star-Spangled Banner. (Lippmann 2004, 47)

Just as Henry Ford captured the spirit of industrial Fordism with his declaration that "any customer can have a car painted any colour that he wants so long as it is black" (Ford and Crowther 1922, 72), the "cultural Fordism" manifest in the ballpark suggests that you can be any colour you want so long as you "act white" – "white" in this case being narrowly identified with the dominant Anglo-Protestant group of Ford's time. And cultural Fordism, like its industrial counterpart, could be found in many countries.

The anti-Ford vision of multiculturalism. For many of its supporters, Canadian multiculturalism was a wager that society did not have to be like this. It was a hope that we could build a society in which people who had come from all corners of the earth could fully participate without first erasing themselves, in which everyone could "act as full and equal citizens in political life, without having to hide or deny their ethnocultural identity" (Kymlicka 2007c, 65). It was a wager that we could build a society in which people don't assume you are from somewhere else just because your skin is not quite the same colour as theirs or your last name is not Smith or Gagnon (or Ryan for that matter); a society where you don't have to change your name, or ditch your turban, your yarmulka, or your hijab in order to participate on an equal basis in the workplace; a society where kids don't make fun of you in the schoolyard because your lunch is different from theirs.

And it was a wager that such a society could be vibrant and unified.

Let us call this the "anti-Ford vision" of multiculturalism. Note its two-sided nature. It's about personal integrity: not having to betray yourself, not having to deny your own history, not feeling ashamed of your parents and grandparents. It's also about making it easier for people to participate in the central aspects of Canadian life: to take part in public education, politics, the economy, without feeling that they're intruding in an alien space that belongs to someone else.

Conservative fears. For many of Canadian multiculturalism's opponents, this was a dangerous aspiration, corrosive of the unity any society needs. For Neil Bissoondath, the most influential of these critics, multiculturalism promoted an "obsessively backward gaze" (1994, 110); it would lead to "imported Old World feuds" (124) and "a slide into ethical chaos" (143). In sum, the "centre of the nation's being" would be "challenged, even effaced" by multiculturalism (45).

I analysed this style of critique at length in *Multicultiphobia* (2010b). I argued there that conservative arguments were generally ill-formulated, blamed multiculturalism for phenomena that clearly predate it, and paid little attention to actual multicultural policies, among other shortcomings.[1]

Progressive critiques. But there is also a critique of the multicultural vision very different from the one presented above. In that one, far from constituting a threat to "our civilization," multiculturalism is trivial and ineffective, or worse. The vision is not sufficiently transformative: it simply leaves too much of our unjust world untouched.

Some of the key progressive critiques of multiculturalism that are taken up in this book can be introduced in the form of questions, questions not addressed in the anti-Ford vision. It is fine to say that identity does not have to be completely erased, but how much does get erased *de facto*, and how does this come about? How closely linked, for example, is a person's identity to their mother tongue? And if that mother tongue is not one of our official languages, what supports for its survival are part of the multicultural vision? Canada has made massive investments to promote the learning of our official languages. Does the multicultural vision call for equivalent support for other languages? If not, how are they to survive? Will they generally be transmitted only within the family and through weekend classes in schools? What incentives will children have to learn the language? And what incentives will they have *not* to learn it (for those pressures are quite real as well)?

And how does the anti-Ford vision address various other painful experiences of minorities? Does greater openness to "difference" somehow overcome discrimination in the workplace? Does it improve the structural location of immigrants in the economy?

And what does the live-and-let-live "recognition" expressed in the anti-Ford vision of multiculturalism do to people's understanding of the realities around them? Could it perhaps even serve to mask power inequalities? Frantz Fanon commented that at a certain point in the national liberation struggle, the colonists will seek to "humanize" their domination, deploying various signs of "politeness and consideration" such as addressing the colonized as "Monsieur ou Madame" (1968, 88). Such "recognition," though, does not constitute liberation, it is a prophylactic against it. Is this the case for multicultural "recognition" as well?

And how might the anti-Ford vision affect the privileged elites' understanding of reality? Might it allow them to give themselves a psychic pat on the back, imagining that the full requirements of justice have been met and that they need trouble themselves no further? Or maybe the whole contrast between multiculturalism and the *American* melting pot is just more fuel for Canadian smugness, akin to the sense of superiority we gain from observing America's gun carnage.[2]

Problematic but necessary terminology. For convenience, I will label the first type of critique "conservative" and the second type "progressive." The labels, and the sharp distinction between the two approaches, are both problematic. There are, first, important overlaps between the two styles of critique. Various progressive critics share the view of their conservative counterparts that multiculturalism somehow "freezes" the identity of members of minority groups. Both types of critic can thus err in attributing extraordinary power to the policy (see chapter 4).

There is also an interesting relationship between the sources of information tapped by the two approaches. Most of us learn about policies from the media, not from official statements or policy evaluations. Naturally, over time, many people's understanding of multiculturalism was shaped not by the policy itself but by op-ed columnists and talk-radio hosts who opposed it. As a result, opposition to multiculturalism often took aim at something merely imagined. Some progressive critics were likely influenced by the media's reproduction of conservative critiques. (There are important differences among the progressives in this respect. Some have done careful documentary research. Others have engaged in fieldwork, seeking to uncover everyday understandings of ethnic relations in Canada. In some cases, however, it is extremely difficult to identify the sources of evidence that shape the critic's understanding of multiculturalism.)

Further, there are political ambiguities in the views of some of the critics that make the "progressive" label an uneasy fit. Consider, for example, Richard Day's statement of the Canada for which he longs: "Instead of being wielded as a tool to build a pre-designed nation, the Canadian state's role would be to create a space of free play. It would be seen, not as the guardian of a perfect yet fragile order, but as providing a minimal field of structure out of which almost anything might emerge" (2000, 225). Day's "minimal field of structure" sounds very much like the "night watchman state," the state that guards lives and property and lets the market operate without hindrance. Similarly, some of the progressives' critiques of the "limits" of tolerance (see chapter 8) suggest a vision of the ideal society that a neoliberal might endorse.

Still, however muddled the terms "progressive" and "conservative" are in contemporary discourse, they play a dominant role in ordering our political reality. In this book, I will work with a fuzzy distinction: I will view as fundamentally conservative those critiques motivated above all by a concern for social order and unity. Progressive critiques, on the other hand, I will view as driven fundamentally by equality concerns. To distinguish the progressive critic from, for example, the person who opposes affirmative action, ostensibly in the name of equality, we could add that the progressive critic does not mobilize equality discourse on behalf of historically privileged groups.[3]

This working understanding of "conservative" and "progressive" is reasonable, given current usage. But if we turn away from that usage for a moment, and think about the roots of the word "conservative," we note that such a political outlook should be concerned with *conserving* something. It will be a key contention of this work that progressives need to understand themselves as *conservative* in that sense and identify publicly the human goods they are fighting to conserve. Environmentalists demanding that we address climate change, for example, are conservative in this sense, while the irresponsible "conservative" politician who thinks we must cleave as closely as possible to the status quo in environmental and economic matters is in fact prolonging a mad and suicidal experiment.[4]

This apparent paradox, of the conservative dimension of progressivism, was explicitly identified by Marx. At the heart of his philosophy of history was the view that a society's fundamental "relations of production" (e.g., lord-serf or the wage relationships) could for a time foster the development of humanity's productive powers. But the very development of those powers would eventually turn the relations of production into "fetters" (Marx and Engels, rpt. 1969, vol. 1, 504). At that point, "as the main thing is not to be deprived of the fruits of civilization, of the acquired productive forces, the traditional forms in which they were produced must be smashed. From this moment, *the revolutionary class becomes conservative*" (Marx rpt. 1977, 117; emphasis added).

So conservatives and progressives are not divided by the fact that one camp wants change while the other wants stability. They are instead divided by questions like: What is most important for society? What must give way to preserve that which is most important? "Conservatism" in current-day electoral politics typically involves a narrow defence of property and privilege, the defence of what some have against others. As the Marx quote suggests, in the progressive vision what must be conserved is something valuable that should belong to all: a shared accomplishment that must become a shared legacy.

My personal sense – which I fervently hope is mistaken – is that, given the unprecedented severity of the climate crisis that is already upon us and that will get much worse, and given the evident unwillingness of political leaders around the world to treat that crisis with the seriousness required, we progressives will find ourselves playing defence much more than we would like in the coming decades. A central struggle will be to prevent the impact of the climate calamity from falling most heavily on those who are already on the losing end of the global and domestic distributions of power and wealth – and who happen to be the least responsible for the catastrophe. Because it will require a profound transformation of economic structures, this "conservative" goal is paradoxically revolutionary, which underscores the wisdom of Walter Benjamin when he commented: "Perhaps revolutions are an attempt by the passengers on this train [of history] – namely, the human race – to activate the emergency brake" (rpt. 2006, 402).

Goals of this book. In *Multicultiphobia*, I touched on the progressive family of critiques only in passing. My justification was that "because I am tracing a debate over time, I will not take up other strands of critique that are interesting in themselves, but have exercised little influence in Parliament or the media" (2010b, 24).[5] I added, however, that "to say that such critiques have had little influence in Parliament or the media is certainly no comment on their quality. When it comes to influencing public debates, the race is not to the swift" (24). If one ignores progressive critiques, then whatever conversations society has about multiculturalism are dominated by conservative critiques and responses to them. This is too one-sided. Progressive critiques can identify real limits of multiculturalism, limits of which we need to be aware, *either* to endorse them *or* to seek to transcend them.[6]

This book, then, is an exercise in *critical listening* to a family of critiques of multiculturalism. *Critical*, because the fact that a critique may be progressive does not entail that it is flawless or even valid. *Listening*, because this book is not motivated by a desire to defend multiculturalism or to rebut its critics, but by a desire to deepen understanding of our multiculturalism and our society.

The third and fourth parts of this book will examine a number of important issues raised by progressive critics. Prior to that, however, comes a "critique of the critique," focusing on general concerns with the thought of some of the progressive critics. Thus, one aspect of the book's critical listening, to be presented in chapter 4, is an examination of the linguistic *opacity* of some progressive critiques. We find claims among some of the critics that involve mysterious actors, endowed with mysterious powers, doing mysterious things to produce mysterious effects. My working assumption is that such opaque writing is a symptom of muddled thought, because thought and expression are intimately related: except when trying to express ourselves in another language, we do not *first* have clear thoughts and *then* struggle to express them clearly. Clear thoughts emerge in the very process of trying to write or speak clearly. As Kant put it: "How much and how accurately would we *think* if we did not think, so to speak, in community with others to whom we *communicate* our thoughts and who communicate their thoughts to us!" (rpt. 1991, 247).

A second fruit of the exercise is the identification of problematic tacit assumptions among some of the progressive critics, assumptions regarding the nature of the state, social reality, the extent to which any policy can transform society, and so on. The book will thus issue a challenge to a subset of the progressive critics, urging them to articulate their critiques of Canadian multiculturalism and society in a form that is clear as well as free of untenable assumptions. A broader challenge is also implied, since both the type of obscurity and the problematic assumptions I will critique are features of much current-day social science and "cultural left" thought. A number of critical observations developed in this work could also be levelled, for example, at *White*

Fragility, Robin DiAngelo's influential bestseller. That book suffers from continual recourse to shadowy collective phenomena such as the "white mind" (2018, 76) and "the collective white consciousness" (91), a one-dimensional understanding of culture, and a resolutely anti-intersectional analytical style.

The spirit that motivates this work. I foresee a predictable misinterpretation of this work. Sociologist Pierre Bourdieu commented that, because approaches are often understood in binary terms, his questioning of objectivism was fated to be read as an attempt to revive subjectivism (rpt. 2000, 225). He was not the first author to lament a misinterpretation of their work provoked by a binary outlook: Max Weber, for example, complained that his *Protestant Ethic* had suffered the same fate (rpt. 2003, 183).

In the same way, some readers concluded from *Multicultiphobia*'s critique of the conservative opponents of multiculturalism that the work must constitute a blanket defence of the phenomenon, little more than an outburst of "moral indignation at those who find fault with this great national tradition" (Frost 2011, 255).[7] But as the book's introduction noted, "I do not view all criticism of multiculturalism as multicultiphobic, and my aim is not to dismiss even those writings that are. They often put their finger on issues about which Canadians need to talk. To talk about them, though, we need to abstain from the rhetorical inflation that has plagued our discussions of diversity issues" (Ryan 2010b, 25). Why abstain? Because

> There is a sort of Gresham's Law that operates in society: bad debates drive out good ones, weak critiques eclipse strong ones. Think, for example, of all the questions that are obscured by the assertion that "they" must embrace "our" values. Or think of the range of complex social phenomena that vanish from awareness when someone claims that because of multiculturalism, immigrants are choosing to live in "ethnic ghettos." This Gresham's Law of debates is no small matter. At its best, a society steers itself over time through open debates. Bad debates gum up the steering mechanism, allowing society to drift, and decisions to be subject to unacknowledged influences or uninformed knee-jerk reactions. (Ryan 2014b, 89)

I mention this previous misunderstanding because this current book may be misread in much the same way. The critical lens turned on certain progressive critiques of multiculturalism may spark the suspicion that this is a fundamentally "anti-progressive" defence of multiculturalism.[8] To clarify where I'm coming from, then: I am a socialist who is also a supporter of many of the efforts of what is often called the "cultural left": I believe that feminism, the struggle for the rights of sexual minorities, and anti-racism, like socialism, all represent, at their best, struggles for human equality and dignity. I also believe, however, that much progressive discourse today is unlikely to reach a *fruitful* target audience.

What do I mean by that? Think, first, of two extremes. The first consists of "the choir" (as in "preaching to the choir"): people who are already in agreement with one's basic position. Writing for such readers can at times be useful: to clarify details in one's shared position; to discuss political strategy; and to strengthen one another's resolve. A work might also provide the already convinced with resources to use in their discussions with people who are unlikely to read the work on their own. (This is more likely if the work is written with that potential use in mind.) Even in an ideologically polarized society, many people interact with others – family members, co-workers, fellow students, neighbours, and so on – who do not share their political commitments. At the other extreme from the "choir" are people who simply *will not* listen. They are in the grip of an exceedingly narrow type of self-interest, with no desire to think about the needs of society as a whole, nor about society's future, and certainly with no willingness to entertain appeals to justice that do not support their narrow self-interest.

The "fruitful" audience is found between those extremes. They are willing to think honestly about the social interest, and about the needs of future generations, and they have *some* openness to questions of political right and wrong, even on "inconvenient" questions. The fruitful target audience then, does not fully accept the positions for which one is advocating, but it might be persuaded to do so. Reaching that audience supports the political task of expanding the range of citizens who accept that we must act on a certain matter. For progressives, reaching the fruitful audience will be impeded by factors such as media bias.[9] But problems internal to some progressive discourse itself also play a role.

Besides not reaching a fruitful audience, some progressive discourse may actually be counterproductive. It may, for example, occlude opportunities for action, levers for change. Indeed, some of the most uncompromisingly "radical" discourse on multiculturalism may induce political paralysis. Discourse can also be counterproductive if it endorses norms that are simply not equality-enhancing, however progressive they may sound at first blush.

My arguments on these points may at times strike some readers as harsh. But how can progressive analysis progress if its claims are not subject to careful scrutiny? That applies to the claims I am making here as well. This book is not meant to be the last word on anything: it is just one more contribution to an ongoing conversation concerning what Canada and multiculturalism are and where they should be headed. I offer many claims in the book, and claims can be challenged.

I believe, in particular, that fruitful challenges might be levelled against certain inferences on which I rely. This book argues that claims to the effect that multiculturalism sought to preserve racial hierarchy presuppose something like a "white supremacy state," akin to the capitalist state discussed in chapter 3; and that many claims concerning the outlook of the ethnic majority presuppose a one-dimensional view of culture, also discussed in chapter 3. But it is logically impossible to assert that these inferences are *necessarily* correct, because that would be equivalent to saying, "There is *no other way* the critics' claims could have come about." To which an obvious reply is, "Prove it!" So in relying on certain inferences, I am simply saying that I cannot see another plausible basis for the claims in question. A critic might legitimately focus their attack right here, and I believe the resulting debate could be quite fruitful.

As to the "white supremacy state," I argue in chapter 6 that the case for its existence is much weaker than the corresponding case for the capitalist state. Thus, I believe it more plausible to hold that multiculturalism arose at least in part as a policy to promote Canadian capitalism, than to believe that it was a ploy to sustain racial hierarchy. One possible line of attack against this argument would be to develop a particularly sweeping version of the racial capitalism thesis, and argue that a state committed to preserving capitalism is *necessarily* committed to preserving white supremacy. I believe it would be very difficult to build a solid case to that effect, but if you think you can do it, I hope you will. And I hope to respond to it as best I can.

Plan of the work. This book has three goals. As noted earlier, it is an exercise in "critical listening" to progressive critiques of multiculturalism. The complexity of the issues raised by those critiques also makes them a perfect vehicle for the book's two other goals: to propose conditions for the intelligibility of social science analysis in general, and to reflect on the requirements for effective progressive thought and writing.

Part I prepares the ground for the rest of the book. Since progressives, as argued earlier, need to both work for a more just society and defend aspects of society from attack, they need a clear sense of current injustices, of the social goods that are under threat, and of the nature of those threats. Chapter 2 tries to contribute to that understanding of our reality through a brief reading of the "signs of the times." The chapter notes the widespread view that Canadians have accomplished something useful – a more relaxed view of national identity and of demographic change – but argues that this is fragile and threatened both by current-day political currents such as pseudo-populist xenophobia and by broader factors such as the global political economy and climate change. It also argues that whatever Canadians may have accomplished is woefully incomplete: Canada remains a country marked by ongoing racism and colour-coded inequality, and we must feel this *viscerally* if we are to even begin to understand the sharpest progressive critiques of multiculturalism.

Chapter 3 shifts from political to conceptual groundwork, analysing four concepts that play a major role in multiculturalism debates: state, policy, culture, and multiculturalism itself. These share an important quality: they are abstract nouns designating complex realities but are regularly used in ways that obscure that complexity. The chapter was written after chapters 4 and 5 had been drafted and with an eye to a core debate examined in chapter 6. Each of the clarifications presented in the chapter, then, is relevant to issues arising from progressive critiques of multiculturalism. The chapter should thus operate like a "time-release" medication, in that the force of certain points will become clearer in subsequent chapters.

I hope, incidentally, that the chapter will contradict its first epigraph, by showing that a clarification of concepts need not suffer from apparent "remoteness from reality." Nothing is more important than understanding the reality in which we are immersed, and solid concepts are essential tools for that understanding. I hope to demonstrate this, not through an abstract theoretical treatise "On the State," for example, but through a lively encounter with specific thinkers, drawing on current events and historical examples.

Part II addresses theoretically and politically problematic features of the writing of various progressive critics. As previously noted, chapter 4 considers "mysterious" aspects of their writing. But why? Does the chapter reflect an obsession with questions of mere style? To the contrary: my concern is not with literary elegance, but with more serious matters. A first problem is that the truth-value of many progressive claims can't be assessed with any degree of confidence. This is not a trivial matter. If we reject the view that insight is the fruit of the isolated genius, then we should recognize that thought advances through an iterative process of claims-making, challenge to claims, leading to dismissal of the challenge, or of the claim, or to a better formulation of the claim, and so on. Mysterious claims block that dynamic from the start. Apart from that, a key political cost of mystery writing is that causes of social phenomena are not identified with any precision. The "mysterious power" claims we will examine in chapter 4, for example, fail to uncover precise mechanisms of subjection and thus also fail to identify resources for resistance.

Chapter 5 examines some key assumptions of various works, assumptions that are not mysterious but are nevertheless problematic. Some critics, for example, assert or imply the existence of a homogenous ethnic majority. In such accounts, little distinguishes supporters and opponents of multiculturalism: both look down on racialized Canadians, viewing themselves as "masters of national space" (Thobani 2007, 154). In addition, while many critics view multiculturalism as a blend of positive and problematic features, others treat it as simply repressive. The chapter examines various implications of the latter position.

Part III concerns the history of Canadian multiculturalism and the implications of that history for today. Chapter 6 asks why the Trudeau Sr. government introduced the policy in 1971. Three stories will be told: a simple, surface-level, narrative; an account favoured by various progressive critics, in which multiculturalism was a response to political pressures "from below," a response that may have sought to sustain racial hierarchy; and a story linking the emergence of multiculturalism to the capitalist nature of the state. Consideration of the second story will lead to a discussion of whether it can plausibly be held that we have a "white supremacy state" in Canada.

Chapter 7 considers that curious hybrid, "multiculturalism within a bilingual framework." The chapter will draw on Eve Haque's account of the Bilingualism and Biculturalism Commission's strained effort to justify a linguistic hierarchy that treated language as a core element of culture for some Canadians but not for others. Was the chosen policy of coast-to-coast bilingualism a fundamental injustice? A necessity dictated by *realpolitik*? Or, perhaps, both?

Part IV gives extended treatment to some key claims of the progressive critics. I call this part "Yes, But ..." to indicate that I seek not to *rebut* these claims but to encourage us to think twice about them, and to strive for some nuance. Chapter 8 considers tolerance. *Yes*, it can be inadequate, unjust, even contemptuous. *But* it is not necessarily so. Even a limited gritted-teeth tolerance can be a bridge to full acceptance. Debates around tolerance are of broader interest for two reasons. They foreground the problem of limits, which greatly trouble some of the progressive critics. And they demonstrate the baleful influence in multiculturalism debates of "gross concepts," notions that are so inadequately specified that one cannot responsibly declare oneself "for" or "against" them without further detail. Tolerance is one such concept, "diversity" and "difference" are two others.

Chapter 9 examines the argument that multiculturalism provides many Canadians with a "psychic prop" and bolsters pride in Canada. Through an analysis of parliamentary multiculturalism discourse during Justin Trudeau's first mandate, we will find that, *yes*, multiculturalism does do this, and that it does mask injustice. *But* we will also find that it is invoked to support calls for justice.

Chapter 10 takes up two important questions suggested by the findings of the previous chapter. First, how should multiculturalism's capacity to mask injustice affect progressives' assessment of it? To answer this, I will argue, we must recognize the ubiquitous and versatile nature of ideology: were multiculturalism to vanish tomorrow, Canadians would not be faced with the "naked" reality of indisputable injustice. Rather, new and existing ideologies would fill the void, masking and justifying social conditions. The second question concerns "national pride." We know that invocations of multiculturalism can bolster this: how should progressives assess that fact, and how should they view national pride in general? I will argue that such pride can be toxic but that it can also take progressive forms, and that it is the task of progressives to figure out just what those forms are, and to promote them, in order both to challenge the influence of more toxic forms and to create emotional support for the effort to create a more just society.

The conclusion, finally, offers some thoughts on three themes related to the book's three goals: the practice of social science, the qualities of progressive thought and writing, and the nature of a just multiculturalism.

That, in brief, is what's in the book. Much is omitted. I had originally envisaged chapters on various other issues, such as "neoliberal" multiculturalism and "illiberal" multiculturalism. As the manuscript grew lengthier, things fell by the wayside. One important omission, however, was planned. While the book touches on relations with Indigenous Canadians at various points, it does not discuss the issue systematically. There are two reasons for this. Unlike in many other countries, multiculturalism policy in Canada emerged in careful isolation from such issues. The weightier reason is personal: while I recognize that many questions can be raised about the impact of multiculturalism on Indigenous relations, I do not think that I am in a position to discuss those issues competently at this time. I take it as given, however, that a justice-pursuing multiculturalism must be compatible with the achievement of justice for Indigenous Canadians, and that this is no simple matter.[10]

PART I

Setting the Stage

Chapter Two

Signs of the Times: A Very Brief Overview

The appeal of demagogues lies in their ability to take a generalized discontent, the mood of drift, resentment, disillusionment and economic shakiness, and transform it into a plan for *doing* something.

Pankaj Mishra, *Age of Anger* (2017)

I argued in the introduction that progressives need to be able to identify just what they are trying to *conserve*: the progressive environmentalist provides the clearest example of this. Conservation requires a reading of our time, to understand just what goods are under threat, and from which direction, and what resources might exist to defend them. Here, I will present three broad sets of important phenomena:

- A globalized "age of anger," manifest in the increasing political success of democratic authoritarians and xenophobic "populism";
- A Canadian exception – real or apparent – to this global political trend; and
- Persistent problems, such as "colour-coded poverty" and ongoing discrimination, that call into question the seriousness and very purpose of Canadian multiculturalism.

2.1 Age of Anger?

"Something is rotten in the state of democracy," wrote Pankaj Mishra (2016) shortly after America's 2016 election shock. The global picture has sparked repeated comparisons with the 1930s, when there was a widespread sense that democracy was vanishing from the planet. Today, we are seeing developments that are different, yet worrisome: in many countries, democracy survives as a *form*, at least for the time being, but serves as a vehicle for various types of authoritarianism. Elected authoritarians are making a sustained effort to weaken the constraints on power that are constitutive of democracy. We see this in the long-established democracy to the south of us, in some of the most populous democracies of the global South, and in some countries that adopted democracy after the collapse of the Soviet Union. As of spring 2020, the best-known examples of the phenomenon included Trump, Putin, Bolsonaro, Modi, Orbán, Duterte, Erdoğan, and Netanyahu.[1] Authoritarian parties represent a powerful electoral force in various other countries: the far-right Sweden Democrats, for example, won the second highest vote count in Sweden's September 2022 election.

Apart from their efforts to weaken democracy, the authoritarians are united by a strategy of demonizing some minority group(s). "Tolerance has undergone core meltdown," as one writer puts it (Merrifield 2020). Their targets are often religious or ethnic minorities, and non-white immigrants in particular. Sexual minorities are also targeted in some cases.[2]

The elected authoritarians also have murky links to even further-right political actors, including right-wing terrorists. At times, these relations involve two degrees of separation. Trump's sense of reality was strongly shaped by an intensive diet of Fox News. Various commentators on that network insist that America is suffering an "invasion" from the south, part of a "great replacement" promoted in part by the Democratic Party. This concept was prominent in the manifestos of the El Paso and Christchurch murderers (Peters et al. 2019).

At other times, the links seem more immediate. On 16 June 2016, UK Brexit leader Nigel Farage unveiled a poster for the Leave campaign: "BREAKING POINT, it screamed above a queue of dusky-hued refugees waiting to cross a border. The message was not very subtle: Vote Leave, Britain, or be over-run by brown people" (Massie 2016). That same afternoon, Jo Cox, a Labour MP active in support of Syrian refugees, was murdered by a far-right extremist. That Cox's murderer is said to have shouted "Britain First!" at the time of his act did not dissuade Trump from retweeting various Islamophobic videos produced by the far-right Britain First group (Parker and Wagner 2017). Nor could he bring himself to condemn the Charlottesville neo-Nazis, many of whom he considered "good people" (Dubenko 2017).

While the exact roster of countries in the hands of elected authoritarians is subject to change, there are two reasons for believing that a xenophobic "age of anger" (Mishra 2017) is not a transient phenomenon.

The first starts with the increasing awareness that our current form of globalization has not protected the interests of the working and middle classes in the developed world. Political elites have shown little commitment to reducing the economic vulnerability of those broad sectors. This may be because of their own entanglements with oligarchic interests, and/or because their states, through international agreements, have set aside many of the economic tools they once wielded: the European economic union is an extreme case of this. This has left the door open for various forms of political manipulation. Donald Trump certainly benefited from appearing to care about Americans' economic insecurity.[3] Among other consequences, the inattention or unconcern of political elites has created space for demagogues to advance xenophobic and misleading diagnoses of citizens' problems. Thus, Orbán claims to be defending Hungary from invasion –"If the dam breaks, the flood will be here, and the cultural invasion will be irreversible" (qtd. in Léotard and Lepeltier-Kutasi 2018) – and warns that "without Christian culture, there will be no freedom in Europe" (Kingsley 2019). But Hungary's true demographic challenge is reflected in the fact that, since Orbán took power in 2010, half a million citizens have emigrated (Müller 2018), continuing a long-standing pattern of demographic decline that characterizes much of post-Soviet Europe: the combined population of "Central Europe and the Baltics" declined by 7 per cent between 1988 and 2018 (World Bank 2019b).

And this brings us to a second factor likely to prolong the political life of xenophobic "populist" movements and parties: demographic patterns. We should expect intensifying efforts by citizens of the global South to gain access to the developed market economies. The UN Population Division's "medium fertility variant" projections show the population of the "more developed regions" declining by 20 per cent between 2015 and 2100 and that of the "less developed regions" increasing by 166 per cent. A subset of that group – the "least developed countries" – is projected to have population growth of ... 880 per cent (2015). We may add to this picture the disruptive effects of climate change, which will most severely hurt the global South, potentially generating "hundreds of millions of new climate refugees" (Wallace-Wells 2019, 60–1). These factors would seem to make a vast global northward flow of people both rational and inevitable. The political consequences of this are *not* inevitable: vigorous political action to make globalization less harmful to the interests of workers in the developed world, for example, might well mitigate the reaction against migrants. But unfortunately, it is reasonable to assume that xenophobic "populism" will continue to enjoy favourable "objective conditions."

2.2 A Canadian Exception?

A mid-2017 *New York Times* article portrayed Canada as a striking exception to xenophobic political trends: "As right-wing populism has roiled elections and upended politics across the West, there is one country where populists have largely failed to break through: Canada. The raw ingredients are present. A white ethnic majority that is losing its demographic dominance. A sharp rise in immigration that is changing culture and communities. News media and political personalities who bet big on white backlash." Despite all that, "not only have the politics of white backlash failed, but immigration and racial diversity are sources of national pride" (Taub 2017).

That Canada is being noticed is partly due to conjunctural factors, in particular the extreme contrast between the comprehensive nastiness of the American leader and the personal style of that grandmaster of the symbolic gesture, Justin Trudeau. Acts such as his personal airport welcome of the first Syrian refugees, and his taking a knee at the June 2020 protest on Parliament Hill, make news around the world. But observers insist that the Canadian difference is not merely transient: "Identity works differently in Canada. Both whites and nonwhites see Canadian identity as something that not only can accommodate outsiders, but is enhanced by the inclusion of many different kinds of people ... Identity rarely works this way. Around the world, people tend to identify with their race, religion or at least language" (Taub 2017). Indeed, Elke Winter's *Us, Them, and Others* focuses on understanding Canada's "multiculturalization of national identity," which has involved "the emergence of an understanding that multiculturalism is not just about 'them' and their rights, but also what defines 'us'" (2011, 39, 195).

Nor is Canadians' general comfort with large-scale immigration from a wide range of source countries merely conjunctural. "Although Canada's high immigration rates have transformed the country in just a few decades," comments Taub, "the public has mostly been calm and accepting" (2017). Pollsters concur: public opinion surveys "show that, almost without exception, in recent decades a majority of the Canadian population has either supported immigration levels or wanted them increased. In most other countries the reverse is true: there is less immigration, and a majority still wants reductions" (Reitz 2011, 3). Indeed, Environics reported in late 2022 that pro-immigration opinion was at its highest level ever recorded (2022).

Further evidence of Canada's unusual landscape is provided by attitudes towards multiculturalism. Real and imagined multiculturalism policies have been a constant target of xenophobic political discourse around the world. And indeed they were long the target of conservative attacks in Canada. But those attacks subsided, and a broad pro-multiculturalism consensus emerged.

Five chapters of *Multicultiphobia* examined conservative critiques of multiculturalism in Parliament and selected news media. Those would be short chapters today. I analysed all mentions of multiculturalism in the House of Commons *Debates* during Justin Trudeau's first government (2015–19). During that period, the only attacks on multiculturalism came from the Bloc Québécois. (Further analysis of multicultural discourse in Parliament is presented in chapter 9.) Even when right-wing politician Maxime Bernier broke with the Conservatives, he at first limited his attacks to a vague beast called "extreme multiculturalism." His party eventually called for an end to multiculturalism ... and failed to win a seat in the fall 2019 election.

As for the media: of the newspapers analysed for *Multicultiphobia*, the *Calgary Sun* and the *National Post* were the two most hostile to multiculturalism. My tally of news articles with substantial treatment of the issue (as opposed to passing mentions), weighted by size, found that in 2006, *Calgary Sun* coverage was 9.1 per cent positive, and 84.1 per cent negative. For the *National Post*, the corresponding figures were 9.8 per cent and 78.3 per cent. Returning to those two sources for the half-year from December 2019 to May 2020, I found *no* substantive coverage of multiculturalism in the *Calgary Sun*. While this hardly points to a love affair with the policy, it does suggest that this generally conservative medium is no longer very concerned about it.

The *National Post*'s coverage is more intriguing. Advocates of multiculturalism are more visible, and the policy is linked to broadly shared values. One article, for example, reports that Italy's Serie A soccer league is using artwork to "spread the values of integration, multiculturalism, and brotherhood" (17 December 2019). Even some of the (no longer very frequent) criticism of multiculturalism in the paper could increase many readers' appreciation of it. Thus, the paper reports that Quebec has abolished the mandatory Ethics and Religious Culture program, which was apparently guilty of "contaminating a generation of young people by making them amenable to Canadian multiculturalism and other pluralist ideas." The evidence? The courses – horror of horrors – have made young Quebeckers more tolerant than their elders. In this regard, the paper cites omnipresent Québécois pundit Jean-François Lisée as arguing that "it's difficult not to see a cause-and-effect connection" in the fact that young Quebecers who have taken the course "are the least favourable to prohibiting religious signs" (9 March 2020).

Outside of Quebec, then, there is little sign of the fervent conservative opposition to multiculturalism that marked much recent history.

I have examined three elements of the "Canadian exception": a "multiculturalization of national identity" (Winter 2011), high levels of comfort with immigration, and a broad consensus of support for multiculturalism, or at least resigned acceptance of it. I will now nuance this picture before turning, in the chapter's third section, to the more fundamental challenges of persistent inequality and discrimination.

Cautions and nuances. We need some qualifiers to the benign picture of Canadian exceptionalism, as well as some cautions to remind us that the exception is not carved in stone. First, to nuance the picture of Canadian attitudes, some realism concerning Canadian immigration. In being generally open to immigration, Canadians are in practice accepting of something rather *closed* by international standards – not in quantitative terms, but in other ways. In 2005, France's interior minister – and future president – Nicolas Sarkozy declared that France needed to move from "a suffered immigration to a chosen immigration" (qtd. in Fassin 2009). Well, this is to a large extent precisely what Canada enjoys, for various reasons.

Geography is one key factor. Unlike Canada, "most Western countries are in geographic proximity to poor and/or unstable countries that are capable of producing large numbers of unwanted migrants seeking to enter the country either by land or sea" (Kymlicka 2007a, 75). But more than geography is at work. Vic Satzewich notes that, much like citizens elsewhere in the developed world, Canadians have reacted with fear and concern when faced with "the unannounced arrival of boatloads of migrants on its borders seeking asylum" (2018, 36). Both the Harper and Justin Trudeau governments have gone to great lengths to prevent such events. A Harvard study noted that "Canada positions Liaison Officers in strategic offshore locations and tasks them with blocking and intercepting improperly documented persons, including asylum seekers, before they board Canada-bound boats or planes" (Arbel and Brenner 2013, 4). The study accused Canada of "systematically closing its borders to asylum seekers and avoiding its refugee protection obligations under domestic and international law" (1). It is alleged that Canadian deterrence efforts have even included working with foreign officials who stand accused of crimes against humanity (Bureau and Robillard 2019).[4]

Three decades ago, I wrote that "successive Canadian governments have sought to submit the compassion of the Canadian people to the dictates of political and economic expediency. Bring in refugees, indeed many refugees, but be careful about it. Bear in mind Canada's 'geopolitical' commitments and alliances. Select those who can most contribute to the Canadian economy. The degree of turmoil in the world generates a large enough pool of candidates for refugee status that one can afford to be quite choosy, all the while maintaining a reputation for one's 'humanitarian tradition'" (Ryan 1988). Under the Harper government in particular, the principle applied for filtering refugees no longer reflected "geopolitical commitments and alliances" alone, but something even more disturbing. As Amira Elghawaby and Bernie Farber noted in the dying days of the Harper reign, "the Canadian government has explicitly stated its intent to grant refuge to religious minorities fleeing Syria, contrary to international norms that assess refugees primarily on the basis of need" (2015).[5]

So Canadians' "exceptional" openness to immigration may depend at least in part on ethically questionable government efforts to admit only "desirable" refugees, along with immigrants selected under the points system in force since 1967. Further, the ethics of the points system itself are open to challenge. Indeed, observers and activists raised important concerns about a skills-based immigration policy even before the points system was implemented. In his classic work from 1965, *The Vertical Mosaic*, John Porter observed that "when emigration of middle and higher level occupational groups is considerable it can strain the educational resources of the society which is losing its trained people. Under-developed countries are placed in this position when advanced societies accept from them only skilled immigrants" (1965, 43). And Kelley and Trebilcock note that groups such as the Canadian Welfare Council and the Canadian Labour Congress "called on the government to admit unskilled immigrants and to train them in Canada" (2000, 356).

One important phenomenon compensates somewhat for the practice of skimming high-skilled people from poorer countries: many immigrants send remittances to family members in their countries-of origin. The World Bank estimates that such remittances exceeded half a trillion dollars in 2019, and noted that they "have exceeded official aid – by a factor of three – since the mid-1990s" (2019a). Still, it can be argued that, to the extent that skilled workers have been trained at public expense, while remittances are sent to private families, some form of compensation is owed to the governments of low income countries.

The fact that Canada has long benefited from immigration that is "chosen," not "suffered," to use Sarkozy's terms, gives credence to Vic Satzewich's contention that "Canada's positive attitude towards immigrants and refugees is, at least in part, contingent on the perception that the state remains in control of the border" (2018, 35). And so it was not surprising that the Conservatives sniffed a political opening when asylum seekers leaving Trump's America began entering Canada at various irregular crossings. Party leader Andrew Scheer often spoke of a "crisis" of asylum seekers, and during the 2019 election campaign he promised a sharp shift in policy. The Conservatives lost the election, but their rhetoric points to some partisan polarization, not just on the asylum question, but on immigration in general. Most ominously, an enormous public opinion gap has opened between Conservatives and Liberals on the question whether "too many immigrants are visible minorities" – 69 per cent of Conservatives agree, and 15 per cent of Liberals (Steele 2019).

Another caution is well illustrated by aspects of the previous one: no country is fully insulated from the world. Not just asylum seekers, but political ideas, fears, and rhetoric, also cross borders. Two years after Nigel Farage's unveiling of a xenophobic Brexit poster was followed within hours by the murder of MP Jo Cox, Canadian Conservatives opted for a similar tactic, posting an image of a Black man carrying a suitcase approaching the border, superimposed on a tweet from Justin Trudeau (Canadian Press 2018). A tragic example of the influence of border-crossing political rhetoric is the fact that the Quebec City mosque terrorist was reported by friends to have "devoured so-called alt-right media from the United States" (Hamilton and Bell 2017). Cross-border influences were repeatedly evident in anti-public-health protests during the pandemic. Protesters targeted Alberta's chief medical officer with chants of "lock her up." QAnon symbols were on display in Quebec protests and during the 2022 Ottawa occupation. Abacus Data, finally, reported in 2022 that 37 per cent of Canadians believe in the great replacement conspiracy, agreeing with the statement that "there is a group of people in this country who are trying to replace native born Canadians with immigrants who agree with their political views." Fully half of Conservative Party voters agree with the statement (Anderson and Coletto 2022). Recall that the mass murderers in Christchurch and El Paso were obsessed with this supposed conspiracy.

A further caution/nuance concerns the "multiculturalization" of Canadian identity, which is subject to regional variations. The demographic profile of Canada is certainly changing, but not uniformly. Statistics Canada projects that "approximately 55% of persons living in CMAs [Census Metropolitan Areas] in 2031 would be either immigrants or the Canadian-born children of immigrants. In Toronto and Vancouver, these proportions would reach 78% and 70%, respectively. They would be at most 10% in the St. John's, Saguenay and Trois-Rivières CMAs" (2010). The projections point to various divides: between most of Atlantic Canada and elsewhere, between urban and rural areas, and, in Quebec, between Montreal/western Quebec and the rest of the province.

Such divides have political implications. In Canada, one of the best-known declarations of xenophobic pride emerged not in Toronto or Vancouver but in Hérouxville, Quebec, a backwater with few if any immigrants. In Eastern Europe, political attitudes in the Visegrád group (Poland, Hungary, Slovakia, Czech Republic) are sharply divided between relatively open capitals and more xenophobic parts of those countries (Bréville 2020). Finally, 2016 exit polls showed that Trump's support was largely drawn from communities smaller than 50,000 people (Saunders 2016). These political precedents suggest that parts of Canada bypassed by the country's demographic transformation could become reservoirs of support for a political reaction against multiculturalism and immigrants.

But if multiculturalism is widely popular today, would not such a reaction meet strong resistance? We cannot be sure, because it is unclear what to make of multiculturalism's popularity, which brings us to another nuance to the benign picture. The problem is not just that the word means many things to its various ostensible supporters, but that there are wildly different depths of attachment to multiculturalism. We can draw an analogy here with patriotism. If it takes the form that I have termed "citizen identification" – recognizing one's fellow citizens as people with whom one is connected in a web of reciprocal rights and obligations – it can demand great sacrifices (Ryan 2010b, 21). But patriotism can also function as a way to put demands on *other* people (e.g., young people shipped off to war). Or it can be a mere tribal value divorced from any idea of personal sacrifice: think of those who will don a MAGA hat and aggressively chant "USA, USA" until they grow hoarse, but for whom wearing a mask to protect others is an intolerable imposition. (We will return to the different flavours of patriotism in chapter 10.)

Multiculturalism likewise can be a demanding ideal, calling for a serious commitment to justice and equality. But many invocations of multiculturalism today seem vacuous: they do not acknowledge it as an unfinished project, and they ignore, for example, the persistence of racism and other forms of discrimination. Such hollow rhetoric was widely manifest in the "ambiguous triumph" of multiculturalism during the early Harper years: Conservatives stopped attacking multiculturalism and instead made use of it to promote their traditional concerns, such as opposition to same-sex marriage (Ryan 2010b, 112–13). This strategy has continued. During Justin Trudeau's first term the Conservatives invoked multiculturalism for their own purposes: to defend, for example, organizations that might wish to discriminate against LGBTQ+ youth (Commons, 21 March 2018). Not all parliamentary references to multiculturalism take this form. Still, one reason the policy may seem very popular today is precisely because many Canadians do not view it as a demanding ideal, believing that "it asks nothing of a White Canadian mainstream, other than tolerance; it mandates no change in the order of social hierarchies, it requires no sacrifice, no territorial concession" (Burman 2016, 363).

Summing up. Despite the foregoing cautions and nuances, I believe there is some truth in the view of Canada as an exception in a time when xenophobic populism is on the rise in many places. Strong evidence of this is the failure to date of the xenophobic political probes being essayed by Maxime Bernier and some high-level Conservatives.

Now the foregoing depiction of the international and Canadian conjunctures could be used to support a "Shut up, things could be worse" response to progressives who criticize multiculturalism. This would be unfortunate, for a number of reasons. It would serve, first, to insulate persistent injustice from critique. To say that such injustice is milder than elsewhere is a cop-out: to the person who says, for example, "Well, we're better than the Americans," an obvious answer is that the injustice that should matter most is the injustice about which *we* can do something, and *that* – to a large extent – is the injustice within our borders. A "shut up" response also assumes that the status quo is stable. But I have offered various reasons for believing that this is not necessarily true. Finally, a casual dismissal assumes that progressive critiques can make no contribution to holding on to whatever progress Canada has made in matters of ethnic and racial justice to this point, nor to identifying the injustices that remain. This is most certainly untrue.

2.3 Persistent Challenges: Racism and Discrimination in Canada

In my original plan, this section would have presented an array of statistics. I believe that statistical analysis is an essential tool for understanding society and that it can sometimes uncover realities that *only* reveal themselves statistically. But I found that, for this chapter, statistics could not convey an adequate sense of the challenges we continue to face as a society.

Consider, for example, the problem of hate crime. We are told that there were 1,719 such crimes in 2018 (Statistics Canada 2020). Is that a lot or a little? How serious are such crimes? And how are those statistics gathered? Deborah Stone notes that "counting always involves deliberate decisions about *counting as*" (1997, 164): we can only arrive at an unemployment rate, for example, through many decisions that this or that type of situation counts as being unemployed. So: what does it take to be *counted as* a hate crime? Consider this incident: "Late one night in April 2015, a drunk man entered a convenience store in the town of Hinton, Alta., and told the person behind the till he didn't want to be served by a Black woman. Riley Bryn McDonald used the n-word. He asked for the manager. He then picked up a cup of hot nacho cheese sauce and threw it in the clerk's face" (Proctor 2020).

The assailant was not *charged* with a hate crime, although the incident may have been *classified* as one. Why the disparity? Because, it seems, "the Criminal Code contains provisions for hate crimes but they're largely reserved for offences involving hate propaganda or the promotion or advocacy of genocide" (Proctor 2020). Statistics Canada, however, uses a broader definition: "criminal offences motivated by bias, prejudice, or hate based on race, national or ethnic origin, language, colour, religion, sex, age, mental or physical disability, sexual orientation or any other similar factor, such as profession or political beliefs" (2020). But the agency depends on data from individual police forces, which may or may not *report* as hate crimes incidents that they do not *charge* as such. (We can also assume that the tally will omit a politically explosive subset of hate crimes: those committed by police.)

Grasping the reality of economic inequality through statistical analysis is yet more complicated. In late 2019, the Canadian Centre for Policy Alternatives issued *Canada's Colour Coded Income Inequality*, an analysis based on 2016 census data. It reports that racialized women earn 59 per cent, and racialized men 78 per cent, of the income of non-racialized men (Block et al. 2019, 13). The corresponding figure for Black men in particular is 66 per cent (13). Part of the disparity arises because racialized workers are more likely to be immigrants. But only part: 25-to-50-year-old racialized immigrant men receive only 71 per cent of the earnings of non-racialized immigrant men (5), and "second-generation racialized men earned 79 cents for every dollar that second-generation non-racialized men earned" (15).

Most analysts of labour force data will ask: but for what does this analysis control? Pretty much nothing, so far as I can see. But an important question is this: for just what *should* it control, if we are to avoid baking racism into the analysis? The standard approach to statistical analysis of earnings gaps proceeds by building a multi-variable equation that can isolate the *specific* effect of race (or ethnicity, or gender) from other factors. An earlier study by Hum and Simpson, for example, controls for "accumulated human capital, current labour market activity, immigration, language, location, aboriginal status, marital status, self-employment status, and occupational level" (1999, 385). On this basis, they conclude that "with the exception of Black men, there is no significant wage gap between visible minority and non-visible minority group membership for native-born workers. It is only among immigrants that the question of wage differentials for visible minorities (in general) arises" (392).

But what are we to conclude from this? It seems reasonable to say, for example, that we should control for differing levels of education (part of "accumulated human capital"): to attribute to race or ethnicity the entire earnings difference between a graduate degree holder and someone whose education ended at high school flies in the face of evidence. Yet would anyone dare suggest that differences between groups in average levels of education are free of the influence of discrimination? It would thus be a serious error to conclude from Hum and Simpson's analysis that, with the exception of Black men, native-born Canadians do not suffer from ethnoracial discrimination. Statistical controls cannot support such a conclusion. They can, however, provide important clues as to exactly *where* the effects of discrimination are turning up. (As a rule of thumb, any statistical control whose application noticeably reduces the "left-over" gap *directly* attributed to racial differences is a topic for further investigation.[6])

A bulletin board of persistent problems. You may at some point have watched a popular cliché scene in a movie or TV show: investigators of something or other stand in front of a bulletin board, on which are posted various photos, comments, and so on. Lines join some items, and the occasional question mark has been scrawled here and there. The investigators stand there, trying to make sense of things, hoping that staring long enough at the board, along with prodigious amounts of coffee consumption, will yield insight. It usually does.

In that spirit, to supplement the fairly limited sense of Canadian reality that we can gain from the sorts of statistics just surveyed, I offer a "bulletin board" of items. I have not tried to cover all aspects of racism and discrimination in today's Canada: that task is beyond me. Still, I think this bulletin board yields insight. Note that its starting point is arbitrary: one could begin this sort of exercise at any moment and work backwards. My version was written in the fall of 2020. It thus does not include major events such as the June 2021 massacre of a Muslim family in London, Ontario, or the white supremacy aspects of the early 2022 occupation of Ottawa.

Item 1. September 2020: "A group of five people yelled racial slurs at a Black man before he was stabbed multiple times in a Brandon, Man., skate park" (CBC 2020a).

Item 2. September 2020: A mother in Russell Township, near Ottawa, reported that her ten-year-old son was attacked by two white boys. After hurling the N-word at him, "one of them hit him in the leg with a scooter while the other jumped on his arm, breaking it in two places" (Jones 2020a).

Item 3. September 2020: In Pembroke, also near Ottawa, 80-year-old Nga Doan was assaulted by some teenagers at her front door. Her granddaughter reported that the teens swore at her grandmother, egged her house, and hit her on the cheek with a rock (CBC 2020b).

Item 4. September 2020: Mohamed-Aslim Zafis is stabbed to death outside the Toronto mosque where he did volunteer caretaking work. An investigation by the Canadian Anti-Hate Network finds that the accused murderer "followed a number of white supremacists accounts." Mustafa Farooq, head of the National Council for Canadian Muslims, comments that "there are 300 (Nazi) groups who are active in Canada, many who are active and mobilized. These are groups that should no longer be able to exist in Canada, plain and simple" (McDonald 2020).

Interlude. "Nasty things happened years ago in Canada. But that is a Canada that no longer exists." Neil Bissoondath (1994, 166).

Item 5. September 2020: A research institute reports that "immigrants, refugees and other newcomers" account for 44 per cent of Ontario's COVID cases, despite representing only 25 per cent of the population and being tested less frequently (ICES 2020). Earlier in the pandemic, the province's Chief Medical Officer refused calls to collect racial data on COVID because "regardless of race, ethnic or other backgrounds, they're all equally important to us" (Kassam 2020). In Ottawa in particular, racialized residents represent 25 per cent of the population but 66 per cent of COVID cases (Jones 2020b). The explanations for this provide a glimpse of some lived effects of urban poverty: those in lower-paid jobs are less likely to be able to work from home and thus are more likely to be at risk during the pandemic; in particular, racialized workers are greatly overrepresented among the staff of long-term-care facilities, the epicentre of the pandemic; they are also more likely to be living in higher-density housing.

Item 6. September 2020: Although dying in a Joliette hospital, 37-year-old Atikamekw woman Joyce Echaquan had the presence of mind to "live-stream the moments before her death on Facebook." The last thing she heard on this earth were the insults of hospital staff (APTN 2020).

Item 7. August 2020: "Tonight, I went on a little stroll in #Saskatoon. A group of young white men rolled down their car windows. One of them made monkey noises at me, while they drove away. Being Black on the Prairies can be violent. It is always unsettling" (Issa 2020).

Interlude. "Don't bring this to Canada you f***in loser." Ed Ammar, founding member of Jason Kenney's United Conservative Party, in response to federal cabinet minister Ahmed Hussen's comment that "anti-black racism does not stop at the border" (CTV 2020).

Item 8. July 2020: A CBC study of "fatal encounters where police used force" from 2000 to June 2020 finds that Indigenous Canadians are nearly four times as likely to be victims as Canadians in general and that Blacks are nearly three times as likely (Singh 2020).[7] An earlier study found that, out of 461 fatal encounters between 2000 and 2017, charges were laid against officers in just eighteen cases, yielding two convictions (Marcoux and Nicholson 2018).

Item 9. June 2020: A video surfaces showing a Nunavut man being deliberately struck by the open door of a slow-moving RCMP vehicle. Indigenous Services Minister Marc Miller declares that "he's 'outraged' and 'pissed' by the continuing pattern of police violence against Indigenous people in Canada," adding that "a car door is not a proper police tactic" (Brown 2020).

Interlude. June 2020: Reversing an earlier denial, RCMP Commissioner Brenda Lucki declares that "there's absolutely systemic racism" in the force. Asked for an example, she points to an RCMP physical test that requires members to long-jump six feet (Kirkup and Leblanc 2020).

Item 10. June 2020: A study by the London-based Institute for Strategic Dialogue finds that Canadians are the highest per capita contributors to 4chan's "/pol/board," which is "hugely important in contemporary RWE [right-wing extremist] culture and mobilisation" (Davey, Guerin and Hart 2020, 33).

Item 11. June 2020: Six in ten respondents in a survey of Chinese Canadians report that they have "adjusted their routines to avoid run-ins or unpleasant encounters since the pandemic began." While the respondents report a high level of attachment to Canada, "only 13 per cent said they think others in Canada view them as Canadian 'all the time'" (Bailey 2020).

Item 12. May 2020: Chinese Canadian organizations that set up a website allowing people to report incidents of racism say that more than 100 such cases have been reported in three months, most of them falling in May. "The three more common types of harassment were verbal insults, denial of access to public areas, and intentional spitting or coughing." Almost all the victims identify as having East or Southeast Asian ethnicity (Mangat 2020).

Interlude. "[Stockwell] Day went on to compare the bullying he endured as a child with the discrimination faced by visible minorities across the country. 'Should I have gone through school and been mocked because I had glasses and was called four-eyes and because of the occupation of my parents?' Day asked. 'Should I have been mocked for all that? No, of course not. But are Canadians largely and in majority racist? No, we are not" (Zimonjic 2020).

Item 13. April 2020: Conservative Party leadership candidate Derek Sloan figures that he can enhance his electoral appeal with Facebook and Twitter posts declaring:

> Dr. Tam must go! Canada must remain sovereign over decisions. The UN, the WHO, and Chinese Communist propaganda must never again have a say over Canada's public health!
> Does [Tam] work for Canada or for China? (qtd. in Harris 2020)

Upon being criticized, Sloan complains that "we are in a culture where political correctness and identity politics are used as a shield to deflect or even outlaw criticism" (qtd. in Rana 2020).

Item 14. April 2019: The *Globe and Mail* reports that it "has obtained a trove of 150,000 messages posted between February 2017, and early 2018 that reveal the private communications of a loosely aligned node of Canadian right-wing extremists ... The discussions celebrate Nazism and joke about the Holocaust. They contain boasts of racist, sexist and homophobic behaviour on the part of participants ... They purchase weapons and discuss training" (Carranco and Milton 2019).

Item 15. March 2019: A report issued by the Nova Scotia Human Rights Commission finds that Black residents of Halifax are 5.7 times more likely to be subjected to police street checks than whites. Between 2006 and 2017, there were almost "two street checks for every one Black person residing in the Halifax region" (Wortley 2019, 104).

Item 16. January 2019: While visiting France, Quebec premier François Legault promises that his government's plan to reduce immigration to the province will not affect France. On the contrary, he comments, "des Français, on en prendrait plus. De même que des Européens" (qtd. in Rioux 2019). The "as well as Europeans" turn of phrase indicates that the premier prefers non-French-speaking immigrants from Europe to the French-speaking ones from Algeria, Morocco, and Haiti who are currently arriving (Patriquin 2019).

Item 17. January 2019: Evan Balgord, director of the Canadian Anti-Hate Network, warns of the "toxic" nature of the "Yellow Vest Canada" Facebook page, which has more than 100,000 followers: "If you go through it at any given moment, you're going to find anti-Semitic conspiracy theories, you're going to find death threats, you're going to find other calls to violence, racism directed to Muslims" (Mosleh 2019).

Item 18. December 2018. The Ontario Human Rights Commission reports that "between 2013 and 2017, a Black person in Toronto was nearly 20 times more likely than a White person to be involved in a fatal shooting by the Toronto Police Service (TPS)." Data obtained from Ontario's Special Investigations Unit (SIU) "reveal a lack of legal basis for police stopping or detaining Black civilians in the first place; inappropriate or unjustified searches during encounters; and unnecessary charges or arrests. The information analysed by the OHRC also raises broader concerns about officer misconduct, transparency and accountability. Courts and arms-length oversight bodies have found that TPS officers have sometimes provided biased and untrustworthy testimony, have inappropriately tried to stop the recording of incidents and/or have failed to cooperate with the SIU" (OHRC 2018).

Interlude. July 2018: Defending the TPS's controversial practice of random street checks, former chief Julian Fantino complains that "demonizing a purely legitimate and effective police initiative with such highly charged inflammatory accusations of police racial profiling, a racist police practice or simply elevating the rhetoric to fraudulently create a moral panic was obviously intended to diminish political courage to come out in support of police simply doing their job" (2018).[8]

Item 19. December 2018: An independent review of the Thunder Bay Police Service concludes that its "investigators failed on an unacceptably high number of occasions to treat or protect the deceased and his or her family equally and without discrimination because the deceased was Indigenous ... Officers repeatedly relied on generalized notions about how Indigenous people likely came to their deaths and acted, or refrained from acting, based on those biases" (McNeilly 2018, 9). The review calls for a number of the cases to be reinvestigated.

Item 20. November 2018: "It's okay to be white" posters show up in downtown Ottawa, apparently originating from 4chan and aiming to "expose anti-white bias and convert 'normies' to the far-right cause" (Gillis 2018).

Item 21. July 2018: Two passers-by scream "f--king Arab people! Terrorists," at Mohammed Abu Marzouk, who had just gotten into his car after a family picnic in Toronto. "Abu Marzouk got out of his vehicle to talk to the men. When he did ... one of the men punched him in the face." When his wife tried to help him, she was kicked as well (Nasser 2018).

Interlude. "Canada is the nation of multiculturalism. It is not just a country of tolerance, but a country of acceptance." MP Sonia Sidhu (Commons, 2 February 2017).

Item 22. May 2018: A woman in a Lethbridge restaurant becomes enraged at four men "who 'started talking in their own language' and began laughing, which she thought was directed at her." She was caught on video yelling "Well shut your f--king mouth then, cause you know what, you're dealing with a Canadian woman right now and I will leap across the table and punch you right in your f--king mouth" (Dormer 2018).

Item 23. April 2018: While job hunting, Salim Kerdougli calls himself Sam. "Salim isn't a Western name, he explains. 'If I say I'm called Salim Kerdougli, I won't even be called for an interview' ... He's had several job interviews. And each time he's asked where he's from, he knows things will go no further" (LaPresse 2018).

Interlude. Three-quarters of Canadians agree that "Canada is a country of equal opportunity" (Jedwab 2015b).[9]

Item 24. October 2017: After sponsoring a motion condemning Islamophobia, Liberal MP Iqra Khalid "received a torrent of hate mail, including death threats" (Khan 2017).

Interlude. "Canada now stands as a supremely tolerant and multicultural society." Ezra Levant (2009, 175).

Thoughts about the bulletin board. After decades of multicultural policy, Canada continues to have colour-coded economic inequality, "streetlevel" outbursts of racism, sometimes verbal, sometimes physically violent, and unequal treatment of Canadians at the hands of agents of the state. We continue to have expressions of the belief that some people are not *quite* Canadian: Dr. Tam, Chinese Canadians in general, a man named Salim, the men in that Lethbridge restaurant who dare to chat in *their own* language. And we continue, as the "interludes" remind us, to have various forms of denial of all of the above.

And this provides, I think, fuel for the anger that many critics feel when they contrast reality with the proud proclamations of Canada's commitment to diversity, the claims that "diversity is our strength," and so on. The sharp contrast between the "brand" of Canada as a tolerant multicultural place and the grim realities depicted on our bulletin board also gives force to the view that multiculturalism is a counterproductive mask of oppression, even that it "upholds white supremacy" (Thobani 2010).

2.4 Conclusion

The three clusters of "signs of the times" surveyed in this chapter present us with an analytical challenge, and a political one. First: how can we account for the contradiction between the "multiculturalization" of Canadian identity, the celebrations of Canadian tolerance and diversity, and the persistence of ethnoracial inequality? One answer is simple and straightforward: everything is going as planned. Multiculturalism was *intended* to mask inequality, and it has largely succeeded. But other, less obvious answers are available. To develop those, I will first need to enter into a closer analysis of various conceptual building blocks. This I will do in chapter 3.

The political challenge is this: the third part of this chapter tells us that things could be much better in Canada, while the first section tells us that they could be much worse. That should not excuse inactivity, since *our* racism is the one we can do something about. But every progressive critique of the current state of affairs, every articulation of a vision for something better, must proceed with an eye to the threat posed by a resurgent far right in this "age of anger." To say that does not dictate exactly *how* this threat must be taken into account. It does not mean, for example, that we must be more "moderate" in our assessments of existing reality. But to the extent possible, the struggle for a more just society must be pursued in such a way as not to increase the chances of movement towards xenophobic authoritarianism. This constraint should affect the discourse progressives deploy, the policies they promote, and the political actions they take.

Chapter Three

Four Concepts

> An introductory discussion of concepts can hardly be dispensed with, in spite of the fact that it is unavoidably abstract and hence gives the impression of remoteness from reality.
>
> Max Weber, *Economy and Society* (rpt. 1978, 3)

The Canadian *state* has a *policy*, ostensibly about matters in some way concerning *culture*, called *multiculturalism*. Each of those italicized words requires some preliminary examination. Why?

Psychologist Daniel Kahneman finds it fruitful to depict mental life through the metaphor of two agents, which he terms System 1 and System 2: "System 1 operates automatically and quickly, with little or no effort and no sense of voluntary control. System 2 allocates attention to the effortful mental activities that demand it" (2011, 20–1). The relevance of Kahneman's metaphor is that *state, policy, culture,* and *multiculturalism* all lend themselves to errors of "fast thinking." Each is an abstract concept, designating not things but sets of complex social relations: such concepts easily lead to reification, personification, and simplification. Thus, I will argue that people often carry around unexamined default assumptions about these concepts, ways of thinking that can weigh heavily on analysis, unless they consciously guard against them. Concepts, including abstract high-level ones, are essential for thought, but unless we are reflexive in their use, they will cast a shadow upon reality.

By associating these tacit assumptions with Kahneman's "fast thinking," I am underlining that their influence is not constant. A person can have a quite sophisticated understanding of a culture they identify as their own, for example, and a simplistic understanding of someone else's. Or they may lean on simplistic assumptions when they are thinking *with* a concept, not *about* it. The claim that multiculturalism was developed to reinforce white supremacy, for example, relies on tacit assumptions about how states do things but does not require that one think directly *about* the concept of the state. As Michael Polanyi notes, we do not focus on our physical or intellectual tools when we perform a task. I cannot, for example, simultaneously type this passage and reflect on the adequacy of the qwerty keyboard: that tool is part of what Polanyi calls my "subsidiary" awareness (1962, 56). So too with our working concepts, except when we try to focus on them.

Thus, we could say that one of the goals of the chapter is to encourage the development of better default assumptions, so that the tools we use more or less instinctively are more solid. But since default assumptions are not always influential, their critique has a strange quality: it must draw on insights that "everyone knows" ... but that many often forget. Let me underline this: a key question as you read this chapter is not whether you think you already know this or that point I am making, but whether you are able to *keep it in mind* when thinking about concrete issues and events.

But why front-load this material? Why not present elements of conceptual clarification as we go along, on an as-needed basis? That procedure, unfortunately, makes it difficult for the reader to assess whether a book's approach is supported by a coherent theoretical framework. It also makes it too easy for the author to indulge in important contradictions: assuming an omniscient state at one moment, for example, and a more constrained state at another. So I'm going to ask the reader to trust me in one respect, so that – paradoxically – you don't have to trust me in another. If you trust that the discussion of concepts developed in this chapter is relevant to the assessment of multiculturalism's progressive critics, you will not need to take it on trust later on that there is some coherent framework in play.[1]

3.1 The State

Consider, first, "the state." Sociologist Pierre Bourdieu comments that "you will find, in books that attempt to be 'theoretical,' that the number of sentences with 'state' as the subject is remarkable." This, says Bourdieu, reflects "an everyday theology" (2012, 158). The analogy is apt, in that both everyday thinking and more rigorous analysis at times manifest a tacit image of the state as something God-like: omniscient, perhaps even omnipotent, at least within the state's borders. The image is tacit, and must remain so: when stated explicitly, its core assumptions look silly, and few people would endorse them. Yet they show up in a variety of contexts.

In *Essence of Decision*, his influential study of the Cuban Missile Crisis, Graham Allison argued that strategic studies often work with this model: "The question of what the enemy will do is answered by considering the question of what a rational, unitary genie would do" (1971, 18). This image of the state is related to two styles of inference. The first can be captured using a chess analogy: A and B are two reasonably competent players, in the mid-game. A makes a move: what goes through B's mind? B infers backwards: what does this move tell me about A's overall strategy? B assumes that their opponent is a rational, competent player, a player, of course, who can see the board and thus has accurate knowledge of the configuration of pieces (inference becomes impossible otherwise). Thus, in strategic thinking as portrayed by Allison, one set of decision-makers tries to figure out the opposing state's objectives and strategy *from the moves it makes*. But the conditions that govern chess do not govern life as a whole. Hence, as Allison showed, the "rational, unitary genie" image of the state could lead to potentially catastrophic errors of inference. One example: the missile sites built in Cuba were "soft" and thus could not survive a US attack. Under the "rational, unitary genie" assumption, this could lead to the inference that the Soviets were developing a first-strike capacity in Cuba (108).

If this first style of inference does not allow for the possibility of error and misinformation on the part of the state, it is tacitly viewing the state as an *omniscient* mind. The second style of inference goes even further, endowing the state with something like *omnipotence*. Here, the objectives of states can be inferred from *what actually came about*. As Benoît Bréville argues, this inference regularly shows up in conspiracy theories, captured in the *cui bono?* question. *Who benefited* from the January 2015 terrorist attack against Charlie Hebdo in Paris? Well, Islamophobia increased and the image of Islam was deeply tarnished, hence the attack must have been the work of "mercenaries recruited by the United States and Israel," as one conspiracy theorist claimed (qtd. in Bréville 2015). The world of the conspiracy theorist is one devoid of strategic blunders, the interplay of multiple actors, pure chance, and sheer craziness.

The "theological" view of the state does not arise solely from a weak understanding of the state alone; it also reflects a broader difficulty that afflicts all of us: how are we to maintain a clear sense of the complexity of social reality? That is why, as we will see throughout this work, elements of the "theological" view turn up in discourse concerning other super-individual actors, such as society, culture, and so on. We often hear, for example, people talking about the culture and traditions of this or that society, as if these phenomena were unified and everyone in the society endorsed them. This way of speaking can both *express* an underlying assumption of unity and *reinforce* that assumption, by further obscuring differences internal to the phenomenon.[2]

The critique of the "theological" view of the state as rational, unified, omniscient, and sometimes omnipotent will be developed around eight key points, with some of the later ones clarifying and nuancing earlier ones:

1. Everything the state does must be done by individuals, who must be *motivated* to carry out the action.
2. Those individuals are not the atomized monads postulated by "rational actor" models. All individuals are carriers of "supra-individual dispositions."
3. These socialized individuals cannot work within The State as a whole, but only in particular organizations within the state.
4. These organizations are not like organs of a healthy body, harmoniously working together towards a common goal. They often compete against one another, and even work at cross-purposes.
5. While these conflicts can arise from the different mandates of organizations, they are also rooted in the interests of the individuals who work in different agencies.
6. The foregoing points wreak havoc with a "basic, linear, transitive vision" (Bourdieu) in which power flows smoothly downward through a state hierarchy and from the state to civil society. More complex and reversible power relations are relevant within government offices and in the dealings of government officials with outside actors.
7. All that said, determined leadership may on occasion discipline the state to some extent.
8. A crucial reason for leaders to seek to impose such discipline arises from the fact that the state we are considering is a *capitalist* state.
8.1 State officials will generally be accepting or supportive of the capitalist nature of the state, which reflects both general ideological conditioning and the way they themselves are selected and promoted.
8.2 Even when this is not the case, officials will feel constrained to sustain the status quo, because of both the state's dependence upon the health of capitalism, and inter-state competition.
8.3 But the state is no more omniscient in the service of capital than it is in other respects. Even a state elite that is entirely sympathetic to capitalism may have no idea of what needs to be done in a time of crisis.

8.4 In Canada and the OECD countries, at least, the capitalist state is also a democratic state, and this imposes further constraints. These can often reinforce the constraints of capital but may at times pull in a different direction.
8.5 The state must thus manage a delicate "minuet," in part to organize high-level compromises between capital and society as a whole. Historically, such compromises can be seen to have stabilized capitalism but not to have been initiated by capitalists themselves.
8.6 Just as the state is not omniscient, neither are capitalist or democratic pressures. In this age of right-wing "populism," we are familiar with the argument that many voters are confused concerning their fundamental interests. But pressure from capital may also fail to promote capitalism's *long-term* interests.
8.7 This reflects in part the fact that "capital" does not pressure the state: capitalists do, and they need not represent the interests of business as a whole, much less the long-term political needs of capitalism.
8.8 Because high-level compromises historically helped sustain capitalism, and because the countervailing forces that helped push for those compromises have been weakened in recent decades, capitalism today may be threatened by "an overdose of itself."

States and individuals. "Does anybody in the world," asked G.K. Chesterton, "believe that a soldier says, 'My leg is nearly dropping off, but I shall go on till it drops; for after all I shall enjoy all the advantages of my government obtaining a warm-water port in the Gulf of Finland'" (1925, 158)? The question reminds us that wars are *discussed* and *planned* at the level of grand strategy but must be *fought* by individual soldiers who may be little interested in broad strategic questions and thus must have other reasons for doing what they do. This is true of everything the state does: someone must give an order to separate children from their families along the US–Mexico border, other people must carry out the order, and they must all have personal reasons for doing so. This simple truth must be kept in mind when we wield other collective nouns: a social class, a church, a corporation.

In the *Communist Manifesto*, Marx and Engels famously declared that "the executive of the modern state is but a committee for managing the common affairs of the whole bourgeoisie." If this is true, then there must be people within the state who for one reason or another are *motivated* to play that role (whether they need *consciously* play it is another matter). Antonio Gramsci wrote that "the State is the instrument for conforming civil society to the economic structure, but it is necessary for the State to 'be willing' to do this" (rpt. 1971, 208), to which we must join the addendum that "the state" is only "willing" when authoritative actors in the state are so willing.

Two clarifications. First, the analysis here does not rule out using "state" and "government" as the subjects of sentences. They can serve as a convenient "shorthand," as Anthony Giddens puts it (1984, 221), so long as we recall that these words stand in for the actions and decisions of authoritative actors. An important condition is that both readers and writer should be likely to share that understanding, to be clear on just what the shorthand is short for. (Some claims that we will examine in chapter 4 fail that test, with important consequences.)

Second, while the state's actions and decisions are *made* by authoritative individuals, they cannot necessarily be *unmade* by them. A government that has made a binding decision – in the form of a law, a court judgment, or the like – has produced an independent reality that must now be taken into account as such. That is, the individuals who produced this independent reality may no longer have the ability to negate it.

Socialized, not "atomized," individuals. Within "the state" it is people who act. Explanation of state action does not *begin* with these individuals, but it must *pass through them* at some point. There is a world of difference between those two assertions. "Methodological individualism" has been described as the belief that "all statements about social phenomena ... can be reduced, without loss of meaning, to descriptions of the qualities of individuals" (Giddens 1984, 214). That theoretical claim is nicely captured in Margaret Thatcher's stern rebuke of those supposedly "casting their problems on society": "There is no such thing! There are individual men and women and there are families" (1987).

In practice, the "individuals" in that approach are not real flesh-and-blood people, but abstract models of egoistic maximizers, such as *homo oeconomicus* or the "rational actor." Explanations of social life based on such constructs can wash out everything of importance: parents may "buy, as it were, the services of children as a particular form of consumption" (Friedman 1962, 33); an act of kindness by A towards B creates "a 'credit slip' held by A to be redeemed by some performance by B" (Coleman 1990, 306); people get married when "the utility expected from marriage exceeds that expected from remaining single or from additional search for a more suitable mate" (Becker 1976, 10), and so on.[3]

Nothing is gained by removing the shadowy abstraction of The State from one's analysis, only to replace it with the shadowy abstraction of "the individual." While societies (and groups, and organizations, etc.) are "made up" of individuals, the latter are also to a large extent "made up" of social materials: "There is not first an individual who then contingently enters social relations; relations are *constitutive* of the individual and their sense of self" (Sayer 2011, 119). The state is "made up" of individuals, but within each of these we find "supra-individual dispositions" (Bourdieu 2003, 225).

Norms are a vital category of such dispositions. It is fruitful to view people in general, and state actors in particular, as manifesting a "constrained normativity": this is a desire to "do the right thing," however they understand it, but a desire constrained by narrow interests. Most people, for example want to hold on to their jobs, or at least leave them only when *they* choose. This certainly shapes the behaviour of state actors. For the politician, it entails an interest in re-election. For the civil servant, it involves at the very least paying attention to certain uncrossable lines. It may also involve working to keep their specific office in business.

But no one is *only* a state actor: we are more than our jobs. A public official can find themselves pressured by family and friends, whose ethical vision is less warped by the constraints of office. And we should not expect the actor's sense of right and wrong to be *totally* remade in function of their work in the state. (We will return to these points in a moment.)

This idea of constrained normativity is not a *model* from which one can derive clear predictions about the behaviour of state actors. This is because the strength of a normative orientation, of a concern to do the right thing, is in no way fixed. It can easily atrophy under particular conditions, such as "close and punitive supervision" (Day and Hamblin 1964), or conditions that provide too much personal advantage to those who engage in unethical behaviour and hence erode the morale of others. This has important implications for how we think about the design of institutions. In most variants of the "rational actor" model, egoism is *fixed*, a given. In the more realistic approach advocated here, the strength of normative orientation is a *variable*. Institutions designed under the "rational actor" assumption, tailored to a "nation of devils" (Kant rpt. 1991, 112), can create an atmosphere that *elicits* such behaviour. When we recognize the variable nature of normative orientation, on the other hand, we attempt to design institutions so that "the requirements of justice are not too much in conflict with citizens' essential interests" (Rawls 1996, 134).

State organizations. While I have repeatedly referred to "state actors," individuals do not work in an undifferentiated State. Rather, they are located in some particular office. The division of the state into individual organizations influences what states do and how they do it. In Nikolai Leskov's short story "The Man on Watch," a palace guard in early nineteenth-century Petersburg hears a man drowning nearby. Private Postnikov realizes that he could easily save the man. Yet he also "remembers his duty and his oath: he knows that he is a sentry, and a sentry dare not desert his sentry box for anything or under any pretext." Eventually, he "could not bear it and deserted his post." The drowning man is saved, and, after a number of twists and turns in the story, Postnikov is punished with "with two hundred strokes of the birch" for this "grave violation of military duty" (rpt. 2014).[4]

Leskov's tale reminds us that the member of any formal organization has a *specific* job to do and that they can expect to be judged on how well they do it. The public official's job is *not* to promote the "public interest," nor is it to defend capitalism, and certainly it is not to work out for themselves what is the most socially useful action they can take at any given moment, as Postnikov did. Depending on the character of their immediate superiors, they may be appreciated for (diplomatically) raising questions about the relation of their specific task to the broader objectives of the organization, but they will win no points by squawking about the irrationality of their work.

So individual officials occupy a specific point in a division of labour. And the same is true for the organization within which they work: like the individual, a particular state office is not tasked with directly promoting the public interest. It has a much more specific job to do, and it is generally up to someone else to ensure that all the specific tasks somehow constitute a harmonious whole. Or not, as we will see.

To break high-level tasks down into mid-level ones, and the latter into lower-level tasks, organizations will implement standard operating procedures. The employee is told not simply to "do your job" but to do it in such and such a way. Thus, Graham Allison, whose study of the Cuban Missile Crisis was cited earlier, offers an "organizational process" model, according to which government behaviour is interpreted as "outputs of large organizations functioning according to standard patterns of behaviour" (1971, 67).

An important implication is that information does not "naturally" flow throughout the state. Information in one office will only be shared with another if there are procedures in place to do that (or if, perhaps, an individual recognizes the exceptional importance of some information and exercises initiative, which may involve some personal risk). Moreover, each office has standardized ways of "seeing" the world outside it. No office, or official, is omniscient; each bypasses the "great blooming, buzzing confusion" of the world (James 1890, vol. 1, 488) by focusing on certain slivers of reality considered relevant. Even these slivers, moreover, are often grasped through simplified bureaucratic categories. As James Scott argued in his classic *Seeing Like a State*, "the functionary of any large organization 'sees' the human activity that is of interest to him largely through the simplified approximations of documents and statistics" (1998, 76).

Post-mortems conducted after particular security failures regularly reveal the serious consequences of these inevitable facts of organizational life. A recurring finding is that all the information decision-makers needed to avert the disaster existed *somewhere* in the state system. In July 2001, for example, an FBI agent based in Arizona sent a memo to headquarters warning of "the possibility of a coordinated effort by Osama bin Laden to send students to the United States to attend civil aviation universities and colleges" (qtd. in Wright 2011, 395). A month later, "a flight school in Minnesota contacted the local FBI field office to express concern about a student, Zacarias Moussaoui. He had asked suspicious questions about the flight patterns around New York City and whether the doors of a cockpit could be opened during flight. The local bureau quickly determined that Moussaoui was an Islamic radical who had been to Pakistan and probably to Afghanistan" (396). (Although he was arrested, FBI headquarters refused to give permission to search his laptop.)

After 9/11, people often said it was the worst attack on America since Pearl Harbor. As it happens, the lead-up to Pearl Harbor manifested similar problems arising from the fragmentation of state organizations. After running through a number of pieces of information that might have alerted decision-makers to an impending attack, historian Roberta Wohlstetter notes that "all of the public and private sources of information mentioned were available to America's political and military leaders in 1941. It is only fair to remark, however, that no single person or agency ever had at any given moment all the signals existing in this vast information network" (1962, 385).

Organizations in conflict. The stories of 9/11 and Pearl Harbor are also relevant to our fourth general point concerning the state: its organs are not like the organs of the body, working together towards a common end. Rivalries among state organizations seem to be inevitable. This naturally affects the flow of information throughout the state. In the case of 9/11, the CIA and FBI weren't sharing intel with each other. The same was true for Naval War Plans and Naval Intelligence prior to Pearl Harbor (Wohlstetter 1962, 395). All this naturally affects the upward flow of vital information. Allison's account of the Cuban Missile Crisis suggests that, prior to the crisis, Kennedy had *twice* ordered US missiles removed from Turkey. The order had not been carried out, but Kennedy only discovered this in the heat of the crisis (1971, 101).[5]

Indeed, matters can go beyond rivalry: state organizations may be working at cross-purposes to one another. On 17 March 1997, the *Globe and Mail* ran a story on Health Canada's anti-smoking campaign: "Government doesn't want you to start smoking. Its increasingly forceful attempts to prevent advertisers from persuading young people to do the wrong thing could turn out to be the biggest free-speech issue of the decade" (Keller 1997). No big surprise there. But *the very same day*, the paper also reported that "federal agricultural scientists have worked for years to help the tobacco industry boost the addictive hit of cigarettes" (*Globe and Mail* 1997). Each organization could claim to be carrying out its mandate: "promote health"; "support agriculture." But the very fragmentation of the state into a multitude of organizations ensures that conflicts between mandates are often not resolved by appeal to higher-level values. The many checks and balances that are an essential part of the modern democratic state also provide ample opportunity for intra-state conflict, as when the Ontario Human Rights Commission, a part of the state, issues a critical report on the behaviour towards Black citizens of the Toronto police, another part of the state.

State offices and individual interests. To account for such conflicts, Allison advanced a third model, the "governmental (bureaucratic) politics" paradigm, according to which "what happens is not chosen as a solution to a problem but rather results from compromise, conflict, and confusion of officials with diverse interests and unequal influence" (1971, 162). The reference to diverse interests is key, and brings us to our fifth general point. While conflicts between state bodies can be expected to arise from their different mandates, they are also rooted in the interests of the individuals who work in different agencies. At the narrowest level, the individual official knows that job evaluations will be written not by The State but by their immediate superiors. They thus have a clear interest in being a "team player."

Apart from this, members of a given organization will generally tend to develop an interest in its survival and expansion. As Weber noted, as soon as a group pays someone to work for it, an interest in the persistence of the group *qua* group emerges, independent of its original purpose, and the group evolves from means to end for those whose livelihoods depend on it (1978, 345). Observing the opposition between those working in the French finance ministry and officials located in bodies such as a housing department, sociologist Pierre Bourdieu observed that "once a 'social conquest' has been built into the state institution, a body [is] constituted whose existence is linked to the perpetuation of that conquest" (2012, 40). So long as there are social ministries, then, there will be some defence of social interests within the state, *unless* other state actors succeed in fundamentally diverting the ministry from its original orientation (which can happen).

Normative considerations can also reinforce the state actor's identification with their specific organization. The official may wish to be loyal to those around them, and to work hard at whatever specific job they've been assigned. Their understanding of what is "the right thing to do" is likely to be shaped to some extent by the shared culture of their office: "Groupthink involves non-deliberate suppression of critical thoughts as a result of internalization of the group's norms," as Irving Janis wrote in his classic article on the phenomenon (rpt. 2016, 162). Indeed, the official's very reading of reality is affected: perception is shaped both by interest and by immediate influences.

The complexities of power. The state is staffed with flesh-and-blood individuals, gathered into particular offices, within particular organizations. Interests operate at various levels of this ensemble: the interests of the individual are linked in various ways to those of their particular office and state organization. All of this entails that it is no simple matter to understand the flow of power within the state, or between the state and society. As Bourdieu put it: "While it is true that, on the surface, the first link in the chain commands all the others, in fact, this basic, linear, ... transitive vision is quite simplistic, to the degree that, at each stage, delegation is accompanied by a loss of control" (2012, 478). This is true of delegation *to* a state bureau and of delegation *within* that bureau. Among other complications, the fact that energy must be expended to exercise formal power – as organization theorist Henry Mintzberg pointed out – renders power more diffused through an organization than one might deduce by looking at a formal org chart (1987, 366). No manager is omniscient and omnipotent, so each must choose *where* to exercise surveillance of underlings; *where* to exercise power; *which* fights are worth fighting, and so on. This shows the need to study power relations "in their multiplicity, their differences, their specificity, their reversibility" (Foucault 1989, 85).[6]

The foregoing analysis further suggests that the relationship between state and outside actors will also often depart from a simple vertical model. Consider the strange case of the "Jr. Jays" debacle, in which Health Canada became part of a public/private partnership that encouraged Canadian children to consume more junk food, play more video games, and watch more television (Ryan 2003). This would be inexplicable were one to assume that the organization's actions were truly governed by its official mandate of the time: "enhance healthy living for all Canadians" (Health Canada 1999). But it would also be seriously misleading to engage in the backward inference characteristic of the "rational, unitary genie" model of the state (Allison 1971, 18) and conclude that the "Jr. Jays" program reveals the *true* objectives of the organization. These opposed interpretations are benign and malign forms of the same theoretical error: one assumes a unified rational state that truthfully declares its objectives and carries them out, the other tacitly assumes a unified malign state whose hidden objectives can only be figured out by focusing on the oddest examples of its practice.

Responding to the fashionable imperative to embrace "reinvented" government, Health Canada conceived the idea of marketing children's health through a profit-making partnership with private companies. It teamed up with a marketing company that set out to sign up sponsors. It appears that no one thought to ask just which sorts of companies market to children. One might have expected Health Canada officials to pull the plug on the program once it realized that any "health" message would be swamped by ads for McDonald's, Nintendo, Cadbury Crispy Crunch, and the like. But that was not consistent with bureaucratic self-preservation: "To walk away from problematic negotiations, or – horror of horrors – to abandon a partnership already in progress, will call into question a whole series of prior decisions, and the official may well be seen as someone not truly committed to the managerial realities of the 90s. Better to let the partnership forge onwards, even if it has at best a peripheral relation to the organization's mission" (Ryan 1998).

The lesson of the story is that the interests of individual officials and government offices can decisively shape relations with outside actors. This means, for example, that funding of "civil society" organizations under the aegis of multiculturalism policy can follow a trajectory only loosely related to grand state objectives.[7]

Discipline from above. To this point, I may seem to be describing a disorganized collection of fiefdoms rather than a modern state. As the frustrated members of the 1969 Task Force on Government Information asked: "Are all the Government departments and agencies, taken together, really more like a Holy Roman Empire of prickly entities than they are like a government administration?" (1969, 13). But we need to balance the foregoing analysis. Despite the complexity of the state, a particularly determined leadership can to some extent bend organizations to its will. Different governments will be more or less energetic in this respect. The Harper decade, when government was held by a party long marked by a deep distrust of the civil service, provides an important illustration of the extent to which political leadership can impose its will. (Andrew Griffith's *Policy Arrogance or Innocent Bias* provides a valuable account of how this imposition of a more conservative direction in multiculturalism policy played out in the relationship between the lead politician, Jason Kenney, and his officials.)

This means that conflicts within the state, as well as differences between top-level goals and actual organizational practice, are in a sense *tolerated* conflicts and differences. They may be tolerated because the leadership does not really intend for certain explicit goals to be carried out, or because they have not tried energetically enough to find out just what is going on at the base, or because they're picking their battles.

The capitalist state. A crucial reason for state leaders to seek to impose discipline on the state arises from the fact that we are considering a *capitalist* state.[8] We need to reflect on just what this means because, first, whatever the state does around ethnic relations, immigration, and so on, it remains always a capitalist state. That crucial fact provides *one* of the lenses through which we must seek to interpret particular state actions. So in chapter 6 we will consider whether the emergence of multicultural policy itself was at least in part a response to imperatives facing the capitalist state. We will also consider whether the Canadian state is a *white supremacy* state, in some way analogous to its being a capitalist state. For this, it will be helpful to be clear on just what it means for the state to be capitalist and what forces prevent it from becoming something else.

It is important to understand the state's capitalist nature in a way that takes into account all of the points developed above. We must understand, for example, how sustaining that capitalist nature can conform to the interests and constrained normativity of state officials. Above all, we must not reintroduce a quasi-magical image, this time of an omniscient and infallible puppet-of-capital state.

We can note, first, that as a rule, few state officials will *want* to challenge the state's capitalist orientation. Most are likely to believe that "the established system, in spite of everything, delivers the goods" (Marcuse 1966, 79). All will have undergone the general ideological conditioning that comes from a system in which we live and move and have our being. One manifestation of this conditioning is that nearly every adult in capitalist society spontaneously thinks of "The Economy" as something the health of which is measured in eminently capitalist terms, via the GNP/GDP, an understanding that greatly sharpens the supposed "trade-off" between Economy and Environment. Few people, conversely, spontaneously think of the economy as a set of social practices whose *fundamental* goal is to meet human needs and provide stable and meaningful work for all who seek it. All of this will hold true in spades for high-level officials. It is fair to assume that they generally do reasonably well in the reigning economic game and hence are particularly appreciative of the goods the system delivers. And the very fact that they have risen to the top shows that they have survived many informal tests of ideological "soundness" throughout their careers. As Ralph Miliband argued in his influential explanation of the enduring capitalist orientation of the modern state:

> The ideological "soundness" of top civil servants (and of many others as well) is not a matter which, in these countries, is now left to chance. Recruitment and promotion are no longer in the main determined on the basis of social provenance or religious affiliation. Nor are civil servants in these systems expected to subscribe to a specific political doctrine or ideology. But they are nevertheless expected to dwell within a spectrum of thought of which strong conservatism forms one extreme and weak "reformism" the other. Outside that spectrum, there lurks the grave danger, and in some countries the absolute certainty, of a blighted administrative career or of no administrative career at all. (1969, 111)

These factors, which shape the subjectivity of state actors, are not omnipotent. Indeed, they may always be in tension with other important influences on subjectivity. One tension can arise from an official's commitment to doing "one's damned duty," as Weber put it (rpt. 1958, 145). A curious feature of Marx's *Capital* is that much of his harrowing description of factory life was based on the reports of government inspectors, whose professional ethos clearly clashed with an imperative to mollify "stakeholders," as today's public management jargon would put it. The official, in this case, is acting as more than a mere bundle of demographic traits.

But even should the capitalism-favouring forces waver – when widespread doubts arise, for example, concerning capitalism's ability to *keep* delivering the goods – other factors reinforce the state's capitalist nature. In his *General Theory*, Keynes commented that "economic prosperity is excessively dependent on a political and social atmosphere which is congenial to the average business man. If the fear of a Labour Government or a New Deal depresses enterprise, this need not be the result either of a reasonable calculation or of a plot with political intent; – it is the mere consequence of upsetting the delicate balance of spontaneous optimism" (rpt. 2007, 162). Accordingly, high-level state actors recognize that they must take the general interests of capital into account, whatever their personal feelings about the matter. They will understand that a state indifferent to the needs of capital will pay a price: capital flight, a decline in business investment and rise in unemployment, political mobilization, and so on.

The "general interests of capital"? The "needs of capital"? The alert reader may sense that I am committing a mistake analogous to that for which I criticized much state-talk, by depicting capital as a rational and unified super-organism. I will rectify this, below. For now, we can note Marx's depiction of class struggle, under conditions of competitive capitalism, as a simultaneous struggle *between* and *within* classes: "Industry leads two armies into the field against each other, each of which again carries on a battle within its own ranks, among its own troops. The army whose troops beat each other up the least gains the victory over the opposing host" (Marx and Engels 1969, vol. 1, 155).

A final crucial constraint on the state is that modern military power is dependent on economic power. Thus, a state that fails in the care and feeding of its business sector may also become more vulnerable in interstate competition. As Pankaj Mishra notes, the fact that the state exists in a world of states has been a driver of much modernization. Of leaders such as India's Nehru and Pakistan's Bhutto, he comments that "they saw progress as an urgent imperative for their traditional societies; they hoped, above all, to make their societies strong and competitive enough in the dog-eat-dog world of international relations" (2017, 134).

Given these multiple constraints, we should expect that state institutions will only be allowed to wander a certain distance from this system imperative, which also constrains clashes between state institutions. As a metaphor for this relationship between subjectivity and objective constraints, imagine a child placed in a room with invisible walls. The walls are always there, but the child becomes aware of this only upon bumping into one. Until then, they may feel they are free to go wherever they wish. Similarly, the constraints that capitalism places on the state are ever-present, but some state actors will be unaware of this.

But the state is no more omniscient in the service of capital than it is in other respects.[9] At the outset of the Great Depression, Keynes wrote: "The world has been slow to realise that we are living this year in the shadow of one of the greatest economic catastrophes of modern history ... We have involved ourselves in a colossal muddle, having blundered in the control of a delicate machine, the working of which we do not understand. The result is that our possibilities of wealth may run to waste for a time – perhaps for a long time" (rpt. 1963, 135–6). The "colossal muddle" illustrates how extraordinarily difficult it can be for a state to change course for the benefit of the capitalist system as a whole. I noted earlier that high-level state officials tend to be survivors of tests of ideological "soundness." This inculcates an allergy to radical ideas, which in normal times can stabilize the capitalist state. But in situations of crisis, the same staffing bias can block the state's capacity to guide capitalism in a new direction. The state elite may be entirely *sympathetic* to capitalism, and intimately entwined with the economic elite, but that in itself does not show them what *needs to be done* in a crisis.

The capitalist state is also a democratic state, however imperfectly so, and this too imposes constraints.[10] Governments must be sensitive to some extent to both voters and organized "civil society" groups. Given the influence upon electoral outcomes of the health of The Economy, the electoral constraint will often *reinforce* the constraints of capital. But not always: at various times, political movements or broad cultural trends have been perceived by state and society elites as system-threatening. A crucial example, which helped set the stage for our neoliberal era, was the supposed "Crisis of Democracy" proclaimed by the Trilateral Commission in the early 1970s (Crozier, Huntington, and Watanuki 1975).

Thus, as Wolfgang Streeck notes, "capitalist democracy is ruled by two diverging sets of normative principles, *social justice* on the one hand and *market justice* on the other" (2016, 213).[11] The state must thus manage a delicate "minuet" (Elkin 1985, 194), often "by addressing the two horns of the dilemma in turn, switching back and forth as a successful response to a crisis of democratic legitimacy results in economic imbalances, and successful measures for economic stabilization in social discontent" (Streeck 2016, 214). While citizens of the global North may rarely notice this "minuet," it has been more fraught – often impossible – outside the core capitalist countries. As Uruguayan writer Eduardo Galeano commented: "In our lands, Adam Smith needs Mussolini" (1981, 146).

To successfully manage the minuet, the state must organize high-level compromises between social groups: an effective capitalist state cannot *only* serve the (narrow) interests of capital. Unemployment insurance, public medicare, a minimum wage, legal recognition of unions, health and safety regulation, progressive taxation: all of these can be seen, in retrospect, to have stabilized capitalism, but none of them came about at the behest of capital. The state thus requires "relative autonomy" from both capital and society as a whole (Poulantzas 1978, 47). The very nature of electoral democracy grants some autonomy from democratic pressures (Nordlinger 1981); autonomy from capitalist pressures is more tenuous.

In any case, neither capitalist nor democratic pressure is grounded in omniscience. In this age of right-wing "populism," it is common to point out that the democratic constraint on government need not reflect the interests of the majority: "People getting their fundamental interests wrong is what American political life is all about. This species of derangement is the bedrock of our civic order" (Frank 2004, 33). But surely the constraint of capital is less vulnerable to confusion around "fundamental interests"? Not necessarily.

Recall Keynes's observation about the "colossal muddle" of the early Depression. A factor that reinforced the conservatism and confusion of the British state elite was the influence of one sector of capital – "The City" – on policy as a whole. We earlier considered Marx and Engels's claim that "the executive of the modern state is but a committee for managing the common affairs of the whole bourgeoisie." A qualifier to this is that when it comes to direct lobbying and explicit threats, the "whole bourgeoisie" is less a factor than this or that sector of capital, this or that large business.[12] Much small and medium business, on the other hand, lacks access to the corridors of power, organized lobbying clout, and so on.

One can thus point to various instances in which business influence on government has not favoured business as a whole. The most dramatic recent case was the American deregulation of the finance industry, which sparked the economic chaos of 2007–8.[13] While the companies and individuals that sparked the crisis generally did very well for themselves, it is hard to see that the deregulation and its consequences were in the interest of business *as a whole*, or that they served the long-term interests of capitalism as a hegemonic socio-economic system.

Perhaps the earliest critic of the dangers of business's political influence for business itself was that rabble-rouser, Adam Smith. Britain's whole colonial policy, he warned, reflected the mentality of "a nation whose government is influenced by shopkeepers" (rpt. 1937, 579–80). In his most famous work, whose 1776 publication coincided with another world-shaping event, Smith argued that "under the present system of management, therefore, Great Britain derives nothing but loss from the dominion which she assumes over her colonies" (581). But the government would never see reason on this question, he added, in large part because to do so was "contrary to the private interest of the governing part" of society (582).

Because business pressure on government may not promote the long-term interests of capital as a whole, because business leaders can be too fixated on "the little and transitory profit of the monopolist," as Smith put it (rpt. 1937, 602), capitalism's success in weathering various crises may have been due to the existence of countervailing forces. But these have been weakened in the neoliberal era. As Wolfgang Streeck comments, "institutional protection of the market economy from democratic interference has advanced greatly in recent decades. Trade unions are on the decline everywhere and have in many countries been all but rooted out, especially in the US. Economic policy has widely been turned over to independent – i.e., democratically unaccountable – central banks concerned above all with the health and goodwill of financial markets" (2016, 53). This raises a paradoxical possibility: "At present, I claim, we are already in a position to observe capitalism passing away as a result of having destroyed its opposition – dying, as it were, from an overdose of itself" (65). Should that seem overwrought, consider that today, the question "Can capitalism survive climate change?" (Wallace-Wells 2019, 162) should be taken seriously. At the time of the Kyoto Accord, the question would have seemed absurd. While business influence has been far from the only factor blocking a serious climate response from the OECD and other governments, it has played an important role.

Summary: the state. The state is not a unified organism. Nor is it omniscient or infallible. Power relations within the state do not obey the simple downward logic of an organization chart, nor do state actors hold all the cards in relations with civil society. As the state is both capitalist and democratic, its elite must manage an often delicate minuet. The capitalist nature of the state is sustained by a variety of factors: by the subjectivity of members of the state elite and of the electorate, and by constraints arising from the domestic and global economy.

Finally, when the state acts it can only do so, one way or another, through individuals. Hence analysis of state actions must "pass through" individuals, although it need not begin with them, and must take into account both the motivations of individual actors and the influence of various types of structures. This is a general methodological point, relevant, I believe, to every "supra-individual" social reality. I have recently heard, for example, a couple of anti-racism activists comment that racism can be systemic *as opposed to* individual. But systemic racism cannot operate without the acts of individuals. Even when it is built into a law or rule, it is up to individuals to decide how to interpret that, whether to apply it or turn a blind eye to it, whether to attempt to challenge it, and so on. (Systemic racism will be discussed in chapter 6.)

3.2 Policy

This section will cover two basic points: the difficulty in conclusively answering some very basic questions concerning a policy, and the complexity of the relationship between a major policy initiative and the society into which it is launched.

The obscure anatomy of policy. Leslie Pal (1992, 7f) suggests that a policy can be seen as composed of:

a. A problem definition: what's wrong here, what are we trying to fix?
b. Goals: what do we aim to achieve? And
c. Instruments: what tools will we use?

It would seem, then, that to understand a policy one must, at a minimum, be able to specify the key elements of this anatomy. This, however, is no easy matter. While those who originally formulate a policy presumably enjoy clarity concerning its goals, outside observers may not.

Consider a historical example. In January 1944, the Governor General presented the W.L. Mackenzie King government's Throne Speech, laying out its upcoming legislative agenda:

> [P]lans for the establishment of a national minimum of social security and human welfare should be advanced as rapidly as possible. Such a national minimum contemplates useful employment for all who are willing to work; standards of nutrition and housing adequate to ensure the health of the whole population; and social insurance against privation resulting from unemployment, from accident, from the death of the bread-winner, from ill-health and from old age. (Commons, 27 January 1944)

The speech declared, in particular: "To aid in ensuring a minimum of well-being to the children of the nation and to help gain for them a closer approach to equality of opportunity in the battle of life, you will be asked to approve a measure making provision for family allowances."

Let us offer, first, a surface-level "anatomy" of this last policy. The *problem* might be the inequality children face in their starting points in life. The policy *goal* is to "approach" equality of opportunity, and the *instrument* is cash transfers to families with children. But *why* was the government proposing such measures at that time? That brings us to a second level of interpretation.

Months earlier, a poll revealed that the Co-operative Commonwealth Federation (CCF) had moved ahead of the Liberals. Gad Horowitz notes that "almost immediately after the release of the September Gallup poll, the Advisory Council of the National Liberal Federation, meeting at King's request, adopted fourteen resolutions 'constituting a program of reform ... of far reaching consequences.' King wrote in his diary: 'I have succeeded in making declarations which will improve the lot of ... farmers and working people ... I think I have cut the ground in large part from under the CCF'" (1968, 38; elisions in Horowitz). From an electoral perspective, we can define (a) the *problem* to be a threat to the Liberal Party's popularity; (b) the *goal* to be the restoration of electoral dominance; and (c) the *instrument* to be the suite of new policies.

But a third interpretation is also plausible. At the time, the CCF could be viewed as an "anti-system" party. Its 1933 "Regina Manifesto" declared: "We aim to replace the present capitalist system, with its inherent injustice and inhumanity, by a social order from which the domination and exploitation of one class by another will be eliminated, in which economic planning will supersede unregulated private enterprise and competition, and in which genuine democratic self-government, based upon economic equality will be possible"; it also promised that "no C.C.F. Government will rest content until it has eradicated capitalism." So one could reasonably infer that (a) the *problem* was a threat to Canadian capitalism; (b) the *goal* was to stabilize capitalism; and, as in the second interpretation, (c) the *instrument* was the set of new policies.

For our second and third interpretations, a broader reading of (c), the instruments, is plausible. The 1944 Throne Speech also promised: "When suitable agreements are reached with the provinces, my ministers will be prepared to recommend measures to provide for federal assistance in a nation-wide system of health insurance, and for a national scheme of contributory old age pensions on a more generous basis than that at present in operation" (Commons, 27 January 1944). In the event, the Canada Pension Plan had to wait another two decades, while national-level public health care began to be slowly rolled out in the late 1950s. Did this reflect a failure of negotiations with provinces? Or, perhaps, was the government announcement itself a crucial *instrument*, one not intended to be followed by serious policy action?

Hans Blumenberg provocatively suggests that "a policy is better, the more it can afford to restrict itself to 'mere words'" (1987, 441), and the possibility that any particular policy declaration *is* the instrument must always be kept in mind. Thus, the seriousness of a policy declaration can only be established retrospectively, and even then without full certainty, because the intentions of those who initially proclaimed a policy do not determine its subsequent fate.

The possibility that policy declarations often "mean less than meets the eye" (Edelman 1988, 24), may help clarify certain apparent contradictions in government action. We noted earlier the surprising juxtaposition of an anti-smoking campaign with efforts to help farmers raise the nicotine levels of tobacco. But perhaps Health Canada's anti-smoking campaigns were not seriously *intended* to reduce tobacco consumption. In the early 1990s, large quantities of Canadian-made cigarettes were being smuggled into Canada from the US, reflecting a large gap in the two countries' tobacco tax levels. Canadian tobacco companies were colluding in this operation by expanding exports to the US, a practice later acknowledged by the chair of Imperial Tobacco (Marsden 1999). An obvious solution would have been to slap high export taxes on tobacco. Instead, the Chrétien government caved in, slashing domestic tobacco taxes in early 1994. It then launched an anti-smoking campaign, which might reasonably be viewed as a mere attempt to give the impression of "doing something."

This dimension of political spectacle must certainly be kept in mind in thinking through multiculturalism: it could well be that a key instrument of the policy is all the speeches that officials and politicians make, announcing it, extolling it, declaring their allegiance to it, and so on. At the same time, we cannot assume that when we have identified a symbolic or rhetorical dimension to a policy, we have pinned down *the* truth concerning it. Eva Mackey provides fascinating excerpts from the *Legislative Briefing Book* concerning the proposed Multiculturalism Act, which the Mulroney government prepared for MPs. For example:

> Question: What does all this mean? Your policy is highly symbolic, lacking practical substance?
>
> Response: Yes the policy speaks to symbolic and emotional issues, as it should. (qtd. in Mackey 2002, 69).

Is *this* the Multiculturalism Act's hidden essence? Perhaps. But we also need to recognize the possibility that it is persuasion aimed at potential *opponents* of the policy. Statements that downplay the policy's significance, in this case, might themselves be "mere rhetoric."

It is no simple matter, then, to pin down the "anatomy" of a given policy. To focus just on (b), note the complexity of the concept of the policy *goal*. It would be naive to assume that the officially stated objective always coincides with the policy's true goal. And what might "true" mean here? We can take it to refer to the objectives of the decision-makers who approved the policy. An obvious difficulty is that we generally do not have access to their inner thoughts, so we are left trying to surmise what those might have been, from various types of evidence (other actions they took, political circumstances at the time, and so on). Further, attempts to pin down the thinking of decision-makers must allow for multiple objectives. It is reasonable to suppose that King hoped to alleviate suffering in Canada, *and* get re-elected, *and* protect capitalism.

The preceding thoughts apply to the original policy launch. After that, other factors add complexity to the concept of the policy goal. The policy will evolve over time – in light of experience, to address new circumstances, because of a shift in government ideology or priorities, and so on. The structural nature of the state is also relevant here: in the process of implementation, the original impetus of the policy gets filtered through organizational routines and interests. Over time, the "goals" of the policy may be reduced to whatever it is the relevant bureaucracies happen to be doing (Wildavsky 1979, 49). Consider, for example, the Department of Canadian Heritage's *Annual Report on the Operation of the Canadian Multiculturalism Act 2016–2017*, issued in late 2018. The report declares that the first of the multiculturalism program's three objectives is "to build an integrated, socially inclusive society by promoting intercultural and interfaith understanding; fostering civic memory, pride and respect for democratic values; and, promoting equal opportunity for individuals of all origins" (Canadian Heritage 2018). Well, is the objective being met? In fact, the report has very little to say on this. It mentions that "62% of Canadians reported concerns over a rise in racism" and that "hate crime motivated by race and/or ethnicity increased by 4% in 2016." But it entirely avoids questions such as the average earnings of various racialized and ethnic groups. Instead, the near entirety of the report is dedicated to what the government is *doing*, leaving aside the question of whether all its activities are bringing us closer to the supposed core policy objective. The report never suggests that all the activities it documents are the *goal* of multiculturalism, but its whole format turns the reader's mind away from the question of goals and substantive achievements.[14]

The question of the nature and goals of a given policy is further muddied by the fact that a major policy opens up a field of play in society as a whole, on which various games are being played for a variety of stakes. Apart from whatever sincere interest they have in the policy, the columnist is seeking to continue an output of articles that sustains their employment, the professor needs another academic publication, someone else is simply making conversation around the dinner table, and so on. And there are actors who think that "There's gold in them thar hills," that there's money to be made in one way or another from multiculturalism. All of these actors can shape the course of the policy, and perceptions of it.

A particular dimension of complexity arises when a government policy becomes associated with a "whole climate of opinion," to borrow

Auden's phrase (2007, 273). This has certainly occurred with Canadian multiculturalism. One implication is that it is not at all clear just what people have in mind when they say they support or oppose multiculturalism. I suggested in *Multicultiphobia* that many Canadians' understanding of multiculturalism had been shaped by its opponents rather than by its supporters or by official statements. It was conservative opponents, for example, who claimed that multiculturalism had no "limits." Opponents further claimed that the failure to set limits to the policy – a failure they themselves had invented – would lead to confusion among immigrants, who might believe that practices such as female genital mutilation (FGM) were acceptable in Canada.

A further implication is that, via the diffuse climate of opinion, a policy could have powerful indirect effects on widely shared "political emotions" (Nussbaum 2013). This can lead politicians, among others, to try out new political appeals, which, over time, can reshape the active political electorate. It can also provide legitimacy and impetus to a range of measures pursued at all levels of government, although they are not formally connected to the central state policy. David Robertson Cameron thus comments that the success of multiculturalism "lies not in a state plan or the application of a comprehensive rational design, but in a thousand accommodations in the schools and communities across the land" (2007, 84).

The incomplete transformation of society. Yasmeen Abu-Laban and Christina Gabriel open their *Selling Diversity* with a wonderful example of the use of multiculturalism as a sales pitch:

> In 2001 the City of Toronto hosted the International Olympic Committee (IOC) in its effort to secure the 2008 summer games. The grand finale of the IOC visit was an evening dinner gala where Prime Minister Jean Chrétien won a standing ovation for his endorsement of the bid by stressing that Toronto's advantage, as opposed to other contender cities, was its "diversity." In an apparent attempt to emphasize this, the evening's festivities included Cirque du Soleil-like acrobats, Slavic and Celtic dancers, hip-hop artists, First Nations drummers, a black choral group, and a conga line dancing to the lyrics "Hot, hot hot." (2011, 11)

But Toronto's mayor provided a remarkable sequel to this story, one that substantially undermined the sales job: "'Why the hell would I want to go to a place like Mombassa?' Mayor Mel Lastman said to a freelance journalist before leaving for a trip to Kenya to pitch the Toronto Olympic bid. 'I just see myself in a pot of boiling water with all these natives dancing around me'" (McIlroy 2001).

The story reminds us that we must be cautious when thinking about a widespread "climate of opinion": society is not homogeneous, and no matter how successful a policy, values and emotions associated with it may never fully transform a population. The rhetoric of diversity had clearly not reshaped the consciousness of Toronto's mayor. Rather, he held on to "a world view shaped in equal parts by Tarzan movies and Bugs Bunny cartoons," as one critic put in (qtd. in McIlroy 2001). Indeed, he had not even learned to keep his racist stereotypes to himself.

Even capitalism, which has had plentiful time and immense resources to remake society in its image, has not fully done so:

> Most human societies continue to adhere to traditional principles of social justice that can all-too-easily come in conflict with market justice. Examples include the idea that someone who puts in a "good day's work" should receive "a good day's wage"; that people should not be poor because of old age; that nobody should starve, remained unattended when ill, or have to live on the streets; that workers in employment should have recourse to some sort of due process against arbitrary exercise of managerial authority; or that employers should give workers notice before they dismiss them. (Streeck 2016, 213)

We see the survival of a "moral economy" in the anger sparked in the wake of natural disasters by "price gouging," which simply relabels the practice of charging what the market can bear, the very essence of market rationality (Sandel 2009, 3–5).

It would seem quite obvious that society is not homogeneous and is never fully transformed by emerging values. Yet there is much confusion on this point. Indeed, our everyday use of various abstract nouns may contribute to it: society, culture, and so on. (Even, among social scientists, "social construction," which can encourage the belief that "society" has a shared construction of this or that.) Recall Bissoondath's claim, cited in chapter 2: "Nasty things happened years ago in Canada. But that is a Canada that no longer exists" (1994, 166). This is an astonishing claim: "nasty things" are entirely a thing of the past; the Canada in which such things could happen has entirely vanished. Believing this will naturally make people less able and willing to perceive racism and intolerance. It can also easily lead to the view that tensions arise not from racism and discrimination but from the behaviour of minorities themselves: "those who see themselves 'marginalized' surely have only themselves to blame," given that Canada is a land of "boundless tolerance" (Byfield 2006). Finally, failing to understand that even the most transformative policy only incompletely permeates a society will lead to surprise and disorientation when outlooks thought long-buried enjoy a political resurgence.

But the incomplete transformation of society also poses a challenge for progressive critics, in that it constitutes a limit on styles of inference. Thus, if one observes a particular expression of racism or discrimination, one cannot immediately infer that this is an *effect* of multiculturalism, nor even that it is *compatible* with the policy. This may well be the case, but the point needs to be argued, and the alternative hypothesis – that the phenomenon is actually in contradiction with the policy – needs to be considered. We will see in chapter 5 that not all progressive critics are sufficiently careful in this respect.

As it transforms a society to a greater or lesser degree, a new social ideal does not remain unaffected by that society's other values and ideologies. First, some actors will seek to make use of the newer ideal, bending it to their purposes. Donald Gutstein cites a lobbying advertisement for "ethical oil" from Canada's tar sands that "showed two men in a Middle Eastern country with nooses around their necks, waiting to be hanged for being homosexuals, with the word 'persecution' stamped on the photo. Next to it was a photo of two men holding hands – in Canada, we assume – with rainbow bracelets and the word 'pride'" (2014, 149). This exemplifies the use of a progressive ideal for quite unprogressive marketing.

So what are we to make of this? It certainly does not mean that the rights of sexual minorities are *nothing but* a marketing tool, or were promoted for that reason. Rather, this is an example of what I have called the "paradox of hegemony" (2019): any broadly supported ideal will become a rhetorical resource to be used for a variety of ends, some of which may horrify those who truly support the ideal. Thus, Canadian multiculturalism has been invoked to: oppose bilingualism (Yaffe 1995); both oppose and support the teaching of creationism in public schools (Hume 1995; Krueger 1995); oppose same-sex marriage (Stephen Harper, Commons, 16 February 2005); oppose land treaties with Indigenous peoples (Jack Ramsay, Commons, 2 May 1994); and even oppose licensed daycare (Nina Grewal, Commons, 15 February 2005).

The linking of a progressive ideal to other objectives may also arise from another direction. Take, for example, the argument that the empowerment of Third World women can slow down population growth. This may be a rhetorical move to build a coalition of support for a set of progressive policies. Yet the move is not risk-free. Presumably, the tactic is used because the value of gender equality is not broadly accepted in a society. Sooner or later, that battle will have to be engaged directly. If one simply allows the goal of equality to "piggy-back" on a goal of population control, other analysts may make the case that there are more "efficient" ways of limiting population growth. In the specific case of multiculturalism, emphasizing the case that diversity "pays" can focus attention narrowly on those forms of diversity that actually do "pay," in some narrow sense. This will lead to the neglect of justice issues, ignoring the specific forms of discrimination suffered by people who *don't* represent an enticing market for advertisers or a pool of potential professional skills. As Abu-Laban and Gabriel note, "on its own terms selling diversity may 'work,' but it does not necessarily guarantee greater equality between Canadians" (2011, 12).

Note the methodological difficulty all this presents. An observed phenomenon could reflect the policy's original goals, or the policy as it evolved over time, or something else altogether. It may actually be a direct effect of the policy. Or it could be a product of those who oppose it, or those who have no particular interest in it one way or the other but who use certain elements rhetorically for other ends, or some combination of these.

When, for example, we see plentiful signs of ongoing racism in Canada after decades of multicultural policy, how are we to understand this? One hypothesis is that it reflects the policy's imperfect permeation of Canadian society. But we cannot therefore conclude that multiculturalism policy is innocent of all connection with racism and other forms of injustice. Doing so could help divert the energies and attention of those who might otherwise struggle against injustice: government funding of civil society groups, for example, might channel energy towards funding applications and activities tailored in light of funding requirements. It might also provide a feel-good distraction for other citizens, who might otherwise have to deal with a certain amount of uneasy conscience. (We will return to this in chapter 10.)

But we may not even be dealing with the problem of a policy's incomplete transformation of society: perhaps it never sought to challenge racism, but simply to make it less visible, more tolerable. But even if one believes this, the story does not end there, since, as we have seen, the original intent of a policy only takes analysis so far, as policy goals will evolve over time. A policy may be progressively tamed, but a contrary movement is also possible, through efforts to develop an ideal's latent potential.

Any policy, in particular, that invokes values of human rights and equality is liable to be pushed further by activists and theorists. Mary Wollstonecraft provided an early example of this. In her dedication in *Vindication of the Rights of Women* (1792), she addresses Talleyrand-Périgord, a member of the French National Assembly: "I address you as a legislator, whether, when men contend for their freedom, and to be allowed to judge for themselves respecting their own happiness, it be not inconsistent and unjust to subjugate women, even though you firmly believe that you are acting in the manner best calculated to promote their happiness? Who made man the exclusive judge, if woman partake with him of the gift of reason?" (rpt. 1993, 67). "Inconsistent and unjust": the demand for moral consistency is a powerful one. Hence we will find activists regularly invoking it: "I have a dream that one day this nation will rise up and live out the true meaning of its creed: 'We hold these truths to be self-evident: that all men are created equal'" (King 1963).

Conversely, *inconsistency* can present those initially aligned with an ideal with a stark choice: either withdraw support or see the ideal turned against them. Marx depicted this dilemma in his *Eighteenth Brumaire of Louis Bonaparte*: the bourgeoisie, he wrote, "understood that all the so-called bourgeois liberties and organs of progress attacked and menaced its class rule at its social foundation and its political summit simultaneously ... The parliamentary regime lives by discussion, how shall it forbid discussion? Every interest, every social institution, is here transformed into general ideas, debated as ideas; how shall any interest, any institution, sustain itself above thought and impose itself as an article of faith?" (rpt. 1969, vol. 2, 435).

We seem to have travelled far from discussion of "mere" policy. But analogous dynamics play out at various levels. It is precisely because Canada has a public health care policy, for example, that critics can condemn the state of health care services on First Nation reserves (Chambers and Burnett, 2017). But what of multiculturalism? Have we seen a similar dynamic of extension? To some extent. It is often noted that multicultural policy was initially aimed "almost exclusively at the European ethnic sector" (Fleras and Elliott 2002, 65). But the changing composition of immigration to Canada, and evidence of a hardening of racist attitudes, led a parliamentary committee to recommend in 1984 that "multicultural policy must now be strengthened and greater emphasis placed on the race relations element, in order to accommodate the new realities of Canada's multiracial society" (Special Committee on Participation of Visible Minorities in Canadian Society 1984, 55). This led to a declining emphasis on celebrating "ethnic heritage" and a greater policy focus on "removal of discriminating barriers, institutional change, and affirmative action to equalize opportunity" (Dewing and Leman 2006, 7).

One may still ask whether that policy extension was (a) effective and (b) lasting. Further, one may ask whether we see multiculturalism being invoked *today* by leaders and citizens who seek to challenge racism. Further still, has the policy helped restructure the public sphere so that different voices are heard, or granted greater legitimacy? We will return to these questions.

Summary: policy. Different readings of the "anatomy" of a policy are often possible. We need to be particularly careful concerning the *objectives* of a policy, since that term can refer to a variety of very distinct phenomena: the non-public goals of the original decision-makers, the officially stated original rationale, the goals that emerged over time, and so on. Finally, even the most far-reaching policy only incompletely changes society. We thus cannot infer back from social phenomena to the policy's "true" objectives.

3.3 Culture

In her 1997 essay "Is Multiculturalism Bad for Women?," feminist philosopher Susan Moller Okin asked, "What should be done when the claims of minority cultures or religions clash with the norm of gender equality that is at least formally endorsed by liberal states (however much they continue to violate it in their practice)?" (rpt. 1999a, 9). Okin raised concerns over practices such as polygamy, which she claimed was tacitly accepted by authorities in France, the use of "cultural defenses" in American courts, and the opinion expressed by some American doctors that FGM should not be criminalized, being "a private matter which, as one said, 'should be decided by a physician, the family, and the child'" (23).

One male critic took particular offence at Okin's opposition to FGM. "Is it possible," asked Sander Gilman, "that the projection of Western, bourgeois notions of pleasure onto other people's bodies is not the best basis for anybody's judgment?" The core of this "Western, bourgeois" view, apparently, is an obsession with physical pleasure, when in fact it is "clear that even sexual pleasure is as much a reflex of the mind as of the body." Against those interfering feminists seeking to abolish "pesky rituals of difference," Gilman insisted that "the question of pleasure should be left to the culture that defines it" (1999, 54–7).

Divine culture? I noted earlier that both everyday thinking and more rigorous analysis at times manifest a tacit image of the state as something God-like. For Gilman, culture also becomes a stand-in for God. It is, first, *omnipotent*: culture can dictate what the mind experiences as pleasure, so the mutilation of one's sexual organs is no big deal. Had Gilman "consulted just a few women," Okin drily replied, "he could easily have found out that there are limits to the power of the mind.

Without a clitoris, a woman cannot experience orgasm, any more than a man could without a penis" (1999b, 125).

Gilman's culture is also godlike in that it gets to define right and wrong, so that the "question of pleasure" can safely be left to the "culture that defines it."[15] Note the profound mystification here: how does a culture "define" anything? *People* define things, and the process whereby a definition becomes widely accepted within a culture is hardly unproblematic. Okin makes what should be an obvious point: that in a patriarchal culture, it is primarily a subset of men who get to "determine and articulate the group's beliefs, practices, and interests" (rpt. 1999a, 12).

Instead of assuming that "culture" – that is, those who succeed in speaking in its name – gets to define what is right and wrong, those of us not in thrall to Gilman's extreme relativism would prefer to say that social practices and institutions should be judged precisely by the extent to which they promote or frustrate human pleasure, happiness, and general well-being, rather than that people should meekly accept as their due whatever fragments of pleasure or happiness this or that culture or institution deigns to allow them.

But there's more: Okin was not writing about the practices inflicted on young women growing up somewhere else. Her concern was with FGM being tolerated in the US. So in his critique, Gilman is claiming not only that culture in general can dictate to the mind what it will experience as pleasure but also that a *minority* culture within a Western country can succeed in doing this. Exposure to popular culture, public education, friends: none of these, he is telling us, have any weight alongside the dictates of the ethnoculture.

In *Multicultiphobia*, I suggested that, rather than think of culture as a "container," we should "apply the metaphor of 'radio waves' to the influences upon us. Each 'frequency' reaches a group of individuals, and yet each of us is attuned to a unique *set* of frequencies. The waves are 'outside' us, yet also 'inside' us. That is, they can shape our view of the world, and even our self-understanding, in myriad ways" (2010b, 14). Gilman will have none of this: his subculture is emphatically a container, and its walls are made of lead, as it were, so that no cultural "radio waves" from outside can penetrate.

A tacit understanding of culture. Now here is a puzzle: Gilman is presumably an intelligent person and as such would immediately reject these tacit assumptions were they made explicit. So why are they made? This brings us back to Kahneman's "fast thinking": default assumptions rule by virtue of *not* being made explicit; they serve, rather, as unexamined tools for thought. Gilman's use of these cognitive tools is particularly repugnant, but the default assumptions themselves are widely shared, as can be seen by the fact that they influence thinkers at multiple points along the political "spectrum."

Exactly how some deeply problematic assumptions about culture became influential is unclear, although sociologist John Porter might have been on to something in noting that "sociology has taken the word [culture] over from anthropology, which has studied small, sometimes isolated, traditional-bound [sic] groups where the transmission from one generation to the next of the established ways of doing things and viewing the world is essential to social survival" (1969, 118).[16]

But how, one might object, can one speak confidently of the influence of *hidden* assumptions? The answer: through a simple inference about the nature of inferences. First, as I argued in *Multicultiphobia*, "since you belong to many groups, one could say that you participate in various cultures. Any group, Saturday afternoon soccer players or book club members, generates standard ways that cover *some* aspects of life, however limited. It is thus quite reasonable to talk of organizational culture, to have Dilbert cartoons poke fun at the culture of engineers, and so on" (2010b, 16). Given this, and the wide range of influences upon us, no single culture can *dictate* what we believe or do: its influence can be no more than a matter of probabilities.

That means we can never reliably infer back from an observed action or belief to a simple cultural explanation. Thus, when someone *does* engage in such an inference, they are drawing on the tacit assumption that culture is an all-enveloping container, asserting that only membership in the culture has explanatory weight, that other dimensions of an individual's identity and experience *do not matter*. As noted earlier, the influence of this tacit assumption is variable. It is likely to have greater weight when explaining the actions of strangers, about whom little is known other than that they "belong" to a different culture. (It is not that the assumption is sleeping at other times. Rather, as stars still shine in the day, yet cannot be seen, its influence is outweighed by the many sources of information we have about those known to us.)

Two views of culture – and their respective affinities. What's at stake in this question? We have two competing understandings. One – the "container" view of culture – is based on the tacit assumption that the individual lives within *one* culture, has *one* important dimension to their identity and *one* important set of affiliations with others – those with whom they share their *one* culture.[17] We are, in Sen's memorable rendering, "inmates rigidly incarcerated in little containers" (2006, xvii). In the other view, the multidimensional approach, each of us lives "within" multiple cultures. We thus have multiple dimensions to our identity, and we can be affiliated with others in a variety of ways. As novelist Amin Maalouf put it, we can enjoy a sense of belonging to

> a religious tradition; a nationality, sometimes two; an ethnic or linguistic group; a more or less extended family; a profession; an institution; a certain social milieu ... But the list is much longer, virtually unlimited: one can have a more or less strong sense of belonging to a province, a village, a neighbourhood, a clan, a sports or professional team, a group of friends, a union, a company, a party, an association, a parish, a community of people who share a passion, or the same sexual preferences, or the same handicaps, or who confront the same nuisances. (Maalouf 1998, 16–17; elision in Maalouf)

To claim that the container view of culture *causes* this or that is to commit the idealist error of assuming that practices flow from beliefs in a unidirectional relation. So we need to seek out, not the "consequences" or "effects" of that view, but the beliefs and practices with which it can enjoy a self-reinforcing *affinity* (Weber 1978, 341). Amartya Sen offers a good example of how a simplistic understanding of culture can fill an ideological need:

> Winston Churchill made the famous remark that the Bengal famine of 1943, which occurred just before India's independence from Britain in 1947 (it would also prove to be the last famine in India in the century, since famines disappeared with the Raj), was caused by the tendency of people there to "breed like rabbits." The explication belongs to the general tradition of finding explanations of disasters not in bad administration, but in the culture of the subjects, and this habit of thought had some real influence in crucially delaying famine relief in the Bengal famine, which killed between two and three million people ... Cultural theories evidently have their uses. (Sen 2006, 106)

The container view of culture and identity can also serve a psychological need. Drawing on his experience covering the Balkan wars, journalist Chris Hedges points to the potential pay-off of viewing oneself as *only* a member of one's nation, which is in a grand struggle with other nations: "To those who swallow the nationalist myth, life is transformed. The collective glorification permits people to abandon their usual preoccupation with the petty concerns of daily life. They can abandon even self-preservation in the desire to see themselves as players in a momentous historical drama. This vision is accepted even at the expense of self-annihilation. Life in wartime becomes theater. All are actors" (2002, 54).[18]

Further, the container view permits casual reference to "the values" of a particular culture, or to "the traditions" of this or that society, in ways that imply uniformity. As I noted in *Multicultiphobia*, such talk has been common among conservative critics of multiculturalism. Some will push this implausible view to an even grander level, speaking of the defining values of a *civilization*. Samuel Huntington's lamentably influential "Clash of Civilizations" essay claimed that "civilizations are differentiated from each other by history, language, culture, tradition and, most important, religion. The people of different civilizations have different views on the relations between God and man, the individual and the group, the citizen and the state, parents and children, husband and wife, as well as differing views of the relative importance of rights and responsibilities, liberty and authority, equality and hierarchy" (Huntington 1993, 25). But the idea that there is a "Western" view of the "relations between God and man" – to take just the first item on his list – is so obviously absurd that the influence of Huntington's essay testifies to the power of the simplistic tacit assumptions being critiqued here.

Now if the world is truly made up of "stark and separated boxes of civilizations or of religious identities" (Sen 2006, 103), it is no wonder that the clash between them is truly titanic, no wonder that many who embrace this vision turn apoplectic about the "great replacement." As we saw in chapter 2, for Viktor Orbán, the El Paso mass murderer, and various Fox News commentators, *we* are threatened with "replacement" by an entirely alien species. And *they* are entirely alien because Muslims, for example, are seen as *nothing but* Muslims. The fact that multiple dimensions of their identity unite them to others is obscured by the one dimension that appears to separate them from those others. From the multidimensional perspective, on the other hand, any risk of a "clash of civilizations" arises only from those who embrace the container view – or act as if they did – and persuade others to embrace it as well. Given the rise of xenophobic authoritarians, the risk today is not negligible.

A further affinity with the container view is the belief that the assimiliation of immigrants is a political imperative. In *Multicultiphobia*, I argued for the importance of "citizen identification, the disposition to view one's fellow citizens, not as an abstract 'them,' but as people with whom one is connected in a web of reciprocal rights and obligations" (2010b, 166–7). The container view favours the assumption that this requires that all citizens occupy a single container. One of the great conservative fears of multiculturalism is thus that it will isolate citizens from one another by emphasizing identification as a member of an ethnic group. Others are concerned that multiculturalism and ethnic pluralism will weaken the welfare state. (See the extensive discussion of this issue in Banting and Kymlicka's *Multiculturalism and the Welfare State*).

But a key element of the multidimensional understanding of culture is that, as Gramsci put it, "each one of us changes himself, modifies himself to the extent that he changes and modifies the complex relations of which he is the hub" (1971, 352). In reality, the sorts of multicultural policies introduced in many countries in the last decades of the twentieth century would at most rearrange the salience of different forms of identification among ethnic minorities. And it is not at all clear that such rearrangements would heighten ethnic identification: if policies lower the discriminatory barriers to participation in various social and economic institutions, they could well have the opposite effect. A rise in inter-ethnic marriages (Kymlicka 1998, 20), for example, would be expected to weaken such identification. (I will return to this question in chapter 8's discussion of the effects of tolerance.)

A progressive variant of the container view, and its dangers. Conservatives hold no monopoly on the container view of culture. In a discussion of Charles Taylor's discomfort with the *demand* that we make "actual judgments of equal worth" of other cultures, Richard Day cites Taylor's rationale for this discomfort: "if the judgment of equal value is to register something independent of our own wills and desires, it cannot be dictated by a principle of ethics" (Taylor 1994, 68). Day then goes on to criticize Taylor for his "reluctance to acknowledge *the equal worth of Others* without some 'objective' basis for the judgment" (2000, 218; emphasis added). So to reserve a judgment of equality between two cultures is to deny equality to some *persons*. But this can make sense only if individuals *are* their culture.

This would seem to be an improbable assumption, but it is not unprecedented in the social sciences. Consider, for example, Marx's disclaimer at the outset of *Capital*: "I paint the capitalist and the landlord in no sense *couleur de rose*. But here individuals are dealt with only in so far as they are the personifications of economic categories, embodiments of particular class-relations and class-interests" (rpt. 1954, 20–1).[19] This allowed Marx to simplify his analysis enormously, and it allows Day to do the same. In both cases, the simplification comes at the cost of misunderstanding complex social identities and realities.

In Marx's abstraction, being a capitalist swallows the entire identity of the person. This is politically vital because – to the extent that the abstraction is confused with reality – the individual is seen as *nothing but* someone who must be fully committed to defending capitalist domination. They cannot be, for example, *also* a religious person with an uneasy sense that there is something wrong with the current state of affairs, or a citizen uncomfortable with the risks that this domination poses to society.[20]

This reduction of the person to "an institution in a single instance" (Arnold Gehlen, qtd. in Habermas 1987, 293) creates important limits to the thought of progressives who indulge in it. Given the hyper-identification of individual and group – whether that group be thought of as a culture or a class – it is hard to see how progressive appeals can gain any hearing in the dominant group. The reductionism also blocks an understanding of people's often puzzling political choices. Commentators such as Thomas Frank have asked how it is possible for so many members of the American working class to vote for a Republican Party that consistently harms their economic interests (2004, 33).

Arlie Hochschild's *Strangers in Their Own Land* offers a possible answer. In a vivid reconstruction of the thinking of many of her Louisiana Tea Party interviewees, she writes: "You haven't gotten a raise in years, and there is no talk of one. Actually, if you are short a high school diploma, or even a BA, your income has dropped over the last twenty years" (2018, 136). In the face of this, people in effect *rearrange their identity*, bringing non-economic dimensions to the fore, dimensions that can confer a dignity that their economic reality does not: "You think of things to feel proud of – your Christian morality, for one. You've always stood up for clean-living, monogamous, heterosexual marriage" (137). And those nasty anti-worker Republicans? Well, they are perceived as "clean-living people" who "put the Bible where it belongs" (47).

This identity shuffle is certainly not a merely individual trick: it has been carefully orchestrated over decades in a process of "interpellation" (Althusser 1971). And it has worked, among white Americans, a focus that reflects another feature of Republican strategy since at least the Nixon presidency: "Among whites without degrees ... 76 percent of those for whom religion is not at all important voted for Democratic House candidates in 2018. At the other end of the spectrum, nearly 4 out of five – 78 percent – of non-college whites who said religion was very important voted for a Republican House candidate" (Edsall 2020).

Implications for multiculturalism. The container view creates a stark either/or view of multiculturalism and its alternatives. Markus Crepaz offers a typical statement of this. He presents a question from the World Values Survey: "Which statement is nearest to your opinion? Immigrants should 1) maintain distinct customs and traditions; 2) take over the customs of the country" (2006, 98). The question clearly assumes the container view. Once one abandons that, a very attractive option is "Both." Further, multiculturalism is depicted from within the container view, as Crepaz claims that "most proponents of multiculturalism would take the answer option 'maintain customs and traditions' as the central goal of multiculturalism" (98).

Indeed, the container view is so influential that many observers view answers to survey questions such as this one as representing attitudes towards multiculturalism as a whole. In *Culture and Equality*, his polemic against what he takes to be multiculturalism, British philosopher Brian Barry writes that "a noteworthy finding was provided by a public opinion poll conducted in Canada in 1993, which showed 'nearly three quarters of respondents rejecting the idea that Canada is a multicultural nation.' The result is especially striking because it amounts to a direct repudiation of the Canadian Multiculturalism Act which was passed in 1988" (2001, 292). But Barry never examined the poll. The quoted words are from a piece by Sebastian Poulter, who also never examined the poll, relying instead on a 1995 article by Kallen, who cites a December 1993 *Toronto Star* article. The latter article, however, shows that the poll question, on which so much second-, third-, and fourth-hand certainty is erected, does not use the word multiculturalism, but asks whether people should "adapt to the value system and the way of life of the majority in Canadian society" (Thompson 1993).

I have noted various problems that arise from the container view of culture. But the multidimensional view itself can pose challenges for aspects of multiculturalism, which must be addressed. I will consider three here. First: in an argument against the prospect of Supreme Court positions being "allotted by sex and race," conservative pundit Andrew Coyne writes: "Each of us is the unique intersection of any number of different group identities. To elevate the relatively trivial differences between different groups over the profound differences between us as individuals can only be achieved by ascribing a false homogeneity to members of the same group: as if there were a woman's view of the law, or a man's for that matter. It is the very opposite of diversity" (2016).

Coyne would appear to be articulating the multidimensional view. But there is nothing in that view of culture that dictates which types of difference are and are not "trivial." Widespread practices of discrimination determine, to a large degree, the importance of specific forms of difference, in terms of both objective life chances and subjective identities. In 2009, Philip Oreopoulos published the findings from a field experiment that involved mailing thousands of fictitious résumés in response to job postings. Among other things, he found that "Canadian applicants that differed only by name had substantially different callback rates: Those with English-sounding names received interview requests 40 percent more often than applicants with Chinese, Indian, or Pakistani names (16 percent versus 11 percent)" (2009, 5). So, after almost forty years of multiculturalism policy, just your name could prevent you from getting through the door, from a serious encounter that would allow you to manifest other dimensions of your identity. However "trivial" you might want your ethnic background to be, others will ensure that it remains important. To answer Coyne, then: if, say, sexism and racism are pervasive in society, structuring social positions and economic outcomes, then a Supreme Court – or a government office, or a newsroom – in which women and racial minorities have at best a token presence is extremely unlikely to be able to understand many fundamental social realities and experiences.

A second challenge arising from the multidimensional view is to the sort of claim advanced by Bhikhu Parekh: "Since human beings are culturally embedded respect for them entails respect for their cultures and ways of life" (1994). The claim seems problematic, resting upon the close identification of person and culture that characterizes the container view. But recall the previous point: in a situation of widespread discrimination, one's ethnic or racialized group may well *feel* like a container, a container erected from the outside. So if you are often treated as *nothing but* a Muslim, and at the same time Islam is subject to widespread derision and suspicion, it is hard to avoid taking this as a personal affront.

Further, "respect" is a very flexible term. To clarify the issue, consider the sort of respect that is involved in a relation of *love*. This may seem an odd approach, but one reason "love matters for justice" (Nussbaum 2013) is that love can provide an epistemological corrective to reflections on justice, which can often work with a conception of equality that is surreptitiously tilted in one's favour. Now, when dealing with someone we love, we know that what matters to them matters, period. We may not share their beliefs, but neither do we casually dismiss or mock them. I think we can view that spirit of *discretion* as a reasonable component of our respect for our fellow citizens.[21] On this basis, we can endorse a later formulation from Parekh: "We can hardly be said to respect a person if we treat with contempt or abstract away all that gives meaning to his life and makes him the kind of person he is" (2000, 240). This formulation avoids the container view's assumption that we are "embedded" in a single culture, and it does not require us to *share* or *like* the other person's life commitments.

Third and finally, it is easy to imagine an objection: "Look, your understanding of culture is all very well and good, but when we speak of multiculturalism, we're definitely not thinking of culture that way.

Multiculturalism is about relations between ethnocultures." But even if one wishes to hold that understanding of multiculturalism, one must not *restrict* the concept of culture to ethnocultures. When we narrow the concept to that particular form, we induce mistakes in our understanding of how culture exists in the world and of how any culture coexists with others, not just within society but within *each human being*.

3.4 Multiculturalism

A puzzling certainty. Let us begin with a puzzle. On the one hand, it would seem obvious that "multiculturalism" means many different things to different people. I noted earlier that in the Canadian context, the term seems to gesture at, not a clear idea, but a "whole climate of opinion." Yet many, especially among critics of multiculturalism, proceed as if their understanding of the term were the only possible one.[22] Richard Day, for example, claims that "the supposition that individuals can 'have' or 'achieve' stable ethnocultural identities is essential to multiculturalism in all of its modes" (2000, 32). The term is thus subject to a mysterious necessity: "Multiculturalism, then, necessarily enacts itself as liberal, statist, capitalist colonialism" (Day 2014, 130).[23] Katha Pollitt goes further, imposing a fixed meaning on not one but two widely contested ideas: "You could say that multiculturalism demands respect for all cultural traditions, while feminism interrogates and challenges all cultural traditions" (1999, 27).

Critic Christian Joppke articulates one of the most widespread dogmatic understandings of multiculturalism: "What multiculturalism *is* has been canonically formulated by Charles Taylor as a 'politics of recognition' that compensates for past injustice and starts with the assumption of the 'equal value' of the culture of the groups that were once denigrated" (2014, 287).[24] This one has been around for a long time: "At the center of the multiculturalist ethos is the contention that all cultures are equally valuable" (Kimball 1992, 64). Similarly, Salim Mansur, an extreme Canadian opponent of multiculturalism, defines it as "the set of ideas that all cultures are equal and deserving of equal treatment in a liberal democracy such as Canada" (2011, 2). (The claim is repeated by one of Mansur's readers: the Norwegian who murdered more than seventy people on 22 July 2011. In his manifesto of over 1,000 pages – which cites Mansur – the murderer revealed an obsession with the proposition that "all cultures are equal," attacking it at least twenty times. The proposition, he claimed, constituted the "essence of multiculturalism," "the foundational concept of multiculturalism.")

Retire the term? Some have – perhaps disingenuously – suggested that the semantic confusion around "multiculturalism" warrants abandoning the term altogether: "The terminology has ceased to have any real meaning," declared the *Globe and Mail* in a 2010 editorial. "It signifies very different things to different people, and has turned into a flashpoint and a distraction. Multiculturalism should be struck from the national vocabulary." The editorial then added that we could somehow "refocus the debate" by talking about "pluralism" instead.

The assumption here is that the confusion arose *for no reason*. In truth, it reflects many factors, none of which would vanish with a change in terminology. Many critics evidently prefer to offer a simplistic caricature of multiculturalism, which is easier to attack. Politicians, for their part, have a notorious preference for ambiguity and imprecision. As noted earlier, in discussing the general concept of "policy," further blurring can occur in the transition from a general policy declaration to actual government actions, as the operative goals of a policy get reduced to whatever the bureaucracy can manage to get done. Academics in particular sub-sub-sub-disciplines, finally, can uncritically adopt terminology (along with claims, speculation, and so on) from others within their narrow circle. So if "multiculturalism" were replaced by "pluralism" or something else ("diversity" is a leading candidate at the moment), we should not expect its meaning to be any more settled than that of multiculturalism.

As evidence of this, consider a discussion paper prepared by Global Affairs Canada for its 2016 international assistance review. Its treatment of the values underpinning Canadian development aid mentions pluralism nine times but entirely avoids the word multiculturalism. But does it *define* pluralism? It does not: it simply keeps using the word, as if we all knew what it meant. We don't. All sorts of nice words – pluralism, inclusiveness, diversity – mask lots of important questions, issues Canadians need to discuss. These are generally the same issues we should be talking about concerning multiculturalism.

Really existing multiculturalism. There are a couple of strategies, which don't exclude each other, that we can adopt to confront the semantic riot. One, fruitfully developed by Will Kymlicka, focuses on "really-existing multiculturalism" (2007c, 108), a phrase that deliberately echoes Soviet-era references to "actually-existing socialism." In *Finding Our Way* (1998), Kymlicka addressed fears around multiculturalism by presenting a list of "thirteen policies –existing or proposed – that are often discussed under the rubric of 'multiculturalism' in the public debate" (1998, 42). This led to his famous summary claim that existing multiculturalism policy was about "renegotiating the terms of integration" (39).

Later, Kymlicka and colleagues developed a multiculturalism policy index, which tracks twenty-three policies that are relevant to Indigenous peoples, substate national groups, or immigrants (Banting et al. 2006).

This book will follow Kymlicka's strategy in this respect: statements about what multiculturalism *is*, and what it *is doing* or *has done*, must be subject to a plausibility check, comparing the claim with what has actually been done in the name of multiculturalism.[25] A corollary to this is that criticisms of multiculturalism cannot be dismissed by invoking lofty policy declarations, if those criticisms are consistent with actual policies.

A normative approach. This book will also pursue a second analytical strategy, based on a question presented in *Multicultiphobia*: "What are we to make of our multiculturalism? Granted that, as a matter of empirical fact, we have become a very diverse nation, how do we wish to *live* this fact? Just what do we want multiculturalism to be for us?" (Ryan 2010b, 208). Now, it is possible that *we* cannot consciously and reflectively decide what we want our multiculturalism to be. Perhaps the matter is effectively decided by a "sociological we": we all share a social space, in which we go about our everyday lives, shaping and in turn shaped by our social institutions. From this perspective, what *we* make of our multiculturalism is decided in millions of everyday actions: in how we interact with one another, in who we decide to love, to marry, to befriend, in where we decide to live, in the assumptions each of us makes about those who we think are not like us, assumptions often made manifest in a glance, a frown, a smile.[26]

Still, on the off chance that discussions of what we want our multiculturalism to be might actually have some small impact on what it becomes, let me offer the following definition, not of what multiculturalism *is*, but of a multiculturalism worth defending: "Multiculturalism should be understood as the ethnoracial dimension of the struggle for a just society."

I will call this multiculturalism-J, where J stands for justice. The definition is certainly vague, because it does not nail down what is meant by justice or a just society. Like Rawls's "original position" thought experiment, the definition simply provides a framework for discussion. But not an empty, *tabula rasa,* framework: the definition presupposes, for example, that any conception of multiculturalism is inadequate if it leads to "trade-offs" with gender equality or the rights of sexual minorities. Practices that endanger those values are antithetical to multiculturalism-J. The approach proposed here would also reject understandings of feminism, for example, that were oblivious to questions of ethnoracial justice. Thus, the approach seeks to avoid practices through which "antiracism reproduces patriarchy and feminism reproduces racism" (Carastathis 2014, 310).

Personally, in a discussion of the nature of a just society, I would on both Rawlsian and religious grounds promote a democratic socialist vision. This would be hostile to a neoliberal multiculturalism, according to which "the society would be just if 1 percent of the population controlled 90 percent of the resources, provided that blacks and other nonwhites, women, and lesbian, gay, bisexual, and transgender (LGBT) people were represented among the 1 percent in roughly similar proportion as their incidence in the general population" (Reed 2013, 54). But the key point is that only by viewing the struggle against ethnoracial injustice as joined with the struggle against economic injustice and other dimensions of struggle can we even grasp that discussion concerning the goal of a just society is a necessary part of pursuing an *unambiguously* just multiculturalism. And only thus can we avoid having the "gravitational pull" of our dominant economic and ideological institutions reduce multiculturalism to an instrument of neoliberal "meritocracy."

It is reasonable to define oneself as a supporter of multiculturalism, *insofar* as it is understood in this way, but not otherwise. That is, one can say that one supports a struggle for ethnoracial justice within the broader struggle for a just society, without committing oneself to supporting multiculturalism understood in other ways. This does not mean that one necessarily *rejects* practices associated with other understandings: they may be normatively and politically ambiguous rather than purely unjust. Such practices may be deeply problematic when they constitute the core and limit of actual multiculturalism policies yet amenable to inclusion within a set of policies pursuing multiculturalism-J.[27]

3.5 Summary: Concepts and the Traps of Language

Words and things. We have examined four concepts in this chapter: State, Policy, Culture, Multiculturalism. These terms have aspects in common. Each is a singular noun, and this masks their internal plurality:

> *The state* can be viewed as a vast set of organizations, as an even vaster set of people working in those organizations, as a set of formal and informal powers, and so on.

A policy can comprise multiple – even contradictory – goals, many tools with which to pursue them, various analyses of the problems thereby targeted, and so on.

A culture can refer to an (almost always) undefined hodgepodge of beliefs and practices, and much else besides.

Multiculturalism carries all the complexity of being a policy, but it can be much more besides: a vague ideology, a set of aspirations, a myth, and so on.

The contrast between the grammatical simplicity of these terms and the messy realities they designate provides endless potential for confusion, talking at cross-purposes, and serious mystification. Pierre Bourdieu comments that "everything conspires to encourage the reification of concepts, starting with the logic of ordinary language" (rpt. 2000, 254). A desk, a chair, a tree: these singular terms refer to single objects ... so shouldn't *a culture* do the same?[28] Errors that arise from this are pervasive and can be quite serious: I have surveyed some such errors in this chapter. More are coming, in Part II.

We can legitimately use the four concepts discussed here – and many others besides – as shorthand, without which it would be hard ever to say anything about politics and society. But both writers and readers must try to remember that shorthand is being used to refer to complex and sometimes shadowy realities.

When "things" come alive: on collective actors. The Bourdieu passage just cited goes on, observing that ordinary language can mislead us in another way: we are easily led to jump from the fact that a term can "act" as the subject of a sentence to the belief that the thing to which it refers really acts in the world. In this case, the "thing" designated by the abstract noun comes alive and does all sorts of things. Social realities, the products of human action, "appear as independent beings endowed with life" (Marx rpt. 1954, 77).[29]

We must not let any collective noun – state, ethnic group, class, and so on – bewitch us into forgetting that all such phenomena are made up of real people, who do not fully submerge their individuality in the whole. They retain their personal interests and passions, and their sense of right and wrong, and these things influence them to some degree and are not fully reshaped by the collective reality. Members of any such reality may simultaneously cooperate and compete with one another. They may aim to further what they understand to be the objectives of the collective, yet also look beyond it, to other objectives, to a time when they are no longer as closely tied to it.

This does not mean, however, that a collective reality is "nothing but" the individuals who comprise it. Some collective phenomena are "going concerns," which will continue to exist after all current members are gone. This is true of any society, which is thus more than the aggregate of its members at any given moment. By extension, the state of health of a society cannot be assessed merely by "aggregating the welfares of different individuals," as some believe (Stokey and Zeckhauser 1978, 257). So it is reasonable and responsible to think of individuals as – along with other dimensions of their identity – *stewards*, responsible for the future well-being of the society, precisely because they are responsible for the well-being of real people who will need that society as their common home.

PART II

On the Writing of the Progressive Critics

Chapter Four

Some Mysterious Claims in the Writing of Progressive Critics

I don't like obscurity because I consider it a form of despotism.
Michel Foucault, "Sexualité et pouvoir," in (1994)

[Bells] have tones that touch and search
The hearts of young and old;
One sound to all, yet each
Lends a meaning to their speech,
And the meaning is manifold.
Longfellow, "The Bells of San Blas" (1882, 61)

Before response, there must be understanding. Before we can assess a claim, we must know what it means. Because of the preferred writing styles of *some* of the progressive critics, this is not always easy. This chapter will examine some mysterious claims advanced by various progressive critics. The next chapter will take up other problematic features in progressive writing.

First, some caveats. I will certainly not be considering *all* progressive critics in this chapter. Nor does the inclusion of claims from this or that author imply that *everything* they write is obscure. Further: I'm drawing from works from varying dates. It is quite possible that some of the authors cited here no longer hold the opinions quoted, either because they have come to reconsider their earlier assertions or because they believe that Canadian realities have significantly changed. So we will take these quotes merely as examples of certain recurring qualities of some progressive discourse. And the style is durable: there are affinities, for example, among the sorts of obscurity that recur in Day (2000), Thobani (2007), various chapters in the Chazan, Helps, and Stanley anthology (2011), and Kanji (2020a, 2020b). (Thobani's book – which I consider important and worthy of careful attention – has been particularly influential: "Thobani + multiculturalism" yields 1,600 hits since 2015 in Google Scholar. Richard Day has also influenced critical Indigenous theorists such as Glen Sean Coulthard.) Conversely, we may take the insights developed here in response to the problematic features as permanently useful insights for the strengthening of progressive discourse. Or so I will claim.

We begin with a rich example:

> Multiculturalism was to prove critical to the rescuing of Euro/white cultural supremacy: white subjects were constituted as tolerant and respectful of difference and diversity, while non-white people were instead constructed as perpetually and irremediably monocultural, in need of being taught the virtues of tolerance and cosmopolitanism under white supervision. (Thobani 2007, 148)

Various questions may be asked of this quote. We have two passive voice phrases. *Who* has done this constituting or constructing? And what does it mean to say that people are constituted/constructed this way? Presumably the particular physical individuals exist independently of these "constructions." So what does it mean? Well, probably that some people have been brought to look at these respective groups of people in the way that Thobani suggests. So *who* exactly are the people who have been induced to see things this way? All of society? Particular people? The "constructors" themselves? Other people? And *how* exactly has this been done, by what means were some people induced to view different groups of people in this way? And, finally, what would be the *evidence* of this construction/constitution?

The quote, in short, illustrates various dimensions of mystery that recur among some of the progressive critics: we have mysterious *actors*, endowed with mysterious *power*, performing mysterious *actions*, to produce mysterious *effects*. I will take up these various dimensions of mystery in a moment. But note, first, that the problem with the illustrative quote is not one of technical "jargon." The latter can certainly be a form of despotism, as Foucault put it, shielding a group of specialists from outside scrutiny (Bourdieu 2012, 280; Lanchester 2016). But it can also have important benefits. Jargon whose meaning is clear and unambiguous can save a lot of time in communication among specialists, who can incorporate the conceptual precision and complexity of a concept into their discourse without having to "reinvent the wheel." In the present case, however, we are dealing with obscurity of a very different type, in which language is so loose and imprecise that people might *think* they are understanding one another or a text, but only because they do not or cannot do an interpretation check with the author of the statement. In this case, we get the cost of jargon – the exclusion of outsiders – but not the benefits, because the obscurity prevents the emergence of a true intellectual community, forged through debate and meaningful interchange. Each reader may find meaning in a mystery sentence, but like the church bells of Longfellow's last poem, "the meaning is manifold." Further, the style does not prepare whoever jointly indulges in it for engagement with those who do not share a taste for their particular flavour of obscurity. This is especially serious if those wielding the problematic language view themselves as progressive and wish to have an impact on society as a whole.

A couple of insights from *Pragmatism*, William James's 1907 collection of essays, help us understand how mysterious writing works. First, James argues that we absorb new claims into our pre-existing network of beliefs: "A new opinion counts as 'true' just in proportion as it gratifies the individual's desire to assimilate the novel in his experience to his beliefs in stock" (rpt. 1995, 25). Hence each reader who accepts a mysterious claim can interpret it so that it is compatible with their own particular belief-set. A claim may thus pass from writer to author without any precise communication having taken place.

Second, noting that most of what we believe has not been personally verified by us, James comments that "truth lives, in fact, for the most part on a credit system. Our thoughts and beliefs 'pass,' so long as nothing challenges them, just as bank-notes pass so long as nobody refuses them" (80). Now the very quality of a mysterious claim makes it hard to imagine anything clashing with it. So once a person has integrated such a claim – however understood – into their network of beliefs, it will prove durable.

Let us now examine various dimensions of mystery.

Mysterious subjects. The subjects of a sentence can be mysterious in a variety of ways. It may be unclear who or what is performing an action (as in passive voice sentences). It may be difficult or impossible to pin down the "existential subject," that is, the real-world phenomenon to which the grammatical subject refers. It may be unclear how the existential subject might perform the sort of action attributed to it.

We considered one of Thobani's various passive voice formulations, above. Richard Day, for his part, claims that "within the Canadian discourse on diversity, recognition is often invoked as a kind of incantation whose mere utterance will ward off social antagonisms" (2000, 34). At first glance, the sentence seems acceptable: we probably all indulge in vague sentences of the form "it is widely believed that ...," or "people often argue that ..." But note what the vague formulation allows Day to do here: he attributes to his unnamed opponents what I have elsewhere termed "a condition closely resembling stupidity" (Ryan 2015). This parallels a lamentable – sometimes even dangerous – trend among conservative critics, that of attributing all sorts of problematic outlooks to unnamed supporters of multiculturalism.

Passive voice formulations may have political effects. Ellen Bresler Rockmore notes how textbooks approved for the Texas history curriculum use sentence structure to "play down the horror of slavery." On the one hand, "the Texas textbooks employ all the principles of good, strong, clear writing when talking about the 'upside' of slavery": "Some slaves reported that their masters treated them kindly," declares one text. This contrasts with textbook sentences like this one: "Families were often broken apart when a family member was sold to another owner" (2015). Here, the passive voice *masks* responsibility.

Some passive voice formulations from progressive critics, on the other hand, may *generalize* responsibility: "Multiculturalism constructs communities as neatly bounded, separate cultural entities, unchanged by the process of migration and dislocation. Such entities *are perceived* as untouched by either the external factors within which their cultural practices take place, which change the histories and destinies of the nation, or by the changing realities within the geopolitical order" (Thobani 2007, 149; emphasis added). Given the lack of qualifiers after the verb (e.g., "by some people"), it is reasonable to read the statement as a claim that pretty much everyone shares the view in question. This raises an obvious political question: when one's target is so shadowy and ubiquitous, how does one go about combating it?[1] And how does one identify potential allies?

Even in active voice sentences, the real-world phenomenon denoted by the grammatical subject may be unclear. Some progressive critics frequently use variants of "multiculturalism" as an active agent:

> Multiculturalism has sought to constitute people of colour as politically identifiable by their cultural backgrounds. (Thobani 2007, 145)
>
> Multiculturalism constructs communities as neatly bounded, separate cultural entities, unchanged by the process of migration and dislocation. (149)

One difficulty here is that it is unclear exactly what "multiculturalism" refers to. As we saw in the previous chapter, this is never obvious. Does it denote some general *theory*? Or "a more diffuse public ethos or discourse of multiculturalism" (Kymlicka 2014, 7)? Or multicultural policy? And if the latter, *which* policies, exactly? And do the claims refer to the *intentions* of those who formulated the policies, or to how they worked out in practice, or to something else?

Some claims are more specific yet no less perplexing: "On one hand, multiculturalism as state policy sought to put in place structures that would perpetuate various forms of dominance. On the other hand, the idea of multiculturalism sought to produce modes of being that might allow for a decolonial project of freedom" (Walcott 2011, 30). This is an example of an "undialectical split": we no longer have one multiculturalism but two, one simply good, the other simply bad. Each is internally unified: there is, for example, *one* "idea of multiculturalism." In the same way, Nandita Sharma claims that "what the idea of multiculturalism does, ironically, is to disavow the notion that we all share a single geopolitical space known as Canada, as well as a long past and present of countless encounters, interactions, and interdependencies" (2011, 96). Note that Walcott and Sharma both refer to *one* idea of multiculturalism, but that their respective renderings of this are quite incompatible.

While using multiculturalism as a sentence subject, various claims *anthropomorphize* it.[2] As we just saw in Sharma's claim, multiculturalism can "disavow" (it can also "imagine," she goes on to claim). For Augie Fleras, multiculturalism speaks, usually in order to mislead: "Multiculturalism rarely means what it says or says what it really means" (2021, 18). Richard Day offers various statements of this sort. Multiculturalism makes claims: "This is, of course, the opposite of the harmonious history of coexistence that is claimed to be the case by liberal multiculturalism" (2014, 136). And it frequently has hopes:

> Unlike aboriginalism, which, as multiculturalism hopes, is relatively on board with the liberal-state-capitalist game plan, indigenism is in contention with almost all aspects of the dominant order. (Day 2014, 137)
>
> As long as it retains the hope of reaching a position of fullness, reconciliation, and rest – even within a liberal-pluralist framework – I argue that multiculturalism will remain a slave to the history of Canadian diversity. (4)
>
> Canadian multiculturalism ... is a reproduction of an ethnocultural economy which takes as its raw material the "objective contents" of Canadian diversity and hopes to produce out of it a simulacrum of Canadian unity. (9)

Now, one might answer that such statements can easily be translated into a less problematic form. Claims about the "hopes" of multiculturalism, for example, might be rendered as: "One of multicultural policy's officially-stated objectives is ..."; or perhaps "One of the goals of those who initiated the policy of multiculturalism was ..."; or perhaps "One of the goals that, over time, came to be pursued by those responsible for multicultural policy, was ..."; or perhaps something else altogether. *But what?*

Moreover, what does it mean to "translate" in this context? We normally think of a good translation as one that accurately renders the original thought in a different form. But is there really an "original thought" here against which our translation might be checked? I suggested in the first chapter that, given the close relationship between thought and communication, opaque writing can be viewed as a symptom of muddled thought, which renders problematic the idea of translation.

Still, we might think of translation here as attempting to arrive at some *plausible* claim, one that might capture the (amorphous) spirit of the original muddled claim. One path for this would be to try to link the claim to the actions and beliefs of concrete human beings. As we just saw, this can certainly be done for claims concerning the "hopes" of multiculturalism. Given that the translation can be done in various different ways, it would be far better for people to write in a way that does not require such translation.

When we do translate, we may find that our construal of a perplexing claim renders it persuasive. Rinaldo Walcott writes that multiculturalism sought "to constrain the movement of mainly non-white migrants into national spaces which had formerly imagined, represented, and performed themselves as entirely white" (2011, 15). What might it mean for a "national space" to imagine and "perform" itself? One might render this as: "Traditionally, most citizens of countries such as Canada, including most members of the state elite, consciously and unconsciously viewed their countries as 'white.' Both policy and everyday interactions were shaped by that view." It would not be easy, I think, to reject that claim.

In other cases, translating a claim shows it to be entirely unacceptable. We earlier met the view that "the question of pleasure should be left to the culture that defines it" (Gilman 1999, 57). We might render this as: "The only legitimate forms of pleasure for men and women are those authorized by the (invariably male) guardians of their culture." The translation highlights the dystopian nightmare masked by an apparent stance of "cultural sensitivity."

At this point, a suspicion might arise in some readers' minds: might talk of "translation" suggest that this chapter reflects nothing more than a "paradigm clash"? That is, are the foregoing observations merely the whine of someone who prefers an "agent-centred" approach, in the face of statements that reflect a structural one? I would answer, first, that paradigms are not self-justifying. Following Michael Polanyi (1962), we may think of paradigms as intellectual *tools*. As with other tools, their fitness for a particular task must be demonstrated in practice. To evade the obligation to assess one's own intellectual tools, and to claim in particular that working within this or that paradigm makes it justifiable to be unintelligible to those outside it (and, probably, to many inside it as well), would seem to be the worst sort of "scholasticism" (Bourdieu 2003).

In any case, to say that we should "translate" and assess claims by linking them to concrete human beings does not mean that we should avoid structural analysis, nor that we must avoid phrases in which human agency is hard to identify. The point is rather that we must always be able to cash in those phrases, convert them into a more detailed form that makes clear the range of human agents that sustain the structure in question. Human agency may seem hard to spot, for example, in the claim that "neoliberal globalization is a major contributor to migratory pressures today," but one can certainly translate that claim into a set of agent-centred ones. By implication, doing our best to keep human agency in mind does not mean that we should view social outcomes as a direct reflection of anyone's *intentions*.

Mysterious power. Various progressive critics display a penchant for claims that attribute a mysterious degree of power to the state and multiculturalism, claims that diminish and even eliminate the agency of citizens. One variant attributes near-omnipotence to official discourses. Of the Bilingualism and Biculturalism Commission, Richard Day writes: "All that the Other Ethnic Groups had in common, according to the writers of the *B & B Report*, was their Otherness" (2000, 187). This view would somehow "allow them all to be *managed* under one policy, while being denied the right to commonly *resist* this policy" (188). So Day jumps from the fact that the B & B Commission stressed the heterogeneous nature of the "other groups" (refused to "essentialize" them, one might say), to the idea that they were losing the *right* of resistance. Eve Haque makes a similar leap. Analysing Pierre Trudeau's October 1971 announcement of the multiculturalism policy, she writes: "Trudeau also couched these rights as individualized freedoms, forever neutralizing the possibility of collective claims made on behalf of a collective third force" (2012, 236).

A number of mysterious power claims revolve around identity:

> Dominant multiculturalism proceeds by essentializing race, ethnicity, and culture in ways that decouple them from the agency of their subjects, thereby neutralizing their capacity to challenge the imposed order. (Galabuzi 2011, 64)

> Unlike the "multi cul de sacism" of a mosaic multiculturalism model that shackles people around their ethnicity and ancestry ... a multiversal model acknowledges ethnicity as but one component of a multidimensional identity. (Fleras 2015, 320)

> Immigrants who might have self-identified along any number and combination of possible identities, including those of class, gender, and age, instead find themselves to be overdetermined culturally, over and above all other aspects of their identities. State-sponsored multiculturalism *compels* them to negotiate and comprehend their identities on very narrow grounds, discouraging and possibly foreclosing the possibility of alliances that might allow a systemic challenge to white dominance, patriarchy, and global corporate capitalism. (Thobani 2007, 175; emphasis added)

These claims should provoke various questions. Do people *feel* "shackled"? Do ethnic minority Canadians identify multiculturalism with a *decline* in personal freedom? If not, are they suffering from false consciousness? This last possibility is suggested by another claim from Thobani: "The policy's reification of culture has *disciplined and transformed* those defined as cultural outsiders such that most have come to accept and reproduce their own classification in just such culturalist terms" (2007, 150; emphasis added). We will return to the question of false consciousness in the next chapter.

Such charges are disturbingly similar to those levelled by conservative critics of multiculturalism. In *Multicultiphobia*, I suggested that conservatives often served up fairy tales instead of analysis: "Apart from splitting reality into malign forces and innocent victims, fairy-tale writing often endows those forces with remarkable powers." Richard Gwyn, for example, "offers a Night-of-the-Living-Dead scenario in which 'people become the stereotypes they are supposed to be.' *How?* How is this dire theft of people's freedom and individuality accomplished?" (2010b, 58).

The progressives cited here share another affinity with their conservative counterparts. I noted in *Multicultiphobia* that the latter repeatedly presented multiculturalism as "the *cause* of something that existed long before it." Multiculturalism was blamed, for example, for "dual loyalties," which in fact are as old as Canada itself (2010b, 54). As for the progressives: claims of the sort that multiculturalism "shackles people around their ethnicity and ancestry" (Fleras 2015, 320) suggest that prior to multiculturalism, ethnic minority Canadians enjoyed greater freedom on matters of identity. Really? Were society and state policy blissfully free of stereotypes and discrimination, or were the targets of those phenomena somehow unaffected by them? We will return to this temporal confusion in chapter 5.

The claims presented by both the conservative and some progressive critics of multiculturalism have interesting implications. If identity can be dictated by government, then it is quite ethereal, rather than something solidly rooted in the material circumstances of one's life and forged in interactions within one's various life milieux. And if the state is so powerful that it can dictate our identity, then it would seem that *society* is simply malleable putty. A never-fulfilled fantasy of technocrats emerges here as a nightmare scenario.

To deny the solidity of social reality is thus also to deny a key claim from chapter 3: that policy only imperfectly permeates a society. This theoretical error licenses the sort of backward inference also discussed in that chapter: existing reality can be read as a manifestation of the *intentions* of state policy. The result is an interlocking set of theoretical errors.

A nightmare take on multiculturalism is most evident in a remarkable analogy presented by Richard Day. After mentioning the wartime internment of "Enemy Aliens," Day goes on:

> With the rise of the first bureaucracy for multiculturalism, the Canadian state began to expand its purview outside of the internment centres set up in times of "national emergencies," to attempt increasing everyday microcontrol of the lives of both canonical Selves and problematic Others. While I would not want to downplay the sufferings of those who have been held in concentration camps, both in Canada and elsewhere, there is a sense in which this form was being extended to cover those who, because of semiotic, financial, and physical limitations, could not be constructed as Enemy Aliens and interned. Rather than constraining the *bodies of some* of those who inhabited its territories, the Canadian government began to try to *constrain the minds of all*. (2000, 165–6)

Day here ignores rather crucial qualitative distinctions. He quotes directly from a 1951 Department of Citizenship and Immigration statement: "The functions of the Canadian Citizenship Branch are to promote unity among all racial groups; to awaken in every Canadian, regardless of race or creed, a deep conviction of the worth of the individual and the principles of democracy; and to encourage a greater consciousness among our people of the achievements of the Canadian nation and the fact that all Canadians actively share in these achievements" (in Day 2000, 170). This sounds innocuous. One might even view it as progressive, certainly for its time. But here's Day's take on it: "everyone, regardless of their 'race or creed,' became potentially subject to Citizenship discipline" (171).[3] Day here is more Foucaultious than Foucault himself.[4] To apply the term "discipline" to describe a rather feeble government effort at persuasion (or, if you prefer, propaganda) is a serious conceptual error.

But it is not enough merely to observe that some progressive critics of multiculturalism deny human agency. It would be unwise to counter that position with an undifferentiated assertion that people always enjoy agency (ergo we need not trouble ourselves about the ways in which policy and social structures can limit their freedom). We need an understanding of human freedom that can do justice both to the reality of human agency and to the sorts of concerns that motivate some of the problematic passages just cited. One possible analysis would examine how government actions and discourses, and those of other social forces, can reconfigure the "menu of choices" facing various actors.

To illustrate how this might help us grapple with some of the progressives' concerns, consider a claim from Grace-Edward Galabuzi: "State policy further imposed a paternalistic relationship on minority cultures from which they could not escape to assert any real autonomy. Their voices became subordinated to a paternalistic funding relationship that muzzled their ability to articulate the experience of racialization as central to their existence" (2011, 75). The claim is overstated: groups representing ethnic minorities *could* "escape" the funding relationship with government, but there were costs to doing so, and the possibility of state funding confronted groups with choices that were often highly divisive.

The menu of choices facing groups was *not* (1) accept state funding, at the cost of adopting a more "pragmatic" and "constructive" (or "domesticated" and "bland") political stance; or (2) carry on as before. Once the state gets involved in extensive funding of civil society groups, any group that chooses to keep its distance from the state will face a different environment. The fact that many other groups are accepting funding can affect its relative status, its ability to be heard in the "marketplace of ideas," even its ability to retain skilled staff, who can be siphoned away by wealthier organizations. So state power in this situation does not *eliminate* anyone's choice, but it can *restructure* the choices people face.

The menu-of-choices approach views the scope of freedom of actors in relation to the quality of choices they face. Marx's account of "original" accumulation provides a striking illustration of this. Marx argued that the modern market game, that "very Eden of the innate rights of man" (rpt. 1954, 172), was both preceded and paralleled by a process of plunder that concentrated landownership and access to other natural resources in a limited number of hands (667–715). In consequence, for the bulk of the population, a choice between wage work and earning a living independently was replaced by the choice between wage work and starvation. So is the worker "free"? Yes, but in a much narrower way than they might have been.[5]

Note then that it is an open question whether state funding improved or not the menu of choices faced by civil society groups.[6] This would have depended on a number of empirical factors: just how much radicalism was there to be tamed by funding in the first place? How socially effective were the voices of these groups prior to funding? And so on. It is also an open question whether multiculturalism expands or narrows the menu of choices in other respects. Recall the simple anti-Ford vision of multiculturalism presented in chapter 1: whatever the limits of this vision, one can argue that a choice of economic marginalization vs. cultural erasure was (to some extent) replaced with a broader range of options, a richer menu.

But the metaphor of the menu should not be understood in too determinist a fashion. Human beings can be quite creative and may seek to expand the range of choices facing them. Marx's proletarian may reject the wage work/starvation choice by turning to a life of crime, organize with others for political resistance, and so on. The civil society group may find subtle ways to apply government funds to radical work.

Mysterious effects. With mysterious effect claims, something or other has been done, but it is not entirely clear *what*:

> Multiculturalism can be seen as a key process by which the state manages difference by maintaining control over the power to name and annex "the other," thus reproducing itself and avoiding a crisis of citizenship. (Walton-Roberts 2011, 106)

> The management of the Other in Canada occurs through the regulative practices of key documents such as the Immigration Act and the Multiculturalism Act. These policies locate the racialized immigrant on the boundaries of the nation and as constitutive elements of these borders. (Haque 2012, 22)

> [T]he socio-economic problems experienced by immigrants became defined in the national imagination as evidence of their innate cultural deficiencies which became a threat to the liberal values of the nation. (Thobani 2007, 162)

> In the Canadian "mosaic," it is said, all the hyphenated cultures – French-Canadian, Native-Canadian, and "multicultural-Canadian" – are celebrated. One problem with this formulation, as many have pointed out, is that multiculturalism implicitly constructs the idea of a core English-Canadian culture, and that other cultures become "multicultural" in relation to that unmarked, yet dominant, Anglo-Canadian core culture. (Mackey 2002, 2)

Let us focus on this last quote. The claimed effect is that an idea has been constructed. But ideas must be held by *someone*. Who, in this case? Everyone? Nearly everyone? (Those familiar with social constructionist analysis will recognize that the vagueness critiqued here is certainly not an idiosyncrasy of this or that writer.)

Some mysterious formulations, such as Walcott's reference to the outlook held by a "national space," imply that an outlook is well-nigh universal. This is also suggested by Thobani's claim. Such phrases seem to manifest the illusion of a society with "only one opinion and one interest" (Arendt 1958a, 39). Yet neither Walcott nor Thobani believe that: both are aware of the existence of sharply conflicting perspectives. So why is *one* of those perspectives given the status of "national"? (We will return to this problem in the next chapter.)

Political implications of mystery writing. As Trump and other right-wing "populists" have demonstrated, vague rhetoric can be very politically fruitful, providing cover to promote policies opposed to what the rhetoric appears to promise. But can mystery writing be politically fruitful for progressive analysis? I doubt it. Certainly, political slogans – which can only be memorable if they are vague – are powerful mobilizing tools: "Black lives matter," "Another world is possible," and "Idle no more" would not benefit by being translated into more precise statements and accompanied by footnotes. But progressive *analysis* has a particular role to play: to uncover the specific phenomena sustaining oppressive structures and suggest possible ways of transcending those structures. And that requires getting beyond mystery. Claims that "multiculturalism" did this or that, for example, often tell us little more than "something or other, in some way connected to multiculturalism, in some sense of the word, has caused this effect." This provides little orientation.

Concluding reflection. While doing the research that led to *Multicultiphobia*, I read hundreds of conservative critiques of multiculturalism: bestselling jeremiads, more than a thousand news articles from the *National Post, Le Devoir*, and other papers, speeches by Reform Party politicians. I will close with a brief contrast between that writing and the material critiqued in this chapter. The latter *is obscure*. Much conservative writing on multiculturalism, for its part, *obscures*. On the surface, it seems clear and user-friendly. But it obscures reality, through a web of claims that are dubious or even demonstrably false. And it creates a community of sorts, an echo chamber in which the dubious assertions of one conservative become the "evidence" of another.

Much of the progressive writing critiqued in this chapter, on the other hand, is pointing to aspects of reality that are not obvious yet are important and worthy of attention. The progressives thus need to be heard. It would help matters if they did their utmost to express themselves more clearly, and turned a critical eye on their most sweeping claims, to see whether they can withstand serious scrutiny.

Another difference between the conservative and progressive should be noted. We can say that the breezy style of the conservative critics, which obscures much of reality, serves their political goal. Conversely, indulgence in mystery writing *frustrates* progressive political goals.

Chapter Five

Other Features in the Writing of Progressive Critics

The previous chapter opened by noting that we must understand a claim before we can evaluate it. The chapter considered a range of claims from progressive critics of multiculturalism that are extremely difficult to grasp. This chapter moves on to assess various *styles* of claim that can be understood but that are nevertheless problematic. As did the previous chapter, this one deals with just *some* of the progressive critics. And however problematic I find some of their arguments, this is not a judgment on the value of their work as a whole.

The first part of the chapter will consider the tendency of some critics to either assert or imply the existence of a homogenous ethnic majority. The second will examine various failures to recognize that policy only partly permeates a society. The third will contrast the dialectical and undialectical approaches to multiculturalism followed by progressive critics. Since an undialectical approach entails a corollary that minorities are in the grip of false consciousness, that concept will be discussed. The fourth part will consider the failure of some critics to suggest alternatives to the current situation as well as the vague or – in one case – distopian alternatives offered by others. Finally, I will speculate on the possible political effects of the styles of analysis critiqued in the chapter.

5.1 The Homogenous Ethnic Majority

In the discussion of culture in chapter 3, I noted the common error of believing that those "inside" a particular culture have a uniform way of seeing the world. Some progressive critics proceed as if the attitudes and practices of an ethnic majority are uniform. This subset of Canadians – whose boundaries are unclear – constitute "national subjects" for Thobani and "canonical" Canadians for Day. Turning the analysis towards these shadowy constructs, rather than towards flesh-and-blood people, facilitates the strategy of imputing homogeneity. This is done in a couple of different ways.

A toenail equals a body. I will term the first approach "DNA discourse." We are told that the tiniest fragment of DNA will yield certain knowledge of the DNA that runs through the entire organism. Analogously, DNA discourse provides a tiny bit of evidence and asserts that it uncovers the truth of the whole. Richard Day, for example, considers the possibility that Canada's turn to multiculturalism represented "an earnest and authentic change of heart on the part of canonical Canadians and their state." Perhaps "Canadians had finally come to consider their Others, though different, to be equal" (2000, 191). Alas, "this was not the case." How does he know? Well, in the year of Trudeau's introduction of multiculturalism policy, British Columbia produced an official history of the province's ethnic groups: "This volume featured Ken Adachi writing on the Japanese, and Rosemary Brown on the Negroes," and so on. So far, so good. But ... "the table of contents was arranged according to the Great Chain of Race, from Americans, British and French, through the European continent from northwest to southeast, then to the Chinese and Japanese, finally ending with the Negroes. The hierarchy of the White, Yellow, Black, and Red races was preserved" (191–2). The table of contents of a single publication offers up enough DNA to prove that nothing has changed. My concern is not with Day's scepticism concerning some widespread "authentic change of heart" in Canada (which I happen to share). My point is that what he considers compelling evidence for his scepticism betrays the workings of an extremely dubious uniformity assumption.

Sunera Thobani, whose analysis centres on the "exaltation" of "national subjects" at the expense of everyone else, asserts that "equally significant to this [national] subject's exaltation are what have been defined as the negative, annoying, and disgusting aspects of these Other cultures" (2007, 169). This she can assert on the basis of a single news article concerning some Vancouverites who tried – and presumably failed – "to shut down a Persian restaurant in their vicinity" (331).

In her discussion of post-9/11 developments, Thobani alleges a profound "reshaping [of] the national imaginary so that assuming a more militaristic presence in the world is deemed as a reflection of the nation's innate masculine nobility, its virile 'goodness'" (2007, 219). Now "national imaginary," one of Thobani's recurring phrases (4, 85, 109, 132), is one of those supremely vague constructs that is everywhere and nowhere. It seems that one can find anything one wants to serve as evidence for it, and be under no obligation to show that the phenomenon in question is truly dominant, let alone universal within a particular social group. Thomas Ricento provides an excellent example. He claims that "the imaginary of Canada as an English-speaking white-settler nation persists" (2013, 480). His evidence? A 1997 speech by Stephen Harper to a conservative American think tank. Ricento does not explain why, if the rhetoric in that speech truly represents the Canadian imaginary, Harper spoke not a word of it as a party leader.

Any claims about a profound shift in "the national imaginary" would have to account for widespread Canadian opposition to the invasion of Iraq and the government's decision not to participate, just eighteen months after the al Qaeda attacks. Now one can argue that the Chrétien government undertook to balance its very public opposition to the invasion of Iraq with a major military commitment in Afghanistan (Bercuson, Granatstein, and Mackie 2011). Since this commitment facilitated the transfer of US troops from Afghanistan to Iraq, the government's public opposition to the invasion seems to have been a hypocritical veil that concealed indirect support for it. By if so, *why the need for hypocrisy in the first place*? If the "national imaginary" had been so thoroughly reshaped, why not wholeheartedly and publicly embrace the invasion of Iraq?

Direct suggestions of uniformity. DNA discourse is a roundabout way of asserting the homogeneity of the ethnic majority. The second way is simpler: directly assert it. Eva Mackey, for example, claims that "those who share in the white unmarked core culture conceive of themselves as 'real' and 'authentic' Canadians, who tolerate and even celebrate the 'colour' and 'flavour' of multicultural 'others'" (2002, 153). There is a double error here. Mackey assumes, first, that a certain multicultural sensibility has totally permeated the "core culture," and, second, that those shaped by this sensibility uniformly wield it to assert their exclusive status as "real" Canadians.

Other authors echo the latter point. For Thobani, there is no difference between "multiculturalist and racist nationals": "Constituting themselves as 'masters of national space,' whether through opposition to multiculturalism and the rights of racial minorities or through support for multiculturalism as the primary political site for minority concerns, both viewed racial and ethnic minorities as 'objects' requiring their control" (2007, 154). Similarly, Khadijah Kanji claims that "white 'multiculturalists' and 'white supremacists' ... share a disbelief that (non-white) immigrants are sufficiently 'civilized' to live among (white) Canadians" (2020a). Slavoj Žižek, for his part, asserts that "multiculturalism is a disavowed, inverted, self-referential form of racism, a 'racism with a distance' – it 'respects' the Other's identity, conceiving the Other as a self-enclosed 'authentic' community towards which he, the multiculturalist, maintains a distance rendered possible by his privileged universal position" (1997, 44).

I believe that statements such as those of Mackey, Thobani, and Žižek simultaneously depict and misunderstand a real phenomenon. A psychic thirst for smug superiority can work with pretty much any raw material, including a supposed "appreciation" of the "Other" – a practice to which we return in chapter 9. But the three authors simply assume that an attitude that may sometimes exist *always* exists. In this, they parallel the "unmasking turn of mind" of so-called rational choice theory (Ryan 2004). The blanket cynicism of that approach holds that all acts of generosity are rooted in self-interest, that all appeals to values such as justice and fairness "are, of course, propaganda devices" (Riker 1982, 205), and so on, and so on. I know of no one who confuses "rational choice" cynicism with progressivism. It is a recipe for passivity and political withdrawal, one that helps create the political room for well-organized efforts to undermine democracy's capacity to regulate capitalism. Indeed, for "rational choice" theorists such as James Buchanan, that was the whole point of the exercise (MacLean 2017).

Thobani offers another example of mistaking the occasional for the inevitable in her treatment of "the immigrant who longs for acceptance": "The fear of 'slipping' back into the 'fresh-off-the-boat' behaviour, of lapsing into the thicker 'immigrant' accent, remains a constant possibility, an ongoing danger against which one is required to remain vigilant. These racial subjects are under constant white surveillance, that watches for just such a slip, just such a gesture, that will confirm what the 'knowing' national subject always already knows: 'they' are all really like that" (2007, 171). Were this depiction transferred into the realm of literature, it could be quite moving and, paradoxically, *more accurate* an account of something real and important. But the amorphous "national subject" would be replaced by a specific character with a specific name, as would "the immigrant who longs for acceptance." (Stephen, in Joy Kogawa's *Obasan*, provides an approximation of the latter, although he was born in Canada.)

The literary work would not make a claim of uniformity, but it could suggest, quite persuasively, that such interpersonal dynamics really do exist and can be significant for those who suffer them, even in a society that many believe is tolerant. That is, such fiction carries an implicit truth-claim, but it is more subtle – and accurate – than Thobani's. It is an *existential* claim – such situations exist – rather than an *essentialist* one – this is the essence of interpersonal relations between "national subjects" and others.

On rare occasions, Thobani departs from her general claim of homogenous "national subjects" – an endnote, for example, acknowledges that "the public advocacy of racial profiling was certainly not unanimously defended among Canadian elites" (Thobani 2007, 357). And in the book's very last paragraph, she points to a path not taken, a very different analytical strategy that might have been very fruitful:

> The key point I have made is that particular subject positions, which exalt the humanity of their claimants, are made available to nationals even as they are closed off to other human beings through the networks of power. As the reproduction of the nation attests, nationals have, in the main, inhabited these subject positions. How enthusiastically and uncritically nationals do this, and whether they choose to contest or reject their nationality is not the question addressed in this study. (Thobani 2007, 252–3)

Thobani is suggesting, in effect, that her "nationals" have been dealt a different hand than other Canadians. How they *play* that hand is another question. To analyse how these differing menus of choice are created and evolve over time, to consider the strategies that different groups of Canadians use in the face of these menus, could have yielded a rich analysis, one that avoided the deadening assumption of a homogenous majority.

But Thobani did not follow that path, probably because of an overarching assumption that the subjectivity of her "national subjects" is unified around that status:

> Providing concrete form to the national subject's humanity, exaltation furthers national formation such that the subject becomes empowered by its bonds with other subjects constituted as its compatriots and, most importantly, with the state as the aggregate of this community of belonging. Inhabiting exalted national subject positions crystallizes this subject's sense of self and of its belonging in the social world ... Exalted characteristics provide an axis for the grounding of the subject, for "fixing" its inherently unstable sense of self, offering a national structure to its humanity that promotes cohesion in the face of the fragmentary and highly dissociative aspects of subjectivity. (Thobani 2007, 10)

In such claims – asserted but never actually argued for – we have a clear expression of the unidimensional vision of human identity that was critiqued in chapter 3's discussion of culture.

Implied uniformity: groups as actors. Finally, one can leave an impression of uniformity by shifting one's level of analysis from individual to group. Barbara Perry's analysis of hate crime views it as "a mechanism of power, intended to reaffirm the precarious hierarchies that characterize a given social order. It attempts to recreate simultaneously the threatened (real or imagined) hegemony of the perpetrator's group and the 'appropriate' subordinate identity of the victim's group" (2015, 1638). The claim is plausible, if one takes it to mean that many hate crime perpetrators really do believe that they are striking a blow for "their" race, religious group, or whatever. But Perry goes on to claim that "The interactions between subordinate and dominant groups provide a context in which both compete for the privilege to define difference in ways which either perpetuate [or] reconfigure hierarchies of social power" (1638). Here the outlook of the perpetrator is unwittingly *endorsed*: there really is a struggle of groups going on, and hate criminals are merely soldiers in this battle. (An analogous error was committed by those who viewed the 9/11 attacks as a symptom of a "clash of civilizations," thereby endorsing al Qaeda's claim to represent an entire "civilization.") Such group-talk can reinforce the assumption that members of the group have a shared view of the situation.

5.2 Policy and Society

Closely related to the assumption that the attitudes of the ethnic majority are more or less uniform is a failure to recognize how incompletely policy permeates social reality. I noted in chapter 3 that even a highly successful policy – indeed, even capitalism itself – does not completely remake a society. Failure to remember this will lead to important misreadings of various phenomena.

In a rich article on "Song and Dance" multiculturalism, Natasha Bakht tells of the repeated failure of critics to make sense of her dance form. She then comments: "Thus, even as multiculturalism encourages cultural diversity, it correspondingly seeks to contain it" (2011, 182). So all of the critics are in some mysterious sense the agents of multiculturalism, furthering its goal of "containing" cultural diversity. Given that critics everywhere can fail to understand innovative or unusual forms of artistic expression, how exactly is multiculturalism – however understood – responsible for this instance of misunderstanding? It would seem that anything done by anyone could be read as a symptom of multiculturalism. Similarly, Thobani claims that "multicultural discourse marks non-western cultures as more patriarchal and backward than the west" (Thobani 2007, 166). But isn't that view a core component of what we now term "Orientalism"? And has not that prejudice long been found in a wide variety of Western nations, many of which have no commitment to multiculturalism?

So the claim suffers from the same tendency of the conservative critics that I critiqued in *Multicultiphobia*, to "blame multiculturalism policy for ills that clearly predate the policy" (Ryan 2010b, 4). Something analogous can be said of a claim discussed in the previous chapter: that "multiculturalism implicitly constructs the idea of a core English-Canadian culture, and that other cultures become 'multicultural' in relation to that unmarked, yet dominant, Anglo-Canadian core culture" (Mackey 2002, 2). This suggests that the "the idea of a core English-Canadian culture" did not exist *before* multiculturalism. But surely Mackey does not believe this.[1] So a more adequate formulation would have claimed that multiculturalism had *transformed* an idea. This would have led to another question: transformed in what way?

I believe that Mackey is pointing to a real phenomenon but is also confusing its roots. In studying multiculturalism-talk during the 2015–19 Parliament, I found many references to a "multicultural Canada." Fine. But there were also references – from all of the three major parties – to "multicultural communities," referring to a *subset* of Canadians. The language in effect updates an older practice that referred to "ethnic groups" in a way that suggested that English and French Canadians were *not* ethnic groups. It thus seems correct to hold that, after decades of multicultural policy, many Canadians still assume the existence of an "unmarked, yet dominant, Anglo-Canadian core culture," as Mackey puts it. But, again, this represents an *updating*, not a "construction."

5.3 Dialectical and Undialectical Analysis

Thus far in the chapter, I have cited from just some progressive critics to emphasize a couple of traits shared by that subset: the assumption that there is a homogenous ethnic majority, and a lack of recognition of the typical relationship between policy and society, which is one of imperfect permeation. In this section, I will cite a broader range of progressives, to note a quality on which they sharply diverge: a leaning towards either dialectical or undialectical styles of analysis.

"Dialectical" has been given many different meanings. Here, I will use the term to designate a few interrelated qualities. A dialectical approach, first, avoids viewing social phenomena as isolated and fixed things.[2] It would thus reject the view of cultures as impermeable containers. A dialectical view of multiculturalism would recognize both that it has changed over time and that it exists in a complex space made up of other policies and a variety of actors, a context in abstraction from which one cannot competently evaluate it. Thus, as was mentioned near the end of chapter 3, the normative quality of a phenomenon can depend on its context. "Song and dance" multiculturalism will have quite different effects depending on whether it is a component of a multiculturalism that is neoliberal, or of one that is consistently egalitarian and anti-racist.

A second quality of a dialectical approach is that it recognizes the "many-sidedness" of a phenomenon, whose various dimensions may be evaluated differently (Hegel rpt. 1977, 403). Canadian medicare offers a simple example. One can be perfectly aware of the problem of long waiting lists for particular forms of surgery, of the seemingly arbitrary regulations, and of myriad other deficiencies, yet be firm on the vital importance of medicare for the quality of Canadian life. More generally, one can feel deep ambivalence towards the welfare state in general, acknowledging the "normalization and surveillance" practices associated with it, yet still assert that "the institutions of the welfare state represent as much of an advance in the political system as those of the democratic constitutional state" (Habermas 1989a, 58–9).

Being many-sided, a phenomenon can contain tensions and contradictions. Institutions, for example, must often try to balance values that are in tension with one another. As has become all too clear in the Age of Trump, an important example is the role of the civil service in a democracy: "the civil servant cannot be placed in a *pure* relation of subordination to the elected official. Were that the case, the civil service would be reduced to being an instrument in the governing party's arsenal. Their relation must rather be a dialectical one, in which the bureaucrat is subordinate in some ways, and autonomous in others" (Ryan 2014c, 461).

Another type of contradiction is between promise and reality: the contrast between the US Declaration of Independence's "All men are created equal" and the political reality that emerged from the revolution is a notorious example. This sort of contradiction may provide resources that actors can use to further different goals, in particular to push reality in the direction of the promise. "We've come to our nation's capital to cash a check," declared Martin Luther King in his "I Have a Dream" speech: "When the architects of our republic wrote the magnificent words of the Constitution and the Declaration of Independence, they were signing a promissory note to which every American was to fall heir" (1963). Yet the contradiction between appearance and reality can also be less fruitful: the one can mask the other, confusing the promise for the reality. As noted in chapter 2, a key claim of many progressive critics is that this frequently happens in the case of Canadian multiculturalism. I think this is correct, though there is much to be said on the subject (see chapters 9 and 10).

A third feature of a dialectical approach is related to qualities of the modern state, discussed in chapter 3. As we saw there, power does not simply flow downward – not within the state, and not between the state and other actors. Some writers either neglect or explicitly deny this, claiming for example that "state-initiated or state-formed organizations are never in conflict with the state" (Carty and Brand 1993, 178). This will surprise observers such as Leslie Pal, whose *Interests of State* was sparked precisely by the fact that "many [women's] organizations were funded in one way or another by the same government that they were attacking" (1993, 3).

More generally, power is not a static "thing," akin to a club, with which those who have "more" can control those who have "less." As Foucault suggested in a 1976 course, power should not be viewed as a matter of "massive and homogeneous domination, of one person over others, one group over others, one class over others" (1994, 3: 180). A dialectical approach should thus be sensitive to ways in which "the tables are turned," the ways those in a generally subordinate position can exercise a counterpower against those generally above them.

Before proceeding to examine the divergent tendencies of the progressive critics, a caution. One may consider a dialectical analysis more "sophisticated" than one that is not. But sophisticated does not always mean *correct*. Some ideas and policies, for example, are toxic enough that we can safely view and treat them in a one-sided way. Further, there can at times be a political cost to trying to see "both sides" of a question, in such a way that commitment is "sicklied o'er with the pale cast of thought." (As a Latin American activist once told me: "Sure, things aren't black and white, but you can't play chess with grey pieces.")

Nor is a dialectical approach always *theoretically* superior: it is not a Swiss army knife appropriate for any task. We should more modestly take it as a heuristic, a possibly useful set of questions: How might the nature of this phenomenon change in a different context? What internal tensions does it contain? How might this power relation contain reciprocal elements? And so on.

Many progressive critics offer a dialectical assessment of multiculturalism itself, and of its political potential. This is one reason why, as I noted in chapter 1, to be a critic does not necessarily mean that one is an opponent. George Sefa Dei, for example, writes that

> many critics would rightly argue that, despite any good intentions, official multiculturalism has been ineffective in addressing broader questions of

structural racism, social oppression, domination, and marginalization of peoples in society. [Still,] as an official political doctrine, multiculturalism has promoted cultural diversity as an intrinsic and valuable component of the social, political and moral order. The policy also seeks to value racial minorities on the basis of a common humanity and envisions a future assured by goodwill on the part of all. Thus, at the very least, the contributions of different cultures to national well-being and destiny are officially acknowledged. (2011, 15)

George Elliott Clarke holds that multiculturalism has yielded various important gains,[3] yet he insists that we need a series of profound constitutional reforms to arrive at "a truly multicultural, multi-faith, and multiracial Canada." In the absence of such reforms, "Canada will be indistinguishable from an ethnocentric hell" (2011, 56–7). James (2012, 33), Winter (2011, 200), and Bakht (2011) also offer dialectical assessments of multiculturalism.

Extensive discussion of the more nuanced critiques would draw us into a range of narrower questions, so I focus here on the undialectical approaches, because they have two important corollaries: the claim that racialized Canadians generally suffer from false consciousness, and the (usually implicit) conclusion that multiculturalism should be abolished. Nandita Sharma offers an extended example of the genre:

Multiculturalism, in short, has helped to produce a culture of neo-racism whereby the idea of ethnic culture has replaced the much discredited idea of race. Like past racisms, neo-racist culture also demands racial separation but organizes this through the supposedly tolerant view that each different culture or ethnic group is best valued when left on its own, with its own supposedly unique basis for social organization. In celebrating the tolerance of white Canadians for these so-called different people who, until recently, had been legal targets for discrimination, a new kind of racist understanding of Canada has been cemented. This is the neo-racist view that, along with continuing vertical hierarchies organized around the racialized duality of superior/inferior, there exist horizontally organized cultural differences. Neo-racist culture, especially after the maturation of neo-liberal politics in the late 1980s, has insisted that these different cultures are best kept apart in fundamental ways. This view has done little to dislodge the centrality of whiteness. Rather, it has insulated whiteness further by representing it as just another culture amongst many, instead of as an emblem of power and a form of dominance over Others. (Sharma 2011, 96)

Like Sharma, Thobani insists that multiculturalism, far from weakening "whiteness," reinforces it:

> Multiculturalism has been critical also in the *reconstitution* of whiteness in its distinct (and historically new) version as a culturally "tolerant" cosmopolitan whiteness. This has facilitated a more fashionable and politically acceptable form of white supremacy, which has had greater currency within a neocolonial, neoliberal global order. (Thobani 2007, 148)

> Multiculturalism actually, from my perspective, upholds white supremacy. (Thobani 2010)

As mentioned in the previous chapter, some writers break multiculturalism in two, reserving their anathemas for the "official" component. Richard Day, for example, distinguishes "multiculturalism as radical imaginary, which tends towards spontaneous emergence" (about which he has little to say), from "multiculturalism as state policy, which tends towards management, discipline, and uniformity" (2000, 4). Following Himani Bannerji (2000), Brian Egan separates "'elite multiculturalism' or a 'multiculturalism from above,' and 'popular multiculturalism,' which emerges from below" (2011, 125).

Here again we find an affinity between progressive and conservative critics. CPC MP Garnett Genuis claims that "multiculturalism is not a product of government policy. It is a concept which our relatively new country drew on by learning from and observing the experiences of other societies through the vast swath of history" (Commons, 29 September 2016). In his parliamentary statements mentioning multiculturalism, Genuis displays a consistent desire to minimize the government's role in its history. Here multiculturalism from below serves a neoliberal end: owing nothing to government, *it requires nothing of it*. This variant cannot be a multiculturalism oriented to justice, unless one believes that justice can come about with no state involvement.

False consciousness? An undialectical assessment seems to require the attribution of something like false consciousness to many of its supposed victims, given multiculturalism's persistent popularity among them. Himani Bannerji, for example, writes: "We demanded some genuine reforms, some changes – some among us even demanded the end of racist capitalism – and instead we got 'multiculturalism' ... It is as though we asked for bread and were given stones, and could not tell the difference between the two" (1996). Thobani too laments this state of consciousness: "I teach and I have young students of colour, they come, and they completely bought into this multiculturalism ideology" (2010).

In the same way, "seduction" plays an explanatory role for the more undialectical critics:

> over the course of the twentieth century, state-sponsored seductive integration of cultural signs slowly replaced coercive assimilation of racialized bodies by civil society as the preferred solution to the problem of Canadian diversity. (Day 2000, 146)

> No longer openly reviled as racial inferiors, immigrants and their descendants were instead seduced by their being celebrated as a source of cultural diversity. This seduction has proved to be potent indeed. (Thobani 2007, 149–50)

"False consciousness" has a very negative ring to it today, through its association with an arrogant and paternalistic form of Marxism.[4] But there are a number of reasonable ways in which we may argue that the consciousness of many – even most – members of a society is false. Let us define the concept in the way suggested by Thomas Frank, cited in chapter 3: "people getting their fundamental interests wrong" (2004, 33). I assume it is in our interest to pay attention to, and maybe seek public action against, more widespread and urgent threats, rather than ones that are unlikely to touch us. But for all of us, our understanding of risks is highly mediated. One can argue, for example, that public understanding of climate change manifests widespread false consciousness, partly as a result of media treatment of the issue. In general, we rely on news media – and social media, and movies, and TV – for much of what we think we know about our present. People's perceptions of the relative threat posed by "Islamic" and right-wing terrorism are certainly influenced by media coverage and political leaders' responses.[5] Some people will also be influenced by political appeals trying to get them to perceive certain real or alleged phenomena as threats: the "Great Replacement," the "threat to the family" posed by same-sex marriage, the "barbaric practices" denounced by the Harper Conservatives, or the hijab-wearing public servant, who apparently threatens the very foundations of "la laïcité."

More generally, we should expect widespread lack of understanding of key dimensions of society, simply because "social evils may stare one in the face, but social structures don't" (Collier 1994, 197). Speaking of the globalization that profoundly shaped people's lives from the late nineteenth century on, Karl Polanyi commented that "the true nature of the international system under which we were living was not realized until it failed" (1957, 20). Today's globalization is surely no easier to understand! This is one factor behind the current appeal of authoritarians, as people lash out against threats that have been identified by right-wing politicians, threats that are plausible simply because the complexity of global structures renders understanding so difficult. In all of these cases, "false consciousness" need not arise from people being "stupid" or being deliberately "duped" by someone, but simply from their not having been exposed to a range of information that would allow them to develop a more adequate understanding of their reality.

Finally, at a more personal level: I assume we all have an interest in happiness. In our pursuit of this, "false consciousness" may be the rule rather than the exception: "what brings true, lasting advantage, if this advantage is to be extended to one's entire existence, is shrouded in impenetrable obscurity" (Kant rpt. 2002, 36). As Robert Lane notes, "people often choose of their own accord paths that do not lead to their well-being: they escalate their standards in proportion to their improved circumstances, choose short-run benefits that incur greater long-term costs, fear and avoid the means to their preferred ends, infer from early failures an unwarranted and disabling incompetence" (2000, 9).

So the questionable claim is not that false consciousness exists: it would be naive to believe otherwise. But it is an entirely different matter to claim that one has access to someone else's *true* consciousness, that is, for an observer to claim that they know better than X what X's "true" or "objective" interests are. This may sometimes be true.[6] But any competent observer must be alert to the temptation to attribute error to X simply because X disagrees with their own view. Before attributing false consciousness to X, one must therefore consider a range of alternative hypotheses.

Let us take a concrete example. Thobani comments that "many people of colour have clearly been very attracted to the multiculturalist discourse despite their everyday experiences of racism and exclusion" (2007, 172). I believe this claim is true. How are we to account for this phenomenon? Let us consider some possible explanations.

(a) As noted above, Thobani's view is that such people are the victims of "seduction." This could take a couple of forms:

(a1) Despite experiencing discrimination, X may mistakenly think, "Maybe it's just me." For people to view their experience as out of the ordinary is not an unknown phenomenon.[7] But is it plausible in this instance? Many of the progressive critics share with their conservative counterparts the claim that multiculturalism has somehow contained people within spaces isolated from "mainstream" society. A corollary to this would be that X spends a fair bit of time with other people who must – on the assumption that discrimination is widespread – also have experiences of this sort. Do they *never talk about this*? Assuming that X does discuss what they've lived with family, friends, and co-workers, they will know that their experience is not theirs alone.

(a2) X may have, not an entirely "false" consciousness, but a somewhat *divided* one. That is, they may hold the belief that discrimination is likely widespread in Canada, yet also that Canada is an "open, tolerant society." I discussed, in chapter 3, our ability to hold apparently contradictory beliefs that become influential in different circumstances. As Alfred Schutz notes, a person "may consider statements as equally valid which in fact are incompatible with one another. As a father, a citizen, an employee, and a member of his church he may have the most different and least congruent opinions on moral, political or economic matters" (1970, 76). This can happen if the person doesn't "notice," so to speak, two contradictory beliefs simultaneously. The implication is that assent to very general statements about society can mask a more critical awareness. Thus, Michael Mann's 1970 review of survey evidence from various countries found that there was a high degree of cross-class consensus around dominant ideological values when these were stated in general terms (e.g., "Ability determines who gets ahead"), but not when concretely related to their own reality: respondents, for example, "are more likely to be cynical about the opportunity structure that confronts them in their actual working lives" (1970, 427).

(b) X may have a reasonably accurate perception of the level of discrimination in Canadian society but believe that multiculturalism is not to blame for this. Even were they exposed to the argument that multiculturalism is "neo-racism" or that it "upholds white supremacy," they would not buy it. They may acknowledge the mystifying effects of multiculturalism – that it leads Canadians to think that their society is much more fair and open than it is – yet still insist that, on balance, multiculturalism serves their interests.

(b1) They may be mistaken in thinking this, which would make it another form of false consciousness.

(b2) They may, on the other hand, have a more nuanced, and on the whole *more accurate*, understanding of Canadian society and the role of multiculturalism within it than do the undialectical critics. They might, for example, point to the increased presence of racialized Canadians in positions of political leadership, compared to a few decades ago, and suggest that multiculturalism must have *something* to do with that. They might also be holding Canadian society to a relatively relaxed standard, recognizing its imperfections but believing that, even if multiculturalism policy is mostly a symbolic affair, that symbolism has created a sense of relative security that has allowed members of ethnic minorities to get on with living their lives. Amarasingam and colleagues' interviews with Sri Lankan Tamil Canadians provide interesting evidence of this relaxed standard of judgment (2016).

To sum up: there are different ways in which X might suffer false consciousness with respect to multiculturalism, and ways in which that might not be the case. But to build the argument that they do suffer false consciousness, one has to demonstrate that their beliefs are in fact false. That is, one must demonstrate that the undialectical assessment of multiculturalism is *true*. But when we consider the range of corollaries to that claim, it seems improbable. We have examined one, the claim that perhaps the majority of racialized Canadians suffer from false consciousness. Let us now consider a second implication.

Majoritarian false consciousness? In suggesting some ways in which X might justify their support of multiculturalism, I passed over one: they might point to the important matter of just *who* is calling for its abolition. They might argue that any ideal that is the target of many conservatives, right-wing terrorists, and politicians such as Maxime Bernier, can't be all bad. That indeed raises an inconvenient question for the undialectical critics. A clear corollary of the undialectical view – unacknowledged by the critics cited here – is that not only do ethnic minorities suffer from false consciousness, but so too do significant segments of ethnic majority groups. After all, organized opposition to multiculturalism, in Canada and almost anywhere else it has emerged, has been rooted in such groups and the political parties that interpellate them. So we are faced with the odd spectacle of conservatives attacking as a dissolvent of social order the very multiculturalism that sustains it, racists condemning "neo-racism," white supremacists denouncing the very policy that "upholds white supremacy." That so many members of the social groups that benefit from multiculturalism are mystified raises interesting questions: Just who is doing the mystifying? *How* exactly have they pulled off this prodigious feat? And *why* have they done so? (Presumably, if one wishes to sustain a policy, one does not undertake to whip up opposition among members of the group that should naturally support it.)

Abolish multiculturalism? Historically, the yoking of an undialectical analysis to belief in the false consciousness of the "masses" has led to the view that one must tear the mask off the dominant mystifying institution. Many Marxists have been influenced by Lenin's claim that "a democratic republic is the best possible political shell for capitalism" (rpt. 1968, 190). An observer of Latin American revolutionary movements, for example, declared that "armed actions by guerrillas were successful in tearing away the veil of democracy used by oligarchies to maintain themselves in power" (Hodges 1974, 217). The left can at times suffer, as Gramsci once put it, from "a failure to grasp what would happen if reaction triumphed" (1971, 225). Paradoxically, an undialectical reading of reality can thus push one to an entirely dialectical – and dubious – theory of social change: once the mask is torn away, people will rise up and sweep away the institutions the mask protected.[8] In the Latin American case, this turned out to be entirely false: the horrors inflicted by Pinochet, the Argentinian generals, and so on, led activists to focus their demands on the return of the "veil of democracy."[9]

So far as I know, no progressive critic has explicitly called for the abolition of multiculturalism. But Thobani is clearly tempted by the idea of ripping off the ideological mask: a chapter epigraph in her *Exalted Subjects* includes the following line from Walter Benjamin: "It is our task to bring about a real state of emergency, and this will improve our position in the struggle against Fascism" (2007, 217). And it does seem reasonable to infer that abolition of a policy that "upholds white supremacy" is a necessary component of the struggle against that oppression.

As it happens, Canada went some distance towards that happy outcome during the Harper years. Andrew Griffith, a Director General within Citizenship and Immigration Canada under the Conservatives, documents the withering of multiculturalism policy during that time and concludes that, cumulatively, the below-the-radar shifts brought the government "closer to the original Reform Party objective of ... abolishing multiculturalism" (2013, 100).[10] So, did that trajectory weaken "white supremacy"? Did it improve the lives of ethnic and racial minorities? Or, perhaps, did it increase awareness of the true racist nature of Canada and the Canadian state? Did it thereby sow the seeds of revolution?

One answer to the last question might be: too early to tell. Amartya Sen argues that "a sense of injustice can feed discontent over a very long period ... The Irish famines of the 1840s may have been peaceful times, but the memory of injustice and the social bitterness about political and economic neglect had the effect of severely alienating the Irish from Britain, and contributed greatly to the violence that characterized Anglo-Irish relations over more than 150 years" (2006, 143–4). Still, the hope that *effective* political militancy might emerge from the tearing away of the veil of multiculturalism seems, at best, a very risky gamble. Tearing away that veil involves having programs such as employment equity, and institutions such as human rights commissions, weakened or abolished, access to the justice system made even more difficult, workplace accommodations eliminated, school curricula returned to their pre-1971 state, and so on. Moreover, political developments in the US and the UK tell us that success for the type of right-wing politicians who will undermine multiculturalism is accompanied by intensified outbreaks of racism at the level of everyday reality: racists feel that they can out themselves, that the hold of "political correctness" is weakening.

This is why other critics of multiculturalism warn against longing for its demise: "The consequence of ridding ourselves of multiculturalism may mean to be left with the opposite, monoculturalism" (Bakht 2011, 220). Slavoj Žižek issues a more general warning:

> The temptation to be avoided here is the old leftist notion of "better for us to deal with the enemy who openly admits his (racist, homophobic ...) bias, than with the hypocritical attitude of publicly denouncing what one secretly and effectively endorses." This notion fatefully underestimates the ideological and political significance of *maintaining appearances*: appearance is never "merely an appearance," it profoundly affects the *actual* socio-symbolic position of those concerned. (1997, 33; elision in original)

5.4 Alternatives?

Whether a critic hopes to abolish multiculturalism, or change it profoundly, it is fair to ask them: abolition followed by *what*? Change *towards what*? Clear answers to this question can be hard to find. Elke Winter comments that various progressive critics "fail to provide us with alternatives," a failing that "seems to be systemic in the epistemological program of critical and anti-foundationalist theories" (2011, 45). Before examining some sort-of-alternatives found in the progressives' writing, I wish to consider some possible reasons to refrain from proposing alternatives.

One good reason to offer a diagnosis but no "cure" is that we often need time to just *sit* with a problem. Awareness of a challenge for which one can see no solution creates a tension, and that itself can be a source of creativity. In *The Act of Creation*, Arthur Koestler argues that this "incubation" is a key ingredient for insight: "the whole personality, on all its levels, becomes saturated with the problem in hand during the period of incubation" (1969, 182). This is true at a collective level as well: "The 'period of incubation,' with its frustrations, tensions, random tries, and false inspirations, corresponds to the critical periods of 'fertile anarchy' which recur, from time to time, in the history of every science" (224). This need for incubation is probably not relevant for every social problem, but it may be important for those that are deep and vast. In such cases, a premature move into problem-solving mode may subtly turn the true and vexing problem into a "tamer" one: "the problem that has no name," to use a famous example, gets named, and misnamed, turned into a mere variant of some other problem.

A further consideration is that hostile reactions to one's proposed cure will often distract from the diagnosis. The climate crisis is perhaps the best example of this. An author who paints a grimly accurate picture of the current situation, and proceeds to make the case for the sort of radical transformation of our global political economy that – at this point – seems necessary, can find themselves dismissed as "naive" and "unrealistic." Perhaps a division of labour is needed on an issue such as this, where some (e.g., the IPCC) specialize in describing and others in prescribing.

A third reason one might refrain from offering an alternative to the policy one is critiquing is associated with Michel Foucault, who frequently refused requests to explain what should replace things such as the carceral system. On one occasion, Foucault claimed that to do so "can only have effects of domination" ("La folie encerclée" rpt. 1994, 3:348). Andrew Sayer is sceptical of such claims: "Foucault fails to notice that critiques typically evaluate rather than instruct. In reducing the normative to imperatives he reproduces that same polarization of thought into is and ought that has made it so difficult for social science to understand our evaluative relation to the world" (2011, 241). Now it is true that Foucault's demurrals often reproduced a simplistic is/ought dichotomy: "It's not up to us to suggest a reform, we simply wish to make known the reality" ("Manifeste de G.I.P." rpt. 1994, 2:175). At the same time, he may have been sensitive to his location in a structure of power and influence, fearful that the ideas of a celebrity intellectual could drown out others.

I have suggested a few possibly legitimate reasons not to yoke one's critique to a suggested alternative, simply to counter the view that works that don't offer solutions can safely be ignored. At the same time, it is unclear how relevant such reasons are to the present case. None of the progressive critics of Canadian multiculturalism enjoy the cult status of a Foucault, so the possibility that their proposals might constitute "domination" seems slight. And the relevance of the first reason I advanced would depend on whether anyone is actually "sitting with" this material. Is *anyone* who was not initially sympathetic to the arguments of the progressive critics actually reading them, and in some way being changed? I do not know.

Whatever the relevance to the progressive critics of the various reasons for not presenting alternatives, there are important reasons on the other side of the balance. At times, a proposed alternative can help clarify the very *meaning* of the critique. Let us say, for example, that the only alternative a critic can identify would not be politically viable without a massive shift in Canadians' political beliefs. In such a case, it would be fair to say that the fundamental target of the critique should be that broader political culture, multicultural policy being merely one manifestation of it.

A second consideration is this: if we cannot see a clear alternative, how do we know that the situation we are critiquing is not better than any other that is viable in the current political conjuncture? And if so, might the very thing we are attacking with full force in fact be worth defending? This is certainly not a trivial question today. Thus, the inability to identify alternatives can contribute to an important practical disorientation.

Richard Day provides an example of this. About the most positive thing he can bring himself to say about Canadian multiculturalism is that it is "preferable to fascism or imperialistic forms of ethnic nationalism" (2000, 15). But Canadians are unlikely to face a stark choice between alternatives such as multiculturalism and fascism. The choices will be more subtle, yet still important for the well-being of Canadians, and for the degree to which Canada approximates a just society. The most influential progressive critics of multiculturalism seem to have no guidance to offer concerning those more subtle choices.

The next couple of arguments for presenting alternatives will draw on two hypothetical characters. Imagine, first, a journalist who is a friend or neighbour of a progressive critic. The critic regularly shares their views with that journalist, who one day asks: but just what do you *want*, exactly? Should the critic say that they aim to weaken "one technique that reproduces nationality, exaltation" (Thobani 2007, 253), or to promote "a new discourse on globalization" (Abu-Laban and Gabriel 2011, 165), or simply to "unsettle multiculturalism" (Chazan et al. 2011, 1), the reporter might observe: So you're in the business of critiquing big ideas. That's great, useful stuff. But I have to tell you: big ideas ain't news. They might also point out that "the *other guys* are quick to promote their alternatives. Check out the Fraser Institute: they're always telling governments what they should or shouldn't be doing, and look at how much coverage they get." The journalist's reasonable reply suggests that some identification of alternatives may be required in order to promote the *diffusion* of a critique in wider circles.

Let us now imagine a citizen/taxpayer, who addresses themselves to the progressive critics (and many other academics besides): "Listen up. We have picked up a large part of the tab for your many years of education, and for your salary. Since you're not doing basic research in physics, or whatever, I think you *owe* us some clear suggestions on how we can make Canada a better society." One might answer that legitimate alternatives can only come about through a truly democratic and egalitarian deliberative process. To which the citizen/taxpayer might well reply: "Fine, then tell us, *concretely* please, just how to set up such a process."

This last reply is telling, as there are good reasons for doubting whether a reasonably perfect deliberative process can develop outside a society that is not itself already fundamentally just.[11] In the meantime, *imperfect* processes of deliberation are not some future event. The writer – by the very act of writing on an issue of public concern – is already participating in ongoing processes of deliberation, however imperfect they may be. I will draw on our citizen/taxpayer one last time: "You have spent countless hours studying this question. Surely you have *something* to propose. Surely you are particularly well placed to make a contribution. So if you were asked to elaborate just *one* of the proposed alternatives on the basis of which a group of citizens could deliberate, what would you say? What *concretely* would you propose?"

I have stressed "concretely," because some of the progressive critics do gesture at alternatives that seem hopelessly vague. Richard Day, for example, offers proposals such as this: "First and foremost, multiculturalism ... must become cognizant of its application within the system of states, and begin to address the ongoing failure of state-sponsored rational-bureaucratic action to solve the problem of diversity" (2000, 221). So far as I can see, this simply means that multiculturalism must somehow become "cognizant" of Day's critique of multiculturalism. Day has other suggestions, for example, "multiculturalism must traverse this complex fantasy of fullness and harmony associated with the nation(s)-state, and allow itself to discover that the history of Canadian diversity in fact does contain what is necessary for its own overcoming" (2000, 223). In chapter 8, we will consider the implications of one of Day's other sort-of alternatives: multiculturalism must "affirm the value of difference and the Other as such" (2000, 224).

Another proposed alternative is worse than vague. At the end of her important *Multiculturalism within a Bilingual Framework*, Eve Haque notes the social challenge identified by her narrative: "We are thus left with the problem of how to promote national unity in a multicultural milieu without establishing a hierarchical relation of rights, without short-circuiting full citizenship rights through a contradiction between language and culture, and without putting into place a racially-based social order." Haque draws on Jacques Derrida's "radical rethinking of *hospitality*" as "an entry point into this issue." Derrida draws a distinction between conditional and unconditional hospitality. The former involves "the welcoming of the Other within the limits of the law whereby the host remains the master of the home and retains his authority." Haque cites Meyda Yeğenoğlu to suggest that this constitutes "racist hospitality." As for the alternative, unconditional hospitality, it "is the ethics, not law, of hospitality, where hospitality is infinite and cannot be limited – that is, regulated – by a nation's political or juridical practices" (Haque 2012, 250).

Note the omission of a third choice: the "other" is welcomed and lives within the limits of the law, and as they attain citizenship, they too participate in the evolution of law (and social custom) over time. (This is not a binary process. Canadian court decisions have shown that, even prior to attaining citizenship, those living in Canada or seeking to do so can influence the structure of law.) While the idea of "hospitality" may initially be relevant, it should become progressively less so over time, because the newcomer is not a "guest," but a *citizen*.[12]

Now Haque allows that Derrida's notion of unconditional hospitality might not have "immediate policy implications." But she endorses Yeğenoğlu's claim that "the very desire for unconditional hospitality is what regulated the improvement of the laws of hospitality." So the claim is that the concept of unconditional hospitality should function as an ideal that reshapes existing practices. In the final sentence of her book, Haque suggests that "perhaps we can use this principled desire for unconditional hospitality in our next, and overdue, exercise of reimagining nation, community, and belonging" (2012, 251).

Now Derrida presents his concept of unconditional hospitality as a contrast with an argument in Kant's *Perpetual Peace*. Kant's hospitality is merely conditional, says Derrida. And the very first Kantian condition mentioned by Derrida is that the welcomed person "must behave peaceably in our country" (1999, 70). And so to oppose this with an "ideal" of unconditional hospitality is to say that people should be welcomed with *no* condition that they "behave peaceably." Derrida makes this explicit:

> It may be terrible because the newcomer may be a good person, or may be the devil; but if you exclude the possibility that the newcomer is coming to destroy your house – if you want to control this and exclude in advance this possibility – there is no hospitality ... For unconditional hospitality to

take place you have to accept the risk of the other coming and destroying the place, initiating a revolution, stealing everything, or killing everyone. (1999, 70–1; emphasis added)

So the "guest" will be given "rights" that no citizen of the country enjoys. Apart from its other drawbacks, "unconditional" hospitality is thus profoundly hostile to equality.

Given that even Derrida acknowledges that unconditional hospitality "could turn into wild war, terrible aggression" (1999, 71), Haque has hit upon an alternative that is spectacularly unsuited to serve as an ideal. It is moreover, entirely unconnected to the first 249 pages of her work. There is simply no actor in her book, no one who appears before the Commission on Bilingualism and Biculturalism, or who makes submissions to it, who calls for anything "unconditional," who has demanded that they be welcomed in an "infinite" way that is unregulated by "juridical practices." So at the end of a long and fascinating story, conclusions are drawn that are not sustained by that story and that only obscure the questions with which it should leave us. What has happened here? My hunch is that this stumble at the finish line points to a tendency among some of the progressive critics: a discomfort with *limits*. I will return to this in chapter 8, when I consider the limits of tolerance.

5.5 Reflections on Possible Political Effects

I will conclude with some admittedly speculative reflections on the political effects of various features of writing discussed in this chapter.

Undialectical reading of multiculturalism. It might seem that a discourse proclaiming that something is simply bad or evil is more radical and progressive than one that says the phenomenon contains a mixture of light and shadow. And some things are quite simply bad. But a tendency to view phenomena in such terms may be more paralysing than progressive, *unless* the blanket dismissal can plausibly be linked to a viable path of action. This does not seem to be the case with the undialectical critics of multiculturalism. A particular concern, which I mention on the basis of my own teaching experience, is that some often quite smart students wish to embrace what seems to them to be the most radical and cutting-edge position, and are easily drawn to undialectical formulations, which they endorse without critical scrutiny.

Uniformity claims. The first example of mysterious writing in chapter 4 claimed that multiculturalism somehow constructed "non-white people ... as perpetually and irremediably monocultural, in need of being taught the virtues of tolerance and cosmopolitanism under white supervision" (Thobani 2007, 148). And "whites," it seems, buy into this: both opponents and supporters of multiculturalism view themselves as "masters of national space" (Thobani 2007, 154).

Let us contrast this to one of the findings of Elke Winter's discourse analysis of the 2008–13 speeches of Jason Kenney, while he was Minister of Immigration, Citizenship and Multiculturalism:

> The Minister very seldom speaks of racism (25 counts) or antiracism (1 count), and if so, then it is in relation to "settlement programs" (and hence related to racism committed by newcomers) ... Hence, in no way is it acknowledged that members of Canada's so-called visible minorities might be victims of racism and discrimination by members of the dominant group(s) ... the overall picture provided paints Canada's Anglo-Saxon, White, Christian majority as uniquely fit to embrace diversity and tolerance, whereas newcomers – of whom 84% are not from European countries – are portrayed as inherently prone to negative attitudes, such as religious "extremism" (7 counts), "violence" (62 counts, all in relation to ethnic minorities within Canada or the countries they come from), and "hatred." (Winter 2015, 649–50)

So Thobani in effect takes one strand of discourse and generalizes it: it applies to Canadian "whites" in general, and it is somehow the fruit of multiculturalism. This hides the reality that it is generally the *opponents* of multiculturalism who emphasize the supposed moral backwardness and other deficiencies of minority cultures. Winter's analysis offers one example of this.

The political implications of this approach are suggested in a 1944 Hannah Arendt article on the state of the Zionist movement. The belief that every Gentile was an anti-Semite, Arendt argued, "led to a very dangerous misappraisal of political conditions in each country. Antisemitic parties and movements were taken at their face value, were considered genuinely representative of the whole nation" (rpt. 2007, 358). And in a later essay on post-war Germany, Arendt pointed to a curious dialectic: the assumption of "collective guilt was of course a very effective, though unintended, whitewash of those who had done something: as we have already seen, where all are guilty, no one is" (2003, 28). To update her argument: since all "national subjects" are responsible for their collective "exaltation," and the disparagement of everyone else, Jason Kenney and his government bear no particular responsibility for this. So the repeated suggestions that there is a homogeneous ethnic majority fail to identify key actors and specific mechanisms of domination. Assumptions about homogeneity also obscure a challenge for the understanding of state actions, a topic to which we will return in the next chapter.

We should also recognize the *isolating potential* of such an approach. It is certainly not a discourse with hegemonic promise, that is, with the potential to be widely embraced as a new "good sense" (Gramsci 1971, 326–8) by wide swaths of Canadians. And perhaps such a potential is an essential marker of authentically progressive discourse.

PART III

Past and Present

Chapter Six

Why Multiculturalism?

Crimes of history, I thought to myself, can stay in history. What we need is to concern ourselves with the injustices of today. Expedience still demands decisions which will one day be judged unjust. Out loud I said, "Why not leave the dead to bury the dead?"

"Dead?" she asked. "I'm not dead. You're not dead. Who's dead?"

Joy Kogawa, Obasan (1983)

This chapter will examine claims to the effect that official multiculturalism came about as a response to compelling political pressures "from below," including the danger of unrest. I will pay particular attention to one suggested answer to the question of what the federal government hoped to achieve in its response to those pressures: the maintenance of racial hierarchy.

We cannot make sense of such claims if we limit our explanandum to the original 1971 policy declaration: the actions that emerged in the *immediate* aftermath of the declaration were just too minimal to be attributed to some grand strategy. So I will interpret the question of "Why multiculturalism?" more broadly, as referring not just to the reasons behind the initial policy declaration but also to the factors behind the slow emergence of multicultural policy as a durable feature of Canadian political life.

The reason to consider this question is simply that many of the progressive critics make claims about it. That is, they do not limit themselves to arguments about what multiculturalism *does*: they also have much to say about how it came about and what it was *intended to do*. A critique of multiculturalism probably does not require such claims: it might have been sufficient to uncover the intended or unintended function(s) of multiculturalism. But in any case, the claims are there, and we will see that they lead us into important questions.

The analysis in this chapter generally has a Canadian focus. Will Kymlicka has argued that "once we recognize the pervasive nature of the trend towards multiculturalism, it seems clear that the main explanation must lie in forces and dynamics that are found across many Western democracies, rather than factors specific to particular countries" (2007c, 87). There is much truth to this. Nevertheless, policies must be enacted by specific governments, for reasons ultimately relevant to those governments. (Despite the Canadian focus, a number of factors that will be adduced in the various accounts developed below were relevant for other countries at the time.)

The chapter begins with a "simple story" of multiculturalism's emergence, a surface-level narrative. It will consider, among other things, the ample evidence that the original declaration reflected a fairly narrow, almost thoughtless, political/electoral calculation on the part of the Trudeau government. I will then ask whether there might have been a deeper logic at work, one that guided and/or constrained the surface-level developments. The arguments of various progressive critics will be used to formulate one narrative based on a deeper logic. The assessment of this narrative will pull us into a thorny question: is the Canadian state a "white supremacy state" in the same durable way that it is a capitalist state? I will then offer a narrative based on a contrasting deeper logic, one focused on the influence of the capitalist state on multiculturalism's emergence.

6.1 Multiculturalism: A "Simple Story"

The story can begin with the June 1960 election of Jean Lesage as Quebec premier, which marked the beginning of the "Quiet Revolution." *Le Devoir* editor André Laurendeau was apparently the first to call for a Royal Commission on Bilingualism in response to Quebec's quickly evolving situation, in a January 1962 editorial (Haque 2012, 50). Two days later, NDP MP Herbert Herridge asked the prime minister whether the government planned to do this. Diefenbaker's reply was clear and concise: "No, Mr. Speaker" (Commons, 22 January 1962). But opposition leader Lester Pearson took up the call in late 1962, warning that the unwillingness of "English speaking Canadians [to] accept the changes which are required to make a reality of full partnership" would lead eventually to Quebec separation (Commons, 17 December 1962). Upon his 1963 election as prime minister, Pearson established the Royal Commission "[t]o inquire into and report upon the existing state of bilingualism and biculturalism in Canada and to recommend what steps should be taken to develop the Canadian confederation on the basis of an equal partnership between the two founding races, taking into account the contribution made by the other ethnic groups to the cultural enrichment of Canada and the measures that should be taken to safeguard that contribution" (Commons, 15 May 1963).

Looking at this first part of the "simple story," we see an intertwining of moves from "above" and "below." That is, initiatives of the new government of Quebec (above), combined with a nascent separatist movement (below?), led to a federal government move from "above," the B&B Commission. But this sparked apparently unanticipated moves from below: as the commission began its public hearings, its members were taken aback by "the vehement statements made by some members of the 'other' ethnic groups" (Jaworsky 1979, 50; see also James 2006, 57). Among other concerns was the unequal status implied by the commission's distinction between "founding races" and "other ethnic groups" (Haque 2012, 57). MP Frank Howard argued that "the very terms of that royal commission are an insult to one group of people in Canada ... the original inhabitants of this nation, those whom we now classify as Indian and Eskimo" (Commons, 10 April 1964).

Raymond Breton would later comment that "the Quebec independence movement and the Royal Commission heightened the status anxieties of many members of other ethnic groups. It increased their fear of being defined as second-class citizens" (1986, 44). This formulation can obscure the very real material interests at stake.[1] Many feared that English-speaking Canadians' *de facto* near-monopoly of mid- and upper-level public service positions would be replaced by a bilingual (i.e., French/English) near-monopoly.[2] And so, in its first public hearings in late 1963, the commission found the very concept of biculturalism countered with the claim that "multi-culture is a necessity" (J.A. Wojciejowski, qtd. in Haque 2012, 56). Calls from "below" for multiculturalism were thus a response to new pressures from "above."

Let us fast-forward a bit. The B&B Commission has issued its multi-volume report, and the Trudeau government is considering its options. Trudeau may well have little sympathy with the concerns of the "other ethnic groups": Manoly Lupul cites a 1964 conversation with Trudeau in which the latter "dismissed the Ukrainian presence in the West with terse fatalism, 'And how long will you last?'" (1982, 97). Yet Trudeau has found himself in a bind, as those concerns have been taken up by the opposition Progressive Conservatives in particular. In late 1968, a Conservative MP calls for a parliamentary subcommittee to "study and report on the possibility of promoting the multicultural aspect of our Canadian society" (Commons, 17 December 1968). During the 1969 debate on the Official Languages Act, various Progressive Conservatives relay arguments from minority ethnic organizations. William Skoreyko quotes a plea from the president of the Ukranian Canadian Committee:

> If ... the languages – and thereby cultures of only two of Canada's ethnic groups are selected for survival – while Canadians speaking other languages are *singled out for virtual immediate assimilation* – then such legislation offends human dignity and contravenes fundamental human rights.
>
> If preservation of language is important and essential to the survival of the French and English, it is equally essential to the Ukrainians, Germans, Italians, Eskimos, Indians and all others for the very same reason. (Commons, 26 May 1969; emphasis added)

Such concerns even find an occasional echo within the Liberal caucus. MP Stanley Haidasz – who will later become the first Minister of State for Multiculturalism – notes that "many doubts and fears about this bill have been expressed by Canadians of other than English and French origins. They would like more assurances from the government as far as the future of their languages and cultures are concerned. There is a danger that while avoiding the United States melting-pot we might fall into another disaster, that of two melting-pots" (Commons, 2 July 1969). At the same time, Trudeau is aware of the "hostility of many in Quebec to any formal recognition of the other groups" (Porter 1987, 118).[3]

This is what may well have led the government to formulate a relatively symbolic multiculturalism policy, one that would mitigate the political fallout from a rather more muscular bilingualism policy. Perhaps, then, multiculturalism really was intended "to be a short-term sentimental transitional phase to calm down the insecurities of ethnic groups," as Keith Spicer later suggested (qtd. in Mazurek 1992, 24). In his response to Trudeau's unveiling of multiculturalism, opposition leader Robert Stanfield characterized the policy as marginal: "There is no indication whatsoever in the Prime Minister's statement this morning that there will be any substantial implementation ... I do not think that members of the other cultural groups with other cultural traditions are at all happy with the relatively pitiful amounts that have been allocated to this other aspect of the diversity about which the Prime Minister spoke this morning, multiculturalism" (Commons, 8 October 1971).

There was little in the aftermath of the 1971 announcement to counter a cynical interpretation of the policy. Through to the end of the 28th Parliament in 1972, Liberals in the House said little about multiculturalism, other than to respond to opposition questions. Nearly half a year after the announcement, the Secretary of State could not answer NDP MP David Orlikow's simple query: "whether the government has yet allocated funds to support the various ethnic and cultural groups in Canada in preserving and expanding their multicultural activities, as announced by the Prime Minister last October?" (Commons, 20 March 1972). Haque notes that in the first year of the policy, spending on multiculturalism was dwarfed by that on bilingualism by a factor of roughly 35 to 1 (2012, 227), a disproportion that proved stable through the 1970s (Lupul 1982, 98). Within the state bureaucracy, multiculturalism held a marginal position and enjoyed little continuity of ministers or staff: Burnet comments that "a complaint made by several people who had to deal with the multicultural directorate was that their letters from Ottawa were never signed twice by the same person" (1978, 110).

And yet ... it persisted. Why? Perhaps the 1971 declaration put an official stamp on a widespread pre-existing sense that Canada was a multicultural country.[4] That sense had crystallized in the wake of Pearson's establishment of the B&B Commission, which put the question of "how many cultures" on the political agenda. As Pearson himself put it: "There is no doubt we are one confederation. We are one state, one country before the world. Are we one nation or two? Are we one race, or two, or many? Are we one culture, or two, or many?" (Commons, 6 April 1965). And so a curious bifurcation developed in the wake of the declaration, between its marginal practical effects and its rhetorical magnification.[5] Together, the widespread sense of Canada's multicultural nature and the official stamp gave legitimacy to efforts to push the policy further. Policies such as multiculturalism may be "apparently hollow, without much monetary commitment, and, ultimately, with little government enthusiasm," Les Pal argues, "but positive symbols give standing" (1993, 260).

Indeed, attempts to push further begin within *days* of Trudeau's policy announcement. In the House, a key figure in this effort is Conservative MP Lincoln Alexander. Four days after the policy unveiling, Alexander asks whether the government will follow up with "a dynamic approach and a dynamic program" for Indigenous Canadians (Commons, 12 October 1971). Weeks later, he urges the government to "deal only with firms and advertising agencies which actively adhere to the general principle of Canada being a multicultural society, and ... ensure that all government publications and advertisements demonstrate the ethnic and racial diversity of Canada" (Commons, 5 November 1971).

Efforts to push further would transcend the statements of lone MPs. During the constitution repatriation debates, civil society activism bore fruit: the Charter of Rights included a reference to multiculturalism, as well as a clause protecting employment-equity-type measures (James 2006). In 1984, the *Equality Now!* report of Parliament's Special Committee on Participation of Visible Minorities in Canadian Society presented its far-reaching recommendations in the name of multiculturalism, even while advocating a profound transformation of the policy.

Reflection on the simple story. Some who have intensively studied the history of Canadian multiculturalism might wish to correct some details, but the foregoing would seem to be a reasonable sketch of an answer to "Why multiculturalism?" But as critical realist Roy Bhaskar has emphasized, every explanation can generate new questions and lead us to dig deeper (2008, 169). We need to keep in mind that not everything that organized groups ask for gets granted, or even taken up by opposition parties as a politically influential demand. What governs the process of selection? What governs the enthusiasm, or not, of the state bureaucracy for different initiatives?

Is there some deeper logic that governs this process, that would shed light on questions such as these? This logic might be one of which state actors are not fully aware, but which occasionally kicks in, in the form of constraints – perhaps the sorts of constraints discussed in chapter 3's analysis of capitalist democracy. Or the logic might be consciously shared within the state elite but not easily detected by the public. To entertain either possibility might appear as indulgence in the sort of mystery thinking critiqued in chapter 4. But, to cite Bhaskar again, the empirical and the real are not coextensive: there are forces that are real and influential yet hard or impossible to detect (2008, 13). This is true in the natural world, and it would be naive to rule out the possibility that it occurs in the political world. (We have Access to Information laws precisely because not everything we need to know about what's going on inside the state is "visible to the naked eye.")

I am introducing the idea of a deeper logic here simply because many progressive critics' claims concerning the origins of multiculturalism omit the various moments of the simple story just presented, but may be identifying less obvious influences on the trajectory of multiculturalism. Still, a criterion for assessing any narrative based on a supposed deeper logic is that it must fit the known facts *reasonably* well.

6.2 A Critical Progressive Story

This section will develop a narrative centred on one possible deeper logic. I will draw on a variety of progressive critics, some of whom may not agree with parts of the story I will present. That story has been fashioned to highlight what I think are important practical and theoretical questions. To arrive at a coherent and plausible narrative, I will leave aside claims that are simply too untethered from any plausible reading of the historical record, such as: "something had to be done to solve the 'problems' of the French, the Immigrant, and the Indian once and for all. This something was called 'multiculturalism'" (Day 2000, 187).

We can begin with a few quotes from Chazan and colleagues' anthology, *Home and Native Land*:

> Western liberal democracies like Canada adopted various forms of state multiculturalism to manage and neutralize post-World-War-II struggles for social and economic justice by racial and cultural minorities, and to constrain the movement of mainly non-white migrants into national spaces which had formerly imagined, represented, and performed themselves as entirely white. State multiculturalism sought to contain such "uprisings" through policies centered on identity and culture while maintaining and retaining the power to authorize and legitimize the late-capitalist material relations of the nation-state. (Walcott 2011, 15)

> The period preceding the emergence of official multiculturalism in Canada represented what Gramsci would have characterized as a passive revolutionary moment, in which contestation of commonsense understandings of the social order, in this case, ethnic and racial orders, proliferated. Some were challenges to the continuity of racism as an organizing principle of social, cultural, economic, and political life. These struggles involved racially and ethnically based organizing as well as class-based formations such as the labour movement. (Galabuzi 2011, 65)

> The very public problem of Canadian diversity was seen to have reached crisis proportions in the 1970s, requiring urgent state intervention in order to stabilize both Canadian identity and the Canadian state itself. If the myth of Canada as a unitary Anglo-white nation or, in some formulations, as a bicultural (English–French) nation, was no longer tenable, what would replace it? Official multiculturalism was devised to fill this gap. (Egan 2011, 126)

A "generic" model. The following generic model will help us sort out the key elements of these types of claims:

a some sort of pressure from below led to
b some sort of response from above, guided by
c some objective(s).

Let us examine variants of each of these components.

Pressures from below. In Galabuzi's account, "insurgent ethnocultural and racialized populations in the 1950s and 1960s ... made common cause with the Canadian labour movement, drawing inspiration from the decolonization processes taking place in Asia and Africa, and from the civil rights struggles in the United States" (2011, 60). Domestic pressures were in a sense amplified by the "widespread minority grievances in the United States that led to urban riots" (69). Thobani's account aligns with this: "It is surely no coincidence that official multiculturalism emerged at a moment when anti-racist and anti-colonial discourses had gained considerable ground internationally" (2007, 155).

The state response. We may think of state response to pressure in general as being located somewhere on a spectrum between two poles. At one end, it may be purely manipulative and cosmetic, a means of defusing popular pressure by mystifying many of those who mounted the challenge, contenting them with "little nothings" (Bourdieu 2003, 294).

At the other pole of the spectrum, the response from above offers something of real value. As Matt James notes of wartime Canada, "by picketing, protesting, and joining intellectuals and farmers in the freshly invigorated CCF, unionists helped forge a new Canadian citizenship regime that recognized – albeit hesitantly, unevenly, and imperfectly – the claims of working people to equal community membership" (2006, 38). This expanded citizenship would eventually include such essential elements as unemployment insurance and a public health system.

Should the response from above offer something of real value, a key question is what comes next. The concession may blunt the popular pressure, undermining the prospects of powerful subsequent challenges. But this is not inevitable: the response from above could give popular challengers energy and confidence, an awareness of their own power, and a sense that the elite has been weakened. Thus, the larger significance of an elite response cannot be read "in itself": much depends on what social actors subsequently do and how they're able to make use of the response.

Finally, outside the spectrum just described is the option of state repression. This can be blended with responses on any part of the spectrum.

Not surprisingly, many progressive critics locate multiculturalism at the manipulative and cosmetic pole of the spectrum of state responses. Two families of critique are recurring. We can call the first the "distraction thesis," which takes aim at "song and dance multiculturalism" in particular, and the second the "disruption-co-optation-corruption thesis," which scrutinizes state funding of civil society organizations.

Regarding distraction, Himani Bannerji argues that "people's memories of the places they have come from persist with them. So this spill of memory has to be contained, and the dominant group contains this spill through various means so it does not take over politics and become anti-racist but remains at the level of song and dance" (1990, 146). Some critics draw on Mullard's alliterative formulation, originally offered in the British context: "saris, samosas, and steel bands" serve to counter "resistance, rebellion and rejection" (qtd. in Mackey 2002, 66–7).

As the cumbersome label I have affixed to it suggests, the disruption-co-optation-corruption thesis attributes various problematic effects to state funding of civil society groups. Thobani argues that "multiculturalism co-opted and derailed the explicitly anti-racist activism of people of colour, splitting their cross-racial alliances as it worked to contain the demands for racial equality that sought to transform the very basis of economic, social, and political power" (2007, 160). Funding was a key tactic in this, as it served to restructure civil society and influence the visibility of its different components:

> State-funded community organizations promoted the emergence of a class of elite cultural "spokes(wo)men," whose primary claim to political space was articulated within the terrain of multiculturalism. This community elite acquired a stake in the preservation of multiculturalism, and they have defended this stake vociferously. State support for community organizations facilitated the state's role as arbitrator of community representatives. These funds designated official insiders and outsiders in communities of colour. (159)

At the extreme, state funding could create what Paul Malvern calls "reverse interest groups," which are little more than government "mouthpieces" (qtd. in Pal 1993, 48).

Regarding the effects of funding on various immigrant and racialized women's organizations, Carty and Brand comment that "state involvement turned them into social agencies, so that now they have become quite bureaucratic. Much of the staff's time is now spent fulfilling the requirements set by bureaucracies" (1993, 173). Leslie Pal is unsympathetic: "Groups themselves constantly lament the time and effort that must go into the application and reporting process. The relevant consideration is not whether resources are expended this way and consequently drawn from other activity, but whether in the absence of grants similar if not greater resources would have to be devoted to fundraising" (1993, 321). But this is surely not the only "relevant consideration": Carty and Brand go on to note that bureaucratic requirements entailed by state funding "do not take concerns of class, the *raison d'être* of these organizations, into consideration" (1993, 173). When a group can access funding to do something *sort of* related to its original mission, the possibility of corruption sets in. I use the term here not in an ethical sense, but to designate a process of goal displacement. Indeed, Pal himself notes that a 1986 Secretary of State review of core funding for civil society organizations expressed the concern that it could pull groups away from their "original mission" (1993, 193).

Finally: in *The Invisible Empire: Racism in Canada*, Margaret Cannon blends the two critiques:

> Multiculturalism is not about cobbling out a consensus between dissenting groups. It is about politics and votes and jobs and power. Once the Somalis are established in Canada, past their refugee period, multiculturalism will give them grants to start up community newspapers, to hold community festivals. There will be grants for salaries to members of the community to serve other Somali newcomers. None of this will do much for the hatred and rancour on Dixon Road, but it will pull the Somalis, along with other ethnic groups, into the multicultural industry. It will also ensure that, when votes are needed, the Somali voters will remember who sent those grants and financed those newspapers and bought advertisements in them, and support the party who provided them. (1995, 240)

The objectives of the state response. And what did the state elite hope to accomplish in its response to pressures from below? We can, first, impute one definite objective to *any* capitalist democracy: to prevent the outbreak of serious unrest. The state elite can expect electoral fallout from such disruption. Further, as Karl Polanyi argued, "the market system was more allergic to rioting than any other economic system we know ... A shooting affray in the streets of the metropolis might destroy a substantial part of the nominal national capital" (1957, 186). So if serious unrest is on the horizon, we can expect some mix of repression and concession (be it cosmetic or valuable).

But this in itself does not entail a commitment to preserve the "status quo," whatever that means. Even a government pursuing radical change could be expected to encounter unrest that might frustrate its objectives. It is easy to imagine, for example, that a government pursuing radical action on climate change would have to contend with many forms of reaction, including violence. (The fascistoid Michigan rallies against coronavirus restrictions in the spring of 2020 give us a taste of what to expect.) Indeed, in some cases, a progressive government will seek to prevent potential unrest sparked by its own allies, particularly should that unrest be little more than "egoistic-passional" outbursts (Gramsci 1971, 366).

Apart from preventing serious unrest, *what else* was the Canadian state elite seeking to accomplish with its policy of multiculturalism? For purposes of this chapter, I wish to focus on the starkest claim of all: that multiculturalism was implemented by the state in order to sustain racial hierarchy, white supremacy. In this vein, Bolaria and Li posit that multiculturalism is a policy "to maintain racism so that coloured labour remains accessible to capital and, at the same time, to give the impression that the state is acting on behalf of the public conscience by combatting racism" (1985, 29). For Richard Day, liberal multiculturalism is "a way of limiting dissent, marketing identity-based commodities and services, perpetuating the power of established racial-national hierarchies, and preserving the current distribution of geographical territories to particular nations and states" (2014, 128). And Thobani argues that "the adoption of multiculturalism helped stabilize white supremacy by transforming its mode of articulation in a decolonizing era" (2007, 146). For Thobani in particular, the claim is not merely historical, but reflects an enduring goal of the Canadian state. Thus, "the U.S. led war on terrorism is a boon to governing elites who have made it the occasion to further consolidate the construct of the true national as a western subject, while constructing the not insignificant presence of people of colour as a potentially deadly threat to the nation" (250).

6.3 Assessing the Critical Progressive Story

How plausible is the above account of the deeper logic of multiculturalism's origins? I will focus on two broad issues. First, the role of pressure "from below," and in particular the role of actual or potential unrest in the rise of multiculturalism. Second, the claim that state elites implemented multiculturalism to preserve race hierarchy.

Pressure from below? At first blush, the claim that various types of pressure from below "forced a reconsideration of the dominant order" (Galabuzi 2011, 61) runs into a contradiction, when combined with the claim made by many progressive critics that the response from above was trivial and cosmetic. An obvious question is this: if actors had so much strength, why were they so disempowered by what would appear to be a relatively trivial response? It would seem that any resistance that can be diffused by cosmetic measures was not a serious resistance in the first place: it is hard to imagine the Frente Farabundo Martí or the African National Congress being deflected by government-funded festivals of ethnic foods and dance.

But that dismissal is too simple. As noted earlier, progressive critics see international trends as a key part of the picture. There is no question that domestic actors can be inspired or worried by events elsewhere. Thus, the 1969 Task Force on Government Information opens with a fearful portrait of the international scene, anticipating the "crisis of democracy" language that would gain traction in the mid-1970s: "We know that among huge minorities in the western countries, there is a new, profound and wide-spread disaffection with the pretensions of government" (1969, vol. 1, 1). Government was thus at risk of being "swamped by rising tides of incomprehension and discontent" (1). Leslie Pal notes that the state elite was particularly attentive to events south of the border: "American unrest and social movements always preceded the Canadian counterparts by a short time, giving officials here a chance to react more calmly and strategically" (1993, 268).

I noted earlier that truly valuable concessions may embolden rather than diffuse popular movements. From an elite point of view, this would argue for addressing anticipated unrest, *before* challengers are particularly strong: "A little fire is quickly trodden out / Which, being suffer'd, rivers cannot quench" (Shakespeare, *3 King Henry VI*, 4.8). So we can tweak the progressive narrative to say that it was the emergence of various popular movements, and a *concern* over where things were headed, based on the international conjuncture, that led to a state response.

Even with regard to the domestic picture, we must remember that a key concern is not simply the "objective" level of threat posed by popular movements, but the *perceptions* of state actors. We must never assume that elites' assessment of threats to the system is accurate, correct to the second decimal point, as it were, or that elites have immunity from different types of panic.[6] One might also argue that political elites will tend to be hyper-alert if they feel they will be called to account for an outbreak of serious unrest, even one whose probability seemed quite small *ex ante*.

The "Sir George Williams affair" provides a case study in elite perceptions of Canadian unrest. In the spring of 1968, a number of Black students accused a lecturer in the biology department of racist grading practices. It seems that the university seriously bungled its response to the claims.[7] Student frustrations continued to mount, and matters were not helped when the professor was promoted in September (Lebel 1969a). On 29 January 1969, students seized the university computer centre. On 11 February the centre was destroyed, resulting in $1.4 million in damage, according to news reports (Balfour 1969).[8] Police made ninety-six arrests, fifty-six of which were of white students, according to the *Globe and Mail* (Balfour 1969).[9] Among the detainees were future senator Anne Cools, and Rosie Douglas, who would go on to become Prime Minister of Dominica. Both served prison terms.

And how was all this viewed from Ottawa? Statements recorded in *Hansard* give us a sense of the fears triggered by the events. From the outset, opposition MPs focused the blame on foreign students. The day after the occupation began, a Conservative member asked whether the government would curtail "grants to foreign students attending Canadian universities under government auspices who engage in activities involving breaches of the peace, bloodshed and other acts of disorder" (Commons, 30 January 1969). After the fire and the arrests, another attacked the government for allowing "a large percentage of foreigners to come into Canada, particularly from the United States, and cause trouble in our universities, thus costing taxpayers of Canada large sums of money" (Commons, 13 February 1969).

An even more ominous culprit was soon identified: "Mao followers were responsible for damages," claimed Créditiste MP Gilbert Rondeau (Commons, 13 February 1969). Indeed, added a Conservative MP, "a sizeable number of students who were involved in the sabotage and destruction at Sir George Williams University were at the time of their arrest carrying and quoting from copies of Mao Tse Tung's little red book" (Commons, 14 February 1969). This led Créditiste MP Henri Latulippe to suggest that the government "put off the approaches made to China" (Commons, 13 February 1969).[10]

Unsurprisingly, the events are interpreted in light of unrest elsewhere. One Conservative commented that "we do not want to have to face what has happened in other countries" (Commons, 13 February 1969). Another condemned the government for its "open-door policy covering the entry into Canada of people like Stokely Carmichael and other agitators who openly urge the overthrow of the government by force" (Commons, 18 February 1969). Conservative Wally Nesbitt also complained that "the notorious student leader, Danny Cohn-Bendit ... is presently in the city of Halifax attempting to foment trouble there" (Commons, 14 February 1969). But not every Conservative MP blamed the unrest on foreign elements: Donald MacInnis identified a fifth column as well, denouncing "the agitation developed by C.B.C. crews which go about the country" (Commons, 18 February 1969).

The opposition MPs were not entirely trading in paranoid fantasies. David Austin details the rich exchanges between Blacks in Montreal (in particular) and American militants (2007). While high-level state officials and members of the government probably had a more nuanced understanding of the events than did the opposition MPs quoted here, the latter's parliamentary statements illustrate a mood of fear and uncertainty that was probably widespread at the time. Further, the opposition MPs created a political vulnerability for the government: it could expect to pay a high price for any further incidents of serious unrest, particularly should that unrest be tied to international students or immigrants.

Multiculturalism: A response to (real, perceived, or anticipated) unrest? Both the Sir George Williams events and state officials' reading of the international situation suggest that, even if *actual* pressure "from below" was not particularly influential, concerns over possible developments could have shaped state decisions. A further question is whether multiculturalism policy itself was a response to a challenge (be it real, perceived, or anticipated) from "insurgent ethnocultural *and racialized* populations" (Galabuzi 2011, 60; emphasis added).

Not initially. As noted in our "simple story," pressure for some form of multiculturalism came from minority ethnic organizations of European descent, in particular from Ukrainian Canadian organizations.[11] All evidence suggests that the focus of these organizations was not on a perceived threat from racialized Canadians, but on their own standing relative to the "founding races." Given the policy's initial focus on minority ethnic groups of European descent, and its relatively "anaemic" qualities (Pal 1993, 54), one cannot see multicultural policy as an effective response to "insurgent" groups, at least during its first phase, which was dubbed "ethnicity multiculturalism" by Fleras and Elliott (2002, 62). Indeed, when Trudeau spoke about the policy in the aftermath of the 1971 declaration, his attention seemed focused on a particular subset of Canadian minority groups. Responding to Conservative MP Steve Paproski's question whether the make-up of the promised Canadian Advisory Council on Multiculturalism would give "recognition of the visible minorities of Canada," Trudeau promised: "I will make sure that members of the Polish community, to which the hon. member belongs, will be given due consideration" (Commons, 6 July 1972).

Still, there is an intriguing passage in the formal document that accompanied Trudeau's declaration, which was included as the Appendix to that day's *Hansard*: "One of man's basic needs is a sense of belonging, and a good deal of contemporary social unrest – in all age groups – exists because this need has not been met. Ethnic groups are certainly not the only way in which this need for belonging can be met, but they have been an important one in Canadian society" (Commons, 8 October 1971). Striking too is a comment from the best-known Canadian theorist of multiculturalism, Will Kymlicka: "we have strong evidence that liberal multiculturalism is consistent with the pacification and domestication of ethnic politics" (2007c, 165). Kymlicka here is discussing the *effects* of policy, not its *goals*, but it is certainly possible that over time multiculturalism came to be seen by the state elite as an important tool for countering potential unrest and challenges from racialized groups.

Multiculturalism: Instrument of race hierarchy? I noted earlier that any state will seek to prevent serious unrest, and that this tells us little about the state's other commitments. So, whether or nor the state elite saw multiculturalism as a tool to head off unrest, did that elite see it as an instrument to preserve racial hierarchy?

Canadian policy history provides strong grounds for suspecting this. Kelley and Trebilcock (2000) exhaustively document the consistently discriminatory immigration policy of Canada's first century. Maintaining a certain racial composition was a core policy objective, although the understanding of that goal shifted over time as different European groups were incorporated into the circle of acceptable immigrants. (Immigration policy is not the whole of government policy, yet it is symptomatic: it would be odd to find a government committed to ethnoracial equality within its borders, while simultaneously preventing alteration of the country's ethnoracial demographics through immigration.)

It is striking that this policy objective survived the Second World War intact. Kymlicka notes that "with the adoption of the Universal Declaration of Human Rights (UDHR) in 1948, the international order decisively repudiated older ideas of a racial or ethnic hierarchy" (2007c, 89). Just one year before that declaration, W.L. Mackenzie King stated that "there will, I am sure, be general agreement with the view that the people of Canada do not wish, as a result of mass immigration, to make a fundamental alteration in the character of our population. Large-scale immigration from the orient would change the fundamental composition of the Canadian population" (Commons, 1 May 1947). King was "sure" of this: the point did not need arguing.

As late as 1956, policy explicitly siloed immigrants from different countries on the basis of their country of origin. The easiest entry was provided to "British subjects born or naturalized in the United Kingdom, Australia, New Zealand, or the Union of South Africa," as well as citizens of Ireland, France, and the US. Somewhat more restrictive conditions applied to those from continental Western Europe. Still more restrictive were the rules applied to would-be immigrants from the rest of Europe and the Americas, and "Egypt, Israel, Lebanon, or Turkey." Everyone else – mostly those from Africa and Asia – faced near-impenetrable barriers to entry (Kelley and Trebilcock 2000, 328).

Kelley and Trebilcock note that "a non-explicitly racist set of admission criteria was adopted in 1962" (2000, 442). Still, official multiculturalism emerged within a state that had manifested a long history of discriminatory immigration policy. It seems naive to imagine that the outlooks that sustained that history had vanished suddenly, leaving no trace within the state elite. At the same time, one cannot assume without further evidence that a policy created within a state with a long history of discrimination was *motivated* primarily by discriminatory objectives. That history actually supports other hypotheses concerning the emergence of multiculturalism, one of which will be developed below. But one hypothesis for which evidence seems entirely absent is that of a collective *metanoia*, a repentance and change of heart through which Canada decisively broke with its racist past.

Thus, to jump directly from the history of the Canadian state to the conclusion that multiculturalism was a defence of white supremacy would be to assume a state marked by some fixed and all-pervasive quality that durably defined it as a race state. What might account for that quality and its fixity? This brings us to complex matters of state theory.

6.4 A White Supremacy State?

American philosopher Charles Mills offers a concise statement of the thesis I wish to consider here:

> The most influential radical critique up till recently [has been] the Marxist analysis of the state as an instrument of class power, so that the liberal-democratic state is supposedly unmasked as the *bourgeois* state, the state of the ruling class. My claim is that ... we need another alternative, another way of theorizing about and critiquing the state: the *racial*, or white-supremacist, state, whose function inter alia is to safeguard the polity *as* a white or white-dominated polity. (Mills 1997, 82)

Against this, I will argue that consideration of the factors that *keep* a state capitalist will call into question Mills's analogy between the capitalist state and a supposed "white supremacy state" (WSS).

Because of the delicacy of this question today, and the various ways in which the ongoing existence of racism in Canada is denied, I wish very carefully to delimit my argument from all the things I am *not* arguing. We must recognize that:

- as we saw in the history of Canadian immigration, the state has historically followed racist policies;
- the state has not vigorously combated racism and the legacy of racism;

- as we saw in chapter 2, even today we have all-too-frequent news reports of agents of the state acting in ways that, I believe, most reasonable people would view as racist;
- the fact that such acts often do not result in firing or even serious reprimands points to a culture of tolerance of racism in some state institutions; *and*
- this, along with the frequency of such occurrences in particular state institutions, forces the conclusion that we are facing systemic racism in organizations such as police forces, including the RCMP. (We will return later to the challenge of systemic racism.)

Granting all of this, the argument I wish to develop here is this: Canada certainly had a racial state. One might argue that in many ways it remains one. But if it is, it certainly is not a racial state in the same way that it is a capitalist state. This is because, to the extent that the state remains a racial state, the main reason for that would have to be sought in the conscious or unconscious racism of its citizens and in the desire of racially privileged citizens to protect those privileges. As both the attitudes and the demographic composition of the citizenry evolve, we can thus expect to see any racial commitments of the state weakened.

With the capitalist nature of the state, things are quite different. As I argued in chapter 3, that nature is supported by widespread attitudes. But it is *also* maintained by structural constraints that prevent the state from wandering too far from a commitment to capitalism. Thus, citizen attitudes may evolve to a great extent without leading to change in the state's capitalist nature. Rather, what we have seen throughout history, when popular attitudes and capitalist commitments are no longer aligned, is a set of efforts to constrain democracy. Today, in particular, democratic pressures are increasingly unable to interfere in the workings of a globalized neoliberal capitalism. This process can be seen at an advanced stage within the European Union (Streeck 2016), as well as in the fine print of various investor protection treaties that Canada has signed (Sinclair 2018).

Before presenting this argument, two delimitations. First, I am leaving aside the overwhelming issue of the Canadian state's relations with Indigenous Canadians, for two reasons. The first is that oppression in current-day relations with Indigenous Canadians involves a "condominium of oppression" in which non-Indigenous Canadians in general are complicit.[12] Those relations thus constitute evidence not of a specifically *white* supremacy, but of colonial domination. My second reason is that, both historically and today, a key factor in relations with Indigenous Canadians has been the state's commitment to secure access to natural resources and thus to "maintain or create the conditions in which profitable capital accumulation is possible" (O'Connor 1973, 6). We thus have a tight interaction between centuries-old racist attitudes and a core objective of any modern capitalist state.

A second delimitation is that this discussion of the state's nature and motives seeks to explain the origins of Canadian multiculturalism. It is therefore focused on past and present: we cannot rule out a very different future. As the climate emergency deepens, and people's lives become increasingly disrupted, it will not be surprising if authoritarian xenophobic pseudo-populism – discussed in chapter 2 – grows ever stronger, as it offers outlets for anger, illusory miracle solutions, and so on. If so, the maintenance of something like white supremacy could become a key ingredient in the logic of many states in the global North. But I suspect that even under this scenario, no *enduring* white supremacy state – analogous to the long-established capitalist state – would emerge, simply because *nothing would be enduring*.

Review: How is the capitalist state locked in? To ground the comparison between the capitalist state and the WSS, let us review chapter 3's analysis of the *anchors* of the capitalist state. That is, what keeps the capitalist state capitalist? We saw that:

- the state elite can normally be expected to share the widespread ideological belief that the capitalist system "delivers the goods," particularly since they themselves are economically comfortable;
- the news media will generally uphold congenial beliefs, for various reasons: such beliefs are taken for granted; high-level journalists belong to a social elite; and the owners of private media have no interest in challenging the capitalist system;
- the general ideological climate – sustained by schools, news media, entertainment, and so on – will rarely question capitalism as a system (although it can challenge various examples of economic injustice). This can exercise practical influence via the electoral sanction and by sustaining the pro-capitalist subjectivity of the state elite;
- capital exercises a structural constraint upon the state: a failure to keep business happy can lead to a variety of unpleasant consequences for the state elite, including an economic downturn that will affect fiscal health and the mood of the electorate; and
- international pressures, finally, keep the state in line. Most immediately, capital flight will punish state elites for straying from policy orthodoxy. At the extreme, political and even military intervention has frequently been inflicted upon countries –particularly in the Third World – that have sought to escape from capitalism.

A vital point is that, in the case of the capitalist state, various factors reinforce one another, such that even someone with no love for capitalism can be pushed to support it once in a position of state power. Is there a similar constellation of forces to sustain a racist state orientation?

Why is this important? No matter how racist the state at any given moment, no matter how many racist crimes are committed by agents of the state – and tolerated or denied altogether by other agents – if the race state is not solidly anchored, in the way that the capitalist state is, then it will have points of leverage for change. The task is to identify those points. Conversely, an approach that simply assumes that the state *is* a WSS, that this is the state's essential nature, can hardly face the task of identifying points of leverage. The approach may *appear* progressive and *be* paralysing. As to the capitalist nature of the state: while citizens and state actors can work to mitigate that, fundamental transformation of the capitalist state requires some dismantling of capitalism itself, which might only be possible at a transnational level.

Let us begin the comparison of the anchors of the capitalist and white supremacist states with the broad structural factors.

International pressures? What equivalent exists for external constraints such as the threat of capital flight or political intervention? Thobani simply asserts the existence of "transnational racial alliances that uphold white supremacy at a global level" (2007, 251), but she fails to provide evidence of this. One can point to specific phenomena such as international cooperation in the "global war on terror." But the fact that states shared a concern to fight terror, and often indulged in a fair bit of Islamophobia when doing so, is not evidence of a defence of white supremacy.

There *is* evidence, on the other hand, that international pressures can challenge race hierarchy. Will Kymlicka points out that "After 1946, Truman instructed the Justice and State Departments to submit amicus briefs supporting legal cases brought by African-American organizations, advising the courts that racial segregation was an obstacle to foreign policy, and a liability in the Cold War struggle with the Soviet Union. In the famous Brown v Board of Education case, for example, the federal government brief said 'It is in the context of the present world struggle between freedom and tyranny that the problem of racial discrimination in the US must be viewed'" (2007c, 117). The story of Sayyid Qutb, who would become a leader of Egypt's Muslim Brotherhood and an inspiration for al Qaeda, is illuminating. Arriving in the US on a scholarship in 1948, He was appalled by America's sexual mores, but also by its racism: "Once, Qutb and several friends were turned away from a movie theater because the owner thought they were black.

'But we're Egyptians,' one of the group explained. The owner apologized and offered to let them in, but Qutb refused, galled by the fact that black Egyptians could be admitted but black Americans could not" (Wright 2011, 22).

Kelley and Trebilcock point to the analogous role of international pressures in challenging Canada's traditionally racist immigration policies: "Canada's credibility in a multi-racial British Commonwealth of newly independent nations, and its role as an honest broker, middle power, and peacekeeper in the larger global theatre, made many of its former immigration policies increasingly anachronistic, and indeed an embarrassment" (2000, 319). One progressive critic sees such pressures as a factor in the emergence of multiculturalism (Galabuzi 2011, 60).

Race equivalent to the power of capital? When capital is generally "unhappy," investment declines, economic activity slows – and government revenue falls along with it – unemployment rises, and the government pays a clear political price. This can even occur with neither a conscious commitment to preserve capitalism upon the part of the individual nor political coordination among capitalists, as a negative "business climate" can emerge on the basis of narrow economic calculations by individual capitalists. Is there any racial equivalent of such phenomena? We have a corporate sector still dominated by white males. We know they will react in various ways to prevent state measures that threaten them as capitalists. But will they also react against state measures that threaten them as *whites*? I doubt it.

Charles Mills would disagree:

> We all have multiple identities, and, to this extent, most of us are both privileged and disadvantaged by different systems of domination. But white racial identity has generally triumphed over all others; it is race that (transgender, transclass) has generally determined the social world and loyalties, the lifeworld, of whites –whether as citizens of the colonizing mother country, settlers, nonslaves, or beneficiaries of the "color bar" and the "color line." There has been no comparable, spontaneously crystallizing transracial "workers'" world or transracial "female" world: race is the identity around which whites have usually closed ranks. (Mills 1997, 138)

A sense of white solidarity has often been important for white *workers*. Race solidarity *from below* might well be understood as compensation for a precarious social situation. Recall the "identity shuffle," mentioned in chapter 3's discussion of Arlie Hochschild's *Strangers in Their Own Land*, through which people choose to focus on any dimension of their identity from which they can squeeze some self-respect.

But does race solidarity exist within the *capitalist* class? Even if an individual capitalist is racist, does that lead them to favour race solidarity over their own economic interests? If white capitalists are imbued with a sense of race solidarity, why have they so enthusiastically embraced the offshoring of production and other forms of economic globalization?[13] And if capital does not rise up in defence of white supremacy, what other social force has an equivalent potential to inflict a wide range of punishments upon a wayward state elite?

News media. The factor of the general ideological climate is too vast to permit a meaningful summary, but let us consider one slice of it, the news media. As with pretty much any institution in a historically white-dominant society, the media elite is predominantly white. This unsurprisingly results in various forms of bias: both clear hostility to the goal of racial equality from some conservative journalists and the more widespread unconscious reproduction of the biases of the surrounding culture. But does such bias represent anything resembling the energy that news media put into sustaining the current economic order? Two concrete comparisons suggest not.

First, politicians or movements that advocate a serious transformation of the economic order can expect to find themselves attacked as naive utopians or dangerous radicals, or simply ignored. This holds true for the whole spectrum of mainstream news media: the "liberal" *Washington Post*'s well-documented hostility to Bernie Sanders provides one example of this (Frank 2016). Does this parallel the treatment of those who work for racial equality? There have certainly been attacks on movements such as Black Lives Matter. But that movement represents one element of a broader push for racial equality. In Canada today, moreover, even BLM is often treated respectfully by conservative media. I examined *National Post* references to the movement for the six months between October 2019 and March 2020 (a period chosen to exclude the widespread shift that occurred in the wake of the murder of George Floyd) and found the treatment surprisingly positive. The paper recognizes that the US movement was sparked in part by the killing of Trayvon Martin and that its Canadian counterpart gained strength after the Toronto shooting of Andrew Loku: acknowledgment that the movement is a response to deadly anti-black violence implicitly legitimizes it.

The second comparison might be more decisive: News media today typically employ a significant number of reporters to cover the "business beat." They write about matters of interest to businesspeople, investors, and so on. But they also monitor the health of "the economy" – understood in capitalist terms – discuss policy ideas affecting it, and so on. *Where are the white supremacy equivalents of such reporters?* The easy invocation of "master narratives" and "social imaginaries" obscures the truth that any form of domination must be *organized*. For this, "organic intellectuals" – including journalists – play an essential role, giving a social group "homogeneity and an awareness of its own function" (Gramsci rpt. 1971, 5). Where in the news media do we find the organic intellectuals of white supremacy?

The electoral factor. I have argued that the stability of the capitalist state rests upon various pillars. An implication is that this state can persist even if one pillar is weakened. Thus, the capitalist orientation of the state does not require that the electorate be particularly committed to it. It is enough that voters be willing to punish governments for economic difficulties such as high unemployment, which can arise from a poor "business climate." And even that is not entirely essential, so long as vital economic decisions can be shielded from democracy. But we have also seen that various pillars of the capitalist state don't have equivalents that sustain a supposed WSS. This entails that the subjectivity of the electorate *must* loom large in any case for the existence of a WSS.

So: might a state's commitment to white supremacy be anchored by a racist electorate? This confronts the difficulty that, after Canada expanded its sources of immigration, we did not see the emergence of a viable electoral strategy of racist political discourse of the sort that has arisen in many countries, including Trump's America. (I will make the case later on that one can plausibly view multiculturalism policy itself as, among other things, an attempt to head off foreseeable backlash constraints that the state might face in trying to diversify Canada's sources of immigration.) Further, over time, the more inclusive pattern of immigration changed the demographics of the electorate itself, making an explicitly racist discourse increasingly unviable.[14]

Two cautions here. First, the changing composition of the electorate does not mean that conservative politicians are entirely unable to appeal to the racist elements of their constituency. This can be tried through "dog whistle" appeals, such as references to "barbaric cultural practices." Further, the electoral sanction can be a factor constraining the state from vigorously *attacking* racism. I will consider this later on.

State personnel. We have seen to this point that various factors sustaining the capitalist nature of the state have no analogue for the supposed WSS. If the WSS in fact enjoys a stable existence, the reason for this seems to come down to the subjectivity of the state elite. Tremendous explanatory weight thus rests on this ideological factor: can it support the weight?

We saw in chapter 3 that the capitalist state is supported by widespread ideological beliefs (e.g., "the system delivers the goods") and by the fact that the state elite lives quite comfortably under the existing economic system. Could analogous factors anchor a WSS? Certainly, a state whose top ranks are predominantly white is run by the "winners" of the racial hierarchy. Will this motivate them to *sustain* that hierarchy? There are a number of reasons to doubt this.

First, an important difference between economic and racial hierarchies rests upon the very nature of modern "genteel" racism, which leaves many people unaware that they personally benefit from racial inequality. Much of the anger that the term *white privilege* sparks among those who benefit from it arises from this. Second, to rest one's explanation on the subjectivity of state personnel ignores probable contradictions in that subjectivity. It tacitly assumes that state actors have been entirely unmoved by decades of struggles against racism and by the worldwide diffusion of discourses for racial equality. We see here the importance of the assumption that there is a homogenous ethnic majority, critiqued in the previous chapter. From that problematic perspective, struggles for racial justice may force strategic manoeuvres upon the majority even while leaving intact their subjectivity. Himani Bannerji's bleak claim that "we will always feel oppressed because it is their intention to oppress us" illustrates this mood of some progressive critics (1990, 149).

A third reason why the state elite's commitment to white supremacy will not compare to its commitment to capitalism concerns the hegemonic – or not – status of associated values. A commitment to capitalism need not be expressed as such. There are a number of nice, polite phrases that will do the trick: "sustaining the business environment," "creating a competitive economy," and so on. The widespread acceptability of such goals, and their interpretation in eminently capitalist terms, remind us that capitalism is supported by a host of hegemonic beliefs and values. It is also true, under this system, that when capital is "unhappy," many people could suffer. So it is very easy to believe that in promoting business interests, one is working for the "national interest."

And what of that other goal, the "Rescue of Whiteness" (Thobani 2007, 150), the maintenance of white supremacy: how is the motivation for that sustained? It is not buttressed by a wide range of hegemonic values. Indeed it is a motive that cannot explicitly be acknowledged in much of the contemporary world, certainly not within the spectrum of influential political discourse. So the state actor who is pursuing this goal is doing something they often cannot talk about to their spouse, their children, their friends.

So while there are various phrases and concepts that support yet mask the goal of supporting capitalism, white supremacy would seem to lack these. "Security" might be one candidate. And in fact we do see definite biases in perceptions of and responses to threats to security, as noted earlier. Yet, although "security" is understood and pursued in an unbalanced fashion, it is not a code word for white supremacy: after 9/11, the targets of security discourse were not racialized people in general.[15]

This points to a related difficulty. When King promised in 1947 to continue restrictions on immigration from "the orient," the marching orders for state personnel were clear: they were written in law, in the form of Orders in Council and various regulations, and publicly acknowledged. What happened to that clearly documented apparatus of racism? Can we have an entire state complex mobilized around an objective that dare not speak its name? When we consider how difficult it is to get different organs of the state working together even around objectives that are publicly proclaimed, the idea seems improbable.

In the absence of smoking-gun evidence of racist policy, those who advance the WSS argument resort often to forced interpretations of official texts. Thobani cites one of the objectives of the 1976–77 Immigration Act: "to enrich and strengthen the cultural and social fabric of Canada, taking into account the federal and bilingual character of Canada." This, she interprets as: "The Act naturalized the character of the nation as bilingual and made its objective the strengthening of the 'cultural and social fabric' of whiteness in the face of increasing non-white immigration" (2007, 157).

None of the points made here deny the undeniable: that we are influenced by a racial or ethnic identity as well as by other dimensions of our identity. Nor do they challenge the fact that a state whose upper levels are predominantly white will manifest racial bias. But bias does not constitute an *active* defence of white supremacy. For this, we need an affirmation of white supremacist values, as well as conscious strategizing around how to promote those values. To return to the question of "organic intellectuals": the capitalist state has a whole army of technicians devoted to promoting economic growth, the smooth working of markets, and so on. Where are the equivalent state technicians for white supremacy? In contrast, one can identify quite a number of such nuts-and-bolts white-supremacy technicians in the United States, involved among other things in coordinating voter suppression efforts (Rutenberg 2020). Note that the existence of such technicians of domination is well-documented, not merely alleged.

Given the lack of clear anchors for a WSS, the argument that the state elite has sought to uphold white supremacy is not well grounded. But

I will conclude this section with two important clarifications. First, the state elite may not seek to sustain racial hierarchy yet not be seriously committed to attacking it either. Second, the foregoing analysis is consistent with the existence of systemic racism in parts of the Canadian state.

Actions versus omissions. I have cast doubt on the WSS construct. But a different claim is more defensible: that the state elite does not seek to tackle racism in a serious and comprehensive manner, or perhaps is constrained from doing so. Now some may view the distinction I am drawing here as trivial. It is not, for a couple of reasons. First, the distinction is relevant to our current discussion, because what we are trying to explain is not an omission, but an action: the introduction of multiculturalism. More importantly, the distinction concerns political strategy, because the claims of action and omission point to different tasks.

In the first case: anyone who remains committed to white supremacy, more than seventy years after the Universal Declaration of Human Rights, and after decades of exposure to discourse on the evils of racism, is an *enemy*: they have proven immune to persuasion, to moral appeals. Whatever power they have as state agents to inflict harm on others must be taken from them. So if the state elite is committed to upholding white supremacy, then that elite is a prime target for political action. *How* one goes about dislodging that elite is unclear to me, and none of the progressive critics address this. (Note that this task is crucial in a way that it is not for tackling the capitalist state, precisely because the latter is sustained by a range of structural factors, not just by the subjectivity of the state elite, as we have seen.)

The claim of omission, on the other hand, first invites an analysis analogous to that done for the capitalist state, to identify what might *constrain* the state elite from seriously tackling racism. Some constraints become clear when we reflect on just what serious anti-racism *means*. It requires quick and effective responses to current manifestations of racism. But it also requires something more demanding: undoing to the extent possible the *effects* of past racism. This should be obvious: we would not be impressed by someone who confessed that they had stolen your car, that they felt terrible about doing so, that they would not steal "going forward," but that they had no intention of giving the car back.

One attempt to compensate to some degree for the legacy of racial injustice has been employment equity, which has been in force in the federal government since 1986. The political constraint from pursuing this policy with vigour was manifest in the backlash against Ontario's NDP government in the early 1990s.[16] A key obstacle is that opposition to employment equity can draw on hegemonic values such as fairness and equality. A *Globe and Mail* editorial, for example, thundered against "the immorality of establishing legal preferences in employment for those of the right race, sex or disability." The Ontario government's "comprehensive, mandatory system of officially-sanctioned discrimination" was "a terrible, monstrous mistake," "utterly repugnant to Canadians" (18 June 1993). But these opponents of employment equity invoke fairness and equality in an ahistorical and asocial way. Ahistorical, because the opponent will often ignore the whole history of injustice that created the need for the policy in the first place; asocial, because they can talk of "fair competition" for jobs while ignoring the multiple disadvantages that arise from having been born into a family victimized by racial injustice. But making these points requires citing complex social phenomena, a task the opponent is spared.

Further, political defence of employment equity is yet more difficult because it is at best a form of rough justice. The parent of a child whose job prospects might suffer from the policy in 1990s Ontario could quite legitimately ask: "Why should my child pay the price for rectifying an injustice to which they did not contribute? Why shouldn't society as a whole somehow pay the bill that has come due?" Could that be done? Certainly. Justice could have been served through a policy of massive job buyouts of senior staff, retiring them a bit early from the labour market, and shifting mid-level staff upwards, to allow for employment for members of designated equity groups without hurting the chances of anyone else. Such a path would be very expensive, so governments everywhere have found it more expedient to download the costs of equity onto youth trying to enter the labour market.

But serious anti-racism requires yet more. Employment equity measures, on their own, run the risk of leaving the majority of racialized citizens to suffer the economic and social effects of past and current racism. Such measures may even serve to co-opt citizens who might have been vital for struggles against racial injustice. Gramsci noted the pacifying effect of transformism, "the gradual but continuous absorption" into the elite of individuals, even from "antagonistic groups" (1971, 58). If this occurs, employment equity could appear successful by all sorts of measures, such as the racial composition of boardrooms and parliaments, yet be compatible with ongoing subordination of vast majorities of various ethnic or racialized groups.

Because economic inequality favours the diffusion of ideologies that justify it (see chapter 10), we can expect any racialized poverty left untouched by employment equity to be a potent stimulus for ongoing racism (which in turn contributes to racialized poverty). This racism can shape-shift without affecting its ideological role of justification.[17]

This means that a serious fight to undo the effects of racism requires a much more active state. It is not enough to tinker with public school curricula, for example: generous spending on education – including early childhood education – and other social services is needed even to partly level the playing field. Serious action against racism thus runs headlong into the political dominance of neoliberalism. The specifically fiscal cost of fighting racism must be paid by current or future taxpayers. At this prospect, many will recoil. Walter Benn Michaels notes that "the obligations of diversity (being nice to each other)" are far less onerous than "the obligations of equality (giving up our money)" (2006, 17). As Nesrine Malik commented in the wake of the protests sparked by the murder of George Floyd, "it is easy to agree that black lives should matter. But it is hard to contemplate all the ways the world needs to change to make them matter" (2020).

So any political party that vigorously advocates comprehensive anti-racism policies will find itself facing a conservative competitor that will talk of "moving on," not obsessing over "past slights," and so on.[18] So both the structural supports of neoliberalism, and the predictable strategies that will be deployed by conservatives in electoral competition, can seriously constrain even those state actors who sincerely wish to attack racism.

Systemic racism. I was drafting this chapter when George Floyd was murdered by a Minneapolis police officer. Suddenly, and to the credit of protest organizers in the US and here, systemic racism became newsworthy. When they attempted to define the concept at all, news stories tended to draw upon definitions that the reporter had found somewhere or other. One result was that, when RCMP Commissioner Brenda Lucki was asked about the matter, she complained that she had "heard about five or 10 different definitions on TV" (qtd. in Leblanc and Kirkup 2020).

Here, I will draw on the useful definition offered in the 1992 report of the Commission on Systemic Racism in the Ontario Criminal Justice System:

> By systemic racism we mean the social production of racial inequality in decisions about people and in the treatment they receive. Racial inequality is neither natural nor inherent in humanity. On the contrary, it is the result of a society's arrangement of economic, cultural and political life. It is produced by the combination of:

- social constructions of races as real, different and unequal (racialization);

- the norms, processes and service delivery of a social system (structure), and
- the actions and decisions of people who work for social systems (personnel). (Commission on Systemic Racism 1992, 39)

Note that as they use the term, "system" can refer to something broad (as in the criminal justice system), or to specific organizations:

> Systems consist of people, their attitudes and beliefs (personnel); values, procedures, policies and informal rules (operating norms); ways of making decisions; and methods of delivering services. These elements continually affect one another over time and together comprise a perceived whole. (45–6)

To support the definition, I will follow the *via negativa*, which "seeks to understand what something *is* by clarifying what it *is not*" (Ryan 2010b, 215). Here, RCMP Commissioner Lucki's disastrous *Globe and Mail* interview is useful. Lucki first stated that "if systemic racism is meaning that racism is entrenched in our policies and procedures, I would say that we don't have systemic racism [in the RCMP]." She then allowed that "if we refer to something like unconscious bias, I think that exists in the RCMP. We are not immune to it and there are times when our members don't act in accordance to our core values, and that includes racism" (qtd. in Leblanc and Kirkup 2020). The contrast with a diagnosis of systemic racism is clear: for Lucki, RCMP racism is simply something that happens from time to time, when officers are not perfect (and who among us is?). Similarly, when Donald Trump finally brought himself to acknowledge that kneeling on a man's neck for eight minutes while he begged for his life, and not letting up until he could beg no more, was perhaps not fully acceptable behaviour, he claimed that "something snapped, I think, with the policeman and the other three watching it" (qtd. in Martin 2020).

We see an analogous flight from systemic analysis in many responses to terrorist acts. Pankaj Mishra notes that "politicians and journalists routinely describe the domestic terrorist as a deranged 'lone wolf', even when, as with Timothy McVeigh, and many other anti-government militants in the United States, he explicitly articulated a point of view – anti-governmentalism – that mirrors mainstream ideas and ideologies" (2017, 78). As then–Prime Minister Stephen Harper put it, we should not "commit sociology" to understand acts of terror. Pierre Poilievre, one of Harper's most faithful lieutenants, helpfully added that "the root causes of terrorism is [*sic*] terrorists" (qtd. in Fitzpatrick 2013).

Lucki's and Trump's comments manifest a wish to view specific cases as isolated incidents that can be understood without reference to anything else. A claim of systemic racism means precisely that such an approach will always fall short. The Commission on Systemic Racism provides ample illustrations of this. It reported that

> many correctional officers routinely use racist language in dealing with black or other racialized prisoners and colleagues. For some officers, this abusive language clearly manifests intense hostility toward black or other racialized people. Other correctional workers who use racist language in dealing with black or other racialized prisoners do not appear to be driven by personal hostility. Some of them told the Commission about their own conduct and that of their colleagues, and were troubled by it. Yet they continued to act in this way. Why? It appears that some correctional officers use racially abusive language because "everyone else does it," or to prove themselves. (1992, 46)

Thus, some guards were in effect being *socialized* into racist practices. Far from it being a problem of "a few bad apples," something about the institution was *making the "apples" bad*. The commission quoted a previous study of the Toronto police that uncovered the same disturbing pattern: "The Force has done a reasonable job of ensuring that those who are recruited do not display an overt bias which would make them unsuitable to be a police officer. What is apparent is that a change occurs after joining the Force. There was significant evidence that many police officers ... develop strong feelings and beliefs as to attributes of individuals, based on factors such as appearance and racial backgrounds" (qtd. in Commission on Systemic Racism 1992, 54; elision in commission report).

Further, an isolating case-by-case approach can only identify the most egregious cases of racism. There are more subtle forms of discrimination that cannot be conclusively identified at the level of the individual case and that only reveal themselves at an aggregate level. Recall the Oreopoulos research discussed in chapter 3, which involved sending employers fictitious résumés that differed only by the applicant's name. No single employer was faced with otherwise identical CVs, so no individual employer can be known conclusively to have discriminated. But that discrimination was occurring is as well proven as anything that statistics can show.

So a claim of systemic racism is first of all a *denial* that the problem can be understood or addressed in a case-by-case manner. It thus also denies that responses that deal with individual cases, such as complaints to Human Rights Commissions or criminal prosecutions, are sufficient, although they are essential components of a solution. But if the systemic racism claim denies all that, what it positively *affirms* is more complicated. The definition crafted by the Commission on Systemic Racism speaks of "actions and decisions," of "norms, processes and service delivery," including "informal rules (operating norms)," and of "personnel." This, in effect, encompasses pretty much everything an organization *is*. Thus, to claim systemic racism is not in itself an analysis: but it is an essential *call* to analysis, which will seek to identify the precise mechanisms by which systemic racism is sustained. To misunderstand this, to view the claim as in itself an analysis or explanation of something, "stops analytic work just where it should begin," as Loïc Wacquant puts it (2022, 187).

I would wager that such an analysis will *always* uncover a mix of race-related factors (e.g., racial prejudices that exist within and outside the organization) and factors that, while not race-specific, need to be taken into account to combat the evil comprehensively. It will help here to recall points made in chapter 3's analysis of the state. I noted, for example, that the very form of bureaucracy gives the individual official a strong personal interest in being a "team player." This helps explain how police who observe a racist act by a colleague may look the other way, even if they disapprove of the act, or how someone who joins an organization can be corrupted, as the Commission on Systemic Racism noted. Particularly within police forces, a heavy price may be paid for not valuing the team above all else. In late 2020, a Toronto police officer filed a human rights complaint stating that "she was subjected to years of intimidation and reprisals by fellow officers and supervisors after she intervened to stop what she said was the unjustified use of force during the arrest of a Black suspect" (Trinh and Baksh 2020).

Other systemic problems can be intertwined with systemic racism. Consider the problem of police violence. A database maintained by *The Guardian* shows that in 2016, US police killed 1,093 people – a total that has stayed roughly constant in subsequent years, according to other media reports. The *Guardian* database reports that the victims were:

24 Native American
266 Black
183 Hispanic/Latino
574 White
21 Asian/Pacific Islander
25 Other/Unknown

On a per capita basis, this means that American Blacks are just over twice as likely to be killed by police as whites, and Native Americans three and a half times as likely (*Guardian* 2017). But even if US Blacks were killed at the same rate as whites, they would still suffer an extremely high number of police killings each year, which demonstrates that the epidemic of police killings arises from both racial and non-racial factors: by my rough calculations, using *The Guardian* figures for 2016 and Wikipedia information for police killings in the UK from 2010 to 2019, American *whites* are roughly eighty times as likely to be killed by police as the average citizen of the UK. Police racism is a systemic problem; police violence is another one: they are distinct but intertwined.

A general point made in chapter 3 is also important here: analysis of what the state and its organizations do need not start with individuals, but it must *pass through them*. That is, analysis of systemic racism will have to identify how it is sustained through the interests, beliefs, and actions of organization members. That something is "systemic" does not mean it can exist independently of individual actors. Further, the people who sustain systemic racism were not created within the organization in which they work, however much they are influenced by it: they carry baggage from the surrounding society. As the Commission on Systemic Racism notes by beginning its definition with the broader phenomenon of racialization, not all the roots of systemic racism lie within a particular organization.

The two clarifications to my rejection of the WSS argument are related, in that one of the symptoms of the state elite's not having attacked racism comprehensively is the failure to combat systemic racism. Any claim of systemic racism, as I noted, is a call to analysis. Such analysis has often been done. But to what effect? How much has changed, for example, in the decades since the 1992 report of the Commission on Systemic Racism in the Ontario Criminal Justice System?

Various constraints, I have argued, can prevent a state elite from tackling racism. Overcoming systemic racism in institutions such as the RCMP, and in police forces generally, presents additional challenges. Power does not flow downward through the state in linear fashion (see chapter 3). This is especially relevant when it comes to forces of order, which have particular sources of autonomous power. The widespread rioting that broke out during the Montreal police strike of 1969, for example, was a stark illustration that the strike threat is particularly persuasive when wielded by the police, even though they are legally barred from striking. In France, more recently, hundreds of thousands of workers demonstrated and struck for months against proposed government pension reforms. It was all in vain. Yet when France's police unions even hinted at job action, that was enough for them to be granted an exemption from the changes (Bonelli 2020).

There are specific political challenges to taming the RCMP. This was manifest in the "very Canadian coup" of late 2005, when RCMP commissioner Giuliano Zaccardelli intervened in the election that brought Harper to power by announcing that the RCMP was launching a criminal investigation of a Liberal cabinet member. That dramatically changed the course of the contest. Linda McQuaig writes that "there is evidence that the RCMP was very unhappy with the Martin government over its decision to call the Arar inquiry, since the inquiry was likely to uncover the RCMP's gross mishandling of the case" (2007, 254). Even at the time, a *Gazette* column detailed the "fishy" qualities of the RCMP's behaviour, including the fact that prior to making public its investigation, it had already conducted an initial inquiry that yielded "no evidence of wrongdoing or illegal activity" (MacPherson 2006). The RCMP investigation did not result in charges. Nor, for that matter, did the FBI investigation of Hillary Clinton, announced days before the 2016 election. Former British Labour cabinet minister Tony Benn once commented that "put crudely the security services have got something on everybody, though they may only use it when it is their interests to do so" (1989, 141). Zaccardelli and Comey demonstrated that, even when they *don't* "have something," they can inflict serious damage on politicians. We should assume that political leaders keep this in mind when they consider how to address systemic racism in an institution such as the RCMP.[19]

Thus, for various reasons, systemic racism can and does exist in state institutions, even if the state elite does not seek to sustain racism.[20]

Let us review the terrain covered in this chapter. I began with a "simple story" about the origins of multiculturalism policy. I then took up a critical progressive account of a deeper logic accounting for the policy. While there are variants of this story, I focused on the harshest account of multiculturalism's origins, which holds that the policy's objective was to sustain racial hierarchy. In assessing the critical progressive case, I noted the plausibility of the view that the policy was – or came to be – an instrument for averting social unrest. But I took aim at the argument that multiculturalism policy was an instrument of race hierarchy, which led into the extended discussion of the hypothesis of a "white supremacy state." My argument rejected that hypothesis, subject to various delimitations and clarifications. I now wish to develop a different account of a possible "deeper logic" behind the rise of multiculturalism. This will overlap in various ways with the critical progressive account but will foreground the capitalist nature of the state.

6.5 Multiculturalism and the Capitalist State: An Alternative Story

The alternative story to be developed here explores how the state elite's understanding of the evolving needs of the capitalist economy may have guided the emergence of multicultural policy. No single lens can explain everything a state does. State actions in a democracy will be directly or indirectly influenced by electoral considerations, the biases of state actors, and those actors' evolving sense of basic decency. But action is also shaped and constrained by the fundamentally capitalist nature of the state. So: without denying the variety of other influences, what light can the state's capitalist nature shed on the emergence of multiculturalism?

We may begin our story with the post-war economy. John Porter notes that economic growth was being sustained in part through immigration. In the 1950s, net migration accounted for roughly half of the growth of the Canadian labour force (1965, 42). This included skilled labour: "about 50 to 60 per cent of the new skilled jobs that came with the industrial development of the decade were filled by immigrants" (48).

We saw earlier in the chapter that Canada had traditionally preferred immigrants of European descent. But international developments increasingly brought that race preference into tension with the needs of the labour force. In 1957 the Royal Commission on Canada's Economic Prospects warned of "serious shortages of many kinds of trained manpower" and of "a dearth [rather] than a plethora of would-be immigrants into Canada from those countries from which they have traditionally come" (1957, 120, 103). The commission thus concluded that "there may be difficulty over the next two or three decades in obtaining as many suitable immigrants as it would be to Canada's advantage to have" (120). And Porter notes that "although it is unlikely that net migration was negative there is little doubt that in the early 1960's it was close to becoming so" (1965, 31).[21] The difficulty, as Kelley and Trebilcock argue, was that "by the early 1960s, Canada's traditional sources of immigrants, in particular Britain and Western Europe, were drying up as the European economies recovered from the Second World War and as the European Economic Community began to gather momentum" (2000, 351).

To situate what happened next, let us first return to another moment of change in Canadian immigration policy. Appearing before a parliamentary committee in April 1900, Deputy Minister of the Interior James Smart declared that "the policy of the Department has been based upon the assumption that it is highly desirable that at the earliest possible moment all the fertile lands of the west should be located, and the country enriched by the general production which will be sure to follow the settlement of a hardy class of settlers" (Select Standing Committee on Agriculture and Colonization 1900, 308). Smart in effect outlined a strategy of agriculture-led national economic development: "Manufacturers, merchants, and working men in all parts of Canada will receive much advantage from the occupation and cultivation of soil which is certain to show a steady increase year by year, not only from the incoming settlers, but from an increase in the production of those who are now settled in the country" (308).

Immigration policy, he continued, must match this development strategy: Canada must "encourage the immigration of *none but agriculturists*" (308). But what of the labour force needed to supply industry, mining, and so on? "The other class no doubt will take care of themselves," commented Smart. And where were those "agriculturists" to be found? "Most Canadians naturally concede," Smart commented, "that the British immigrant is by far the more desirable if it is possible to secure him, but the difficulty is, that in Great Britain, especially in England and Wales, it is said that there is only about one million people all told, who are engaged in agricultural pursuits ... It is therefore necessary to look to other countries" (308). He then ran through the challenges of recruiting from the US and various places in Northern and Central Europe. Smart insisted that "in France we have also done considerable work." Alas, "the population is practically stationary and the work of French emigration has not shown the best results, nor is it likely to do so. Frenchmen in France seem to prefer the homeland" (308).

A later defence of the immigration strategy that ensued from this analysis gave us one of Canadian history's most famous quotes. Clifford Sifton, Minister of the Interior for a decade during the Laurier years, wrote: "When I speak of quality I have in mind, I think, something that is quite different from what is in the mind of the average writer or speaker upon the question of Immigration. I think a stalwart peasant in a sheep-skin coat, born on the soil, whose forefathers have been farmers for ten generations, with a stout wife and a half-dozen children, is good quality" (Sifton 1922).

The continuation of Sifton's statement is perhaps less famous: "A Trades Union artisan who will not work more than eight hours a day and will not work that long if he can help it, will not work on a farm at all and has to be fed by the public when work is slack is, in my judgment, quantity and very bad quantity. I am indifferent as to whether or not he is British born. It matters not what his nationality is; such men are not wanted in Canada, and the more of them we get the more trouble we shall have."

Sifton's statements are striking for the clarity with which his criteria of economic desirability outweigh those of "race" desirability. Race preference did not disappear. We might say that Sifton sought to widen somewhat the circle of ethnic desirability and narrow that of class desirability. For Sifton, Canada needed those who "have been bred for generations to work from daylight to dark. They have never done anything else and they never expect to do anything else" (1922). The ideal immigrant would work hard and demand little.

Apart from telling us something about debates over immigration policy, Sifton's comments are revealing in another way. His invocation of the "stalwart peasant" produced by generations of breeding drew on a then-influential blurring of race and class in which supposed racial differences were cited to justify class inequality. For the aristocrat, claimed Tocqueville, "the poor is a being of another species" (1986, vol. 1, 322). Eric Hobsbawm notes that in the late nineteenth century, "humanity was divided by 'race,' an idea which penetrated the ideology of the period almost as deeply as 'progress' ... Even in the 'developed' countries themselves, humanity was increasingly divided into the energetic and talented stock of the middle classes and the supine masses whose genetic deficiencies doomed them to inferiority. Biology was called upon to explain inequality, particularly by those who felt themselves destined for superiority" (1994, 32).

Indeed, the Nazis' Aryan race theory originated with Count Arthur de Gobineau, who held the French aristocracy to which he belonged to be part of a race superior to that of the rest of society. As Arendt notes, "all the loose race talk that is so characteristic of French writers after 1870, even if they are not racists in any strict sense of the word, follows antinational, pro-Germanic lines" (1958b, 174). This exemplifies a point to which we will return in chapter 10: just as many things can mask racism, racism itself can serve as an ideological mask for other forms of injustice.

Sifton's arguments were presented in a *Maclean's* article published in 1922, seventeen years after he left the Laurier cabinet. He was in fact defending a policy since rejected. Canada, he lamented, had instead accepted "the off-scourings and dregs of society ... ne'er-do-wells and scalawags who desire to get away from Europe" (1922). And this reminds us of a point noted in chapter 3: it is not always obvious what is required to sustain economic growth. Thus even actors who share that objective can be sharply divided on policy. Smart and Sifton evidently believed that growth in the non-agricultural economy would be gradual enough that natural population growth could meet those needs. In a 1910 defence of the post-Sifton policy, P.H. Bryce, Chief Medical Officer of the Interior Ministry, disagreed: Canada required labour "willing to do the rougher work of opening up new areas by building railways and canals" (1910). Bryce's assessment of the post-Sifton immigrants differed from Sifton's own. Deportations, he insisted, had "removed from amongst the newcomers the derelicts, until it is probable that fewer defectives per 1,000 actually exist in the immigrants than in an equal number of the same class amongst the native born."

Fast-forward to the early 1960s, and we see Canada facing an analogous situation: the supply of "desirable" immigrants is limited, hence the understanding of desirability must expand.[22] But, as at the turn of the century, uncertainties remained about the best way to support capitalist growth.

First, the policy shift: "Admission policies which explicitly discriminated on the basis of race or country of origin were largely eliminated by 1962 and were replaced by criteria for independent immigrants which emphasized skills, education, and training" (Kelley and Trebilcock, 315). This was ratified by the introduction of the points system in 1967, which reduced, but did not eliminate, the discretion of immigration officers, and of the minister. The short-term effects of the policy change were notable: "the proportion of immigrants coming from Asia and the Caribbean increased dramatically, from 10 per cent in 1965–6 to 23 per cent in 1969–70" (348); the longer-term effects even more so: "Ninety per cent of immigrants who arrived in Canada before 1961 were born in Europe, compared with only 25 per cent of those who arrived between 1981 and 1991" (442).

As to different views of the needs of capital, Kelley and Trebilcock note a division within the state: "the Department of Citizenship and Immigration tended to argue for reliance on long-term factors bearing on adaptability, such as age, education, and training, while the Department of Labour tended to take the position that selection criteria should be adjusted on a regular basis to reflect current labour-market shortages and surpluses" (2000, 351–2). The Department of Labour was in effect advocating that short-term criteria determine choices with long-term effects: the granting of permanent residency and eventual citizenship. This probably reflected the influence of narrow sectoral interests: "Both the Canadian Federation of Agriculture (CFA) and the Mining Association of Canada (MAC) were less enthusiastic about the emphasis on skilled over unskilled (and cheaper) labour" (357).[23]

Margaret Walton-Roberts comments that "immigration has moved from being a domestic policy of nation-building to one that is primarily a response to international competition for talent" (2011, 104). But to some extent, Canada has always found itself in competition with others in the effort to attract *and retain* the types of immigrants it sought. In his 1900 testimony, James Smart enumerated the challenges of attracting "desirable classes" of immigrants from various places. Countries such as Germany and Russia restricted emigration. In the case of Sweden, Smart commented that "a general tendency towards the United States where Swedes have been highly successful and occupy many prominent places, [has] been difficult to overcome" (Select Standing Committee on Agriculture and Colonization 1900, 310). And Clifford Sifton's 1922 *Maclean's* article was a response to public concerns that the Canadian population was 1.8 million smaller than "it would have been had we retained all our immigration and the natural increase of the population" over the previous decade (1922). The 1957 Royal Commission, finally, acknowledged that Canada was in competition with "other countries which provide alternative settlement opportunities for possible immigrants" (1957, 103).

A clear implication of this long-standing international competition for talent is that public policy needs to address factors that make Canada *un*attractive. An important one is the prospect of economic marginalization. This was not really addressed by the 1971 multicultural policy declaration, except through the emphasis on encouraging learning of one of the official languages. Perhaps it was believed that, with proper selection criteria for immigrants, this problem would look after itself.

A second unattractive factor would be a widespread ideology of assimilationism, an adherence to the "Fordist" model of collective life with which this book opened. Even more unattractive would be outright racism. It would have been clear to policy-makers that a turn to worldwide sources of immigration could foment various forms of xenophobia. Just as policy-makers were aware of racial unrest in the US, they certainly knew of nativist reactions against immigration, exemplified by British Conservative MP Enoch Powell's infamous "rivers of blood" speech, which described the UK as "a nation busily engaged in heaping up its own funeral pyre" through immigration (rpt. 2007).

Within Canada itself, "in the mid-1960s, anti-Jewish and anti-black hate propaganda was widespread in Canada, especially in Ontario and Quebec. Simultaneously, neo-Nazi and white supremacist groups, based largely in the United States, became active in Canada. The Canadian Nazi Party made its first appearance in Toronto in 1965" (Cohen-Almagor 2006, 157). This led the government to strike the Special Committee on Hate Propaganda in Canada, which led in turn to the 1970 addition of provisions on hate propaganda to the Criminal Code (Walker 2018,

3). Note too that the Sir George Williams affair, discussed earlier, could be viewed as an illustration of how minority unrest would arise from majority prejudice. There were vivid signs of that prejudice during the affair itself: "At a tense moment on the street someone shouted: 'Get rid of the n-----s.' The marchers passed by, one carrying a sign reading: This is Montreal, Alabama" (Balfour 1969).

So we can safely assume that elites within the state were aware that they faced a ticklish challenge of "managing diversity." But managing in what sense? Would it be enough to bring in a wider diversity of immigrants and step up assimilation efforts? No, for two reasons. The first was the aforementioned international talent competition in which Canada found itself. The second was that, if the government was concerned at the prospect of a racist reaction against immigrants, assimilation would never be enough, because *racism doesn't work that way*. Racism being what it (often) is, racialized immigrants who conformed to "white" patterns of behaviour in every respect would still be the targets of resentment and resistance.[24] So the management of diversity would have to attempt to make members of the dominant ethnic groups less rigid, less xenophobic, less tied to narrow images of Canada and Canadians.

Now the whole idea of managing diversity can raise hackles. Richard Day, for example, takes frequent aim at the idea of "management of the problem of Canadian diversity" (2000, 26). His criticism, and his book as a whole, are premised on a puzzling assertion: "The problem of the problem of diversity, then, is that *the assumption of an objectively existing and problematic ethnocultural diversity covers over the work of differentiation itself*. Because it is a discursive construct with no basis in an empirical reality - not a 'thing' of any sort at all – Canadian diversity 'does not exist'" (2000, 5). I would counter that extremely narrow understanding of existence with Charles Taylor's "What is real is what you have to deal with" (1989, 59).[25]

When we move away from the excessively abstract claim that it is somehow problematic to view a single thing called "diversity" as a single problem, we notice a host of interrelated issues that a society must deal with and that won't magically vanish by being labelled a mere "discursive construct." For example, multiple religions coexist in Canada. Should public funds be available to the schools of some faiths but not others? Should religious ministers be allowed to preach hate against followers of other religions? Against atheists, or homosexuals? Should sex-ed curricula be influenced by homophobic religious beliefs? Should the practices of one religion be favoured, through public holidays or state symbols? And so on. These are all issues that "diversity" inevitably raises. And there are a thousand others. And yes, they must be "managed," one way or another.

But if the government has sought to affect the beliefs and practices of the dominant ethnic groups, multiculturalism policy also appears to have taken aim at the "other ethnic groups" of European descent. An oft-quoted part of Trudeau's 1971 policy declaration holds that "national unity if it is to mean anything in the deeply personal sense, must be founded on confidence in one's own individual identity; out of this can grow respect for that of others and a willingness to share ideas, attitudes and assumptions" (Commons, 8 October 1971). The view that respect for others is grounded in self-confidence has been termed the "multiculturalism hypothesis" or "multicultural assumption" (Berry, Kalin, and Taylor 1977, 225). It is certainly plausible that members of the "other ethnic groups," long subject to discrimination, slights, and slurs, will inflict upon others what they themselves have suffered, unless the cycle can be broken.[26]

Perhaps the multiculturalism hypothesis was reasonable, but the actual policies enacted after the 1971 declaration were too anaemic to put it to the test. Or perhaps it was simply too indirect a way to attack racial prejudice. In any case, there were continuing signs of tension in the mid-1970s. Kelley and Trebilcock note that a 1974 government green paper pointed to "the increase in racial tensions that accompanied the changing ethnic composition of Canada as a direct result of the 1962 and 1967 changes to immigration policy" (2000, 372).

So in late 1975, John Munro, the minister responsible for multiculturalism, told the *Globe and Mail* that the policy would be changing direction: "'Combating discrimination,' Mr. Munro said, 'will become the major over-all objective of the program ... 'We would no longer put such emphasis on the folkloric aspect'" (Johnson 1975). "As he outlined the new concept," the *Globe* article went on, "Mr. Munro suggested that large, well-structured minorities with established leadership will not require the support of the multiculturalism program ... Instead, the program will address itself to helping smaller groups and 'the real minorities of this country' such as black people, the Portuguese community, people from the Caribbean, India or Pakistan, and the native people."

As unlikely as it may sound when discussing a Liberal cabinet minister, it seems that Mr. Munro was suffering from a simple "transitive" vision of power – that is, he was making the assumption that the government held all the cards in its relations with outside groups. But the "well-structured minorities with established leadership" whose demands he was dismissing were precisely those with serious political clout. The head of the government-created Canadian Consultative Council on Multiculturalism

(CCCM) was quick to react, expressing "shock" to the *Globe* reporter and declaring that "what the minister has said is incompatible with the multiculturalism program." Munro lost his tussle with a "civil society" organization stacked with Liberal Party activists, and his policy proposal never made it to cabinet (Jaworsky 1979, 125).

As noted at the outset of this "story," the state is not *only* capitalist. However much a capitalist logic might have encouraged a more muscular attack on discrimination, the very constitution of the CCCM suggested the degree to which multiculturalism policy had been subordinated to electoral calculations after the Liberals nearly lost power in 1972. Still, most observers agree that the program did eventually shift, particularly in the wake of the 1984 *Equality Now!* report, and in 1987, "a new parliamentary standing committee on multiculturalism proclaimed that multicultural policy had indeed evolved from cultural preservation to the promotion of equality" (McRoberts 1997, 127).

But note the contradiction in which the state was caught: if the government was seeking to *retain* immigrants, not just attract them in the first place, then a purely superficial approach that improved Canada's "brand" but failed to improve realities on the ground would seem inadequate. At the same time, as argued above, both electoral considerations and the constraints of neoliberal capitalism (in particular) limit the state's ability to attack racism in a serious way. This is an example of a more general predicament faced by states, noted by a number of writers (e.g., O'Connor 1973): support for capitalism is never free of contradictions. Still, within those constraints, multiculturalism – taken broadly – might be credited with some weakening of attachment to the "Fordist" model of collective life, some broadening of widespread notions of what it means to be a Canadian, so as to sustain high levels of support for immigration over several decades.

We can summarize the alternative story in seven points: (1) The Canadian economy was reliant on immigration. (2) Traditional sources of immigration were drying up. (3) Recourse to new sources was thus required. (4) This led to the 1962 shift in immigration policy, but (5) there was international competition for skilled immigrants. (6) The government was aware that immigrants from new sources could lead to a racial backlash, which would harm the government and the economy and reduce Canada's attractiveness as a destination country; thus (7) the 1971 multiculturalism declaration was *in part* a response to this danger. ("In part," because the narrative does not deny the influence of elements discussed above, such as international pressures, the B&B Commission, pressure from civil society organizations, and so on.)

In *Becoming Multicultural: Immigration and the Politics of Membership in Canada and Germany* (2012), Triadafilos Triadafilopoulos offers an account at odds with the one just summarized. He in effect argues that (1)–(3) had nothing to do with (4). For Triadafilopoulos, the 1962 policy shift did not aim at "attracting skilled immigrants to Canada"; rather it was meant to "offer critics proof that Canada's positions on anti-discrimination and civil rights were not empty gestures" (2012, 87–8).[27]

Triadafilopoulos offers two types of evidence in support of his account. The first is official statements, including Minister of Citizenship and Immigration Ellen Fairclough's presentation of the new immigration regulations to the House, which, he argues, proved that the policy shift "would serve a distinctly political end by granting the government a more effective means of countering accusations of racism and discrimination" (90). The second is the bureaucracy's "decision to interpret the 1962 reforms passively," for example, by continuing to focus recruitment efforts on traditional source countries (90).

The most curious aspect of this argument is that Triadafilopoulos acknowledges that economic concerns had a strong influence on immigration policy in the post-war era (57) and in the 1970s (107). For a plausible account, he would thus need to explain the puzzling *absence* of economic influences during the 1962 policy shift. What led those influences to take a nap, so to speak, during this momentous transition in immigration policy? How can a policy that had always been shaped by the perceived needs of the Canadian economy suddenly float free of such considerations? Triadafilopoulos does not say. The implausible idea of economic influences being suspended and then revived points to the importance of having one's explanations disciplined by some coherent theory of how the state works.

In truth, economic concerns weighed heavily on the policy shift. As noted above, the 1957 Royal Commission – ignored in Triadafilopoulos's account – explicitly argued the points I have labelled (1), (2), and (5): the Canadian economy was reliant on skilled immigrants; traditional source countries were less likely to supply them; and Canada was in competition with other immigrant-receiving countries. Further, leaving aside the fact that it is always risky to take a politician's public statements as a reliable guide to a policy's goals, in the Fairclough speech presented by Triadafilopoulos as a key support to his argument, the minister refers to "the government's basic objective which remains to foster and encourage, wherever possible, changes and improvements which will result in the immigration of larger numbers of suitably qualified immigrants to Canada" (Commons, 19 January 1962). A statement in response to the policy announcement by New Democrat MP Harold Winch also noted: "Inquiries of the Ministry told us this afternoon we shall find that as an immigration policy carried out by regulation in Canada it will be determined by the status of the economy" (Commons, 19 January 1962). The most plausible view of the 1962 policy change, then, is that it was the government's answer to the challenges articulated by the 1957 Royal Commission.

A secondary feature of the 1962 policy reinforces this interpretation: it did not eliminate discrimination in the sponsorship rights of immigrants. Triadafilopoulos contends that this also demonstrates "the political nature of the 1962 reforms" (2012, 90); in fact, it does precisely the opposite. Why maintain discrimination if the policy's goal is to proclaim Canada's "anti-discrimination" to the world? That choice is *exactly* what one would expect from a policy driven by economic concerns, given the government's oft-stated perception that sponsored immigrants contributed less to the economy than independent ones.

As to Triadafilopoulos's other strand of evidence: the bureaucratic response was not as muted as he suggests. By 1966, admissions from non-traditional source countries had more than tripled relative to 1961.[28] Triadafilopoulos appears to feel those admissions might have increased faster. Perhaps. But however one assesses the bureaucracy's response, it would be rash to draw inferences from that response to the goals of the policy itself. The bureaucracy may have been at a loss as to how to proceed, or simply *opposed* to the new policy.[29] Could the government not have imposed its will? In theory, yes. But: what government? Between the 1962 policy shift and the 1967 introduction of the points system, Canada had three general elections. Such a period of governmental fragility is not ideal for imposing a change of direction on a bureaucracy.

Thus, the argument that the momentous immigration policy shift of the 1960s was not shaped by economic concerns cannot be sustained. To say this is not to fall into economic determinism. As chapter 3 argued, state decision-makers are not merely servants of capital: they are always shaped by a variety of considerations. But it is hard to imagine anyone oblivious to the economic implications of policy choices making it into the upper reaches of the public service, or into the cabinet. Nor can we expect the state elite to ignore the fact that a serious change in immigration policy would deeply affect society – not just the labour market – and would require other policies to address those effects. Multiculturalism was, in part, one such policy.

6.6 Just-So Stories?

"Frog, did this really happen?"
"Maybe it did and maybe it didn't."
       Arnold Lobel, *Days with Frog and Toad* (1979, 34)

Taken from the title of one of Kipling's children's books, the dismissive label of "just-so story" is often applied to accounts contrived to fit some available facts, but lacking in any real explanatory value. Does the label fit the stories presented in this chapter? Did any of this really happen?

The "simple story," which stays close to the level of political journalism, would seem to be on reasonably solid ground. The other two stories are explicitly based on contrasting "deeper logics," each one attributing a grand objective to state action (maintain white supremacy, or encourage capitalism). So of those two stories, the sceptic might indeed say: none of this happened, the whole multiculturalism policy emerged step by incremental step, guided by little more than a simple electoral calculation.

But as I noted at the outset, a deeper logic may or may not be consciously embraced by state actors: it may simply appear in the form of constraints upon their choices. Imagine, for example, a politician exclusively and utterly guided by public opinion polls. We would still have to ask: what shapes the content of those polls? Poll outcomes can be biased by question wording and sequencing and by other factors. But there are limits to this, if various social realities turn sufficiently dire. And that can happen precisely when the state elite has ignored crucial constraints.

For reasons I presented at length above, we gain a better understanding of those constraints – and of the deeper logic that guided the emergence of multiculturalism – when we view the state as capitalist rather than as white supremacist, because the very existence of the capitalist state rests on more solid grounds. Just how fundamental is the state's capitalist orientation? Consider Justin Trudeau's 2017 promise to a group of fossil fuel executives in Texas: "As I said on that first trip to the oil patch back in 2012: no country would find 173 billion barrels of oil and just leave it in the ground. The resource will be developed" (Trudeau 2017). Here, a leader who works to display his progressive credentials in so many areas is in effect promising that the tar sands oil will be extracted, although he should be reasonably well aware of the implications of this for humanity.[30] We will continue this practice, he effectively promises, no matter what catastrophes are unleashed. There is no, simply no, equivalent level of determination to protect race supremacy in any developed capitalist state today, nor probably anywhere in the world.

The comparative value of the two deeper logics may also be contrasted by looking at specific policy choices. Himani Bannerji claims that multiculturalism emerged because "the Canadian state had to deal with a labour importation policy which was primarily meant to create a working class" (2000, 44). Thus, immigrants who arrive in Canada quickly learn "that they are here to primarily reproduce the under classes" (46). This in fact would have been an excellent strategy to sustain white supremacy: ideology both justifies and is reinforced by material realities (see chapter 10), hence policies that guaranteed a marginal economic status for racialized people would have furthered the goals of a WSS.

This strategy could have been pursued in various ways. Germany, for example, opted for a massive reliance on guest workers, who had little prospect of attaining citizenship. To further cement their marginalization, "special education arrangements were set up for the children of Turkish guest-workers (even if they were in fact born in Germany), on the assumption that they did not really belong in Germany" (Kymlicka 2007c, 73). The US took a different route, opting for long-standing toleration of economically marginalized undocumented workers.

But the Canadian state elite opted for neither of these paths.[31] Tom Kent, a key architect of the 1967 shift in immigration policy (see Kelley and Trebilcock 2000, 353), wrote in his memoirs of his concern with the "potential for explosive growth in the unskilled labour force" (1988, 408). The 1967 points system, combined with a tightening of sponsorship rules, aimed to avoid this outcome.

The points system has not been without problems. A capitalist government in a federal state has limited influence over labour market outcomes. As Kymlicka notes, there has long been a

> mismatch between the points system under which immigrants are selected and their subsequent access to the labour market. We admit immigrants on the basis of their foreign credentials and work experience, but these credentials and experiences are not properly recognized in Canada. This is partly the result of provincial licensing and accreditation policies, which refuse to recognize foreign credentials, and partly the result of the hiring policies of private sector employers, which unduly discount foreign work experience. (2007b, 148–9)

In a WSS intent on promoting the economic and social marginalization of racialized Others, multiculturalism policies focused on integration would also seem inexplicable. In the 1971 policy declaration, Prime Minister Trudeau stated that "the individual's freedom would be hampered if he were locked for life within a particular cultural compartment by the accident of birth or language" (Commons, 8 October 1971). A white supremacist might well answer, "You say that as if it's a bad thing!" An emphasis on integration and the learning of official languages is exactly what we would expect of a policy that aims to expand the pool of skilled workers, but the opposite of what we would expect of one that aims to sustain a racialized underclass.

Now one might object: a skilled labour strategy – to the extent that the federal government pursued it – does seem to undercut the thesis of a WSS. But it also undermines a capitalist state narrative, because capitalism requires cheap labour. But as we saw earlier, there were debates in the 1960s concerning the labour needs of Canadian capitalism. Since then, it has become clear that a cheap labour strategy is increasingly dangerous in a globalized world. For any economic sector that can be offshored, cheap low-skilled labour can always be "outbid" by cheaper labour elsewhere. Over time, we have seen industries migrate to places like South Korea, then to China, then on to Vietnam, Bangladesh, or Burma. It is said that Vietnamese factory wages are now between one quarter and one third of Chinese wages (Bulard 2017).

Further, serving the needs of capital involves far more than managing the labour supply. Unrest is expensive (recall the Polanyi quote, earlier, regarding the economic effects of a "shooting affray"). Elrick comments that "in the case of the United Kingdom, members of the Department [of Citizenship and Immigration] perceived the country's long-standing history of 'racial riots' as being directly linked to immigration by 'unskilled persons' who settled in urban areas and fell victim to 'poverty and squalor and created a social problem'" (2022, 107).[32] Whether the officials' analysis was correct or not, it suggests that they were not confusing a cheap-labour immigration strategy with a pro-capital one. Thus, for both economic and sociopolitical reasons, the pursuit of a cheap labour strategy for sectors such as industry would seem evidence not of a capitalist state but of something very different: state capture by particular economic interests.[33]

The integration focus of Canadian multiculturalism, and in particular the emphasis on official language learning, raises other issues and concerns.

To these we now turn, as we examine the paradoxical nature of "multiculturalism within a bilingual framework."

Chapter Seven

Multiculturalism within a Bilingual Framework?

"A policy of multiculturalism within a bilingual framework commends itself to the government as the most suitable means of assuring the cultural freedom of Canadians," declared Prime Minister Trudeau in unveiling his multiculturalism policy (Commons, 8 October 1971). Most of us are so surrounded today by myriad depictions of what multiculturalism *is*, and so little aware of what it *might have been*, and of what its early advocates *hoped it would be*, that we have little sense of how odd was the term "multiculturalism within a bilingual framework." Eve Haque has taken those words as the title of her valuable book. Through her detailed analysis of arguments and debates centred around the B&B Commission, she delineates a moment when other paths might have been pursued. This is important, because it naturally leads to the question of whether the path followed was the most just and the most rational. And this in turn should raise the question of whether at least some elements of other paths could or should be embraced now and in the future.

The first part of this chapter will loosely follow Haque's account of the debates that swirled around the B&B Commission from its inception. The second part will examine that commission's response to the demands of various representatives of the "other ethnic groups," a response that displayed a contradictory position on the centrality of language to culture, depending on just whose language was being considered. I will then consider justifications for that contradiction and suggest that the political reality of Quebec's exit option was a much more binding constraint on policy than Haque recognizes. Finally, in the fourth section, I will consider viable alternatives to the path taken, ones that might have been compatible with political constraints yet more just and inclusive.

7.1 Contemporary Arguments and Debates

I noted in the previous chapter that the B&B Commission faced an immediate challenge to its mandate to identify "the basis of an equal partnership between the two founding races." There were a number of possible lines of challenge to those terms. Two obvious ones would be, first, to point out that talk of "races" in this context was an offensive anachronism, and, second, to argue that *any* formulation that seemed to favour giving some Canadians more rights than others was unacceptable, and that the idea of grounding such rights on "founder" status was particularly suspect. As Conservative MP Steve Eugene Paproski later commented: "It would be fatal to accept as a principle that there is some kind of chronological priority of rights which applies to those who came earlier. If this were the case then the Indians and the Eskimos would have more rights than anyone, but as a matter of fact they have fewer" (Commons, 20 June 1969).

But one could broadly accept the settler-colonial framework of the "founding" while arguing that there were *more than two* founding groups. Haque cites various instances of this strategy. For example, the Ukrainian Self-Reliance League of Canada argued that "those pioneers of Ukrainian origin who broke the virgin prairies, cleared the bush, built the roads, worked the mines, were unquestionable 'founders' in their own right" (qtd. in Haque 2012, 108). Perhaps these spokespeople sincerely believed this, or perhaps they were adapting to the ideological terrain as they understood it.

A sense of that terrain, and of the difficulties it presented for the "other ethnic groups," had been articulated almost five decades earlier by Conservative MP Gérard Girouard: "If there is talk of biculturalism today in Canada, it is because the French and the English nations have built something in Canada. Immigrants coming to Canada today do not bring Canada anything; they come to get what Canada can give them" (Commons, 10 April 1964). This is but one example, and few politicians today would put things so crudely regarding contemporary immigrants. But the first part of Girouard's statement, that Canada was built by some groups (only), seems to have been a core assumption made by the B&B Commission, whose terms of reference apparently rested on what we might call a "triad of dualities": "*two* founding groups, *two* cultures, *two* official languages." Each element can be read as a positive or a normative claim. The claim that there *are* two founding groups, for example, can be read along Girouard's lines as saying that only two groups have achieved anything *worthy* of being called a founding. Note too that the "connective tissue" between each duality is implied rather than stated. For example: there *are* two founding people, thus there *should be* recognition of two cultures and two official languages.

A key figure in the challenge to this cluster of claims was Paul Yuzyk, appointed to the Senate by John Diefenbaker in 1963. In his first Senate speech, in March 1964, Yuzyk stated that

> in less than two decades before World War I, most of the arable land in the prairie provinces was settled by a considerable number of several European peoples, a very large proportion of whom were neither of British nor French origin. They fully accepted the laws of Canada, brought civilization to vast areas hitherto uninhabited, greatly aided the expansion of Canadian economy and prosperity, loyally and fully participated in the Canadian armed forces of the two world wars, and conscientiously performed their duties as citizens in every respect, even though there was some discrimination against them for quite a long time. The third element, ethnic groups, now numbering approximately five million persons, are co-builders of the West and other parts of Canada, along with the British and French Canadians, and are just as permanent a part of the Canadian scene. (Senate, 3 March 1964)[1]

Yuzyk also challenged the fact claim of biculturalism: "The word 'bicultural,' which I could not find in any dictionary, is a misnomer. In reality Canada never was bicultural; the Indians and Eskimos have been with us throughout our history; the British group is multicultural-English, Scots, Irish, Welsh; and with the settling of other ethnic groups, which now make up almost one-third of the population, Canada has become multicultural in fact" (Senate, 3 March 1964).[2]

And what were the practical implications of the sorts of counter-claims advanced by Yuzyk? Later in his Senate speech, he declared that

> the third element ethnic or cultural groups should receive the status of co-partners, who would be guaranteed the right to perpetuate their mother tongues and cultures, which should be offered as optional subjects in the public and high school systems and the separate schools of the provinces, and the universities, wherever there would be a sufficient number of students to warrant the maintenance of such classes. (Senate, 3 March 1964)

Similar education proposals were frequently presented to the B&B Commission. The Mennonite Society for the Promotion of the German Language, for example, urged that "either French, German, Ukrainian, Jewish or Icelandic – depending on the decision of the respective school district – should be introduced in schools as a second language from grade one" (qtd. in Haque 2012, 257).

How much support was there for such proposals? Haque has studied the briefs from minority ethnic groups, as well as many articles in minority ethnic community newspapers, and documents the variety of positions concerning multiculturalism and multilingualism. Her assessment is that the German Canadian community generally supported multiculturalism but did not support language preservation (2012, 103); the Italian Canadian community did not support the idea of multiculturalism (105); and the Japanese Canadian community "advocated not multiculturalism but rather a pan-Canadian identity" (103). But the Ukrainian Canadian community was by far the most active minority ethnic group in its engagement with the commission (96), so its forceful advocacy of multiculturalism garnered attention. At the same time, support probably varied within the Ukrainian Canadian community itself. It is reasonable to expect that those who are most concerned about cultural preservation will be the most active in organizations devoted to that end. Also, in matters of education, it is always possible to have a "contradiction between the parents' rights and choices [and] those their children might prefer" (Porter 1987, 126).

7.2 The B&B Commission Response, and Its Contradictions

Speaking on behalf of a multi-ethnic umbrella group at the November 1963 preliminary hearings of the B&B Commission, Walter Bossey challenged the commissioners. After noting the 1961 census finding that the "British" and "French" together made up just 74 per cent of the Canadian population, Bossey asked: "Are you going to make Confederation of your own two groups?" (qtd. in Haque 2012, 69).

Leaving aside qualifications and nuances, it is fair to say that the B&B Commission answered, in effect, *Yes*. As far as the commissioners were concerned, Canada was marked by a duality, and the latest census findings did not change this fact: "The other cultural groups are scattered all across the country, and not one of them – even the biggest and most active – represents as much as 20 per cent of the population of any of the ten provinces " (1969, 10). The commission dismissed claims that members of these groups represented a "third force" (or, in Yuzyk's language, a "third element"): their "only common feature is not being of either British or French ethnic origin. Can the aspirations of those of Chinese origin in Vancouver be amalgamated with the aspirations of those of Ukrainian origin in Winnipeg?" (10). Thus, any immigrant must be "made aware of certain fundamental principles that will bear upon his citizenship in his adopted country. In particular, he should know that Canada recognizes two official languages and that it possesses two predominant cultures that have produced two societies – Francophone and Anglophone – which form two distinct communities within an overall Canadian context" (4).

With respect to education in particular, the commission insisted that "the learning of third languages should not be carried on at the expense of public support for learning the second official language" (1969, 139). A multilingual vision would thus not be allowed to replace bilingualism, although there might be limited room for it in "the broader context" of bilingualism and biculturalism (138).

Haque's work helps clarify the relationship between the B&B Commission's vision and the one embodied in Trudeau's 1971 multiculturalism policy declaration. Kenneth McRoberts expresses the widespread view that "the Trudeau government adopted its multiculturalism without the commission's blessings" (1997, 123). Yet Canadian multiculturalism policy's integrative focus seems well captured by the commission's statement that "those of other languages and cultures are more or less integrated with the Francophone and Anglophone communities, where they should find opportunities for self-fulfilment and equality of status. It is within these two societies that their cultural distinctiveness should find a climate of respect and encouragement to survive" (1969, 10).

We might say that the Trudeau policy embodied the spirit of the B&B Commission's approach but slapped the name "multiculturalism" on it. Jean Burnet, research director for the crucial Book IV of the B&B Commission report (see Jaworsky 1979, 48), later suggested that "the policy makers wished to endorse polyethnicity." The term "ethnicity" being out of favour, however, "the accurate term polyethnicity was replaced by the misleading term multiculturalism" (1975, 36).

One of Haque's central arguments is that a massive contradiction ran through the B&B Commission's treatment of the relationship between language and culture: its report presented language as a "fundamental element of culture" for the "founding races" but merely a "private and peripheral element of culture" for everyone else (2012, 6). So in making the case that bilingualism was essential, the commission reported that "during our hearings we often heard Anglophones overstating, with understandable complacency, the possibilities of survival for a culture even after the language has been lost"; the commission countered with the assertion that "original cultural traits survive only partially after the adoption of the English language, especially when several generations have passed" (qtd. in Haque 2012, 161).[3] The commission also argued that "nobody will maintain that a group still has a living culture, in the full sense of the term, when it is forced to use another language in order to express to itself the realities which make up a large part of its daily life" (qtd. in Haque 2012, 160). Note that this argument did double duty for the commission: it supported the case for official bilingualism, as Haque notes, but it also served to deny the claims of those such as Yuzyk who insisted that Canada was *in fact* multicultural.

In its discussion of "the other ethnic groups," however, the commission advanced a much more relaxed view of the language/culture relationship: "Many seem to believe that the members of a group who have adopted another language have *completely* lost their original culture. This is yet another illusion which has given rise to many misunderstandings. In Canada we can observe the indisputable survival of *some* cultural traits among native groups and among a number of groups of other ethnic origins" (qtd. in Haque 2012, 160–1; emphases added). It seems that the commission was formulating a "consolation prize" vision of culture for the minority groups, and *only* for them. One can only imagine how delighted the Québécois would have been had the commission declared that they should stop fretting about the Anglicization of the province, because they could still enjoy "some cultural traits."

So the B&B Commission held that those whose mother tongue was French should have a right to the preservation of their language, but that Canadians with minority mother tongues should not. Some sort of hierarchy was being presented. But what sort? Leaning heavily on the "two founding races" phrase in the commission's terms of reference, Haque suggests that the hierarchy in question was in fact a *racial* one: the commission's "shift to language and culture in no way refuted the racialized hierarchy of the terms of reference; rather, racial differentiation was shifted onto the terrain of language and culture" (137–8).

Given the vast multitude of ways in which the term "race" has been used over the centuries, it is hard to know what to make of this claim. The previous chapter discussed that word's use as a term of *class* distinction. Consider as well a speech that John A. Macdonald made in the Commons in 1890:

> I appeal to all our friends in this house, without reference to party ... to merge everything in the great desire to make Canada, French and English, one people without any hostile feeling, without any difference in feeling, further than that which arises from the different literatures and the different strains of mind that run always in different races and which sever the Scotsman and the Irishman from the Englishman as much as they sever the Frenchman from the Englishman. (20 February)

Here we have Canada's two main something-or-others, who must become one *people*, comprised of a proliferation of *races*, such as the Scots, Irish, and English.

7.3 Justifications

In any case, there is no question that (a) the B&B Commission vision endorsed a hierarchy between two official languages and all the rest, and (b) any such hierarchy necessarily favours those whose mother tongue has official status.[4] More specifically in the Canadian case, official-language minorities would have more access to education in their mother tongue – and to other language supports as well – than other linguistic minorities. How was all this justified?

One argument was that the hierarchy was necessary for purely practical reasons. Speaking to the Ukrainian Canadian Congress on the day after the 1971 policy declaration, Trudeau stated that "an overwhelming number of Canadians use either English or French in their day-to-day communications with one another and with government. It is for this practical reason – not some rationalization about founding races – that these two languages have attained an official character in Canada" (1972, 33–6).

The B&B Commission also advanced a pragmatic justification: it acknowledged a precedent for education proposals of the sort being advanced by various groups. In Manitoba in 1897, the "School Act was amended to state: 'Where ten of the pupils speak... any language other than English as their native language, the teaching of such pupils shall be conducted in ... such other language and English upon the bi-lingual system'" (1969, 104; elisions in B&B). The commission argued that this provision – abolished in 1916 – might have been appropriate "in earlier times," when "people originally settled among other members of their cultural group, and when they could expect to be born, live, and die in one particular community." But "in our mobile and changing society, with the increasing scope, sophistication, and complexity of modern educational facilities and curricula, it is not feasible for Canada's public education systems to employ languages other than English and French extensively as languages of instruction" (1969, 139). Education policy must centre on "the overriding goal of ensuring that all children have the best possible education as preparation for a productive adult life," the commission argued, adding that "parents who choose to have their children instructed in a language that is not useful in the work world or in our institutions make a choice; in effect, they may be choosing for their children a knowledge of the language and culture of their own cultural group at the expense of instruction in other fields which are perhaps more relevant to Canadian society" (1969, 140).

Such arguments were disingenuous. So far as I know, no one was proposing state support for schools that limited themselves to teaching the languages and cultures of "back home." The proposals were, rather, for thoroughly modern schools with space for bilingual education, the second language being determined by local demographics and preferences. Against this, Canada opted for a model of coast-to-coast French–English bilingualism. *That* was what needed to be justified, and the sorts of pragmatic arguments just cited did not do that. For a Prairie Canadian in particular, the B&B Commission's argument that French, but not German or Ukrainian, was "useful in the work world or in our institutions" (1969, 140) *assumed* the prior choice of coast-to-coast French–English bilingualism: it could not *justify* that choice.

A very different type of pragmatic justification was also offered, one that appealed not to the demands of modern life but to the messy realities of Canadian politics. In *Federalism and the French Canadians*, Trudeau argued that

> if French Canadians are able to claim equal partnership with English Canadians, and if their culture is established on a coast-to-coast basis, it is mainly because of the balance of linguistic forces within the country. Historical origins are less important than people generally think, the proof being that neither Eskimo nor Indian dialects have any kind of privileged position. On the other hand, if there were six million people living in Canada whose mother tongue was Ukrainian, it is likely that this language would establish itself as forcefully as French. In terms of *realpolitik*, French and English are equal in Canada because each of these linguistic groups has the power to break the country. And this power cannot yet be claimed by the Iroquois, the Eskimos, or the Ukrainians. (1968, 31)

On this argument, the fundamental difference between the B&B Commission's treatment of French Canadians and that of the "other ethnic groups" is that the Québécois in particular had a viable exit option from Canada. One could try to soften this *de facto* situation by reference to supposed privileges emerging from being a "founding race," but the undeniable fact is that the willingness to move on language at the national level only emerged along with the exit option itself. The rationale for bilingualism and biculturalism would thus be not so much considerations of justice or equality, as the Québécois' *de facto* status as a "national minority," in contrast to the geographically dispersed "other ethnic groups."

Haque downplays this factor, suggesting that the B&B Commission manufactured a crisis. She cites co-chair André Laurendeau's opening speech: "We are in a state of emergency –an emergency that can jeopardize the very existence of Canada" (qtd. in Haque 2012, 56), and argues that this "establishment of a singular crisis became the first step in consolidating the centrality of the founding races with the marginalization of other ethnic groups and the erasure of Indigenous concerns" (92).

Much hinges on this. Was the exit option actually on the political agenda at the time? If not, if the crisis was constructed more or less *ex nihilo* as Haque suggests, then we are faced with a textbook application of the "garbage can model": invoke or create a problem in order to advance one's preferred "solution" to it (Cohen et al. 1972). I believe the exit option was an increasingly live one at the time and that Haque is underestimating the warning signs within Quebec.

As argued in chapter 6, states regularly respond to *anticipated* as well as actual threats. As the 1960s progressed, there were various reasons to fear growing separatist strength in Quebec. As we saw in the previous chapter, the federal government viewed significant immigration as key to economic growth. For many French Canadians, this sparked questions about the future of Canada's linguistic balance. As one Quebec nationalist wrote:

> In Montreal, which receives 85% of immigrants to Quebec, 90% of the children of new Quebeckers study in English. This pace of assimilation of immigrants to the Anglophone minority, along with the declining birthrate among Francophone Quebeckers (a decline of 23% since 1964), allows Francophone protestors to conclude that a "minoritization" of French Canada is imminent, Montreal becoming an English city within ten years, and Quebec an English province about twenty years after that. (Rioux 1976, 153)

Tensions around this exploded in the 1968–69 school controversy in Saint-Léonard, a south-shore Montreal suburb. In late June 1968, the local school board voted to impose French-only education in the fall, starting in the first grade and progressing annually. The measure sparked protests by anglophone parents, many of whom were Italian Canadians, as well as counterprotests. In the fall of 1969, Quebec's Union Nationale government introduced a law guaranteeing parents the right to choose their children's language of education, sparking more widespread protests, as well as bombings of Loyola College and the home of the (Italian Canadian) deputy-mayor (Lebel 1969b). It also contributed to the government's ouster in the spring 1970 election (and the permanent eclipse of the Union Nationale). The Parti Québécois won 24 per cent of the vote in that election, its first. There seems little question that language fears strengthened the political prospects of the exit option.

It is also reasonable to suppose that the separatist movement would have been further strengthened had the B&B Commission and the federal government made choices more aligned with the hopes of many spokespersons for the "other ethnic groups." As we saw earlier, such groups urged a break with the concept of two founding peoples.[5] Such a break seems eminently reasonable and just, but it could also have further strengthened the exit option.

But it is another question whether the coast-to-coast bilingualism model was the best response to the actual or latent crisis, or whether another strategy might have met the separatist threat effectively *and* been more compatible with a deeper multiculturalism. Ralliement Créditiste MP Gilles Grégoire offered a striking early statement regarding why many Quebec nationalists would view nationwide bilingualism as an irrelevance:

> When we from the province of Quebec come into Ontario, the first road sign we meet when entering the province of Ontario on the road from Montreal to Ottawa says: "Observe speed limit." We do not require that a road sign should be written in both languages. It might be a courtesy, but that is not what we want. We want the opportunity and the facilities to develop ourselves, and to develop by ourselves in our country. We do not require anything from English speaking Canadians. They can develop themselves as they wish, but let us have the same opportunity. (Commons, 19 November 1963)

And it was not bilingualism that the Quebec nationalists in Saint-Léonard were fighting for; indeed, it was precisely what they were fighting *against*. One anglophone protester against the Saint-Léonard school board's decision concisely expressed both the attraction of English for immigrants and why Québécois nationalists could reasonably view bilingualism as a path to Anglicization: "We don't personally prefer English to French ... I do believe in bilingualism 100 per cent. I think there are fantastic opportunities for people who are bilingual in Quebec. But English is the international language. Most of the business done in Montreal is in English ... It's just an economic situation that has been established for a number of years" (qtd. in Seale 1968; elisions in original).

A very different option was the territorial bilingualism envisaged by some representatives of the "other ethnic groups" (Haque 2012, 66).

But this one had a practical implication that was not addressed by any of the groups cited in Haque's book. Recall the education proposal advanced by a Mennonite group, which resembled various others presented to the B&B Commission: "Either French, German, Ukrainian, Jewish or Icelandic – depending on the decision of the respective school district – should be introduced in schools as a second language from grade one" (qtd. in Haque 2012, 257). This would seemingly entail one of three paths for the future of the federal civil service. Either English would dominate as the unique *lingua franca*, particularly at the upper levels, or those outside central Canada would be largely frozen out of a French–English–bilingual civil service, or the federal state would in practice be carved up into fiefdoms "belonging" to either the anglophone national majority or the francophone minority. Each option corresponded to a serious long-term political problem: increased Quebec alienation, increased alienation elsewhere in Canada, and/or intensified state fragmentation.[6]

Reflection on the justice of "multiculturalism within a bilingual framework," and identification of viable paths not taken, must recognize the political constraints under which the federal government was operating in its choices. Given the constraints posed by Quebec's exit option, what could and should have been done? It is important to note, first, that the submissions from different ethnic communities to the B&B Commission did not advocate an abolition of all language hierarchy. In the idea, for example, that Ukrainian–English bilingual education would be publicly funded where numbers warranted, or German–English bilingual education, there was a common denominator. It was assumed across the board that English would be the *lingua franca* for most of Canada. Could this have been otherwise? If one answers *No*, then one is accepting a language hierarchy. So what was really in question was the *specific* form of linguistic hierarchy, not hierarchy as such, which exists by law or *de facto* in every country on earth.

Another immovable constraint was the constitutional status of English and French: no better gift could have been given to the separatist movement in Quebec than to attempt to alter that constitutional constraint. Some proponents of multiculturalism explicitly granted this. In his influential Senate speech, Paul Yuzyk stated: "As the founding peoples of our country, the British and the French should be regarded as the senior partners whose special rights include the recognition of English and French as the official languages in accordance with the British North America Act" (Senate, 3 March 1964).

But language policy need not be a binary matter of a language being official and promoted, or not-official and thus ignored: there can be many levels of state support for other languages. We saw in the previous chapter that after the 1971 introduction of multiculturalism, state support for the non-official languages was minuscule compared to that for the two official languages. When one reads that the federal government had the resources to support French–English translation services for the "Fraternity of Canadian Astrologers" (Pal 1993, 160), one has to wonder whether more money might have been found for the non-official languages, and support given in ways that would not displace the development of official bilingualism throughout the country.

An important practical question is whether it was already too late for minority languages – even with serious government support – to be vibrant components of the Canadian landscape. John Porter noted that

> the 1971 census asked not only a mother-tongue question but also one on the language most often spoken at home. The assimilation to English has been very marked. While the English-speaking ethnic origin constituted 45 per cent of the population, English as the language most often spoken in the home was 65 per cent. While the non-English, non-French ethnicities made up 28 per cent of the population, only about 12 per cent had the same mother tongue as their ethnic origin, and only about 6 per cent spoke their ethnic origin language most often in the home. (1987, 115)

This may be why the B&B Commission was quite sceptical about potential demand for official/minority-language bilingual education (1969, 140).[7]

Nevertheless, there has been much immigration to Canada since then, and a different policy emphasis could have fostered a much richer development of Canadian multilingualism.[8] Also, a less binary approach to official and non-official languages might have better negotiated the tensions "between Canada's English–French bilingualism on the one hand and the principles of substantive, multiculturalist egalitarianism on the other" (Ijaz and Boon 2018, 390). Nadine Ijaz's research on the regulation of traditional Chinese medicine (TCM) in Ontario provides a stark example of failure to seek such balance. "Ontario's regulated health professions require that their members demonstrate proficiency in either English or French in order to be registered" (374), and this requirement was applied to TCM with little attention to its particular nature and clientele. Experienced practitioners, often older and with limited English proficiency, "play a key role in transmitting knowledge and skill to more junior practitioners," (376) yet they can be barred from the practice of TCM. Note the odd result: "the regulator justified its linguistic entry requirements on the basis of two key points:

patient safety and interprofessional collaboration" (382), but one could practise knowing only French, although this would be far more of an impediment to those two regulatory goals than a knowledge of Chinese alone. Does state support of French–English bilingualism really require such rigidity?

7.4 Conclusion

At the outset of this chapter, I noted that Haque's analysis pointed to paths not taken and the contingency of that outcome known as multiculturalism within a bilingual framework. We arrived at the conclusion that perhaps *sharply* different paths were not in fact available, because of the political constraint posed by the Quebec question. But this does not mean that the path chosen was therefore a just one. Rather, it suggests that a certain degree of injustice is baked into the Canadian political system. At the very least, greater acknowledgment of this on the part of the B&B Commission and the Trudeau government might have led to more creativity in efforts to support non-official languages in ways that were politically viable. Such an option is still available to us today.

PART IV

Yes, But...

Chapter Eight

On Tolerance (and Other "Gross Concepts")

Tolerance:

"1. a. The action or practice of enduring or sustaining pain or hardship; the power or capacity of enduring; endurance. *Obsolete.*"

"2. The action of allowing; licence, permission granted by an authority. *Obsolete.*"

"3. The action or practice of tolerating; toleration; the disposition to be patient with or indulgent to the opinions or practices of others; freedom from bigotry or undue severity in judging the conduct of others; forbearance; catholicity of spirit."

Oxford English Dictionary (2000)

Here's a puzzle: when a person says that some politicians are "fanning the flame of intolerance" (Wong 1997), I would wager that no one will consider this a compliment. Yet there is no corresponding unanimity around "tolerance" and "tolerant." Indeed, various progressive critics are not at all enamoured of tolerance. This chapter will consider their critiques. The question is of interest because in much public discourse multiculturalism is closely associated with tolerance. The puzzle of tolerance is also worthy of attention because some progressive critiques reveal styles of thought on the question that are relevant to other issues related to multiculturalism. The question, for example, of whether "mere" tolerance is a *barrier* to something more than tolerance, as opposed to a *gateway* to that something more, is close to one that can be asked of "song and dance multiculturalism."[1] Finally, the critiques have the benefit of demonstrating the vagueness that plagues most key terms related to multiculturalism: not just "tolerance," but "diversity" and "difference" as well.

The first section of this chapter will examine progressive critiques of tolerance. I will then discuss some conceptual problems that affect, not just those critiques, but appreciative invocations of tolerance as well. The third section will respond to the critiques.

8.1 Critiques of Tolerance

The progressive critics to be examined here are working with a particular understanding of tolerance, clearly expressed by Mackey, who cites David Theo Goldberg as her authority: "Tolerance, as Susan Mendus makes clear, presupposes that its object is morally repugnant, that it really needs to be reformed, that is, altered" (qtd. in Mackey 2002, 162). In the same vein, Richard Day asserts that tolerance "appears only as a defence against what is repulsive" (2000, 224).

I will return to this claim after examining various critiques of tolerance. For now, note that this understanding implies that states (one agent of tolerance), and individuals (another class of agents) must divide phenomena into three categories:

- The "intolerable": from the perspective of the state, this should not be permitted; from that of the individual, it should be opposed.
- The "tolerable": however "repugnant" it might be, we should put up with it.
- The neutral or positive: this can be "accepted," "encouraged," and so on.

This division suggests various possible types of critique. One might argue that lines have been drawn in the wrong places, or that they have been drawn by an unjust exercise of power. Or, in one surprising argument, one might argue that such lines should not exist at all.

Tolerance is less than ... acceptance, support, equality, respect. The first critique arises immediately from the link between tolerance and repugnance, or even merely dislike: tolerance is a very limited and condescending perspective. Lori Beaman cites Jakobsen and Pellegrini, who ask: "What does it feel like to be on the receiving end of this tolerance? Does it really feel any different from contempt or exclusion?" (qtd. in Beaman 2012, 17). Similarly, Stanley Fish asks: "Do you really show respect for a view by tolerating it, as you might tolerate the buzzing of a fly?" (1997, 388). The claim is a venerable one: Goethe wrote that "toleration should, strictly speaking, be only a passing mood; it ought to lead to acknowledgment and appreciation. To tolerate a person is to affront him" (1893, no. 356).[2]

It is not just the progressive critics who voice this objection. Neil Bissoondath complains that multiculturalism has "preached tolerance rather than encouraging acceptance" (1994, 192). Even Canadian politicians sound the theme. In a commencement address at NYU, Justin Trudeau stated:

> Sometimes people talk about striving for tolerance. Now, don't get me wrong: there are places in this world where a little more tolerance would go a long way, but if we're being honest right now, right here, I think we should aim a little higher.
>
> Think about it: Saying "I tolerate you" actually means something like "Ok, I grudgingly admit that you have a right to exist, but just don't get up in my face about it. Or date my sister."
>
> There's not a religion in the world that asks you to Tolerate thy neighbour.[3]
>
> So let's try for something a little more like acceptance, respect, friendship, and yes, even love. (Trudeau 2018)

Various Liberal MPs offered similar statements during Justin Trudeau's first term: John Aldag said we must move beyond "mere tolerance" (Commons, 6 June 2018). Arif Virani likewise hoped we could "move beyond tolerating difference and move towards celebrating difference" (Commons, 20 March 2018). Randy Boissonnault feels that "we are moving beyond tolerance to acceptance" (Commons, 18 October 2016), while Sonia Sidhu believes Canada has *already* accomplished that: "Canada is the nation of multiculturalism. It is not just a country of tolerance, but a country of acceptance" (Commons, 2 February 2017).

My goal in inflicting these repetitive claims on the reader is to show that, in certain circles at least, the deficient nature of tolerance is common wisdom. But I will argue below that the claim is conceptually dubious and relies on fuzzy thought and speech for its plausibility.

Tolerance is a power relation. Eva Mackey claims that "tolerance actually reproduces dominance (of those with the power to tolerate), because asking for 'tolerance' always implies the possibility of intolerance. The power and the choice whether to accept or not accept difference, to tolerate it or not, still lies in the hands of the tolerators" (2002, 16). Lori Beaman goes further, critiquing "the hierarchies *created* by the concepts of tolerance and accommodation" (2012, 16; emphasis added). Thus, for Beaman, the frameworks of tolerance or accommodation "create a hierarchical positioning of 'us' and 'them' that is *conceptually unavoidable*" (2012, 17; emphasis added). Bhikhu Parekh, for his part, critiques liberalism's "persistent tendency to avoid a dialogue with other cultures by viewing them as nothing more than minority cultures whom it would 'grant' such rights as it unilaterally determines" (1999, 74).

Tolerance as a "spoonful of sugar." Richard Day describes eighteenth-century British toleration in North America as "the necessary counterbalance while waiting for assimilation to have its effects" (2000, 104). In this view, tolerance functions as the "spoonful of sugar that helps the medicine go down," as Mary Poppins sang. In this case, the medicine of assimilation. This dynamic is hinted at in a conservative observer's comment: "One reason that Canada's experiment with multiculturalism is succeeding is that no one tells newcomers to abandon their beliefs or way of life. We don't demand that they embrace the mainstream. We don't expect them to adopt Canadian habits *overnight*" (Gee 2016; emphasis added). The dynamic makes psychological sense. When we believe a dimension of our identity is under attack, we are pushed to defend it: "When people feel their faith is threatened, their religious identification seems to be their entire identity. But if it's their mother tongue or their ethnic group that is threatened, they will fight ferociously against those of the same religion" (Maalouf 1998, 20). Conversely, one might expect tolerance to foster assimilation. So the spoonful of sugar critique suggests that tolerance is a manipulative ploy, a roundabout way to make others conform.

Tolerance has limits. In chapter 5, I discussed Eve Haque's discomfort with limits to tolerance and her invocation of Jacques Derrida's concept of "unconditional hospitality." Haque's is perhaps the most explicit expression of a more widely shared view. While Eva Mackey never quite says there should be no limits, "limit" and its variants play a uniformly negative role in her *The House of Difference*.

Richard Day goes further: Canadian multiculturalism, he says, must "affirm the value of difference and the Other as such ... To affirm difference as such is to have no need of tolerance, which appears only as a defence against what is repulsive" (2000, 224). So, for Day, there is simply *nothing* that we should find "repulsive." This is a remarkable claim, for it erases *two* categories of phenomena: both the intolerable and the (merely) tolerable.[4]

Other writers suggest that limits necessarily make tolerance superficial. Slavoj Žižek, for example, claims that "liberal 'tolerance' condones the folklorist Other deprived of its substance – like the multitude of 'ethnic cuisines' in a contemporary megalopolis; however, any 'real' Other is instantly denounced for its 'fundamentalism'" (1997, 37). Fleras and Elliott draw on Stanley Fish to define an "abstracted multiculturalism" that claims to support difference, but only "in principle, not in practice," backing off when "other cultures insist on intolerance"

(2002, 23). (While Fleras and Elliott are uncomfortable with Fish's framework, they fail to identify the conceptual errors that give rise to it. I will consider those errors in a moment.)

8.2 The Concept of Tolerance

The foregoing critiques all depend on a particular understanding of tolerance. Recall Goldberg's claim, cited by Mackey: "Tolerance, as Susan Mendus *makes clear*, presupposes that its object is morally repugnant, that it really needs to be reformed, that is, altered" (Goldberg 1993, 7; emphasis added). But Mendus does not in fact "make clear" the nature of tolerance: she simply *asserts* a claim about it, which is not the same thing. Whenever one author's assertion becomes another's proven claim, we are glimpsing a problematic "longing for certainty" (Albert 1985, 31).

Moreover, in the passage Goldberg cites, Mendus goes on to show – in spite of herself – that her understanding fails to capture much usage of the words "tolerance" and "toleration":

> The very first example of toleration discussed in this book was racial toleration, and I mentioned there the fact that there is a slight oddity in speaking of toleration in a racial context. One reason for the oddity is that toleration implies that the thing tolerated is morally reprehensible ... But that implication is false in the racial case: there is nothing morally reprehensible about belonging to a different race or being of a different colour. (Mendus 1989, 149–50)

But people do in fact regularly speak of racial tolerance or toleration. So on exactly what basis can Mendus dismiss common usage as mistaken?

Peter Balint points out a further problem with assuming that tolerance requires that one have some objection to the phenomenon tolerated: it opens a strange gap between noun ("tolerance") and adjective ("tolerant"). Imagine two people. The first is bothered by all sorts of things: the music other people like, the clothes they wear, and so on. But she grits her teeth and "puts up with it." The second person is easy-going, enjoying the variety of the world. It would seem strange to say that the first person is the more tolerant one. We need a conception of tolerance, Balint argues, that "captures significant ordinary language uses of the term" (2017, 79). But ordinary language does not have the objection component as a necessary element. Tolerance with that component, which Balint calls forbearance-tolerance, is important and necessary in our world, but it is just one category of tolerance.[5]

This problem is made particularly vivid by the dimension already discussed, racial tolerance. How would we describe a person who seriously dislikes, say, Blacks, but refrains from acting on that dislike in any way? Would we view them as tolerant? We are more likely to see them as racist. And we are likely to fear that their hidden racism could "erupt" any time, given certain conditions – such as a racist in the Oval Office. Tolerance "with clenched teeth and pinched nostrils," as Forbes nicely puts it (2019, 30), does not appear to be a stable or reliable condition.

I would suggest, then, that we think of specific acts of tolerance as located within a two-dimensional range. One dimension concerns the underlying attitude: from opposition to neutrality. Note that, often, such neutrality reflects a prior commitment to tolerance. That is, I decide that "I will not interfere with X, whatever I may feel about it." This renders one's subjective assessment of X moot. For example, I don't need to arrive at a sophisticated understanding of a particular religion to decide to tolerate its practice. (That prior commitment itself applies to some range: it does not preclude viewing some religious practices, for example, as *intolerable*.)

A second dimension, relevant to forbearance-tolerance, concerns the specific meaning of "putting up with it." At one end, it can mean offering no visible sign whatever of one's negative view. Philosopher-novelist Iris Murdoch presents a hypothetical case of a woman who really does not like her daughter-in-law, feeling "that her son has married beneath him." Yet "the mother, who is a very 'correct' person, behaves beautifully to the girl throughout, not allowing her real opinion to appear in any way" (1997, 312). But forbearance might be considerably less complete than this. One might freely express one's negative opinion of a practice yet forbear from interfering with it. Analogously, state tolerance can involve varying degrees of "putting up with it." Consider marijuana: its consumption is now legal in Canada, but only under very restricted conditions.

Gross concepts. Understanding that acts of tolerance are located within a two-dimensional range helps us avoid treating tolerance as what Ian Shapiro calls a "gross concept" (gross here being contrasted with fine, as in "fine-grained"). To discuss the value of freedom in the abstract, suggests Shapiro, is to stay at the level of a gross concept. In contrast, faced with any invocation of freedom, we need to ask: "*Who* is free, *from* what restraint ... *to* perform which action?" (2005, 154).

Shapiro's contrast is fruitful. Suppose someone tell me I should "practise tolerance," or "be more tolerant." It is fair to ask:

- Just what thing or range of things are you asking me to tolerate?
- In just which sense of tolerate? Put up with? Fully accept and respect?

- If in the sense of "put up with": How completely? Are you asking me to be like Murdoch's hypothetical mother-in-law? Or may I speak out against the phenomenon I am being asked to tolerate? May I try to persuade someone, for example, that the phenomenon (belief, practice, or whatever) in question is wrong, or mistaken?

Tremendous confusion in "political correctness" debates, which periodically flare up like a bad case of the shingles, arises from ignoring the wide range of responses that can constitute "putting up with" something, thus conflating – probably deliberately – *censuring* and *censoring* (Hunter 1991, 246). The confusion continues. After a tweet from Liberal MP Celina Caesar-Chavannes telling Max Bernier to "check your privilege and be quiet" (qtd. in Wherry 2018), Bernier told his supporters that "I guess she wasn't aware that we lived in a democracy with free speech as one of its building blocks" and urged them to send money so that he could "defend free speech" (2018). But to tell someone to "be quiet" is not to shut them up, unless one has power over them, which was certainly not the case in this instance. Indeed, far from shutting Bernier up, Caesar-Chavannes unwittingly served as his publicity agent.

In moving beyond gross concepts, one's take on certain issues can shift by becoming finer grained. Consider Kymlicka's observation that "the adoption of liberal multiculturalism rests on what Nancy Rosenblum calls the 'liberal expectancy' ... – that is, the hope and expectation that liberal-democratic values will grow over time and take firm root across ethnic, racial, and religious lines, within both majority and minority groups" (2007c, 94). That would seem to be a prime example of the spoonful of sugar tactic: multicultural tolerance, it is hoped, will change both majority and minority groups – change in a direction thought most compatible with a shared democratic life. Is the tactic legitimate in this instance? Or is it normatively problematic? If so, why? The expectation is not that members of various ethnocultures will become "just like us," but that cultures can "bend" somewhat – as Rawls put it (1996, 246) – so as to harmonize with values required for a shared citizenship. So one can respond to the critic by arguing that, sometimes, a spoonful of sugar is just what a healthy democracy needs. (There is more to be said about the spoonful of sugar critique, which contains an important implicit insight. We will return to it, below.)

Now some critics do reject this, but their position is weak. Stanley Fish charges Kymlicka with an "inability to see the contradiction between maintaining a tradition and setting out to soften it and blur its edges" (1997, 389). He claims that Kymlicka "is trying to be a strong multiculturalist but turns boutique when the going gets tough" (389), boutique multiculturalism being "the multiculturalism of ethnic restaurants" (378). But the supposed "contradiction" only arises from what I have previously termed a "primitive ontology," according to which "a culture is 'preserved' only if every last piece of it is left unchanged" (2010b, 44). For Fish, there is no middle ground between a frozen culture and one reduced to "ethnic restaurants."[6]

Tolerance is not the only gross concept in play in multiculturalism debates: "diversity" and "difference" often suffer the same status. Consider a couple of declarations from Liberal MPs:

> As Canadians, we know that diversity is not an obstacle to be overcome or a collective difficulty to be tolerated, but rather it is a tremendous source of strength. (Commons, 21 March 2016)

> We know that it is not sufficient to simply talk about championing our diversity. We need to be vigilant in defending it so that we can move beyond tolerating difference and move towards celebrating difference. (Commons, 20 March 2018)

Agree? Disagree? It depends. Parliamentary discourse generally limits itself to the empty and vague level of celebrating "diversity," a vagueness that is perhaps an inescapable job requirement for politicians. Diversity sounds nice, but when we drill down to the level of detail, we must acknowledge that "diversity" covers a wide range of practices that we can consider normatively problematic, or, worse, practices that are intolerable or that we have to "put up with" but cannot honestly "celebrate." Forbes identifies the unspoken elements in most diversity discourse: "diversity has become something to celebrate only by virtue of a tacit agreement that the word is to be used to refer only to desirable deviations – and an unspoken determination to do away with some undesirable ones, that is, to decrease diversity (strictly speaking) and to increase uniformity" (2019, 2).[7]

8.3 Response to Critiques

The need for limits. There is an odd relationship between conservative critics of multiculturalism and the particular progressive critics being considered here. The former attack multiculturalism for failing to establish limits, while the latter attack it for having done so. The simplest reply to those who attack limits to tolerance is that one can believe in tolerance without limit or one can believe in human rights. Not both.

An interesting question is why Haque, Mackey, Day, Žižek, and Fish either explicitly endorse a limitless ideal, or express disdain for limits.

We see here an academic form of *thoughtlessness*, in which authors advance assertions that they can't possibly apply consistently in their writing, much less follow in their lives.[8] Now, when we are thoughtless, we *drift*. But where? My sense is that the current on which those uncomfortable with limits are being carried has a distinctly neoliberal direction.

What is the main target of neoliberal theory and action? A self-governing community that makes policies, laws, and rules, creating restrictions in the name of the common good. This ideal is attacked in the name of unbounded property rights and capitalist globalization. Thus, Buchanan and Tullock's influential *The Calculus of Consent* argued for "the protection of something approaching the unanimity rule" for "collective or public decisions which modify or restrict the structure of individual human or property rights" (1962, 73). As noted in chapter 3, much "progress" has occurred in this respect in recent decades. Strikingly, some progressives share the same target. In the critiques of limits, the possibility of a just democracy establishing limits is never envisioned. Thus, Mackey comments that "by the 'democratic will of the people', it is 'the people' (historically defined as white assimilated 'Canadian-Canadians'), who should have the authority to define the limits of difference and the project of nation-building" (2002, 154). The possibility of "the people" having shifted from its "historically defined" form, and the prospect of further shift, are absent from her analysis. In like spirit, some progressives critique, not unjust laws, but law itself. Thobani approvingly cites Walter Benjamin's claim that law is "an immediate manifestation of violence" (Thobani 2007, 36), as well as Foucault's critique of the belief that "power must be exercised in accordance with a fundamental lawfulness" (37). Slavoj Žižek, for his part, urges us to "suspend the neutral space of Law" (1997, 49). But while the neoliberal attack on democratic constraints on property is linked to a clear political project, the progressive critics' discomfort with limits appears aimless and free-floating.

What needs to be demonstrated and critiqued is not the existence of limits, but the unjust and biased nature of those limits. (I will return to this in a moment.) Restricting one's analysis to a mere attack on limits as such is indistinguishable from a libertarian flight from responsible normative reflection.

Asymmetrical tolerance? We saw that Mackey, Beaman, and Parekh critique what they see as the asymmetry of tolerance. Mackey, for example, complains that "the power and the choice whether to accept or not accept difference, to tolerate it or not, still lies in the hands of the tolerators" (2002, 16).[9] Now in one sense, this cannot be otherwise. How could the matter of whether *I* am willing to tolerate some behaviour rest with anyone other than me? The same can be said for acceptance, respect, and so on. But that in itself does not render tolerance or respect asymmetrical: each member of a couple, for example, can identify things they have to "put up with" in the other. Nor does Mackey's observation entail that society can be divided into the givers and receivers of tolerance. Members of conservative religious groups in Canada, for example, are called upon to be tolerant of the practices of those outside the group, and of sexual minorities. So the member of such a religious group at the same time hopes to benefit from the tolerance of others, and is called upon to exercise tolerance.

Throughout history, key instances of toleration have been asymmetrical. Early modern policies of religious toleration, for example, exemplified what Rainer Forst terms the "Permission Conception": "According to it, toleration is a relation between an authority or a majority and a dissenting, 'different' minority (or various minorities)." Thus, "the situation or the 'terms of toleration' are nonreciprocal: one party allows another party certain things on conditions specified by the former" (2012, 140). But Forst also notes the existence of an "alternative conception of toleration that evolved historically and still is present in contemporary discourse – the respect conception – ... in which the tolerating parties recognize each other in a reciprocal, 'horizontal' way" (141).[10]

Thus, tolerance *can* be asymmetrical, and *has been* so, but this is not the only form it takes.

Nevertheless ... To reject the progressive critics' suggestion that tolerance is necessarily asymmetrical should not lead us to forget that it often is and that a critical stance is necessary to help erode asymmetries. Thus, the strongest critique, not of tolerance as such, nor of limits as such, but of "actually existing tolerance," would be that many limits are specified in an asymmetrical fashion, one that privileges some views over others. Habermas observes that "every act of toleration must circumscribe the range of behavior that everyone must accept, thereby setting limits to tolerance itself. There can be no inclusion without exclusion. And as long as this line is drawn in an authoritarian manner, i.e., unilaterally, toleration bears the stigma of arbitrary exclusion" (2008, 253).

A clarification is necessary here: as a society transitions from being (more-or-less) authoritarian and excluding to being (more-or-less) democratic and inclusive, it does not jettison all its inherited social norms. Similarly, as a society's demographics change, its norms do not automatically change in parallel. So at any given moment, there will be norms – and hence limits – that do not adequately take into account the perspectives and legitimate interests of different types of citizens. A serious injustice can arise when such limits are insulated from critique. This insulation can take various forms: lack of effective channels to express objections to the status quo, excessively rigid public opinion, politicians who pander to that opinion, and so on. In regard to tolerance, the problem of unjust limits can be analysed at two points: the line between the tolerated and the not tolerated, and the line between the *merely* tolerated and the fully accepted, even supported.

Language policy, discussed in the previous chapter, provides an example of the latter type of injustice. Shortly after the 1971 multiculturalism policy declaration, Liberal MP Allen Sulatycky boasted that "we throw open our doors to the world and allow newcomers to retain that from their past which they value, and even allow them to retain their former language, to a greater extent than is possible anywhere else in the world" (Commons, 2 March 1972). In this vision, multiculturalism is entirely *permissive*: we don't support, but we *allow*. This is not a trivial good, as we see when we contrast it with active attempts to eliminate the use of Indigenous languages in the residential school gulag of earlier times. But this form of tolerance cannot be confused with equality: in the matter of languages, two are *supported*, others are *allowed*.

Another common type of unjust limit bans or discourages practices that are accepted when performed by the majority group. Political activism is one example. A young woman interviewed for Amarasingam and colleagues' study of Toronto-area Tamil Canadians comments that "the fact that they're [Tamils] exercising their rights to protest doesn't make them Canadian anymore. I feel like, you know, people tend to pick and choose when you can be Canadian or not. Ya, I think multiculturalism probably is not as it is advertised" (2016, 135). Rafeef Ziadah explores the Harper government's decision to cut funding for immigrant integration programs delivered by the Canadian Arab Federation (CAF) and Palestine House. Ziadah notes that "CAF and Palestine House were not assessed on their programme delivery (in fact both had received high ranking for this). Rather, the judgment was on their positions, actions, and events regarding Canadian foreign policies, and specifically their criticism of Israeli state policies" (2017, 18).[11] While the government's actions were regularly presented as a rejection of "extremism," this concept was deployed asymmetrically. Thus, for example, in a letter to Palestine House warning that their funding was under review, Multiculturalism Minister Jason Kenney objected to "the presence on your website of a map showing a Palestinian state encompassing all of Israel" (qtd. in Ziadah 2017, 18). While appearing to advocate for Palestinian sovereignty over all of pre-1947 Palestine is "extremism," advocating for continued *de facto* Israeli sovereignty over the same territory is quite acceptable.

But unjust limits can operate in a contrary direction: tolerating the intolerable. As we saw in chapter 6, for various reasons governments in Canada have tolerated police violence, particularly against Indigenous and Black Canadians. Politicians often *condemn* it, but the grim constancy of incidents of police violence shows that in practice state leaders *put up* with it. The reader can no doubt think of various other examples of such "culpable tolerance" (Tocqueville 1986, vol. 1, 338). Foucault observed that the state worked hard to punish "outrages to morals" but seemed indifferent to threats to "employment, health, the environment" (1994, 4:203), a broad category of intolerable things that are frequently tolerated. (Indeed, the Ottawa police force offered a master class in culpable tolerance during the city's early 2022 occupation.)

I have touched on just three types of unjust limits: *mere* tolerance of things that merit active support; inconsistent *in*tolerance of practices, such as political activism; and *tolerance* of the intolerable. In the absence of serious social deliberation, which hears from all affected parties, unjust limits will remain undetected and/or unaddressed. It is important, then, to *spark* such deliberation, by pointing to *specific* instances of unjust limits rather than talking vaguely about limits to tolerance. Canada has seen various important examples of such deliberation in recent decades, such as the RCMP turban debate and the debate on same-sex marriage.

These specific debates concern exactly where certain lines should be drawn: they do not challenge the need for the lines themselves. In particular, they do not erase the category of "tolerable" practices – things that an individual or a society cannot fully accept, but should (or must) put up with. Thus, even ideal social debates will not eliminate the need for the forbearance-tolerance that bothers some critics so much. The tolerance required of religious believers provides a rich example. A liberal society can demand various forms of tolerance from such persons, but not that they fully accept the doctrines of other citizens that are incompatible with their own. The latter demand, as Balint suggests, manifests serious *in*tolerance of some religious believers (2017, 110).

But religious practices also demand forbearance-tolerance on the part of society as a whole, and here things get complicated. Although employment discrimination is illegal in Canada, for example, the sexist hiring practices of the Catholic Church are tolerated. But the line between intolerable and tolerable religious practices can shift over time and can at times be identified only with difficulty. Consider religious preaching against homosexuality. We can visualize a spectrum here.

At one end might be simple preaching that homosexuality is "sinful." Depending on how this "sin" is stigmatized, how frequently it is condemned, whether it is included or not in a broader catalogue of sins, including things such as greed and so on, the preaching's effects on a young person could range from discomfort, to contempt for others, to dangerous self-hatred. But the spectrum continues, to *de facto* encouragements of violence, or ostracism. At some point, religious practice will cross the line between the tolerable and the intolerable. Further, state and society need not be entirely "neutral" in the face of (barely) tolerable homophobic doctrines.[12]

But in any case, religious belief will likely always require the double forbearance-tolerance discussed here: on the part of believers towards other citizens, and on the part of state and society towards some religious practices.

Forbearance-tolerance: obstacle or gateway to full acceptance? However necessary forbearance-tolerance may be, it remains true that people can exercise such "mere" tolerance when they should be more generous and accepting. In such cases, it is right to critique tolerance for being "less than" something else, such as acceptance or encouragement. An important practical question is this: from a dynamic perspective, what is the relation of such forbearance-tolerance to a more generous response?

Beaman argues that "although many people agree that the language of tolerance and to some extent accommodation can be problematic, they also insist that accommodation can imply or be part of equality. My worry is that these terms *fix us* in place in a way that does not ever quite reach equality" (2012, 17; emphasis added). As she does not explain precisely how this "fixing" occurs, we seem to have here a mysterious-power claim. Still, one can imagine situations in which the tolerator thinks they have done enough by putting up with something, and commends themselves on their virtuous tolerance. Such smug forbearance-tolerance might then be an *obstacle* to full acceptance.

But the error here – explicit in the case of Beaman, implicit for other critics – is to associate the problem with the very *concept* of tolerance and ignore the possibility that tolerance might have more positive effects. According to the critics, we must pass beyond toleration to true acceptance, which toleration supposedly rules out. But what is the path to this true acceptance? How is it supposed to come about, in concrete terms? Rather than constituting an obstacle to acceptance, even a very limited, gritted-teeth sort of tolerance can serve as a bridge to full acceptance, in two ways.

The first path is rooted in the psychology of beliefs and actions. I argued at length in a previous work that "beliefs can flow from actions as much as actions from beliefs" (2014a, 69). As that close observer of psychology Marcel Proust put it, "everyone seeks reasons for their passion" (1988a, 402). Thus, a limited forbearance-tolerance, nothing more than an attempt not to indulge in manifestations of hostility, can at least stop reinforcing the beliefs that would justify those hostile deeds. When such limited tolerance is exercised towards those within one's social circles, it can also prevent a rupture or poisoning of relations, thus preserving the possibility for a reassessment of one's inner sentiments.

Another way in which forbearance-tolerance might lead to fuller acceptance is through its impact on the public world. Consider the evolution of attitudes concerning same-sex marriage. Christian Joppke notes that in just one decade, Americans shifted from 65 per cent opposition to 60 per cent support. One factor in this shift, he suggests, is that "in 1985, less than 20% of Americans had gay friends, relatives, or colleagues. By 2013, the proportion had leapt to 75%" (2017, 83). As Michael Gerson comments, "a human face always makes harsh judgment more difficult" (2010). But Joppke should have said that in 1985, less than 20 per cent *knew* they had gay friends, relatives, or colleagues. Why did that proportion rise so quickly? Growing tolerance certainly played a role, by reducing the potential suffering associated with "coming out."

The argument can be generalized: if a majority group becomes more tolerant, even if that is initially limited to forbearance-tolerance, those outside that group can become more willing to "be themselves," not to inflict "cultural Fordism" on themselves. This can often prod members of the majority to a more generous stance. So while it is true that toleration can work as a "spoonful of sugar" that facilitates assimilation, it can also function in precisely the opposite way.

I have suggested two paths by which forbearance-tolerance can serve as a gateway. Those who assume it to be an obstacle should ask themselves this: would Canada be better off without *any* laws restricting hate speech? After all, such laws aim to enforce tolerance. In the 1970 parliamentary debate on the law, Progressive Conservative Lincoln Alexander noted that "this bill points out that which is unacceptable to the Canadian way of life. It is not a code for love ... It is a code directed towards conduct, towards overt action" (Commons, 7 April 1970). Laws against hate speech involve a double forbearance-tolerance, analogous to that discussed above (concerning religious belief). First, society puts up with something ugly. As MP Ian Grant Wahn noted, "this bill does not attempt to outlaw hatred" (Commons, 9 April 1970). Second, the law *demands* restraint from racists, antisemites, and so on. *Of course* such laws do not eliminate the "root causes" of hate and prejudice. Rather, they treat various forms of hatred as ills that must be contained, "like war and disease – so that they do not overturn political justice" (Rawls 1996, 64). The disease metaphor is a useful reminder that things like hate speech do not simply *express* hatred, they also spread it. Thus, laws against hate speech attempt to protect a society's shared public space (second gateway path) and may also influence the subjectivity of haters and/or of those who might have been seduced by them (first path). Thus, law may not immediately target subjectivities, but it can influence them over time. As Martha Nussbaum argues, "law often precedes and guides the creation of decent sentiments. We certainly don't want to wait until most people love each other before we protect the civil rights of the vulnerable" (2013, 315).

8.4 Conclusion

Essence and accident. Aristotle distinguished between the *essence* of things, "the attributes which belong to them in virtue of what they are" (*Physics* 192b), and their "accidents." The "essence" of a circle, to take a simple example, is that all points on it are equidistant from its centre. The size of any particular circle, the colour in which it is drawn, and so on, are "accidents." The progressive critics of tolerance have included various "accidents" of tolerance within its essence. They assume that tolerance must always relate to something "repugnant" or "repulsive" and suggest that it is *by definition* asymmetrical. Neither claim is correct.[13]

Gross concepts. But as I noted, this is far from the only conceptual problem. Many invocations of tolerance and intolerance are so general that they effectively treat these as "gross concepts." When we push for precision, asking questions such as "tolerance *of what*?," we see that one cannot responsibly be "for" or "against" tolerance or intolerance in the abstract. We noted in particular that tolerance of the intolerable is one important form of injustice.

The fact that justice often requires intolerance, yet political discourse tends to trade in vague concepts, allows the value of tolerance to be invoked in morally problematic ways. Those who rail today against "political correctness," for example, are often accusing people who protest against speech they consider racist – or sexist, homophobic, and so on – of being intolerant, under the assumption that this must be a bad thing. Thus, Andrew Macdougall, Harper's former communications director, accused a Liberal MP of an "anti-Christian sneer" for pointing out that Conservative leader Andrew Scheer "is somebody who has voted against every single civil rights advancement in the last 25 years." "So much for tolerance," huffed Macdougall (2017). So to be "tolerant" in this case would be to refrain even from pointing out that Scheer, in opposing same-sex marriage, for example, has sought to impose legal rules binding on *all*, on the basis of allegedly religious convictions held by *some*.

But the fact that it can be invoked in morally problematic ways does not count against tolerance in general. As Nicholas Wolterstorff argues, "all moral language is susceptible to distortion: the language of love, the language of duty, the language of virtue – and the language of rights" (2008, 388). The call to move *beyond* tolerance to something better, as it happens, is just as vulnerable to problematic usage. During Justin Trudeau's first term, various Bloc Québécois MPs charged multiculturalism with promoting *mere* tolerance, claiming that the Quebec they wanted aimed much higher: "We want to welcome others in our own way and not as Canada does ... We want to truly live together, not just tolerate one another" (Gabriel Ste-Marie, Commons, 6 November 2018); "Here, we support recognizing and respecting all differences, not just tolerating them" (Luc Thériault, Commons, 26 September 2018). In practice, this glorious transcendence of mere tolerance entails that a hijab-wearing Québécoise must choose between a practice she considers integral to her faith, and becoming a teacher or public servant.

Tolerance and democratic deliberation. The previous paragraph might be condemned by some Québécois. Yes, I am claiming that intolerance of the hijab is ethically wrong, as well as a violation of human rights, and that spinning the failure to offer even forbearance-tolerance as a more advanced attitude is Orwellian. Perhaps others could put forward arguments to the contrary.[14] There is much to discuss here. But I doubt if the issue will ever be adequately discussed.

And this leads to a final observation: to arrive at a just practice of tolerance, and to identify just limits, we need something more than tolerance as it is usually understood. Consider Jürgen Habermas's claim that "citizens can agree on where to draw the boundaries of a reciprocally demanded tolerance only if they submit their decisions to a form of deliberation that compels the parties involved, who are also those affected, to adopt each other's perspectives and to give equal consideration to the interests of all" (2008, 254). "To adopt each other's perspectives" demands much more than what people usually think of as tolerance.[15]

So the critics are correct in saying that we must go *beyond* tolerance. But we must do this, not to leave tolerance behind, as various progressive critics believe, but to establish the contours of a just tolerance, through respectful social deliberation that hears from people representing a wide variety of viewpoints.

Chapter Nine

Multiculturalism as Psychic Prop

"I revelled in my own nature, and we all know that that's where happiness is found."

Camus, La chute (1956, 24)

9.1 Introduction: Material and Ideal Interests

Augustine notes that "the eye is attracted by beautiful objects, by gold and silver and all such things. There is great pleasure, too, in feeling something agreeable to the touch, and material things have various qualities to please each of the other senses. Again, it is gratifying to be held in esteem by other men" (*Confessions*, 2.5). The quote nicely distinguishes between what Max Weber termed "material" and "ideal" interests (1958, 280; 1978, 1129). The former are perhaps more obvious: we know that we need food and shelter, for example. But we also need love, respect, self-esteem, and much else. We *may* physically survive even when our ideal interests are neglected, but we will not flourish.

But "ideal" here does not mean "nice." Pursuit of our ideal interests can be a very ugly affair. In fact, the Augustine quote continues: "It is gratifying to be held in esteem by other men and to have the power of giving them orders and gaining the mastery over them. This is also the reason why revenge is sweet." *Ideal*, in this usage, is simply contrasted with *material*. But the contrast does not mean that the types of interests are unrelated. Thorsten Veblen argued that our consumption typically pursues both: some rudimentary shelter is a material need, but a fancy home satisfies both types of interest (rpt. 1994).

Moreover, success or failure in the pursuit of one type of interest has consequences for the other. William Goode notes that "all people share the universal need to gain the respect or esteem of others, since without it they can not as easily elicit the help of others" (qtd. in James 2006, 114). Conversely, it has been recognized for millennia that material poverty often leads to social marginalization. The Book of Proverbs states that "The poor are disliked even by their neighbors, but the rich have many friends" (Pr. 14.20), an assessment seconded by Aristotle's observation that "Men who are well-born are thought worthy of honour, and so are those who enjoy power or wealth" (*Ethics* ¶ 1124). "Mankind's greatest error," as one of Orhan Pamuk's characters puts it, is "to confuse poverty with stupidity" (2005, 298).

At the same time, the pursuit of ideal interests can run counter to material ones. Earlier points in the book have touched on this. As we saw in chapter 2, for many poor white Americans the search for self-respect has led them to support political leaders who consistently harm their economic prospects. Race solidarity *from below* (see chapter 6) is for that reason not conducive to the clear-eyed pursuit of material interests.[1]

As this shows, ideal interests have important social and political implications. Consider also Georg Lukács's claim: "the fighting power of a class grows with its ability to carry out its own mission with a good conscience and to adapt all phenomena to its own interests with unbroken confidence in itself" (1971, 66). Why? Perhaps any group with a clear conscience can adopt a more hard-nosed stance in confronting other groups, perhaps there is less internal dissension, fewer second thoughts. Perhaps, finally, the clear conscience reduces the chance of defections from the group, which can play a vital role in revolutions. This chapter is more concerned with such social and political effects than with purely psychological ones.

Plan of the chapter. I wish to examine various hypotheses from progressive critics concerning the role of Canadian multiculturalism in the ethnic majority's pursuit of its ideal interests. The next section (9.2) will briefly consider various claims. The section after that (9.3) will examine Elke Winter's argument that we should analyse multiculturalism in terms of various triangular relations, through which the "multiculturalization" of identity allows the ethnic majority (outside of Quebec) to view itself as different from *them* (e.g., Americans) because of its way of relating to "its" minority groups. As one empirical approach to the question of the ideological effects of multiculturalism, I will then analyse parliamentary discourse in Justin Trudeau's first term, which will shed some light on the various progressive hypotheses.

9.2 An Assortment of Claims

Smugness. A first claim is that multiculturalism provides Canadians with a smug confidence in their collective virtue: "Multiculturalism makes the Canadian population think they're doing really nice things: isn't it nice that we can accept 'these' people? But 'these' people remain 'these' people" (Brand 1990, 274). This is not a trivial matter. I have suggested throughout this work that multiculturalism can serve as a focus of contestation, as various groups try to push the policy further, to use it, for example, as a critical resource in anti-racism struggles. Smugness on the part of the ethnic majority can block that dynamic. It can, for example, quell debates about the justice of existing lines between "mere" tolerance and acceptance.

Imagined superiority. A psychic benefit closely related to smugness is that of imagined superiority. This can take various forms. One alleged by some critics is assumed superiority with respect to ethnic minorities. We examined Thobani's claim to this effect in chapter 4: "white subjects were constituted as tolerant and respectful of difference and diversity, while non-white people were instead constructed as perpetually and irremediably monocultural" (2007, 148). Similarly, Slavoj Žižek claims that "the multiculturalist respect for the Other's specificity is the very form of asserting one's own superiority" (2007, 44).

Erasure of history. Sunera Thobani writes that "as in Australia and Britain, the embrace of multiculturalism allowed Canadians to resolve the crisis of whiteness through its reorganization as tolerant, pluralist, and racially innocent, uncontaminated by its previous racist history" (2007, 154). This is a plausible claim: multiculturalism could well allow many Canadians to draw a line under the past, blithely denying Faulkner's famous claim: "The past is never dead. It's not even past" (1953, 85). Multiculturalism might thus create space for the claim that the Canada where "nasty things happened" is dead and gone (see chapter 2).

An assessment. As we will see in reviewing the parliamentary record, there is certainly evidence that invocations of multiculturalism can foster smugness. The claim that multiculturalism induces a sense of superiority towards ethnic minorities is much weaker: those who advance the claim fail to provide serious supporting evidence. In Žižek's formulation in particular, we see again the problem of assuming a uniform reality. There is no doubt that members of majority groups often assert or assume their superiority to others. But a key question is whether such assumed superiority is in fact observed most often among Canadians who *support* multiculturalism.

198   Part IV: Yes, but …

As to the third claim, multiculturalism could well contribute to the erasure of history. It can also do the opposite, as we will see in a moment. We must also remember that countries everywhere erase inconvenient elements of their history, and they do not need multiculturalism to do it. They simply need to bypass those parts of history in school curricula, public commemorations, and so on. That is, collective memory does not need to be *erased*: it dies unless it is deliberately sustained.

9.3 Us, Them, and Others

As mentioned in chapter 2, Elke Winter's *Us, Them, and Others* seeks to explain the "multiculturalization of national identity" in Canada, the path by which a country becomes "normatively pluralist" (2011, 39, 77). Her answer suggests that multiculturalism provides for a sense of superiority. But here, that sense is more complex and flexible than in Žižek, for example.

Winter bases her explanation on a key claim taken from Max Weber, that groups are only formed on the basis of a "confrontation with outsiders" (2011, 60). In the Canadian case, this has taken on a peculiarly triangular form: "This book examines how a pluralist 'national we' is bounded by opposition to a real or imagined 'Others' with a capital O. These Others are constructed as 'them.' It also traces whether and how this 'national we' includes references to 'others' (lower case) in our midst, that is, alongside of 'us'" (5–6). Winter's terminology is not always easy to follow.[2] But the core insight I will take from her triadic analysis is this: the multiculturalization of identity is embraced because it allows *us* (designating, in effect, ethnic-majority Canadians outside Quebec) to understand ourselves as different from *them* because of our way of relating to "our" *others*: "Pluralism is thus best understood as overlapping and dynamic sets of triangular relations, where the conditional association between 'us' and 'others' is rendered possible through the exclusion of 'them.'" (6).

Winter focuses her triadic analysis on two "thems" in particular. The first is long-standing. In a speech given the day after his 1971 policy declaration, Trudeau argued that "each of the many fibres contributes its own qualities and Canada gains strength from the combination. We become less like others; we become less susceptible to cultural, social or political envelopment by others" (1972, 32–3). And *who*, exactly, might "envelop" us? Trudeau was clearly alluding to the US. He did the same in a March 1972 speech: Canada, he claimed, is "a different country from any other; we have a different outlook, different attitudes, and different values. We are this because the social evolution of Canadians has not been identical to the patterns pursued, consciously or unconsciously, by other societies elsewhere. For a number of reasons there has not developed in Canada a pressure to conform and, in my view, we are the better for it" (qtd. in Commons, 26 June 1972).

Thus, as Randall Hansen drily puts it: "Successive governments have told Canadians that what makes them different from the United States is multiculturalism: the Americans are the melting pot, we are the mosaic. Canadians have, somewhat unremarkably, responded positively. Put another way, when we affirm multiculturalism, we affirm ourselves" (2014, 84).

The second "them" became more salient in the 1990s. As I commented in *Multicultiphobia*: "On the night of the 30 October [1995] referendum, Quebec Premier Jacques Parizeau declared that 'money and the ethnic vote' had led to the victory of the 'No' camp. Subsequently, two multiculturalism supporters argued that minorities in Quebec 'remained loyal to Canada in large part because they perceive it as accommodating and accepting of their cultural identity.' PQ Cabinet minister Louise Harel seemed to agree that multiculturalism had helped save Canada on referendum night" (2010b, 93).

Parizeau's comments gave a strong push to the dynamic analysed by Winter. She quotes from a *Globe and Mail* editorial published days after the referendum, which gives full expression to the us–them–others relation:

> On radio phone-in shows, on newspaper letters pages, in every public forum they could find, Canadians both inside and outside Quebec have poured forth their outrage and disgust. We are deeply offended. And being offended is one way we learn about ourselves. By showing us what we are against, Mr. Parizeau, Mr. Bouchard and Mr. Landry have given us a rare opportunity to affirm what we are for ...
>
> We are against ethnic nationalism, in which people of common ethnicity rule themselves – masters in their own house. We are for civic nationalism, in which people of different backgrounds come together under the umbrella of common citizenship to form a community of equals. Ours is a modern nationalism: liberal, decent, tolerant and colour-blind. (*Globe and Mail* 1995).

The contrast is overstated. But that's the point: the Québécois, like the American "melting pot," provide a caricaturized "them" that supports a caricaturized and contrasting image of "us." And that yields psychic benefits, which provide support for a "conditional inclusion of ethnically diverse immigrants" (Winter 2011, 27).

Few Americans lose much sleep over what Canadians might think of them. But the other triangular relation sparks strong reactions among the "them." We can distinguish two modes. The first is resentful. BQ MP Monique Pauzé, for example, complains that "the Liberal heritage includes disdain for Quebec French. If we oppose multiculturalism, we are racist. If we want a secular Quebec, we are racist. If we want a French Quebec, we are racist. If we want newcomers to integrate with us, we are accused of using an 'us' based on colour. The Liberal heritage includes denigrating and insulting anyone who does not think like them" (Commons, 30 January 2019). Columnist Richard Martineau draws a surprising parallel: "'Speak White,' says Martineau, is what 'the English' used to say to Quebeckers who insisted on speaking French.[3] And today we have: 'Speak White, do as we do, embrace multiculturalism, stop clinging to your culture and history, open yourselves up to the point of forgetting yourselves. Speak White, stop trying to impose your archaic language on the newly-arrived'" (2020). Note that both Pauzé and Martineau equate criticism of intolerance with ... intolerance. The discourse aims to make intolerance – of the hijab, for example – impervious to critique. Resentment, too, can serve psychic interests.

The second mode is boastful. Various Bloc Québécois statements in Parliament, for example, present Quebec as the place that has got diversity right: "we are a tightly knit diverse nation" (Gabriel Ste-Marie, Commons, 6 November 2018). As I noted in *Multicultiphobia*, the Quebec nationalist critique of multiculturalism relies on a depiction of that policy created by its conservative critics. Thus:

> Confining people to these virtual fortresses, so typical of Canadian multiculturalism, does not allow for cultural osmosis ... In the summer of 2017, I met an Italian diplomat while I was travelling. He had stopped in Toronto and wanted to gather people from all walks of life around his table. He said no one would talk to anyone else. Everyone was suspicious of everyone else. No one would start a dialogue. He said that multiculturalism was like building a bunker for each culture. (Commons, Monique Pauzé, 6 November 2018)

To interpret the triangular relations that Winter dissects as a source of psychic benefits – which I am emphasizing much more than does Winter –does not mean that "our" view of the contrast with America or Quebec is purely illusory. Winter's core thesis is specific and focused and can be combined with a number of other arguments. It is compatible with a view of multiculturalism as an initiative "from above" or as a response to pressure "from below," with a view of multiculturalism as pure manipulation or as a real concession to minority groups, and everything in between. Winter's own view on the latter point is dialectical: "Did the dominant group try to co-opt minority members by granting specific rights to the most vocal and powerful immigrant groups? Most likely, it did. Did the dominant group try to contain minority demands by pitting one group against another? Most likely, it did. Did, nonetheless, some minority groups and/or individuals benefit from this process of pluralizing Canadianness? Most likely, they did and still do" (2011, 200).

The argument can also be understood in strong and weak forms. Winter prefers the strong variant: "the conditional association between 'us' and 'others' is rendered possible through the exclusion of 'them'" (2011, 6). In my view, this cannot be sustained, because it is logically equivalent to asserting that the "multicultural we" that emerged in Canada could not have emerged in any other way. This cannot be demonstrated. The weak variant is thus more plausible: the triangular relations analysed by Winter played some role in the emergence of a widespread view that multiculturalism was a core element of Canadian identity.

Finally, Thobani mentions another type of triangular relation, one that should not be neglected. Citing analysts of Australia and Britain, she notes that "upper and middle classes have been able to utilize their support for multiculturalism as cultural capital in the age of globalization, unlike the working classes whom they have depicted as irremediably racist and uncouth" (2007, 153). Although expressed in Thobani's customary homogenizing style, the point is important, and relevant to the serious – and self-serving – misreading of shocks such as Trump's election and the Brexit vote. Viewing these as *nothing but* expressions of racism and xenophobia provides a convenient alibi for globalizing elites (Klein 2016; Piketty 2019, 927).

9.4 Parliamentary Multiculturalism Discourse

Earlier in this chapter, we examined three hypotheses concerning the relationship between multiculturalism and ideal interests:

- it contributes to smugness;
- it supports a sense of superiority over ethnic minorities; and
- it erases history.

We then considered Elke Winter's argument that two triangular relations have helped solidify support for multiculturalism and reshape Canadian identity.

This section will use the parliamentary record as a body of discourse with which to test these various claims. It will also offer other observations on parliamentary discourse in order to shed light on how political elites view and make use of multiculturalism. The analysis is based on statements in the House during Justin Trudeau's first term (3 December 2015–11 September 2019). This is just one body of discourse and so cannot offer conclusive proof or disproof of any of the claims. But it does have the merit of being a well-defined body of content, taken from a relatively influential institution.

Using the official website of Parliament (www.ourcommons.ca), I first searched for all mentions of "multiculturalism" or "multicultural." From the results, I pruned all purely incidental mentions – statements, for example, where the only appearance of the terms is of the form "Minister of Canadian Heritage (Multiculturalism)," or where the "Multicultural Council for Ontario Seniors" is mentioned in a long list of organizations. I was left with a total of 310 interventions (speeches, very short statements, and so on).

Of the 310, I classified 187 (60%) as "celebratory." These interventions celebrate multiculturalism, or Canada for being multicultural, or something closely related. Thus:

> We Canadians are generally accepting and tolerant people. We celebrate our multicultural and pluralistic society, we value our diversity and we live in relative harmony with many different traditions, religions and cultures. (Gordie Hogg, Lib, 5 June 2019).

> The Festival Laval Laughs is all about diversity and inclusion. It celebrates the multiculturalism that defines our community and our country. (Angelo Iacono, Lib, 19 September 2018).

There were 53 (17%) interventions that used multiculturalism as a critical resource, to make a case for stronger anti-racism efforts, for example. Thus:

> Canadians understand that diversity is our strength. While we have much to celebrate, there are still real challenges for many people in the country. Let me be very clear. Throughout history, and even today, there are people in communities who experience systemic racism, oppression and discrimination, preventing them from fully participating in our society. These experiences are still felt today by many Canadians, and we can and we must do better. (Pablo Rodriguez, Lib, 19 October 2018)

The following table summarizes the profile of the interventions by party:

		Celebratory	% of total	Critical resource	% of total
LIB	190	126	66	36	19
CPC	63	34	54	5	8
NDP	44	27	61	12	27
BQ	13	0	0	0	0
Totals	310	187	60	53	17

Note the BQ profile. Ten of the BQ's thirteen interventions expressed opposition to multiculturalism: *no other party offered oppositional statements.*

Celebratory statements. The frequency of celebratory invocations of multiculturalism is to some extent built into the institution. MPs are elected locally. And so they regularly stand up to mention an organization or event in their riding, after which their staff dutifully publicize the speech. Or they line up to speak in favour of a declaration concerning some month or other: Sikh heritage month, Tamil heritage month, Latin American Heritage Month, Jewish heritage month, and so on.

Because they are often event-focused, some celebratory interventions highlight "song and dance" (and food) multiculturalism:

> Montreal is all about multiculturalism. It has something for everyone and is the place to go for everything, from smoked meat and Vietnamese noodle soup to poutine. (Marc Miller, Lib, 15 May 2017)

> This is one of the largest multicultural festivals in Canada, and we have it right in Oshawa. These are places to experience the Ukrainian culture, dance, and of course their food. (Colin Carrie, CPC, 10 February 2017)

> Edmonton is a place of risk takers, where we happily wrap ourselves in rainbows for the Pride parade, proudly don head coverings for the Vaisakhi Sikh march, and gleefully gobble up food from around the world during our multicultural heritage festival. (Randy Boissonnault, Lib, 7 October 2016).

Most celebratory statements, then, are relatively innocent. But some, in my view, cross a line, in the sense that they provide support to some aspect of the progressive critique of multiculturalism. I counted seventeen in this subcategory. As we pass from a general tally of interventions to more specific questions like this one, the count becomes more tentative: other researchers might locate the "line" – or classify individual cases – differently.

So, what puts these statements over the line? Some are one-sided portrayals of Canadian reality:

> Thanks to this country's multiculturalism, new Canadians from all parts of the world enjoy harmony, cross-cultural understanding, and mutual respect. (Geng Tan, Lib, 14 February 2018)

> My riding of King-Vaughan is a shining example of Canada's diversity, where people from all around the world live together in harmony and prosperity, celebrating our different cultures and traditions. (Deborah Schulte, Lib, 21 September 2017)

Others reference specific communities with no mention of the challenges they face, such as ongoing discrimination:

> We celebrate February as Black History Month, and this is the kind of diversity that makes our Canada strong. (Ramesh Sangha, Lib, 12 February 2018).

Others extol Canada's greatness, painting it as the envy of the world:

> I would suggest that we are envied by countries around the world because of our great diversity. (Kevin Lamoureux, Lib, 18 June 2018)

> Today, in a world of resurgent xenophobia and nativism, Canada stands as an aspirational city on the hill amongst liberal democracies. (Borys Wrzesnewskyj, Lib, 7 February 2017)

These recurring claims about how we might be seen from *outside* the country are striking.

In my view, the moral and political error of this "over the line" celebratory rhetoric is that it seeks to bolster a national identity around very problematic claims about who we are *today* as a nation, rather than around what we should *aspire* to be; in fact, it profoundly confuses the two.

Some celebratory interventions go even further, arguably becoming offensive. Here, for example, an MP simply erases the existence of Canadian *citizens* of Latin American origin:

> We have Latin Americans to thank for being able to enjoy things like strawberries, oranges, grapes, watermelon, and much more in the midst of our Canadian winters. We also welcome many people from Latin America

to help fill our labour gaps in different regions of Canada. (Cathay Wagantall, CPC, 13 June 2018)

On the other hand, other celebratory statements, of roughly the same frequency as the "over the line" ones, contain a critical component, although I did not include them in the "critical resource" tally:

> Ours is a land of many faiths, many languages and many cultures. It is a place where Muslims, Sikhs, Buddhists, Hindus, Jews, Christians and members of numerous other religious groups live in harmony ... Even as we move toward a more diverse and inclusive society, there is a considerable amount of evidence on the persistence of racism and discrimination in Canadian society. (Andy Fillmore, Lib, 26 September 2018)

> This is the bill that would designate the month of April as Sikh heritage month. New Democrats have long been supporters of multiculturalism and celebrating the diverse backgrounds that make up the Canadian mosaic ... Racism and legal restrictions often stood in the way of Sikh progress in British Columbia. Fears of Asian immigration to B.C. among Anglo-Saxon residents escalated in the early years of the 20th century, often based on fears that economic competition would lower wages, but nearly always also fuelled by simple racism. (Randall Garrison, NDP, 4 October 2018)

These mixed critical–celebratory interventions came only from NDP and Liberal M.P.'s.

As noted above, 17 per cent of the parliamentary interventions used multiculturalism as a critical resource. Because I am analysing discourse in light of the progressive critiques, this category is defined to cover interventions that tend to counter those critiques, invoking multiculturalism, for example, to advocate for action against racism or Islamophobia in Canadian society. Other interventions in this category condemn antisemitism or argue for support for Indigenous languages.

Some examples. Iqra Khalid, the Liberal MP who presented Motion 103 condemning Islamophobia, declared:

> We can either let our differences of race, creed, and religion that speak of discrimination or hatred, exclusion, and suspicion divide us as Canadians, or we can work with our differences to make us stronger and help us progress as a multicultural, secular, strong nation. (21 March 2017)

Liberal Sukh Dhaliwal used multiculturalism to argue for reforms to the justice system:

> The defining value of our country is our respect for equality and commitment to promoting multiculturalism, but we continually need to do more to make sure that this value remains in place, and one of those areas that has long gone unchanged is our justice system. It is a fact that we have lower levels of representation of indigenous and minority communities in juries, and that needs to change to ensure the integrity of the justice system. (5 June 2018)

Even celebrations of song and dance multiculturalism can provide an opening for critical interventions. Jenny Kwan, the NDP's multiculturalism critic, used a speech on Latin American Heritage Month to criticize the treatment of seasonal workers:

> Let us not just recognize the importance of diversity and the joy of attending beautiful festivals and celebrations, but examine how our policies prevent the people whose heritage we say we appreciate from staying in Canada and calling it their home. (19 March 2018).

In another speech, Kwan warns that

> anti-immigrant, anti-refugee, and anti-Muslim rhetoric had truly taken hold in some places ... Given the rise globally in anti-immigrant and anti-refugee rhetoric, as Canadians and especially as parliamentarians, we must do more than just rest on our humanitarian laurels to prevent these ideas from taking hold here. (28 February 2018)

The invocations of multiculturalism just discussed argue for things that we must do, things that appear integrally linked to multiculturalism. We might say that the logic flows from multiculturalism as premise to the fight against Islamophobia, for example, as conclusion. But there is a different use of multiculturalism: as a rhetorical prop for a party's policies.

I noted in chapter 2 that the Conservatives have continued to use multiculturalism in this way. Further examples during the period under study include the use of multiculturalism to:

- critique current immigration policy (Michelle Rempel, CPC, 10 May 2018);
- express support for Israel, "a pluralistic, multicultural democracy" (Garnett Genuis, CPC, 6 June 2017)[4]; and
- attack the BDS movement (Kelly McCauley, CPC, 18 February 2016).

Again, my classification of interventions could be contested. Consider, for example, the argument by Conservative MPs that organizations should be able to access summer job funds without having to pledge that they would not discriminate against LGBTQ+ youth. Can one not plausibly argue that the government's "values test ... has no place in a tolerant, diverse, multicultural society" (Karen Vecchio, CPC, 1 March 2018)? One can, precisely because the claim relies on three "gross concepts" (see chapter 8), and in effect argues that a "tolerant" society must tolerate intolerance. But one cannot plausibly argue that it is multiculturalism that brought the Conservatives to this position. Rather, it is the party's long-standing reliance on a fundamentalist Christian constituency that was decisive. Thus, while "critical resource" interventions run from multiculturalism to plausible implications of it, the "rhetorical prop" invocations run in the opposite direction, from party policy on an issue to multiculturalism as a rhetorical device to support it.[5]

And what of the other parties? Do they not also use multiculturalism in this way? Not really. The Liberals do, however, invoke multiculturalism as part of their attacks on the CPC, on issues such as:

- their "barbaric cultural practices" discourse and legislation (John Aldag, Lib, 28 February 2018);
- their "unjust, two-tiered citizenship model" (Ali Ehsassi, Lib, 19 June 2017); and
- their anti-Muslim refugee policy in Syria (Arif Virani, Lib, 10 May 2017).

In such cases, the link to multiculturalism is more evident than in the case of the "rhetorical prop" interventions.

Assessing the progressive hypotheses. What light does the parliamentary record shed on the various progressive hypotheses concerning multiculturalism and ideal interests? There is plentiful evidence of invocations of multiculturalism that can contribute to smugness, but there are also many interventions that work in the contrary direction. I found no evidence of multiculturalism being used to assert superiority over ethnic minority groups.

What of the claim that multiculturalism has contributed to the erasure of the "inconvenient" elements of Canadian history? On the one hand, such elements are certainly absent from this curious defence of multiculturalism:

> Canada is built on multiculturalism. When people think about our country, they think about French Canadians, English Canadians, and indigenous

Canadians, who all have their own languages, religions, cultures, and nations. That shows that the country has always been the same. Canada has been a multicultural country for over 250 years. (Frank Baylis, Lib, 6 November 2018)

But other interventions acknowledge the historical record: "Canada does not have an unblemished record when it comes to citizenship. In fact, the record on citizenship in our country has been checkered with discrimination, racism, and sexism" (Don Davies, NDP, 10 March 2016).

Since the most painful aspect of Canada's history is its relationship with Indigenous peoples, one important test is to examine how invocations of multiculturalism relate to this. Again, the picture is mixed. Some interventions erase, not just history, but Indigenous people altogether:

> Our cultural fabric is made up of Canadians from all over the world. We are all immigrants. (Todd Doherty, CPC, 13 June 2018)

NDP M.P. Scott Duvall offers a multicultural updating of the founding races rhetoric:

> We live in a multicultural society, a country that has been built by those coming here from other countries and building new lives, new communities. (20 May 2016)

Former Liberal leader Stéphane Dion manages a simultaneous mention and erasure of Indigenous Canadians:

> We enjoy among the highest quality of life of any country, with two international languages recognized as our official languages, a strong indigenous people who remind us of our history, and a multicultural population that allows us to influence the world. *Our roots are in Europe*, we form part of the Americas, and we are open to Asia. (31 January 2017; emphasis added)

But interventions that work in the opposite direction are somewhat more plentiful than the problematic ones:

> Recognizing and making reparations for the historical abuse and mistreatment of indigenous peoples is a fundamental part of building a more inclusive society and promoting the diversity of Canada. (John Aldag, Lib, 18 June 2018)

In a major foreign policy speech, Chrystia Freeland argued that by embracing multiculturalism and diversity, Canadians are embodying a way of life that works. We can say this in all humility, but also without any false self-effacement ... We say this in the full knowledge that we also have problems of our own to overcome, most egregiously the injustices suffered by indigenous people in Canada. We must never flinch from acknowledging this great failure. (6 June 2017)

Presenting a petition to the House, Liberal MaryAnn Mihychuk linked multiculturalism to anti-colonialism discourse:

The petition points out that when local indigenous cultural artifacts are removed, it irrevocably damages the diverse regional and cultural traditions that have created a multicultural Canada and that the forcible removal of cultural property from the reach of indigenous communities is an act of colonization, which is wholly incompatible with the Truth and Reconciliation Commission's calls to action. (19 March 2019)

Shortly after the Quebec City massacre, New Democrat Jenny Kwan linked the recent and episodic to the long-standing and systemic:

Canada's multicultural society can flourish in the context of cultural diversity only if we are united in condemning and remedying issues of racial and religious discrimination, be that overt instances such as the recent and devastating Quebec City mosque attack; or be that systemic, long-standing discrimination, such as that faced by too many members of the indigenous communities. (16 February 2017)

And what of Elke Winter's claims? I found some contrasts with the US, although they were not plentiful. New Democrat Wayne Stetski contrasted multicultural Canada with "Trumpland," adding, "We are not that melting pot" (31 January 2017). Liberal Randeep Sarai also referenced the supposed melting pot to the south:

In Canada we have a diverse range of cultures. We have indigenous culture, we have Quebec culture, we have a multicultural culture, so we are not a melting pot of culture, where everything merges into one. We celebrate a diverse range of cultures, and I am proud of living in Canada. (10 March 2016)

I did not detect claims of superiority towards Quebec. This may reflect the constraints of electoral competition. All the parties are competitive in Quebec and so cannot be expected to make arguments at its expense. (As the Bloc Québecois only runs in Quebec, on the other hand, it is not surprising to find BQ MPs engaging in triangular discourse, declaring that Quebec's model of integration is superior to that of the rest of Canada.) Some MPs work instead to distance Quebec from the BQ's anti-multiculturalism stance:

> I have a hard time imagining myself in the Quebec described by my colleague. First off, the Quebec I know welcomes all kinds of cultures. (Frank Baylis, Lib, 26 September 2018)

> Both multiculturalism and [Quebec's] interculturalism place a high degree of importance on integration and respect for common civic and democratic values, and both have been invaluable to Canada's social fabric since the 1970s. I believe strongly that Canada's federal multiculturalism policy is flexible enough to allow for their coexistence. (Andy Fillmore, Lib, 26 September 2018)

As to Winter's basic premise, concerning the multiculturalization of Canadian identity: many interventions do proclaim the multicultural nature of Canada, with a frequency that is probably without parallel elsewhere in the world. We also see the occasional formulation that points in the contrary direction. Liberal Pam Damoff uses "multicultural" as a synonym for foreign:

> It is interesting to note that in recent years, the profession has become increasingly female and multicultural. Women now account for 41% of physicians in Canada, while those who acquired their medical degrees elsewhere constitute 26.5% of all physicians in this country. (17 May 2019)

A few interventions refer to "multicultural communities" to denote minority groups of various types. Overall, statements that undermine the claim that multiculturalism involves all Canadians are not plentiful: I counted just six. But they do testify to the durability of the idea that "multicultural" is somehow about minorities alone.

But do we really need multiculturalism? In assessing the progressive critiques in light of my analysis of parliamentary discourse, in most cases I delivered a mixed verdict. But I need to address a legitimate grounds for scepticism. One might respond to the idea that the various "critical resource" invocations of multiculturalism somehow balance the "over the line" ones, by asking: but do we really need multiculturalism to condemn things like racism and hate crimes? Consider a couple of the critical resource statements:

> Cowardly hate crimes such as the one we witnessed in Quebec City on Sunday have no place in our society. (Ali Ehsassi, Lib, 31 January 2017)

> Over the past few years, we have seen an escalation of division and intolerance in this country. Despite the fact that the majority of Canadians value our diversity and pluralism, we have witnessed a rise in hate crimes, particularly those that target the Muslim community and continued anti-Semitism. (Arif Virani, Lib, 20 March 2018)

Now: do MPs really need to appeal to multiculturalism in order to condemn antisemitism or to say that it's wrong to murder people in a mosque? Isn't racism a violation of core principles of liberal democracy, whether or not one subscribes to multiculturalism?

But perhaps a widespread attachment to multiculturalism, however vaguely understood, is a practical requirement to create the desire and political space for governments to address issues that really should be addressed, even without multiculturalism. For Banting and Kymlicka, what multiculturalism policies "all have in common is that they go beyond the protection of the basic civil and political rights guaranteed to all individuals in a liberal-democratic state" (2006, 1). If that be so, then the argument here is that the invocation of multiculturalism may be necessary to defend *something less* than multiculturalism. Consider a statement from one Liberal M.P.:

> I rise today with a sad and heavy heart to speak about the hate crimes committed in Ottawa in the recent past ... These hateful acts have no place in Canadian society. I know that these heinous acts do not reflect the Canadian values of openness and inclusiveness. Our Canadian society is truly multicultural and inclusive. (Chandra Arya, 18 April 2018)

Chandra Arya believes, and I think he is right, that the reference to Canadian values, and to what our society "truly" is, gives the condemnation more bite. Perhaps it shouldn't, but it does. Why?

One clue might be what claims of this form *avoid*. American writer Arthur Schlesinger Jr. argues that "we don't have to believe that our values are absolutely better than the next fellow's or the next country's, but we have no doubt that they are better *for us* ... and that they are worth living and dying for" (qtd. in Michaels 2006, 148). The underlying assumption is that it is easier to argue that certain values are in fact "ours," and to draw certain inferences directly from that, than to advance "absolute" moral claims. Again we must ask: but why?

One reason, I suspect, is a mistaken understanding of what moral argument entails, a foundationalism that leads to fear that claims of the form "this is wrong" – as opposed to "this is against our values" – will drag one into an endless and vertigo-inducing debate. I discussed this mistaken foundationalism at length in *Facts, Values, and the Policy World* (2022) and will thus leave it aside here.

Another reason is particularly relevant to progressives. There is today an awareness that absolute and/or universal claims concerning right and wrong have often been parochial and oppressive. This naturally leads to a strong suspicion of such claims, as well as a more-or-less conscious avoidance of them in one's own arguments. As a result, a certain form of relativism is influential. In *Multicultiphobia*, I labelled this "Relativism (3)," the claim that "propositions can be judged only within their framework: ethical norms, for example, are always held *within* a culture, and cannot be assessed from outside it" (2010b, 137).[6] As a theoretical claim, Relativism (3) is indefensible (146–50). But I believe it is very influential as a *practice*. That is, by avoiding simple moral claims – "This is wrong, period" – and referring to "our" values, or perhaps to progressive values, as the case may be, people proceed *as if* Relativism 3 were correct. (As I stressed in *Multicultiphobia*, this is certainly not limited to the "left," or to "multiculturalists," as some conservatives allege.)

So perhaps it is no longer enough simply to say that a given practice is *wrong*, as an everyday unreflective relativism-in-practice has become too widespread. If so, a somewhat mythologized view of "our values" may be an essential tool for progressive critiques, for example, to condemn hate crime and discrimination. Anti-hate expert Barbara Perry provides an interesting example of this. On the one hand, she writes in a scholarly article: "For more than a quarter century, Canadians have clung to the mythology of multiculturalism. It has become the mantra of this nation to proclaim itself among the most diverse and inclusive countries among its peers" (2015, 1637). Under the influence of this ideology, "the rhetoric of inclusion" obscures "the reality of exclusion" (1642). But Perry also holds that "the rhetoric of multiculturalism still has some capacity to provide a foundation for critical discourse" (1637). When called upon by the media to comment on a 47 per cent increase in hate crimes in 2017, Perry did exactly that: "It's an assault on our core values of inclusion and equity" (qtd. in Grant 2018).

A delicate balancing act is involved here: to sustain the sense of the *aspirational* nature of our identity, to do our utmost to prevent it from masking the elements of reality that deny it, yet be able to invoke "our core values of inclusion and equity" as a critical resource. We will return to that challenge in the next chapter.

9.5 Conclusion

We have seen that in many invocations, multiculturalism does function as a psychic prop, and that it can mask ongoing injustice. But it can also be used to support calls for justice. This leads to two types of questions, which will receive more extensive treatment in the next chapter. First, concerning masks: how should the masking function shape our political and normative assessment of multiculturalism? While critics often seem to assume that this function is enough to damn multiculturalism, I will argue that such a view misunderstands the nature and ubiquity of ideology.

The second set of questions concerns national pride: what are we to make of all the statements praising multiculturalism, and praising Canada for having embraced it? Leaving aside the very problematic "over the line" comments analysed earlier, how should progressives view statements that express pride in the nation for its multiculturalism? Part of the answer to that question comes down to how we assess the very idea of national pride. Its dangers are well-known. But does it have any progressive potential?

Chapter Ten

Of Masks, Nations, and Nationalism

One cannot see the modern world as it is unless one recognizes the over whelming strength of patriotism, national loyalty. In certain circumstances it can break down, at certain levels of civilization it does not exist, but as a *positive* force there is nothing to set beside it. Christianity and international Socialism are as weak as straw in comparison with it.

George Orwell, "The Lion and the Unicorn" (1941)

During a webinar a few months into the pandemic, the moderator asked panellists to comment on how multiculturalism has acted to "obscure, recreate, and perhaps embed, systemic racism and white supremacy." They were all happy to oblige. The view that Canadian multiculturalism masks ongoing realities of racism and discrimination is perhaps the most durable progressive critique. Other charges, such as the claim that "song and dance" multiculturalism provides scraps of pseudo-recognition rather than true equality, have become less relevant with shifts in multiculturalism policy and funding over the decades.[1] But the salience of particular elements of multiculturalism policy can decline over time without affecting the policy's broader ideological impact.

I have touched on the masking question at various points in this book. In this chapter, I will take it as given that multiculturalism often masks ongoing racism and discrimination. But I will argue that this fact tells us surprisingly little about the stance progressives should take towards it, or about its potential as a critical resource.

To the extent that multiculturalism successfully masks reality, it can bolster national pride. Such pride has throughout history been used to support aggressive nationalism, military adventures, and much else. But I will argue that there are forms of national pride that do not require a refusal to acknowledge injustice and that progressives can welcome.

Thus, progressives need to recognize national pride not as something to be countered, shunned, and derided, but as yet another stake to fight over. That is, progressive forms must be nurtured to challenge the influence of more toxic ones and to create emotional support for the effort to build a more just society.

To avoid repeatedly inflicting upon the reader the cumbersome phrase "national pride/nationalism/patriotism," I will use "national pride" as an umbrella term that denotes both sentiments as well as the political commitments linked to them. The *Oxford English Dictionary* defines pride as "A sense of confidence, self-respect, and solidarity as felt or publicly expressed by members of a group" (as in gay or Black pride). Pride as used here thus includes elements such as affection and loyalty.

10.1 On Masks, and Ideology

Injustice and ideology: a universal relation. As a mosquito secretes venom, every form of injustice secretes an ideology to justify it. Let me restate this in less mystifying language. Recall a point mentioned earlier: while our beliefs often guide our actions, our actions and our social location in turn shape our beliefs. In particular, we perhaps unconsciously seek beliefs that will sustain our self-image and calm our conscience. When we hit on a belief that does the trick, we have good reason for clinging to it. Those convenient beliefs will naturally be sought first from those available in one's society.

All this regularly occurs at a purely individual level, for example, when one person has done wrong to another (Tavris and Aronson 2007). But the dynamic also operates at a broader level. *Every* system of domination, claimed Weber, "attempts to establish and to cultivate the belief in its legitimacy" (1978, 213). This *would* be true of a hypothetically just system, and *is* true of all existing forms of unjust domination. Drawing on one definition of ideology (Eagleton 1991, 30), I will call beliefs that justify social injustice "ideological."

Multiculturalism as a handy tool. And so, Canada being what it is, the image of our country as a multicultural, tolerant place will inevitably be seized on to mask the messy reality of colour-coded inequality, racist patterns of "carding" and police violence, and so on. Ideology working the way it does, this will be done even by people who *oppose* multiculturalism. I have previously cited dismissals of ongoing injustice from Neil Bissoondath, Ezra Levant, Ted Byfield, and others. One cannot plausibly argue in such cases that a belief in multiculturalism causes obliviousness to reality. Rather, multiculturalism is ready-to-hand as a tool of denial. There is evidence, in fact, that those who oppose multiculturalism are *more* prone to deny racism and discrimination. A 2015 study found that, among those who say they have a "very negative" view of multiculturalism policy, 69 per cent agree that "if there is discrimination against Muslims, it is mainly their fault." This drops to 27 per cent among those with a "very positive" view of multiculturalism (Jedwab 2015a). The corresponding results are 41 versus 18 per cent when the question concerns Jewish Canadians, and 29 versus 19 per cent for Black Canadians.

But multiculturalism is not the only available mask. Many Canadians share the meritocratic ideology that is influential throughout the world, simply because it is personally flattering for them, as well as ideologically useful, providing convenient "explanations" for the presence of wealth and poverty. And that reminds us of a crucial point: it is not only ethnoracial inequalities that require justification, but class ones as well. Some justifications of the latter are in fact quite close to those deployed around race. After citing Harry Chang's comment that "the political economic raison d'etre of racial categories lies in the iron-clad social validity that is possible if relations are objectified as the intrinsic quality of 'racial features,'" Adolph Reed adds: "This formulation applies equally to populations stigmatized as feebleminded, natural-born criminals, 'white trash,' poverty cultures, the underclass, crack babies, superpredators, and other narratives of ascriptive hierarchy" (2013, 51).[2] The view of the poor as "a being of another species" (Tocqueville 1986, vol. 1, 322), mentioned in chapter 6, persists today.

Recall Thobani's interesting observation, noted in chapter 9, that many have embraced multiculturalism because it offers them a sense of superiority over the "irremediably racist and uncouth" working class. This is one convenient mask of economic inequality. Many others are available. Another mask, which a multi-nation study by Kuppens and colleagues found to be widespread, is the belief that those with less education are mostly to blame for their situation (2018).

Other places, other masks. Multiculturalism shapes one specific form of denial of racism in Canada. Elsewhere, denial requires other resources. Hochschild's *Strangers in Their Own Land* (2018) uncovered a prevalent assumption among the Louisiana Tea Party supporters she studied, that Blacks have benefited from unjust privileges granted by the federal government. So if they are still poor, that is mostly through their own fault. During the first wave of "political correctness" controversies, William Greider drily commented that the foreigner who relied only on media to understand America would conclude that a major problem was "Blacks and their privileged position in the American system" (1994, 180).

Racism as mask. When we analyse masks in relation to the injustice/ideology relationship, an intriguing insight emerges: racism is not just masked, *it masks*. Go back through history: whenever we find expressions of race-thought – distinctions between Greeks and barbarians, between civilization and savagery, and so on – these are almost always offered when some form of domination was in need of justification. So was the race-thinking a cause or a consequence of the state of domination? Or was it a bit of both? Both, certainly, if we take into account "permissive causes."[3]

Two radical Black theorists have commented on racism's masking function. In *Black Marxism*, Cedric J. Robinson argues that "in the seventeenth and eighteenth centuries ... Race became largely the rationalization for the domination, exploitation, and/or extermination of non-'Europeans' (including Slavs and Jews)" (rpt. 2020, 27). Similarly, Eric Williams claims in *Capitalism and Slavery* that "slavery was not born of racism: racism was the consequence of slavery" (rpt. 1964, 7).[4]

This certainly does not mean that racism is *only* a mask. Even if it emerges in particular contexts as an ideological justification for domination, it can become embedded in a wide range of institutions and practices, beyond those that gave rise to it. Hence the struggle against racism must proceed on several fronts: racism must be attacked directly, *along with* the range of social conditions that it legitimates and sustains and that sustain it in turn.

So to say that something is a mask does not mean it is *only* a mask. This is true of racism. And it is true of multiculturalism: were it only a mask, progressives would be bound to do our best to eradicate it. But it is not.

But there is a great danger for multiculturalism: the more often it performs a masking function, the less it may be able to do anything else. This is true of any social ideal, which can be fatally *bent*. An important example is patriotism, to which we will turn in a moment. Nussbaum, in this vein, wrote that "the Vietnam War made a whole generation of Americans shrink from appeals to patriotic emotion" (2013, 381).

This is another reason for heeding the progressive critics: doing so may help prevent multiculturalism from *becoming* what the most pessimistic among them insist it already *is*.

10.2 Of Nations and National Pride

To mask injustice is to be complicit with it. But while such masking can prop up national pride, not all such pride requires denial. I will argue that the normative and political effects of national pride – and of multiculturalism as a support of it – depend on its specific form. (Keep in mind that "pride" here refers to more than a sentiment: it also embraces political commitments.)

A post-national world? A prior question is whether one believes that nations can play some essential progressive role, or at least whether we are, in any case, stuck with them.[5] I'll begin with the second question. In a 2015 article, Augie Fleras argued that nations are becoming irrelevant: "technology transforms borders into paper-thin membranes," so that we now live in "a globalizing and postnational world of transmigration and hyperdiversity" (2015, 317). Fleras draws from this the conclusion that multiculturalism is now obsolete and that we need a "post multicultural governance model" (313).

As with many writings on "post-" this or that, the analysis suffers from a fatal one-sidedness. Are borders now "paper-thin membranes"? Yes and no. *Ideas*, certainly, now travel the world with disconcerting speed. Gilles Kepel notes the challenge to French authorities posed by the shift of radical preaching from particular mosques to the internet (2015). The "Three Percenters," who have penetrated the Canadian armed forces (Taylor 2020) and have been labelled one of Canada's most dangerous right-wing extremist groups, are an American import (Hutter 2018). And a journalist covering an anti-mask protest in Canada's distinct society noted that "the most popular symbols at the protest – be it on t-shirts, placards or flags – belonged to QAnon, a far-right conspiracy theory started in the United States that claims a satanic, pedophile cabal secretly controls the U.S. government" (Montpetit and MacFarlane 2020).

Economic globalization also appears to have erased borders. As noted in chapter 3, the global mobility of capital is now a major constraint on the ability of states to tame capitalism. Remittances play a major role in the economies of many nations. Economic crises – like pandemics – are rapidly transmitted across borders.

And yet ... we continue to live in a world of sovereign nations. Authoritative policies and laws are formulated exclusively within nations, or through multinational agreements or bodies authorized by sovereign national states. Despite economic globalization, the wealth gaps between different national spaces remain enormous. The desire of people to transfer from one space to another remains constrained by migration controls.

It is also important to recall David Harvey's observation that even in an age of globalization, spatially fixed capital such as real estate, natural resources, and so on are core components of national economies (1982, 420). In the same way, global population flows should not obscure the fact that the great majority of the world's people will never migrate from the nation of their birth: "The intersections of rich and poor world are relatively slight, in terms of proportions of populations" (Bhattacharyya 2018, 20).

So, reports of the nation's demise are greatly exaggerated. But should we celebrate this fact, or lament it? The question is whether the nation remains essential to meet important human needs, if not perhaps forever then at least for the foreseeable future. On this, I would agree with Martha Nussbaum that the nation has "pivotal importance in setting life conditions for all on a basis of equal respect, and [is] the largest unit we know until now that is decently accountable to people's voices and capable of expressing their desire to give themselves laws of their own choosing" (2013, 17).

We need, first, to recognize that the nation is the broadest current community within which people actually have legally binding obligations to one another, often reinforced by emotional ties. As Hannah Arendt commented on the fate of people made stateless, the Rights of Man "had been defined as 'inalienable' because they were supposed to be independent of all governments; but it turned out that the moment human beings lacked their own government and had to fall back upon their minimum rights, no authority was left to protect them and no institution was willing to guarantee them" (1958b, 292).

As well, humanity is living a great paradox today: we confront a number of global problems, solutions to which will only come about through actions initiated at the national level. Because enforcement mechanisms are lacking, international agreements on climate change have been ineffective, perhaps worse than useless. Indeed, such agreements have served as masks, offering "the comfortable illusion that serious progress is being made" (Gardiner 2011, 140). A serious alternative is the "climate club" proposal, in which a core group of nations agree to binding emissions targets, and to sanctions to enforce those, and then create incentives for others to join. Because "countries who are outside the club – and do not share in the burden of emissions reductions – are penalized," for example, through higher tariffs, national interests can be aligned with climate action (Nordhaus 2015).[6] Thomas Piketty is promoting an analogous proposal as a way to begin to tame capitalism and inequality within the European Union and to counteract the EU's neoliberal commitments (2019, 1033ff).

Critics who are allergic to ideas such as these, which accept the reality of sovereign states as a binding constraint, and who wish to transcend the narrow framework of the nation and arrive at a global community, must recognize that to date, the principal international bodies that have *effectively* constrained national sovereignty have done so in the name of neoliberal "fair competition." The critics thus need to specify the political forces that might plausibly emerge to constrain sovereignty for more progressive ends. In my view, it is almost certain that, if capitalism is to be tamed, the resistance to it must work *through* national institutions, even as that resistance strives to coordinate action internationally.

On citizenship and self-determination. It would thus seem to follow that "the nation has a valuable role to play, as the largest unit we know so far that is sufficiently accountable to people and expressive of their voices" (Nussbaum 2013, 212). But that immediately raises a problem, as the nation is *at best* only truly accountable to those within its borders: citizens, first, and (to a greater or lesser degree) other residents. Nations restrict entry into the national space, and in our current world, such restrictions are one mechanism sustaining wildly unequal standards of living. Given how profoundly this state of affairs violates human equality, it is safe to say that a world whose core rules had been designed behind a "veil of ignorance" would not look like ours. What practical conclusions flow from this, however, is unclear.

Thobani recognizes this problem but not the dilemma with which it confronts us. Faced with Seyla Benhabib's comment that "I am made uncomfortable by the imposition of a global redistributive principle to create economic justice among peoples, unless and until the compatibility of such a principle with democratic self-governance is examined" (2004, 105), Thobani asks: "Whose self-governance, one might well ask? That of the powerful communities of enfranchised citizens? Or that of their disenfranchised and powerless Others?" (2007, 70). Since, by definition, if one is engaging in self-governance, one is no longer "disenfranchised and powerless," Thobani would seem to be advocating that the undefined "Others" join the community of the enfranchised. But she goes on to criticize Benhabib for her failure to "support demands that the rights of the dispossessed supersede those of the possessors" (71). So that, presumably, is her alternative to current global injustice. *How* such a power reversal might come about, Thobani does not say. As does Mackey (see chapter 8), Thobani casually dismisses the great progressive value of democratic self-governance as an obstacle to justice. But for progressives, the challenge today is to imagine paths that might strengthen such self-governance, and also to persuade democratic communities to commit to international and environmental justice. To say that is not to offer a solution, but merely to name a *practical constraint* on possible solutions.[7] To deal with the constraints that democracy places on the pursuit of justice is indeed a vexing challenge for anyone who takes that pursuit seriously. Benhabib, to her credit, grapples with this. Thobani, and some of the other progressive critics, do not.

National pride. As the nation continues to have an essential role to play, progressives need to think about the question of national pride. But to do so drags us into uncomfortable territory: the word "nationalism" is associated for many of us with negative images, from goose-stepping troops to shrieking fascistoid Trumpistas. The "imagined communities" we call nations, noted Benedict Anderson, can "generate such colossal sacrifices" (1991, 7). Many have come to bitterly regret those sacrifices.[8]

Some try to divide light and shadow through a terminological distinction:

> Sometimes people confuse nationalism with patriotism. There's nothing wrong and all kinds of things right with loving the place where you live and the people you live with and wanting that place and those people to thrive, so it's easy to confuse nationalism and patriotism, especially because they once meant more or less the same thing ... Patriotism is animated by love, nationalism by hatred. To confuse the one for the other is to pretend that hate is love and fear is courage. (Lepore 2019, 12).

The *Oxford English dictionary* offers less tendentious definitions of the two terms: patriotism is "The quality of being patriotic; love of or devotion to one's country," whereas nationalism is "Advocacy of or support for the interests of one's own nation, esp. to the exclusion or detriment of the interests of other nations. Also: advocacy of or support for national independence or self-determination" (2000).

For our purposes, the patriotism/nationalism distinction is not very helpful, because the difference between progressive and reactionary forms of national pride cuts across the line between the two. So I will revert to earlier usage, when "the two appear to have been more or less interchangeable" (ibid.), using, as noted earlier, "national pride" to designate both political commitments and feelings of pride in and attachment to one's country.

Lepore, who identifies nationalism with hatred, writes from America, where the exaltation of the nation *against* other nations has inflicted endless calamities upon humanity. Elsewhere, things look different. A Sandinista leader once commented that "for us, nationalism is a shield, not a knife." A shield from what? In the case of a tiny Central American nation, the answer is obvious. Indeed, the name of his movement was not an accident: the Sandinistas formed a front for "National Liberation." Such movements, as Eric Hobsbawm notes, "were the main agents for the political emancipation of most of the globe" in the twentieth century (1992, 169).

Although Canada is much larger and wealthier than Nicaragua, the view of nationalism as a shield is relevant here and always has been. Observers often deride "smug Canadians" and their condescension towards Americans, yet this may have supported a spirit of independence and resistance to attempts to import some of the loonier ideas hatched by the American right – to which some Canadian politicians today are very attracted. Smugness, certainly, also has its dangers, to which we'll return, below.

So nationalism can serve as a shield. But is it good for anything else? Benedict Anderson, although well aware of the dangers of nationalism, writes: "In an age when it is so common for progressive, cosmopolitan intellectuals ... to insist on the near-pathological character of nationalism, its roots in fear and hatred of the Other, and its affinities with racism, it is useful to remind ourselves that nations inspire love, and often profoundly self-sacrificing love" (1991, 141). But there is a tension between competing goals. We need, argues Martha Nussbaum, "to engender and sustain strong commitment to worthy projects that require effort and sacrifice." But we also need, she adds, "to keep at bay forces that lurk in all societies and, ultimately, in all of us: tendencies to protect the fragile self by denigrating and subordinating others" (2013, 3). And that is a key challenge: to develop a spirit of solidarity that is free of a narrow understanding of "we," a spirit that has banished what R.L. Gabrielle Nishiguchi calls "our image of the ideal Canadian face" (1997, 112).[9] "We, the people," as Seyla Benhabib puts it, "is a tension-riven formula" (2004, 82).

One might fear that a strong sense of national identification will block attachment to the global human community. Certainly, when broader affiliations *already* exist, nationalism can harm them. This was the case with the sense of community held by European working-class movements prior to the First World War, which evaporated once war was declared. But if a sense of identification with global humanity is not already widespread, there is no reason to believe that a decline in nationalism will of itself foster it. We need to be wary of what Charles Taylor terms "subtraction stories," which hold that, if people can only free themselves of X, then Y will *naturally* emerge without "constructive effort" (2007, 169). A rather different consequence, as Tocqueville suggested, is that people "retreat into a narrow and unenlightened egoism" (1986, vol. 1, 354). Thus, the real alternative to some widespread attachment to the nation is not necessarily a liberated or cosmopolitan citizenry: it may well be an atomized one, shattered and "available" for immersion in a neoliberal life. A dramatic illustration of this is the fact that those Canadians who have so angrily rejected calls to be in solidarity with their fellow citizens by taking proper safety precautions during the pandemic have clearly not done so in the name of global solidarity.

The need for discernment. Foucault notes Plutarch's warning that "diseases of the soul" can be mistaken for virtues. The possibility of confusion arises from close similarities between virtues and vices: "anger and courage ... cowardice and prudence" (1984, 74). One thus needs a well-developed vocabulary to capture just what is virtuous about particular virtues, or vicious about particular vices, as well as a keen "eye" to discern whether a particular phenomenon is virtue or vice. So it is with national pride, which can take both progressive and toxic forms. These are not firmly isolated from each other: it is easy to imagine a gradual transition in either direction, and the contrasting forms may not always be easily distinguished. Progressives thus need careful discernment to untangle the potential implications of various types of appeals to national pride.[10]

One aid in this might be to distinguish *dimensions* of differentiation between progressive and regressive appeals, not to arrive at simple "this type good, that type bad" distinctions, but to identify different questions to ask of nationalist appeals, as a basis for discernment. We might ask, among other things:

- Pride *in what*?

The Harper government went to great lengths to focus Canadian pride on a history of military achievements. A typical instance was the new citizenship guide's exaltation of a First World War battle: "The Canadian Corps captured Vimy Ridge in April 1917, with 10,000 killed or wounded, securing the Canadians' reputation for valour as the 'shock troops of the British Empire.' One Canadian officer said: 'It was Canada from the Atlantic to the Pacific on parade ... In those few minutes I witnessed the birth of a nation'" (CIC 2009, 21). This celebration of Canada as a "warrior nation" (Ryan 2010a, 29) sought to centre national pride on what, exactly? On a hierarchical enterprise, based on obedience, on sacrifice in the name of objectives one may not share or understand: on "shock troops," as the citizenship guide bluntly put it.[11]

A very different appeal to national pride focuses on what Canadians have accomplished *together*. Here's an example from Pat Bird's *Of Dust and Time and Dreams and Agonies: A Short History of Canadian People*:

> Nor were a few prominent Canadians responsible for the development of Canadian society. It was the labour and effort of thousands and thousands of very ordinary Canadians that created the wealth and institutions of this country. The clearing of land, the planting of crops, the development of

technology, transportation and communication networks, the production of goods and services: all these were the achievement of generations of Canadian men and women. One cannot read Canadian history without getting a sense of the tremendous contribution earlier generations of Canadians have made. Those accomplishments deserve to be remembered and celebrated. (Bird 1975, 155)

One may find fault with any such appeal, but the basic line of contrast with a militaristic and hierarchical appeal is clear. Much of the Bird quote focuses on material development as a shared achievement. But social achievements can also be celebrated. A 2014 Association for Canadian Studies poll asked "What keeps Canada united?" The Charter of Rights and Freedoms and health care topped the list of answers (Jedwab 2014). These achievements need to be "recovered" as shared accomplishments, not as "boons" graciously bestowed from above.[12]

- Vertical or horizontal appeal?

Closely related to the previous distinction is one between vertical and horizontal visions of national pride. Nussbaum comments that in Rousseau's vision of patriotic love, "the person-to-person dimension is missing, since the approved sentiments of communal bonding do not lead to or rest upon any sentiments directed at individuals, even sentiments of concern and respect." Rousseau's "civic love, like feudal love, is obedient, hierarchical" (2013, 45). But we need "a sense of a common fate, and a friendship that draws the advantaged and less advantaged into a single group, with a common task before it" (345). This helps clarify why Lepore's patriotism versus nationalism contrast is not helpful for progressive purposes. Even in the absence of the "hatred" she associates with nationalism, efforts to build loyalty and affection to the abstract nation may do nothing to build "civic solidarity" (Habermas 2006, 13), or what I have termed "citizen identification," our sense of being bound to – and responsible for – one another (Ryan 2010b, 21).

- Pride *and* what?

A further distinguishing question is whether the appeal to national pride seems to discourage critical reflection and comment, or welcome, even encourage it. Is the pride being evoked enriched by an awareness of our society's past failings and its ongoing injustice? Or is it fearful of that awareness? Is the pride being sought *prickly*, or *textured*?[13] The just-cited *Of Dust and Time* book is explicitly framed as an attempt to foster the latter type: "if you feel proud, as I do, to belong to this country and proud of its people, and encouraged to try and make our present society a different and better one, after reading this book, it will have served its purpose" (Bird 1975, 4).

Jack Granatstein's *Who Killed Canadian History?*, in contrast, strives for something more prickly. He laments that students are being taught the history of "the grievers among us" rather than "that of the Canadian nation and people" (1998, xiii). The prickliness emerges from the assumption that "the nation is fragile indeed, and one reason for this lamentable state of affairs might be the lack of a history that binds Canadians together" (xvii). This binding history, it appears, is incompatible with students being taught "that Canada was anti-Semitic and turned away the Jews of Europe fleeing Hitler. That blacks have been persecuted in Canada" (94).

Nussbaum argues that those who promote what I am calling prickly pride "fear that presenting the nation as it is will undercut love. But really, what they are saying is that the human heart can't stand reality, that lovers can't stand the real bodies of those they love, that parents can't embrace children who do not live up to an idealized picture of achievement" (2013, 255). They endorse, one might say, the view that:

> human kind
> Cannot bear very much reality. (Eliot 1963, 190)

While rejecting attempts to build a prickly pride that ignores the crimes our society has committed in the past, and today's injustices, we still need to recognize that a society in which citizens take no pride in their country and its past is not healthy. I suggested in chapter 6 that the long-term effect on progressive movements of concessions granted in response to popular pressure depends on whether those are remembered as a *victory*, a memory that can spur a group to ongoing efforts. This logic can hold at a national level. Just as an appreciation of natural beauty is a vital prerequisite for environmental defence (McCarthy 2015), a sense that we have accomplished something together in history would seem to be an important basis for a collective willingness to address injustice today.

- Smug or aspirational pride?

Clearly, though, there is a fine line between a historical pride that helps the struggle for justice to be sustained and deepened, and smugness. And there is also the danger of believing that serious injustice is *only* historical in Canada, part of a Canada that we have thankfully left behind. So a further question to ask is whether appeals to national pride embody a call to action or merely offer psychic jollies. For Martha Nussbaum, the object of affection and pride should be "an aspiring yet imperfect society" (2013, 6). She argues that the speeches of Abraham Lincoln and Martin Luther King often evoked that, expressing "a profound love of America and a pride in her highest ideals" yet "showing that America has failed to live up to her ideals" (239). She also offers a striking quote from a speech given by Nehru as India gained independence: "The service of India means, the service of the millions who suffer. It means the ending of poverty and ignorance and disease and inequality of opportunity" (qtd. in Nussbaum 2013, 247).

Comparisons with the US are an unending source of Canadian smugness, as if it is good enough to do better than a country that trails the rest of the developed world in a wide range of social indicators. A comment from British journalist Gary Younge will sound familiar to Canadian anti-racism activists: "In my experience, drawing connections, continuities, and contrasts between the racisms on either side of the Atlantic invites something between rebuke and confusion from many white European liberals. Few will deny the existence of racism in their own countries but they insist on trying to force an admission that it 'is better here than there' – as though we should be happy with the racism we have" (2020).

National pride, and the rest of the world. A final set of questions concerns the relation of national-pride appeals to the broader world. At least three issues may be distinguished here.

- Hostility towards, fear of, or solidarity with, those beyond our borders?

We know that nationalist appeals often emphasize the dangers beyond our borders, the malevolence of some real or imagined foe, and so on. Such nationalism can justify militarism and a narrow understanding of the national interest. But appeals to national pride can be joined to a concern for global justice and to recognition that we are members of a shared humanity, confronting a common future.

- Obsession with what *distinguishes* us?

A friend responded to the previously cited Pat Bird passage that urges us to take pride in "the labour and effort of thousands and thousands of very ordinary Canadians" (1975, 155) with the comment: "but people everywhere can say something like that." They can. And they should. Implicit in Bird's argument is the view that pride need not focus on things that supposedly distinguish us from others.

The stakes here may be clarified by way of analogy. There is a long-standing belief that the dignity of humans rests on what distinguishes us from "mere brutes." This has generated an endless series of anxious claims that *only we* can do this or that, claims often reflecting little more than human ignorance, the fact that we are not "smart enough to know how smart animals are," as Waal puts it (2016). It has led as well to deprecation of our "merely" animal functions, of our bodies, and of those alleged to be deficient in the rationality thought to constitute human dignity.

One cannot say that humanity has done itself any favours in all this. Nor is an obsession with what is supposedly distinctive a good basis for national pride. Keeping in mind that the broad meaning of pride being used here includes affection and loyalty, it should be clear that those sentiments should above all focus on the aspects of our shared reality that are essential for our happiness and well-being, whether or not they are particularly distinctive. We should take pride, for example, in our democratic freedoms, even if there is nothing "uniquely Canadian" about them. We need pride in such things, especially because they need defending and their loss would impoverish us.

- Dependence on view of others?

In the previous chapter, I noted that various "over the line" celebrations of Canadian multiculturalism made claims about how the rest of the world sees us. But must national pride really rest on the belief that "Canada stands as an aspirational city on the hill amongst liberal democracies" (Commons, 7 February 2017)? Herder's advice is useful here: "Every nation must learn to feel that it becomes great, beautiful, noble, rich, well ordered, active, and happy, not in the eyes of others, not in the mouth of posterity, but only in itself, in its own self" (rpt. 2002, 406).[14]

And multiculturalism? I have suggested various dimensions of differentiation with which we can evaluate appeals to national pride. In light of those, how do expressions of pride that invoke multiculturalism fare? Reasonably well, I think, with an important exception: the "over the line" appeals.[15] As just noted, these often manifest a dependence on the supposed views of the rest of the world. They also promote smugness and thus make it harder to acknowledge ongoing injustice.

Once we accept, however, the need for national pride, many invocations of multiculturalism seem progressive. Few invocations focus on the government's role in promoting multiculturalism: they are more likely to celebrate it as an achievement of Canadians in general. Further, they encourage pride in relations *among* Canadians, rather than being centred on the abstract nation, the flag, and so on. Many appeals make room for recognition of historical injustice and acknowledge ongoing challenges.

10.3 Concluding Thoughts

This chapter has considered two closely related issues: how we should assess multiculturalism in light of its capacity to mask injustice, and, more generally, the political and normative qualities of appeals to national pride. On the first, I urged the need for realism concerning ideology, and recognition of its ubiquitous nature. The call to abandon illusions, wrote a young Karl Marx, is a call to "abandon a condition which requires illusions" (rpt. 1963, 44). So long as injustice exists, so will justifications of it. Slay one, and another will soon emerge to replace it. But as we saw, to mask is not to *be* a mere mask. Racism itself, as various authors have argued, can function as a mask. It is, however, much more solid than mere ideological illusion. So Marx's claim concerning illusions should not lead one to conclude that if we, say, abolish capitalism, racism will automatically wither away in consequence.

For many progressives, the chapter's arguments concerning national pride will be harder to accept. I argued that the nation is crucial for meeting many essential human needs and will continue to be so for the foreseeable future. I also suggested that a progressive form of national pride is an important resource for action in pursuit of a just society.

I know this can be hard to accept, because I found it very hard to write. It goes against the grain, so the grain must be analysed. One source of discomfort is the desire to avoid the boosterism that characterizes so much official discourse today. More importantly, it is hard to take pride in a country whose wealth was and is supported by colonial dispossession. Canada also belongs to the First World and, as such, is implicated in unjust economic structures, upon which our standard of living depends.

These sources of resistance to national pride are legitimate. But so too are the arguments for the progressive importance of such pride. This is why, as I noted earlier, discernment is vital, along with the development of criteria that help us distinguish the political implications of different appeals to national pride.

Chapter Eleven

Conclusion

Talk of heroic downfall in view of an inevitable defeat is actually very unheroic, as it does not to look into the future. The responsible question is not how I will heroically get out of the affair, but how a future generation should continue to live.

Dietrich Bonhoeffer, *Widerstand und Ergebung*

I set out in this work to develop not one but three themes. The first is the obvious one: issues arising from progressive critiques of Canadian multiculturalism. A second concerns the nature of society and the practice of social science. The final theme concerns what I believe are necessary qualities of progressive thought and writing. In this conclusion, I will comment on the last two themes, before ending with brief thoughts on multiculturalism.

11.1 Society and Our Attempts to Understand It

I wish to say a bit more about two key challenges for understanding reality: the relation between individuals and structures, and the role of concepts, which organize reality ... and uncover, hide, and distort it.

Analysis must "pass through" individuals. People act. Institutions and structures act *through* people. Social structures and practices are reproduced by the acts of individuals, who are "always already" shaped by their various social milieux. Thus, for statements concerning the actions of institutions, social structures, and collective entities, it should be possible to "translate" the claim into one concerning human agents, endowed with plausible powers, and acting from plausible motives. This, I am claiming, is not a personal "preference" for a particular *paradigm*, but a condition of intelligibility for all statements about society.

If one's claims cannot be translated so as to make visible the actions of plausible human agents, one is not analysing, but mystifying.

To see that this condition of intelligibility is capacious, able to accommodate a wide variety of approaches and outlooks, consider Karl Polanyi's influential claim concerning the nineteenth-century "countermovement" that resisted the development of market society: "Society protected itself against the perils inherent in a self-regulating market system – this was the one comprehensive feature in the history of the age" (1957, 76).

What might it mean for a *society* to protect itself? We might reasonably view this as actions by some individuals that meet certain conditions:

- The actors believe that they're pursuing the good of society.
- They have given some thought about what society as an ongoing concern needs over the medium and long term, and they have discussed that question with others.
- Their view on this question is not *merely* a rationalization of their class or other partial interests.
- They advance claims that such and such is in the interests of society, and there are many other individuals, in a wide variety of social locations, who accept the claim; these others repeat it, work it into their own discourse and analysis, and so on.
- Over time, the claim comes to be seen as self-evident within an influential portion of the population, and guides major policy choices.

Clearly, there's much room for delusion, deception, and self-deception here. Nevertheless, there are times – such as today – when some threats to society's long-term well-being are so manifest that those who confront those threats may reasonably be understood to be embodying the actions of society. Thus, I believe that Polanyi's countermovement claim can pass the "translation" test.

Concepts should be tools, not sirens, and not blinkers. Even before a child learns to speak, they are organizing their impressions of the world into a set of "well circumscribed objects" (Schutz 1970, 72). Soon, the child learns language and begins to name that world of objects. (When all goes well, the child learns the word "love" quite early, and the practice of naming is extended into the world of feelings and abstract realities.) "By this one single trick in which it surpasses the animal," notes Michael Polanyi, "the child acquires the capacity for sustained thought and enters on the whole cultural heritage of its ancestors" (1962, 69).

With that same trick, however, comes "the shadow cast by language upon truth" (Auden 2007, 306). The very words that connect us to reality serve to hide parts of it: "The names by which we designate things always reflect a concept held by our understanding, foreign to our true impressions, which forces us to eliminate from those impressions everything unrelated to that concept" (Proust 1988b, 399). The social scientist in particular, thinking and writing about complex phenomena, will always struggle to keep concepts in their place as tools for understanding and talking about reality, rather than sirens that draw the thinker into an obsessive focus on sharpening an ax that never gets used, or blinkers that hide the messy reality "out there" and hide the very fact that it is hidden.

Four key concepts were the focus of chapter 2. I stressed in particular the importance and difficulty of keeping in contact with reality when discussing collective actors. We also examined the normative and empirical confusion around the idea of "culture." Writing on multiculturalism often seems to be working with an understanding of culture more appropriate for an isolated pre-industrial island community, entirely cut off from the rest of the world. This is the case for almost all the conservative critics, who take aim at multiculturalism's supposed tendency to lock minority groups in bunkers. Unfortunately, many progressive critics suffer from the same confusion. Recall, for example, various claims quoted in the chapter 4 critique of "mysterious power" discourse, such as the assertion that multiculturalism "shackles people around their ethnicity and ancestry" (Fleras 2015, 320), as if such a thing were possible in a complex modern society.

One implication of the messy complexity of the realities covered by these key concepts is that we must be very careful about "backward inferences." The leap from observed state actions to the "true" objectives of decision-makers; from a person's actions to their culture; from any social phenomenon to a particular policy and its objectives: these are all risky, and often misleading.

The challenge of concepts was foregrounded again in chapter 8's discussion of "gross concepts." I noted that people often take a stand for or against tolerance, diversity, or "difference." But this cannot be done responsibly without further detail: tolerance *of what*, for example, must be specified.

One gross concept not discussed in the book, but that has had a particularly confusing impact on discussions of multiculturalism, is "recognition." A remarkable number of writers describe multiculturalism as a "politics of recognition," but without explaining just what they understand by that. As with other gross concepts, many questions might be asked: recognition *of what*? Recognition expressed *in what way*? Recognition as an *alternative* to redistribution (Fraser 1995), or as a *motive* and *support* for it?

The lesson here is a difficult one: the fact that a term seems familiar to us does not entail that it is *meaningful*. In the presence of grand abstract concepts, we need to ask: what *concretely* does this term mean to me? What might it mean to the author? Can I answer that without more information? If not, we are probably in the presence of a gross concept. The lesson is hard to apply, because this is not how we usually read. We read – as we do everything else – as sense-making creatures, and when a text is lacking in meaning, we will often supply it ... if we can: "A person who is trying to understand a text is always projecting. He projects a meaning for the text as a whole as soon as some initial meaning emerges in the text" (Gadamer 1989, 267).

So clarity in discussions of multiculturalism – and of many other social issues – may require that we "recule pour mieux sauter": that we "back up" from the level of smooth, fast, confident readers, to that of stumbling, puzzled ones, in order to be able to "jump" to the level of truly critical readers, able to stay grounded in our reality while negotiating complex analyses of it.

11.2 On Progressive Thought and Writing

"*On the other hand.*" This phrase captures the approach I have emphasized throughout this work. From the outset, you should have often felt the argument pull first in one direction, and then in a somewhat opposed one.[1] This is done in the hope that we may thereby arrive at a richer understanding of reality. Some specific examples:

Yes, power often flows downwards through the state, and yes, the state holds a lot of cards in dealing with civil society. *On the other hand*, power relations can be reversed, for better (as when equality-seeking groups push a policy further than foreseen by state elites), or for worse (as when police forces exercise autonomy from control).

Yes, the state is a capitalist state. *On the other hand*, it is also a democratic one. Yes, the state is made up of individuals. *On the other hand*, these are socialized individuals, gathered in specific organizations that shape their interests and their outlook.

Yes, we are all subject to cultural influences. *On the other hand*, we do not "belong" to a single culture. We are influenced by many cultures, which gives us some autonomy from any particular one.

Yes, national pride can be invoked to support oppressive projects. *On the other hand*, it can also be an essential resource for progressive struggles.

Yes, multiculturalism can mask injustice. *On the other hand*, it can also support calls for greater justice. It can hinder challenges to existing structures. *On the other hand*, it can provide resources for such challenges.

The last points highlight the importance of *discernment*, discussed in chapter 10. Reality does not present itself to progressives neatly divided into Good and Bad, Light and Shadow. The lines between progressive and regressive forms of national pride, or between just and unjust forms of tolerance and intolerance, are subtle and not entirely stable. The point that Foucault drew from Plutarch – that virtue and vice are not easily distinguished – applies as much to social realities as it does to the individual spirit. This is certainly true of multiculturalism, and of many other policies.

Some maxims for progressive thought. In his *Critique of Judgment*, Kant articulated three "maxims of common human understanding": "(1) to think for oneself; (2) to think from the standpoint of everyone else; (3) always to think consistently" (rpt. 2007, 124). The need for careful discernment might analogously be termed a maxim for *progressive* thought and writing. Let us consider other maxims closely related to that one. But note, first, that I am not *dictating* these: I have neither the inclination nor the power to do so. I am simply claiming that these maxims represent standards for useful progressive work, a claim that anyone is free to challenge. Second, these are not maxims that I myself find particularly easy to follow. Finally, to the reader who might consider some of what follows too obvious, I would answer that there is great value in recalling to mind that which is obvious, yet easily forgotten in practice. Everyone understands that physical skills develop through repetition, and the same is true for intellectual skills (Ryan 2022, 108).

AVOID THOUGHTLESSNESS. I have suggested that some positions advanced by progressive critics reflect thoughtlessness. One guard against this is to imagine one's judgments being acted upon, and think through the implications of that. "Unconditional hospitality"? How would that play out? Limitless tolerance? Same question. Multiculturalism is "white supremacy"? Think through the possible consequences of its abolition. To be precise: try to imagine consequences, but don't *fantasize* about them. Unless there are solid reasons for believing that a strong and radical progressive political movement is well-positioned to take advantage of worsening conditions, to assume that a sharpening of oppression – or the ripping away of the "mask" of multiculturalism – would spark an effective revolutionary response, is to fantasize. Which is fun ... but not harmless fun.

REPEATEDLY ASK "WHAT IS TO BE DONE?" It might seem obvious that progressives should regularly be thinking about the short- and long-term alternatives towards we should be working. But it is easy to forget the importance of this question when one is focused on critiquing social conditions or dominant patterns of thought. It is also easy to forget the need to accompany critical thought – focused on what can and must be changed – with appreciative thought, to identify what must be defended and sustained.

AVOID MYSTERY WRITING. There are various reasons for this. One is that the previous maxims depend on this one: they all require reasonably precise thought, but mystery writing prevents that from developing. Further, writing that wallows in mysterious power and effects is very hard to link to political action, as neither specific targets of such action nor points of leverage for change can be identified by such writing. Finally, steering clear of mystery helps open one's writing to critique by others. This in turn may facilitate further "translation" for other purposes, so as to reach broader audiences.[2]

LEARN FROM THE OTHER SIDE. Languishing in prison under Mussolini, Antonio Gramsci was acutely aware that fascists had succeeded where socialists had failed. This made him willing to take lessons from his enemies. To confront the challenge of constructing hegemony, for example, he paid careful attention to the relationship of the Catholic Church of his time to the broad masses of Italian people (e.g. 1971, 328). One area in which progressives should learn from their opponents today concerns "interpellation." The architects of the rise of neoliberalism recognized that personal identity can have multiple and contradictory dimensions. These offer an important lever for political appeals and change. As we saw in chapter 3, the American right addressed (interpellated) the white working class as god-fearing patriots, in order to gain support for a political project that would gravely hurt the economic interests of that class.

While Gramsci learned from the Italian church, however, he was certainly not willing to imitate it in all respects (1971, 332, 340). So "learning from the other side" does not mean that progressives should learn to manipulate others as well as the right does. Rather, we must recognize how particular dimensions of some actors' identities can create an opening for progressive appeals. Chapter 2 offered an example: the historical role played by officials doing "one's damned duty" (Weber 1958, 145). That is, injustice can be challenged by individuals who believe that their official position – as factory inspector, in Marx's time, as government auditor, human rights investigator, judge, or the like, in ours – imposes ethical responsibilities on them, as well as specific forms of concern for the social good.

KEEP CAPITALISM IN MIND. Max Weber famously argued that to "fight its way to supremacy against a whole world of hostile forces" (2003, 56), early capitalism needed support from a "Protestant ethic." But he also argued that once well-established, capitalism "no longer needs the support of any religious forces" (72), because "the capitalist economy of the present day is an immense cosmos into which the individual is born, and which presents itself to him, at least as an individual, as an unalterable order of things in which he must live. It forces the individual, in so far as he is involved in the system of market relationships, to conform to capitalistic rules of action" (54). We must never lose sight of that "cosmos." Whenever we do, we will misunderstand whatever phenomenon we are examining.

This does not mean that capitalism is "at the root" of everything else, nor does it mean that we can focus all our attention on countering it and let other problems look after themselves. But to ask, for example, how the emergence of multicultural policy was influenced by the capitalist nature of the Canadian state yields important insights, as I argued in chapter 6. Further, inquiring into the complex relations between capitalism and ongoing racism can help us avoid the idealist error of viewing racism as *only* a matter of discriminatory attitudes, or attributing it to an abstract and ahistorical "whiteness."[3]

Keeping capitalism in mind should also lead us to keep the climate emergency in mind. As we reflect on a path to a more just society, we must always remember that any such path will have to be found in a context of extreme challenge. To keep capitalism in mind, finally, is to remember the enormous range of people who suffer injustice in our society and world, as well as the wide variety of mechanisms that impose suffering. This has important implications for the political landscape. I noted at the end of chapter 2 that a key challenge for progressives today is to push for justice while trying to minimize the danger of a xenophobic authoritarian backlash. Joining anti-racism work with promotion of a comprehensive economic equality agenda, and with those pursuing that agenda, or at the very least being sensitive to those parallel struggles, might help. Many components of such an agenda are obvious: greater public investment in early childhood education, a more adequate minimum wage, strengthened labour laws, especially for part-time and precarious workers, a union-friendly legal framework, expansion of mental health services, in particular to tackle drug addiction, measures to develop alternatives to incarceration. All such policies can "disproportionately" benefit communities that are disproportionately affected by the problems they target, yet do so in the name of social progress for all.[4] Derenoncourt and Montialoux similarly argue that the most immediate way to reduce American racial income disparities is to raise the minimum wage and increase its coverage, measures that proved their effectiveness in the mid-1960s. By comparison, they argue, corporate diversity initiatives benefit only an "elite stratum" (2020).

But just what the practical implications of this should be for political organizing will depend on specific histories and conjunctural conditions, and can certainly not be captured in a simple maxim. It clearly does not mean that movements for racial or gender justice (among others) should be abandoned. Indeed, the claim that "group-based" movements will "split the potential coalition for broad-based egalitarian reform" (Barry 2001, 325–6) may be as absurd as the old conservative complaint that Karl Marx invented class struggle. To the extent that class-based movements have often ignored the specific concerns of women or racialized members of the class, it is not the "politics of identity" that has created division, but a narrow politics of class.

BEWARE THE ATTRACTION OF UNDIALECTICAL DISCOURSE. Not just progressives, but anyone who feels that there are serious ills in their society, can be tempted by a stance articulated in the biblical Book of Ezekiel: "Whether they hear or refuse to hear (for they are a rebellious house) they shall know that there has been a prophet among them" (Ezekiel 2.5). The attraction of this position is clear, as it too can yield psychic benefits: *I* have said my piece, and *I* am in the right. If no one listens, that's on them. (We should never forget that writers in general, and academics in particular, pursue ideal interests as much as anyone else. Academics who wish to be progressive would do well to identify the particular ideal interests that move them and assess their compatibility with progressive practice.)

But consider an analogy: throughout the pandemic, there was much discussion of whether experts had succeeded in communicating the risks and the current state of scientific knowledge on the virus. No one, I think, would be impressed with an expert who said: "I've spoken the truth on this, whether anyone pays attention is not my concern." This would probably be viewed as a dereliction of duty, as we assume health experts have a moral obligation to do their outmost to be effective. And progressives? Do we not also have such a moral-political duty? The point, as Marx might have said were he writing today, is not to deconstruct the world, to disrupt its social imaginaries, to unsettle its narratives: "the point is to change it."

So progressives need to be free of a dangerous assumption: that the more uncompromising their criticism of Canada, the more complete and free of nuance their rejection of phenomena such as multiculturalism, the more progressive they are. This assumption simply ignores the task of *hegemony*, of gaining a hearing for one's positions in a wide section of society, of expanding the circle of people who accept a critical analysis and are prepared to act on it. The final stanza of "The Mask of Anarchy," Percy Bysshe Shelley's poem on the Peterloo Massacre (rpt.

1842), calls on the people to "Rise like Lions after slumber," and ends with the memorable line: "Ye are many – they are few." One should avoid framing political issues in such a way that "They are many – we are few."

An objection. Consider a hypothetical objection to the foregoing:

> You seem to believe that a carefully modulated discourse will somehow reach "a wide section of society." Typical: your entire book is permeated by assumptions about "fruitful audiences," all those people supposedly ready to change their views on justice issues. You seem to forget that politics is not about persuading open-minded people of the rightness of one's position, it's about power and *struggle*, which must be the struggle of organized groups. What you glibly dismiss as "preaching to the choir" in fact helps consolidate a political force. It's effective, even if only those who are part of that force read it or find it persuasive.

There is an element of truth in this objection, and some error. It raises important questions: What are human beings like? How does change happen? These questions are relevant to this book as a whole, because in the works of a fair number of progressive critics, I find little or no mention of ethnic majority Canadians (or "canonical Canadians," or "national subjects") having been moved by ethical arguments, or being open to them. And so it would seem that a bleak vision is tacitly assumed.

The vision is a venerable one, concisely articulated by the Athenian envoys to Melos, in the chilling debate recounted by Thucydides. The Athenians dismiss ethical appeals as mere noise, "a great mass of words that nobody would believe" (¶5.89). The stark truth, they declare, is that "the strong do what they can and the weak suffer what they must" (¶5.89).[5]

Were it really true that people are not moved by considerations of justice and the rights of others, no just world would be possible. Indeed, human civilization would be doomed, because an adequate response to the climate emergency will *never* occur on the basis of self-interest alone, in large part because of the time lag between emissions and their climate effects. *Today*'s climate crisis is the result of *past* emissions, not current ones. Because of this, as Stephen Gardiner has conclusively demonstrated, no matter how severe the climate crisis at any given moment, self-interested politicians and citizens will continue to avoid serious *mitigation* measures and focus their efforts on local and short-term *adaptation* (2011).

But people are generally not amoral selfish individualists, although they are *assumed* to be such in "rational choice" models. I have previously noted the generally reactionary implications of those models (chapter 5). They should also be dismissed on empirical grounds. The "rational choice" vision accounts for some observable phenomena in the political world but ignores much more. It correctly notes that many appeals to values in politics are purely cynical vote-getting tactics, "propaganda devices" (Riker 1982, 205), but it fails to ask why they are necessary in the first place. In the "rational choice" universe, voters are unconcerned about lofty matters such as the public interest: "The benefits voters consider in making their decisions are streams of utility derived from government activity" (Downs 1957, 36). So for a politician to carry on about fairness, "family values," and so on, is akin to a sports car salesman extolling his product's benefits for world peace. Yet values talk is ubiquitous in politics.

But so too are cynicism and naked appeals to voters' narrow self-interest. So we must not counter the bleak vision of a world full of "rational actors" with a naive vision of sensitive citizens always willing to be swayed by what Habermas terms "the authority of the better argument" (1989b, 36). To steer reflection between those two visions, I will draw on a case study of activism. At the end of his *The Skin We're In: A Year of Black Resistance and Power*, Desmond Cole tells the story of the mobilization to save Abdoul Abdi from deportation. Born in Saudi Arabia, Abdi was brought to Canada as a child. From the age of seven, he was under the control of child services in Nova Scotia. After his conviction on various charges, he discovered that he was liable to deportation, because Nova Scotia's Department of Community Services had never bothered to apply for citizenship on his behalf (Cole 2020, 211).

The normative case against deporting him seems clear-cut: the government agency that had controlled Abdi's life for almost his entire childhood had failed to execute a core duty of responsible guardianship. Indeed, even a federal politician told his sister that "the care system failed your brother" (Cole 2020, 216). (The politician, as it happens, was Justin Trudeau.) Yet the deportation process rolled on, even after that admission. But after a second reversal in federal court, Public Safety Minister Ralph Goodale announced that the government was throwing in the towel. The outcome, Cole observes, "happened because we fought ... Folks from Goodale's constituency in Regina, Saskatchewan stood in the snow to demonstrate on Abdoul's behalf when he was in CBSA custody. Supporters in Ottawa wrote letters to and called their members of Parliament. Black Lives Matter–Toronto took over [immigration minister Ahmed] Hussen's office and held a press conference demanding that Abdoul be released" (2020, 219).

They won because they fought. Most certainly. But how are we to interpret this fight and its outcome? It would seem that the story supports the *realpolitik* view: the supporters of Abdi had right on their side all along, but they only prevailed when they created enough trouble for the government.

But three challenges might be put to this interpretation. First: why did the core group who led the protest dedicate so much effort to this? The question reminds us that, unless one grants members of a progressive political movement a magical exemption from amoral self-interest, it is unclear how one expects a principled political movement to emerge in a world of selfish agents, because of the well-known collective action problem: "rational, self-interested individuals will not act to achieve their common or group interests" (Olson 1965, 2) – let alone act to defend the interests of *others*. Second: Cole comments that "people across Canada we didn't know stood up for a young man they'd never met" (2020, 219). Why? Can *their* actions be explained in *realpolitik* terms? Or were they motivated by the view that what was being done to Abdi was *wrong*? Finally: Why didn't political leaders just sic the police on those occupying a minister's office? Could it be because people would have been shocked by this, that the action would have *outraged the conscience* of a politically worrisome number of people?

Cole's account, and the questions I have raised, tell us something about how change can occur. The actors in the story were influenced by considerations of right and wrong, but in different ways. Some of the core group were Abdi's family and friends (his sister Fatouma was a key force). The injustice of his deportation would have affected them *viscerally*. For others, his treatment was another instance of an injustice they were already committed to fighting. Perhaps still others had been previously uninvolved in justice issues but were hit by the egregious unfairness of the government's actions. Politicians and officials, finally, might have been quite unmoved by ethical appeals. But the potential reaction of the broader public to a muscular response to the protesters stayed their hand and eventually led them to concede.[6]

Recall the discussion in chapter 10 of the political importance of a clear conscience, which can increase a group's "fighting power" (Lukács 1971, 66). This reduces the risk of a gradual erosion of the group. (Such erosion is an important element even for revolutionary change, which never involves the defeat of an *intact* dominant group.) Even the most cynical politician or official might at a certain point have recognized that the tenacity of the support for Abdi could undermine the public's acceptance of a tough deportation policy, as more Canadians became aware of the injustices that can arise from that stance.

What persuasion requires. But if ethical arguments can sway people under certain conditions, why not always? Why was all the pressure organized by Abdi's supporters needed? We can link the question to two concepts previously discussed in this work. One is constrained normativity. The politician or the official need not be a heartless ogre: it may simply be that factors arising from their understanding of their jobs limit their willingness to accept a moral appeal. The official may be fearful of setting a precedent and thus "opening the floodgates" to a host of other appeals. The politician may fear appearing "soft on crime," and so on.

But constrained normativity affects all of us, and one of its dimensions is that we have limited time, attention, and energy. The working days of many people are so long and exhausting that they have little inclination to spend energy on news and reflection on issues such as the Abdi case during the limited time they have available to recharge their batteries. The limits of time and attention affect activists as well. If anti-racist work can reproduce patriarchy and feminist work can reproduce racism (Carastathis 2014), this reflects in part the constrained normativity of many activists themselves.

The second concept previously discussed is ideology, which can cover all sorts of human suffering with layers upon layers of abstraction and fog. The very effectiveness of the "soft on crime" charge, which can easily be thrown at people trying to prevent miscarriages of justice, is one example of ideological fog. And this is why *persuasion requires more than persuasion*. As the Abdi case showed, activist pressure can burn away ideological fog by replacing abstractions with a human face and a concrete moral claim. There is a striking exchange early in Plato's *Republic*:

> Well, you must either prove stronger than we are, or you will have to stay here.
> Isn't there another alternative, namely, that we persuade you to let us go?
> But could you persuade us, if we won't listen? (327c).

To induce politicians and officials, and a dominant group in general, to *listen*, to attend to the arguments of neglected others, will often depend on a measure of disruption, of force, that makes a blind adherence to the status quo seem unsustainable, imprudent, or unreasonable.

Note that such force generally does not quite *force* elites to do something. Rather, it can reconfigure the "menu of choices" facing politicians and officials. The tenacity of the Abdi protest confronted decision-makers with a choice between doing what they should have done in the first place, or continuing to ignore the appeals – perhaps even unleashing the police – and facing the prospect of more widespread protest.

Now if the force in question necessarily involved physical violence, or purely transactional threats and bribes, then we would be back at the grim *realpolitik* vision of how change happens. But this is not the case. Foucault once suggested that power is a set of mechanisms "which seem likely to induce behaviors or discourses" (rpt. 1997, 51). There are many such "mechanisms."

The setting for one of the stories in Cory Doctorow's *Radicalized* (2019) is a luxury high-rise in which a few floors have been set aside for subsidized housing. The building is configured so that those on the "poor floors" are *invisible* to the others: they can never get on an elevator if a rich person is using it, and they can only exit the elevators at the back entrance. Why this set-up? In his *Theory of Moral Sentiments*, Adam Smith declared that "the fortunate and the proud wonder at the insolence of human wretchedness, that it should dare to present itself before them, and with the loathsome aspect of its misery presume to disturb the serenity of their happiness" (rpt. 2009, 64). So visible suffering disturbs the *serenity* of the dominant. Depending on the form of suffering, it might trigger *fear* that they might one day be in the situation of the suffering person.[7] Or the visible suffering might spark an uneasy awareness that the contrast in their situations is unjust, or that their own well-being comes at a high cost for others, or that the public policies they support are not benign, do not merely give people "what they deserve." These last reactions all depend on *conscience*. And so much of the force wielded by activism, far from being an exercise of *realpolitik* for which conscience and morality are irrelevant, in fact relies on those factors. (Perhaps a distinction can be drawn between forms of activism and pressure that have the potential to move the conscience of others not already on board, and those that *merely* pressure. The line between the two is no doubt unclear, but the distinction is worth keeping in mind, not least when activists are thinking through the likely effects of particular actions.)

Using force and trying to "reason with someone" are conventionally seen as disjunctive tactics. In practice, the first may be a necessary prelude to the second. Force – including efforts to make suffering and injustice more visible and less abstract – is not an *argument*, but it can encourage an openness to heed argument.[8] And because force usually requires organized action, there is some validity to "preaching to the choir," if this in fact helps strengthen a progressive force. (Preaching to the choir with the sort of "mystery" writing I critiqued in chapter 4, however, seems destined to fail, if it cannot pin down "what is to be done.")

Still: progressive thought and writing at some point has to reach beyond the already convinced and aim at a broader public. Mere pressure tactics that garner grudging concessions from political leaders and officials but do not persuade broad segments of the public will always be vulnerable to backlash. Even normative persuasion of elites *alone* is not enough to guard against backlash, if elites are persuaded to implement measures whose cost lands on particular parts of the public.

And this has implications for the analysis of reality. Because some analyses remove texture from the political landscape, grouping people who hold – or could hold – quite different attitudes towards justice issues into a homogeneous blob, they ignore the resources for change already offered by existing attitudes.

Summary. I have argued that a combination of arguments and disruptive force can favour progressive social change. As some progressive critics do not appear to believe that normative appeals can reach the ethnic majority, they need to explain just how *they* believe progressive change might come about. If, on the other hand, the argument presented here is plausible, then the challenge will be, in any given situation, to identify the actions that will create a willingness to listen, along with the normative and prudential arguments that will persuade people *once* they're listening. And that last task suggests that progressives must make a normative reflection that might reach broad segments of the public an ongoing component of their analysis.

11.3 Multiculturalism: Concluding Thoughts

Progressive critics. I have presented various similarities between two broad families of critique. Some progressive critics, like their conservative counterparts, blame multiculturalism for phenomena that pre-existed it. Some from both camps attribute excessive power to a policy and to the state, for example, the power to freeze identities.

But there is a particular value to the progressive critics: collectively, they are engaging in "ideology-critique," pointing out the contrast between widespread images of multiculturalism and of Canada and some persistent aspects of our reality. I have argued that some of them do this in a one-sided manner that obscures the levers of change offered by the Canadian attachment to multiculturalism. Nevertheless, I consider their ideology-critique an essential corrective to many Pollyannaish depictions of our society.

But progressive critiques could certainly be strengthened. One general means to this would be to yoke critique to the articulation of a vision of a possible future. Dissection of the contradictions and hypocrisies of "actually existing multiculturalism" needs to be accompanied, as I have previously stressed, by reflection on what we want multiculturalism to *become*. The world of speech, Foucault once wrote, has known much "plundering" (1994, vol. 2, 136). Rather than merely observe or lament this, progressives need to join in the game. Multiculturalism is clearly a popular idea in Canada, so why not push that idea in as progressive a direction as possible?

Multiculturalism-J. In chapter 3, I used "multiculturalism-J" to denote – in deliberately broad terms – that towards which we should be working: "Multiculturalism should be understood as the ethnoracial dimension of the struggle for a just society." I will end this book with some thoughts on that.

Note, first, that to view multiculturalism as part of a struggle means that it is not a condition of society, but an *activity*. And it will always be one, because a just society is never fully established. (And even if it were, we would have to struggle to sustain it, to adapt it to changing circumstances, and so on.) Still, the activity has a goal: in what general direction would multiculturalism-J tend? And in what sense would its goal actually *be* multiculturalism? Let us view it in light of three claims about the necessary core of any multiculturalism. Would multiculturalism-J involve "the promotion of group identities and institutionally supported diversity" (Winter, 2011, 213)? Would it "proceed by means of 'recognizing' the 'culture' that constitutes a minority as a distinct group" (Joppke 2004, 238)?[9] Would it "go beyond the protection of the basic civil and political rights guaranteed to all individuals in a liberal-democratic state, to also extend some level of public recognition and support for ethnocultural minorities to maintain and express their distinct identities and practices" (Kymlicka 2007c, 16)?

In truth, there is much that we don't know concerning the nature of an increasingly just society, charting its course into the future through a just and inclusive ongoing deliberation. What would be important to people, who themselves would be changed in the very movement of society? Which types of attachments and identifications would people continue to treasure? What new types would they develop?

I suspect that most people will always have an attachment to their mother tongue. Beyond that, speculation is easily led astray by assumptions about "core" and "peripheral" parts of culture. Many consider religion a core element of cultures, even of "civilizations" (Huntington 1993). But we have certainly seen that attachment to the religious identity into which one is born varies tremendously between individuals and groups. Indeed, many people may be more attached to foods with which they grew up.

But there is also much, I think, that we *do* know about what multiculturalism-J will look like. As, by definition, it harmonizes with other dimensions of the struggle for justice, any culture – religious, ethnic, or other – that harboured prejudice against women, sexual minorities, or those "outside" would be called upon to "bend" (Rawls 1996) in the direction of justice.

As to the question of whether multiculturalism-J would go beyond the traditional liberal schedule of rights: yes, but not necessarily in the way that Banting and Kymlicka had in mind when they defined multiculturalism in that way. I assume that a just society would give ever-increasing importance to a wide range of social rights, *in addition* to civil and political ones. This would include practical recognition of a human right to have meaningful and dignified work. We would expect society's occupational hierarchy to be quite a bit flatter than today,[10] and we would *not* expect to find patterns of ethnoracial "sorting" into different slots in that hierarchy. There would be, that is, a right *not* to have one's ethnoracial – or class – background significantly influence one's economic position.

A number of years ago, we inflicted on our two sons a lecture on Caravaggio's *Supper at Emmaus* at London's National Gallery. They were grabbed less by the lecture's content than by the rather quirky art historian delivering it. He would often raise a question about the painting's history or symbolism. He would pause, then say "Don't know, doesn't matter."

And so: a just multiculturalism in a just society would be a beautiful and humane treasure. Would it be a "true" multiculturalism, according to many current views of what that entails? *Don't know, doesn't matter.*

Notes

Chapter 1

1 In retrospect, the critics I discussed in *Multicultiphobia* seem relatively benign. While they themselves were not engaging in reasoned debate with supporters of multiculturalism, they generally avoided a rhetoric that would undermine the very possibility of dialogue. Such rhetoric, unfortunately, has been deployed by more recent critics. For Salim Mansur, multiculturalism is "an insidious assault on freedom in the West" (2010, 20). Indeed, he compares this "assault" to that "mounted by the twin forces of totalitarianism – fascism, or Nazism, and Soviet communism – in the last century" (2011, 3). Mansur is cited in the gargantuan manifesto of a Norwegian man whose response to the supposed threat of multiculturalism was mass murder.

2 We would do well not to assume that the Ford English School ceremony was representative of American *reality*. It is probably more accurate to view it as an expression of an assimilationist *aspiration* on the part of at least some American elites.

In relation to the supposed contrast between the Canadian mosaic and American assimilationism, it is striking to read Hannah Arendt's comment that "what influenced me when I came to the United States [in the 1940s] was precisely the freedom of becoming a citizen without having to pay the price of assimilation" (2003, 4).

3 Still, ambiguities remain. If someone's belief in equality leads to the view that we must defend existing group cultures, and thus favours a *laissez-faire* attitude towards oppressive practices within those cultures, then they are simultaneously promoting equality *between* groups and inequality *within* groups.

4 F.A. Hayek, one of the key theoreticians of neoliberalism, insisted that he was a liberal, not a conservative, because "the main point about

liberalism is that it wants to go elsewhere, not to stand still." Stasis, for Hayek, was not the goal: "what is most urgently needed in most parts of the world is a thorough sweeping away of the obstacles to free growth" (2011, 521). As Ayad Akhtar notes in *Homeland Elegies*: "The so-called conservatives of the past half-century have sought to conserve almost nothing of the societies they inherited but instead have worked to remake them with the vigor reminiscent of the leftist revolutionaries they despise" (2020, 234).

5 By way of example: consider the presence in the *Globe and Mail* of two critics of multiculturalism, each representing one of the broad approaches depicted here. In each case, I searched a four-year period, beginning with the year of publication of the critic's book. Neil Bissoondath, whose *Selling illusions* appeared in 1994, is mentioned in 101 articles in the 1994–97 period. Himani Bannerji, author of *The Dark Side of the Nation* (2000), is mentioned in exactly ... 0 articles in the subsequent four years.

6 It is important to note that the progressive critics of multiculturalism are not in all cases *opponents* of it. As we will see, many acknowledge multiculturalism's emancipatory potential. Others view it more starkly as an obstacle to progressive change.

7 Balancing this misreading with its opposite, Robert Maciel labels *Multicultiphobia* a "significant attack" on multiculturalism (2014, 383).

8 Two other binary misinterpretations can be addressed here. To insist, first, that the effects of structures are mediated through the actions of individuals is not to adopt an "agent-centred" approach: it is simply to argue that we cannot understand structures otherwise. To argue, second, that a white supremacy orientation is not as deeply and enduringly anchored in the state as is a capitalist ethos, is not to advance the absurd claim that the state is free of racism.

9 Apart from ideological bias, the news media generally have various style preferences: for keeping things simple, for easily digestible types of analysis, and for novelty. As Rodney Benson notes in his *Shaping Immigration News*, such preferences work against systemic or structural arguments (2013).

10 For a sense of how fraught discussions of this challenge might be, contrast Lawrence and Dua's "Decolonizing Antiracism," which argues that "people of color are settlers," because they "live on land that is appropriated and contested, where Aboriginal peoples are denied nationhood and access to their own lands" (2005, 134), with Nandita Sharma's sharp dismissal of such claims as "neo-racist arguments" (2011, 99).

Chapter 2

1. By late 2022, Netanyahu had lost power, then regained it. Trump clearly hopes to replicate that feat. Bolsonaro apparently wishes to replicate Trump's strategy: he has authorized a transition to President Lula but has not conceded the legitimacy of the electoral outcome. Duterte has been succeeded by the son of the long-time dictator Ferdinand Marcos. Orban, for his part, appears to have consolidated his hold on power, while Modi has survived his disastrous response to the COVID crisis.

    Note that I do not have a sharp set of criteria that would definitively distinguish such cases from others. For my purposes here, it is enough to note that the phenomenon is widespread.

2. The preoccupation of the global right with issues of sexuality is striking. In Warsaw, a conservative magazine distributed "LGBT-free zone" stickers for its readers to post on their homes and businesses (Lawrynuik 2019). The Archbishop of Kraków warns that the "red plague" has been succeeded by "a new one that wants to rule our souls, hearts and minds. It is not Marxist or Bolshevik … It's not red, but rainbow" (qtd. in Santora 2019). And the speaker of the Hungarian Chamber of Deputies equates "gender studies" with Nazi eugenics (Almássy 2018). A member of Jason Kenney's United Conservative Party compared the rainbow flag to the Nazi and Soviet ones (Rieger 2018).

3. A moment in the first 2016 presidential debate vividly illustrated the opening through which Trump walked: "We have to stop our companies from leaving the United States and with it firing all of their people. All you have to do is take a look at Carrier Air Conditioning in Indianapolis. They fired 1,400 people. They're going to Mexico. So many hundreds and hundreds of companies are doing this. We cannot let it happen." To which Clinton replied: "Well, I think that trade is an important issue. Of course we are five percent of the world's population. We have to trade with the other 95 percent" (Presidential Debate Transcript 2016).

4. Of the similar tactics being used within the EU, Seyla Benhabib comments: "Since, in many cases, individuals seeking asylum and refuge are escaping the oppressive, illegal, and even murderous regimes of their own countries, enhanced cooperation with these governments can have disastrous effects upon their lives" (2004, 152).

5. The government may have been following the advice of a conservative critic of immigration policy. Speaking before a Senate Commitee in 2011, former CSIS senior manager David Harris commented that some refugees from Muslim-majority countries "may, indeed, be bona fide refugees. Think of Christians, Jews and moderate Muslims who for years have been

persecuted under the Islamist apartheid systems prevalent in a number of Muslim lands." But he also warned that "one in five Egyptian Muslims sympathizes with our al Qaeda enemy" and complained that "roughly 20,000 permanent residents came from Egypt in the past 10 years" (Canada, Standing Senate Committee 2011, 3 February).
6 I focused on the question of education. Consider another of Hum and Simpson's controls, "current labour market activity." Again, it is reasonable to compare hourly – rather than overall – earnings. But if one finds that different groups work significantly different numbers of total hours, this is *prima facie* evidence of another dimension of discrimination, which must be investigated.
7 The study also found that "68 per cent of people killed in police encounters were suffering with some kind of mental illness, addiction or both" (Singh 2020).
8 My student Camille Strippoli drew Fantino's article to my attention.
9 But the same survey found that 60 per cent agree that "immigrants have more difficulty than 'Canadians' finding employment in their field of expertise" (Jedwab 2015b).

Chapter 3

1 A coherent framework should be free of contradictions. That does not mean it is free of tensions, as we will see below. Nor need a framework be easily labelled. In the discussion of the state, for example, I draw on Weber, Bourdieu, Marx, and many others.
2 This relates to a criticism levelled against the term "visible minority," which can both assume homogeneity and lead to bureaucratic practices that further it. Jedwab and Satzewich comment that "it may be a mistake to lump all Canadians into one of two broad analytical categories: 'visible minority' and 'non-visible' minority (or White) ... Groups with dramatically different migration histories and class statuses in Canada are lumped together in such a way as to blur important differences between groups and make the categories sociologically meaningless" (2015, xxvi).
3 Such claims, which seem the stuff of satire, account for the strong reactions against the "rational actor" construct: nearly a "social moron" (Sen 1977, 335); nearly "psychopathic" (Rawls 1996, 51). Commenting on Friedman's cost/benefit approach to childrearing, Franz Hinkelammert observed that Friedman "forgot to take into account the cost of psychiatric therapy for a child produced in this way" (1981, 84).

Despite the influence of such extreme models, methodological individualism in general need not deny that people can be constrained by ethical norms. But the approach will seek to explain the emergence

of those norms in function of the interests of initially atomized rational actors. They attempt, that is, to "derive the reasonable from the rational," to use Rawls's terms (1996, 52).
4 Leskov is not depicting a pathology of public bureaucracies alone. In a case of life imitating art, a Florida *lifeguard* was fired ... for saving a man from drowning. The lifeguard's offence was to "save a swimmer in distress outside his designated zone." A spokesperson for the company that fired him commented that "we limit what we do to the protected swimming zones that we've agreed to service" (Lynch 2012).
5 Other historians question this point (Alterman 2004, 114).
6 If we do study power in the way Foucault recommends, we will call into question one of his most famous claims, that we live in a Panopticon society (e.g., 1994, 2:437). That vision exaggerates the linear downward flow of control, and the upward flow of information arising from surveillance at any given level.
7 Consider Zuhair Kashmeri's *The Gulf Within: Canadian Arabs, Racism, and the Gulf War*. He opens with the claim that Canada "claimed moral high ground in the world and promised to show other nations how different nationalities and cultures could live peacefully under one roof. After giving the world multiculturalism for decades, Ottawa unleashed its security forces against Canada's Arabs and Muslims" (1991, x). This does not sound like government propaganda. A couple of pages later, however, comes an acknowledgment of research funding from the Department of Multiculturalism and Citizenship.
8 The scholarship on this topic is immense, and I will not summarize it here. My goal is merely to highlight certain points that will prove relevant to our consideration of the progressive critiques of multiculturalism. (The reader familiar with debates concerning the capitalist state will recognize that, consistent with the overall approach I am taking, my account here will address both "agency" and "structure.")
9 Why keep repeating the point? Because it is so easy to forget when working within particular theoretical frameworks. Antonio Gramsci commented that "mechanical historical materialism does not allow for the possibility of error" (rpt. 1971, 408). Before attributing this to the blinkers of one particular ideology, we should recall that much of the economics profession was captured by a vision of omniscient markets embedded in assumptions of "rational expectations" and "efficient-markets" (Skidelsky 2009, xv; Wolf 2015, 136). One underlying factor is that assumptions of omniscience make thinking about states or markets *easier* than if error is taken into account.
10 I am working with a very minimal definition of the term: democracy is government elected by "the people" – which often does not represent

the entire adult population. The point of this limited definition is that the need for the state to reconcile the demands of capital and those of "the people" arises even when there are important restrictions on adult suffrage. For many other purposes, one would want to add the criterion of "an electorate consisting of the entire adult population" to the definition (Therborn 1977, 4). Using that criterion, Therborn determines that Canada only became a democracy in 1945 (11).

11 Some hope that indoctrination in neoclassical economics will reduce the tension. To free people of "perilous fallacies," argues Steven Pinker, we must "give high priority to economics, evolutionary biology, and probability and statistics in any high school or college curriculum" (2002, 235). Bryan Caplan's *The Myth of the Rational Voter* identifies the sorts of "fallacies" that might be targeted by such indoctrination: "Why are inefficient policies like the minimum wage popular? Voters' rational ignorance: few bother to learn enough economics to understand the policies' drawbacks" (2006, 96). Thus, rejection of a position that is debated even among economists, and that can be questioned on normative and policy grounds (Ryan 2018), is attributed to simple "ignorance."

12 That is true for *explicit* threats. As Wolfgang Streeck notes, business as a whole also exercises uncoordinated but quite effective pressure: cutting back investment, exporting capital, and so on (2017, xvii).

13 Deregulation here refers to both publicly observable rule changes and less obvious shifts in *enforcement* of regulations. Various sources recount, for example, the revealing story of Brooksley Born, head of the Commodity Futures Trading Commission, who was forced to resign after seeking to bring the derivatives market under serious regulatory control (Häring and Douglas 2012, 90–2; Lessig 2011, 74–5). One of her nemeses was Robert Rubin, whose career trajectory included, in succession: Goldman Sachs, US Treasury Secretary, Citigroup.

14 Dickens presents a classic send-up of such government information in *Little Dorrit*, when the minister for the Circumlocution Office announces in Parliament that "within the short compass of the last financial half-year, this much-maligned Department (Cheers) had written and received fifteen thousand letters (Loud cheers), had written twenty-four thousand minutes (Louder cheers), and thirty-two thousand five hundred and seventeen memoranda (Vehement cheering)" (1867, 93).

15 There is an influential antecedent to the theology in which Gilman is confusedly wallowing. As Lovejoy notes, William of Ockham – famed for his logical "razor"– held that "a thing was *made* good merely by God's willing it, and evil, or not good, by his not willing it" (1964, 70). Substitute "culture" for "God," and one arrives at the most extreme cultural relativist position.

16 I thank Will Kymlicka for pointing me towards Porter's critiques of multiculturalism and the Bilingualism and Biculturalism Commission (hereafter B&B Commission).

17 Some opt for a more organic metaphor than "container": to show his commitment to serious dialogue with Britain's Muslims, then Prime Minister Tony Blair expressed his desire to "get right into the entrails of the community" (qtd. in C-Span 2005).

18 As a journalist covering the post-Yugoslavia civil wars, Hedges witnessed first-hand the catastrophic effects of a one-dimensional view of culture and identity. Yet there are contexts in which that view can play a positive role. Coulthard notes that "Indigenous scholars and activists defend what would appear to be essentialist notions of indigeneity in their attempts to provide radical alternatives" (2014, 98). One can certainly make the case that *one stage* in a group's political development requires that its members view their group identity as foundational.

19 Orthodox neoclassical economics, so hostile to Marx in most respects, has followed his lead on this, consistently erasing flesh-and-blood human beings in its analysis, replacing them with "rational actors" who are nothing more than consistent representations of a particular maximization logic. This substitution is so pervasive that many rather obvious findings arising from the partial return to real human beings, undertaken by "behavioural" economics, seem revolutionary in relation to economic orthodoxy.

20 Later in life, both Marx and Engels grew uneasy with those followers who confused their abstractions with reality. Much of Marx's "Critique of the Gotha Programme" took aim at such confusion. At one point, he appears to express second thoughts concerning the specific abstraction being discussed here: "unequal individuals ... are measurable only by an equal standard insofar as they are brought under an equal point of view, are taken from one definite side only – for instance, in the present case, are regarded only as workers and nothing more is seen in them, everything else being ignored" (rpt. 1969, vol. 3, 18; see also Amartya Sen's discussion of this passage, in 2009, 247).

21 The claim is not that we "owe" respect to all fellow citizens: I do not owe respect to white supremacists nor to their value commitments. But if we do respect someone, respect includes this restraint.

22 It has been suggested that multiculturalism is an "essentially contested concept" (e.g., Crick 2004). Would that were true! In coining the phrase, W.B. Gallie defined such concepts not merely as those that lack a "correct or standard use," but as concepts for which "each party recognizes the fact that its own use of it is contested by those of other parties" (1955–56, 168, 175). In the case of multiculturalism, such shared recognition would be an important advance.

23 And yet, the same author can wistfully refer to "what multiculturalism is supposed to be about – that is, *equal reciprocal recognition* between *all* of the peoples whom a history of violent conquest has cast within the purview of the Canadian state" (Day 2000, 210).

24 This claim arises from a double misunderstanding of Charles Taylor's "Politics of Recognition" essay. First, the claim of cultural equality is attributed to Taylor. Second, it is assumed that the essay can be viewed as a *canonical* statement of multiculturalism.

25 This is not to *reduce* the concept to a set of policies: it is reasonable to include under the label "multiculturalism" phenomena that might plausibly be viewed as effects of specific policies, of official discourse concerning multiculturalism, and so on. Thus, we can safely assume that what Elke Winter calls the "multiculturalization of national identity" (2011, 39) has *something* to do with decades of policy and official discourse. So while we can and should distinguish "a more diffuse public ethos" (Kymlicka 2014, 7) from specific multiculturalism policies, we should not assume that these dimensions of multiculturalism are unrelated.

   At the same time, a virtue of the "policy index" is to show that the federal government's Multiculturalism Directorate (or Ministry, or whatever) has not had a monopoly on multicultural policy practice.

26 Typically, we do all these things with no awareness of our infinitesimal yet real impact on social reality. As Bhaskar puts it, "people do not marry to reproduce the nuclear family or work to sustain the capitalist economy," yet these effects are "nevertheless the unintended consequence" of their actions (1998, 35).

27 These reflections are relevant to "song and dance" multiculturalism. The progressive critique of this is certainly important. At the same time, as Emma Goldman (sort of) said: "If I can't dance, I don't want to be part of your revolution" (Shulman 1991). Song, dance, and shared meals can all be joyful elements of life, and a just multiculturalism should celebrate them.

28 Andreas Schedler comments that "our paradigms of objects are still concrete, material things with observable properties. Very few objects of political research correspond to this model" (2011, 372).

29 Yet Marx himself did portray collective phenomena as agents: "The English bourgeoisie acted for its own interest quite as wisely as did the Swedish bourgeoisie" (1954, 677); "Mankind always sets itself only such tasks as it can solve" (rpt. 1969, 1:504). Is this simply loose talk, or can we make sense of such claims? The first statement can probably be "translated" into a form that identifies human agents. The second seems more problematic.

Chapter 4

1 Nancy Maclean makes a similar point: "Scholars and journalists in many nations are now grappling with how numerous democracies have been, in effect, losing sovereignty and responsiveness to voters, and hence popularity. Yet most write in the passive voice, focusing on impact more than sources, and attributing the action to abstract nouns rather than human agents" (2017, 242).
2 Progressive critics have no monopoly on this. Jürgen Habermas even endows multiculturalism with self-consciousness, referring to a "multiculturalism that understands itself in the right way" (2008, 270).
3 Similarly, "the extension of 'rights' and 'equality'" has led to "further penetration of state forms into the daily lives of Canadians" (Day 2000, 179).
4 "Foucauldian" is the more common adjective. I term "Foucaultious" the tendency to imitate one of Foucault's modes of discourse, in which he casually tosses out extremely general and provocative claims. In relation to these, Foucault had a revealing tendency, when later challenged, to disavow all responsibility: "Stop harping on things I said before! When I say them, they're already forgotten. I think in order to forget" (1994, 2:304).
5 The libertarian sees the free choice and says that the transaction must therefore be beneficial to both parties and should not be interfered with. The critic sees the background conditions that constrain the choice and sees unfairness and *de facto* coercion (Rawls 2001, 53; Sandel 2012, 45).
6 The state officials who make funding decisions also face a menu of choices: they are not in a position of absolute power over those they fund.

Chapter 5

1 The idea of a national core has a long pedigree. Writing in 1922, Walter Lippmann referred to "that assimilated mass which always considers itself the 'nation'" (2004, 29).
2 For Engels, dialectics "comprehends things and their representations, ideas, in their essential connection, concatenation, motion, origin and ending" (Marx and Engels 1969, vol. 3, 129). For Bertell Ollman, "above all else Marx's dialectic is a way of viewing things as moments in their own development in, with, and through other things" (1976, 52). A nice contrast is provided by Bishop Butler's assertion that "everything is what it is and not another thing" (qtd. in Taylor 1975, 116).
3 For example: "Whatever the electoral possibilities that political parties sought to exploit by doling out grants and favors, it is still true that the first anthologies of literature by racialized and so-called ethnic minorities

(and several of the first books) were assembled by intellectuals who took the state's money – which was also their community's money – and used it to commence a conversation that has immeasurably enriched Canadian literature" (Clarke 2011, 51).

4 In my study of the political economy of Nicaragua's revolutionary decade, I note a number of clear expressions of this. One example: Victor Tirado, member of the Sandinistas' nine-man ruling junta, "informed a group of workers that old ideas of democracy were now obsolete, 'although you, being workers, are not aware of this yet'" (Ryan 1995, 36).

5 A study of US terror attacks from 2006 to 2015 found that "controlling for target type, fatalities, and being arrested, attacks by Muslim perpetrators received, on average, 357% more coverage than other attacks." The researchers added that "the disparities in news coverage of attacks based on the perpetrator's religion may explain why members of the public tend to fear the 'Muslim terrorist' while ignoring other threats" (Kearns et al. 2019, 985).

6 Even if so, it is yet another matter to claim that X's mistaken understanding of their own interests justifies taking decisions out of their hands.

7 Years ago, I was active in the Association Coopérative d'Économie Familiale in Montreal. One long-time activist in the group had a standard argument that she used in meetings with indebted adults, which ran something like this: We want to do for debt what Kinsey did for sex. Before Kinsey, many people thought that they were weird, unique, shameful. Today, many people in debt think the same. But I can tell you that at least half the families in your neighbourhood are struggling with debt problems.

8 In language that was unusually harsh for her, Hannah Arendt commented: "No one in his right senses can believe – as certain German student groups recently theorized– that only when the government has been forced 'to practice violence openly' will the rebels be able 'to fight against this shit society (*Scheissgesellschaft*) with adequate means and destroy it' ... This linguistically (though hardly intellectually) vulgarized new version of the old Communist nonsense of the thirties, that the victory of fascism was all to the good for those who were against it, is either sheer play-acting, the 'revolutionary' variant of hypocrisy, or testifies to the political idiocy of 'believers'" (1972, 195).

9 Foucault and Chomsky had a striking exchange on the question of "unmasking" power. After Foucault declared that "in a society such as ours, the true political task is to critique the set of apparently neutral and independent institutions, to critique and attack them so that the political violence that was exercised in obscurity is unmasked" (1994, 2:496),

Chomsky offered an understated warning: "You know, if a great Leviathan like the United States were really to become fascist, a lot of problems would result" (2006, 44–5). (This is a prediction that might soon be tested.)
10 For a detailed analysis of one dimension of the Conservatives' undermining of multiculturalism, see James (2012).
11 On this, see the striking exchange between Fraser and Habermas in Calhoun (1992, 469).
12 I noted in *Multicultiphobia* that the image of the immigrant as "guest" justifies much unequal treatment: "The analogy tells the immigrant: even after committing to this country, even after taking out citizenship, *you* will never enjoy the full autonomy and voice that *we* take for granted. When *we* complain about some aspect of our society or government, we are simply exercising our democratic rights. But when *you* complain, a spoken or unspoken question will always hang in the air: So why did you come here?" (2010b, 216).

Chapter 6

1 Through an examination of social movements' interaction with various official commissions from the 1930s on, Matt James persuasively argues for the material interests at stake for movements often depicted as "postmaterialist" (2006).
2 Some years later, after the B&B Commission had issued all its reports, an opposition MP would quote Minister of National Revenue Jean-Pierre Coté to the effect that "henceforth bilingualism would be a necessity in the public service and the chance of a unilingual person being hired, let alone promoted, would be nil" (Donald Mazankowski, Commons, 7 July 1969). By "bilingual," Coté was not referring to those who spoke Ukrainian or Chinese, along with English.
3 An early foretaste of how fondly a multiculturalism policy might be viewed in Quebec was offered by Ralliement Créditiste MP Charles-Arthur Gauthier: "And when I hear the New Democratic party members talk about multiculturalism, I say to myself right away that they have never understood the true meaning of confederation, never knew why they were coming to Canada" (Caanada, House of Commons [hereafter Commons], 10 April 1964).
4 Whatever the government's intentions, the "stamp" itself had a certain dignity. Trudeau's 8 October 1971 policy announcement does not appear to have been drafted casually: it is thoughtful, expressing a coherent vision of a somewhat multicultural society.
5 Here is Liberal MP Allen Sulatycky speaking five months after the declaration: "in the last few days the very basis of confederation has been

challenged. I refer to three particular elements: the idea of equalization payments, the concept of an accommodation between the two major language groups in the country, and some question has been raised about the value of the government's new multicultural policy. It strikes me that if we challenge these factors in our national existence we are really challenging the idea of confederation itself" (Commons, 2 March 1972). It is rather startling to see how quickly a still-marginal policy initiative has been elevated – at least by some – to the rank of an essential component of Confederation!

6 Such assumptions betray the "God-like" image of the state critiqued in chapter 3. A fateful historical example of elite panic emerged in the face of an upcoming *peaceful and unarmed* march in 1819 in Manchester, England. One journalist condemned the organizers for bringing together "into one body so frightful a multitude of diseased minds," and warned that they "are answerable for all of evil [sic] that may follow" (*Times of London*, 17 August 1819). The "evil" proved great indeed: elite panic led to the infamous "Peterloo Massacre."

7 The Dean of Science "concluded that the charges specifically relating to racial discrimination had no substance. *It is true that his decision was not communicated to the complaining students*, but there had been a careful though informal hearing" (emphasis added). This from the acting vice-chancellor, in a *defence* of the university's actions (Clarke 1969).

In late 2022, Concordia University – formed by the amalgamation of Sir George Williams and Loyola College – formally apologized for the university's response to the protest, which Concordia president Graham Carr described as a "stark manifestation of institutional racism" (Nerestant 2022).

8 The previous sentence's passive voice structure is deliberately used to bypass the question of agency (see chapter 4). According to the *Globe and Mail*, the destruction was the work of "militant students" (Balfour 1969). David Austin simply notes that "the computer center of the university caught fire with many of the protesters still inside" (2007, 521). I was a paperboy for the *Montreal Gazette* at the time, generally believing what I read as I delivered the paper every morning but Sunday, for the princely reward of 10¢ per customer weekly. I thus accepted that the fire was the work of the protesters. But the fact that they were *inside* the centre at the time, and emerged "running, choking, through smoke into the arms of waiting police" (Balfour 1969), casts doubt on the official story.

9 Earlier in the day of the computer centre seizure, "more than 300 blacks and about 70 white Marxists had used force to take over a hearing that was investigating charges of racism directed at a teacher" (Mcdonald 1969). It is unclear how the reporter knew that all the whites were Marxists, but this claim proved important, as we will see.

10 That same day, Mr. Latulippe offered an unusual policy solution for racial unrest: "Many wives refuse to bear children because they would not know where to accommodate them. Children would crowd their homes. Besides, some have to work to support themselves or their family, to pay their rent and their debts" he began. Thus, "someway should be found to change the conditions making pregnancy undesirable." Were this done, "we would not have to bring over millions of immigrants. We could go on building up our society, which would develop and also be healthier. We might never witness again what happened at Sir George Williams University" (Commons, 13 February 1969).

This is an interesting expression of a political strategy that combines advocacy of redistributive measures with anti-immigrant rhetoric. Piketty terms the approach "social-nativism," noting that it has been deployed by Poland's governing PiS party, by France's Rassemblement National (previously the National Front) under Marine LePen, and, to some extent, by Viktor Orbán's Fidesz party in Hungary (2019, 1007). The redistribution need not be particularly substantial: the xenophobic party simply needs to promise more than is on offer from its social-democratic competitor, which these days is not a big ask.

11 I noted earlier that any argument for a deeper logic to explain multiculturalism must fit the known facts. Himani Bannerji's account fails that test: "Note the time around which multiculturalism and the diversity discourse is invented in Canada. Multi-ethnic European immigrations of the past did not inspire it, nor are the present-day European immigrants the targets of this discourse" (2000, 43). Bannerji also shifts Trudeau's policy declaration back a decade, to "the very early 1980s" (44).

12 Thobani's *Exalted Subjects* acknowledges this tangled situation: "The immigrant is a much more complex and ambiguous figure in settler societies like Canada than has generally been suggested. Propelled into the circuit of migration by structural conditions within the global economy, as well as by their desires for economic advancement, migrants have been party to the ongoing colonization of Aboriginal peoples ... The more immigrants have sought their own inclusion and access to citizenship, the more invested they have become, with very few exceptions, in supporting the nation's erasure of its originary violence and its fantasies of progress and prosperity" (2007, 16).

13 Claims of white solidarity that ignore economic realities are not new. Wilson Jeremiah Moses cites late nineteenth-century Black leader William Hooper Councill's claim that "the white man ... throws his powerful arms around every little red-headed freckled-face, poor white girl and boy in the land and makes the way possible for them to rise in the world." This, Moses comments, was "pure nonsense in an age characterized by the

degradation of labor and the exploitation of women and children by the forces of free enterprise" (1978, 76; see also Robinson 2000, 376).

14 I earlier cited Thobani's claim that the 9/11 attacks gave "governing elites" the opportunity to portray "the not insignificant presence of people of colour as a potentially deadly threat to the nation" (2007, 250). But it would be electoral suicide to go after "people of colour" *in general*, at least at the level of national politics.

15 Note also that security and anti-terrorism discourse was mobilized in defence of Canada's resource-based capitalist economy, particularly with the Harper government's treatment of environmental protest. After Harper's Natural Resources Minister Joe Oliver accused environmentalists of using "funding from foreign special interest groups to undermine Canada's national economic interest," the National Energy Board, "an ostensibly independent regulatory agency, coordinated with the nation's intelligence service, police and oil companies to spy on environmentalists" (Leslie 2014).

16 For a concise history of employment equity in Canada, including the Ontario backlash, see Abu-Laban and Gabriel (2011, 129ff).

17 Thomas McCarthy notes that racism turned "scientific" in the late nineteenth century, under the influence of Darwinism and genetics. When that was no longer sustainable, emphasis shifted to "differences of culture and character. While these latter differences are no longer regarded as innate, they are regarded as deeply ingrained; and though they are not inherited biologically, they are passed on from generation to generation" (2009, 11).

18 "Moving" on is always an attractive idea to those who profit from the legacy of injustice. Richard III, who in Shakespeare's account has murdered his nephews to gain the throne, wants to move on: "Look what is done cannot be now amended." When Elizabeth mourns for her "poor infants, in their graves," Richard dismissively replies: "Harp not on that string, madam; that is past" (*Richard III*, 4.4).

19 It is interesting that one recommendation of the *Equality Now!* Parliamentary Committee explicitly rejected by the Mulroney government was that "Solicitor General Canada should increase the representation of visible minorities in the RCMP through the removal of artificial barriers and the initiation of an active recruiting strategy. Other police forces should do likewise" (Canada 1984).

20 Two important events since the writing of this chapter may or may not be instances of systemic racism in state institutions. Each warrants further study. The first is the passivity of the local police force in the face of the prolonged occupation in downtown Ottawa in early 2022. It was often suggested that the police non-response reflected the overwhelmingly

white nature of the protesters. This may well be true. Counter-evidence might be the brutality inflicted by police on protesters at the Toronto G20 summit in June 2010. The Toronto police force eventually had to pay $16.5 million in compensation to protesters who were illegally detained, and video of the police attack on the protesters that I have examined suggests that most of those protesters were white.

The second event is the generous response of the Canadian government towards those fleeing Ukraine, particularly when contrasted to the timid response to Afghan refugees. It would appear that (racialized, Muslim) refugees towards whom Canada has concrete obligations arising from our presence in Afghanistan are being treated less generously than (mostly white) refugees from Ukraine.

21 Note Porter's emphasis on *net* immigration. He comments: "It is unlikely that any other society has resembled a huge demographic railway station as much as has the non-French part of Canada. As well as a society receiving immigrants it has been one producing emigrants, either naturally or by harbouring the 'birds of passage' who have stopped over in Canada while making the move from Europe to the United States" (1965, 33).

22 Elrick's granular documentary study of individual immigration decisions (2022) demonstrates that immigration practice was loosening racial criteria prior to the official policy changes of the 1960s.

23 Whatever the orientation of the points system, the government did not neglect these narrow economic interests: "The government met the demand for cheap labour without recourse to increased immigration by issuing visas for temporary work to migrant workers, many of whom were seasonal workers from Mexico and the Caribbean, or domestic workers, a class which previously had been able to enter the country as landed immigrants" (Kelley and Trebilcock 2000, 361).

24 That reality provides some justification for the much-reviled concept of "visible minority," which designates precisely the person who could be the target of racism even if all behavioural characteristics differentiating them from the racial majority had disappeared.

25 It is probably impossible to rely consistently on the narrow ontology that Day invokes here. He certainly doesn't think another "discursive construct" – multiculturalism – is unreal. Indeed, as we saw in chapter 4, he endows it with remarkable powers: it makes claims and has hopes.

26 Anderson references mid-1970s research by Frances Henry on racism in Toronto that found that "persons who had migrated from Southern and Eastern Europe tended more towards racist attitudes than did those who were born in Canada, Great Britain, the U.S.A., or Western Europe" (1978, 144).

27 While the word "economy" does turn up once in his discussion of the 1967 shift, Triadafilopoulos's principal emphasis continues to rest on political considerations, such as the need to mollify domestic constituencies, and the points system's potential for "demonstrating the purity of Canada's intentions to the rest of the world" (2012, 103).
28 My calculations based on *Canada Year Book* data on immigration by country of birth show a 276 per cent increase over the five-year period (Dominion Bureau of Statistics 1962, 1968). Calculations based on Statistics Canada data on immigration by country of last permanent residence yield an increase of 291 per cent (Statistics Canada 2021).
29 On the first possibility: Triadafilopoulos himself notes that "administrative capacity stood far below that needed to carry out a truly global immigration program" (2012, 92). On the second: he cites a *Globe and Mail* editorial that warned that the new policy was vulnerable to bureaucrats whose "whole training and tradition" inclined them to oppose it (2012, 91).
30 As NASA's James Hansen puts it, full exploitation of the tar sands represents "game over for the climate" (2012). The claim has become more solid in the decade since it was made, as humanity's remaining "carbon budget" has inexorably dwindled.
31 As noted earlier, the guest worker strategy was used for particular economic sectors. In 2015, there were 45,000 temporary foreign workers in the agriculture sector (Statistics Canada 2019).
32 Elrick is citing a 1958 memo from the Assistant Deputy Minister to the Deputy Minister.
33 The massive reality of globalization can obscure the fact that much production is *not* mobile (Harvey 1982, 420). Depending on the specific nature of such production, a cheap low-skilled labour strategy may work, at least in economic terms: hence the reliance on temporary foreign workers in Canadian agriculture, the clamour of restaurant owners for temporary visa workers, and so on.

Chapter 7

1 The claim to have "brought civilization to vast areas hitherto uninhabited" reproduces the doctrine of *terra nullius*. On the role of that doctrine in the European conquest, see the Truth and Reconciliation Commission (2015, 46). Yuzyk's reference thus exemplifies a point stressed by Haque: the harmonization of Canadian multiculturalism discourse with settler-colonialism assumptions.
2 Yuzyk was taking aim at biculturalism within a month of his Senate appointment. A *Globe and Mail* article on a March 1963 Yuzyk speech

noted: "The Senator added that Canada is not a bicultural country, but a multicultural one" (*Globe and Mail* 1963).
3 The latter quote is used in a 1973 publication of the Ukrainian Canadian University Students' Union in order to chide those who "were not aware of the paradox between their being interested in maintaining Ukrainian identity and gradually losing their language skills through not speaking Ukrainian" (Zaputovich 1973).
4 In his history of feudal Europe, Marc Bloch noted how Latin facilitated communication throughout Europe (rpt. 1989, 124). But it was not the language of inner thought, hence its use involved "perpetual approximations" (*de perpétuels à peu près*). But that was the case for everyone. Now: replace Latin with English, say, and the advantage of the native speaker is obvious.
5 As I noted in *Multicultiphobia*, even the relatively innocuous multiculturalism policy eventually chosen by the government was regularly condemned by nationalists as precisely such a break. A complaint from Bloc Québécois MP Michel Daviault is typical: "The new Canadian multicultural identity which the government is trying to impose is in fact a ploy to acculturate Quebecers ... In the promotion of this glorious Canadian multicultural mosaic, the government is rather quick to forget the concept of two founding nations" (Commons, 27 October 1994).
6 And what did we in fact end up with? As of the end of March 2019, there were 5,626 executive (EX) positions in the federal government's "core public administration." Of these, 85 per cent were designated bilingual. While the bilingual EX positions are held coast-to-coast, some 83 per cent are in the National Capital Region. Just under two thirds (64.4 per cent) of the bilingual EX positions are held by anglophones. Visible minorities remain underrepresented at the executive level, holding just 10.1 per cent of all EX positions and 10.8 per cent of the bilingual ones.

Those figures are all based on data provided by the Treasury Board Secretariat (11 January 2021.) But there is much that we cannot know on the basis of TBS data. What is the province of origin of government executives? How many of them learned French growing up outside Quebec, eastern Ontario, or New Brunswick? Did anglophones and "allophones" from outside those regions learn *enough* French in school to allow them to build on their French-language skills while in the civil service?

These unknowns make it hard to judge whether coast-to-coast bilingualism was *in fact* necessary for a bilingual civil service that was not a central Canadian monopoly. Still, it probably *appeared* necessary at the time.

7 Children whose parents wanted them to receive such an education – if they had any say in the matter – might have offered the objection of Joyce's Stephen Dedalus: "My ancestors threw off their language and took another ... Do you fancy I am going to pay in my own life and person debts they made? What for?" (rpt. 1994, 147).
8 And it need not have hampered integration: Kymlicka notes that "there is now a voluminous literature in the United States suggesting that Hispanic children whose parents do not speak English will learn English better over the long term if they enrol in transitional bilingual programs" (1998, 51).

Chapter 8

1 Walter Lippmann quotes a "kindly gentlewoman" who asks: "What kind of American consciousness can grow in the atmosphere of sauerkraut and Limburger cheese? Or what can you expect of the Americanism of the man whose breath always reeks of garlic?" (2004, 47). If the food sharing that often takes place at multicultural festivals can help loosen up people's views of "appropriate" smells and tastes, it might serve as a gateway to fuller acceptance. For other potential benefits of "cultural spectacles," see Bramadat's interesting account (2001).
2 Though speaking of "respect" rather than tolerance, Ishmael in Melville's Moby Dick nicely captures the same mix of giving and taking away in one breath: "I cherish the greatest respect towards everybody's religious obligations, never mind how comical" (rpt. 1988, 84).
3 In their fascinating 2012 work *Racecraft*, Fields and Fields mock the same "tolerate thy neighbor" phrase (rpt. 2022, 104).
4 A comment in a later piece suggests that Day's strange claim arises from a profound confusion: between *people* and their *actions*. Offering his take on Will Kymlicka's views, Day writes that "there are [for Kymlicka], of course, 'limits of tolerance' that must also be respected. It is here, I would suggest, that liberal multiculturalism clearly reveals itself, despite its willingness to give gifts, as a fighting creed. Some Others are simply too different to be tolerated" (2014, 132). Day's confusion transforms the rather unarguable point that limitless tolerance is incompatible with life in society into an expression of xenophobia.
5 We might say that the idea that tolerance involves disliking something but putting up with it, as opposed to not disliking it in the first place, reflects the spirit of Kant rather than Aristotle. That is, it emphasizes the idea of doing the right thing against one's inclinations, which for Kant is the criterion for a specifically *moral* action (*Groundwork*, viii, 10), as opposed to having – and developing – the right inclinations. (The latter point *is* recognized by Kant but is not as central in his ethics.)

Notes to pages 186–91 263

6 Fish, who became famous during the first wave of political correctness debates by declaring that "free speech does not exist" (1994), went on to declare that "multiculturalism does not exist" (1997, 378). In both cases, he suffers from an unsustainable assumption according to which things only exist when they exist in what he happens to consider their pure form. Ryan (2001) critiques Fish's views on free speech.

7 An incident in early 2021 points to an analogous delimitation of another relevant term. Conservative leader Erin O'Toole had Derek Sloan tossed from the caucus when it became public that his leadership campaign had received a small donation from white supremacist Paul Fromm. Fromm commented that the party leader's "bluster and outrage give the lie to his promise to build an 'inclusive' party" (qtd. in Jones 2021). If we find the comment absurd, it is because there is normally a tacit recognition that there are limits to "inclusion."

Fromm's membership in the Conservative Party is another example of the connections between right and far-right that were discussed in chapter 2. The man who murdered nine Blacks in a Charleston, South Carolina, church in 2015 praised the "Council of Conservative Citizens" for helping radicalize him. Fromm at the time was the group's international director, and he described the massacre as a response to the "frustration of Whites faced with their ethnic cleansing and replacement in the U.S. and Canada" (qtd. in Logan 2015).

8 I have previously discussed the analogous paradox of writers who sneer at the very idea of truth, yet litter their writings with claims that begin "in fact," "it is clear that," and so on (Ryan 2015).

9 Preston King likewise declares that "if one concedes or promotes a power to tolerate, one equally concedes or promotes a power not to tolerate. Tolerance presupposes a liberty of action in regard to those matters or persons which are tolerated" (1998, 9).

10 Yet he warns of "how strong the permission conception still is in liberal-democratic societies, holding the political imagination captive" (Forst 2012, 150). We will return to this in a moment.

11 This political chill has bipartisan support: "In the run up to his successful 2015 election victory, the current Liberal Prime Minister, Justin Trudeau, tweeted 'The BDS movement, like Israeli Apartheid Week, has no place on Canadian campuses'" (Ziadah 2017, 19).

12 In *Multicultiphobia*, I discussed the possibility of "a common charter of obligations for any religious organization operating in Canada." This could seek to rein in practices such as homophobic religious preaching. Religious groups would not be *forced* to comply, but Canada could legitimately "make adherence to the charter a condition for enjoying the various public privileges already granted to religious organizations: tax

benefits, access of clergy to institutional populations, and so on" (2010b, 250).

13 Note that I chose a geometric example to illustrate "essence," precisely because it is uncontroversial. In the case of social concepts such as tolerance, identification of essential attributes is always tentative, and dependent to some degree on ordinary language usage. This argues against overloading one's core definition with elements that might prove to be "accidents."

14 What the Legault government itself thinks about this, however, is indicated by its invocation of the notwithstanding clause within the bill itself.

15 The First Amendment to the US Constitution offers a classic declaration of state tolerance of speech: "Congress shall make no law ... abridging the freedom of speech." As Simone Chambers points out, "the First Amendment does not enforce the reciprocal requirements of practical discourse. It does not require us to *listen* to what others have to say; it does not require us to attempt to *understand* the other's point of view; it does not require us to *refrain* from manipulating or deceiving others; it does not require us to be *swayed* by the force of the better argument" (1995, 246).

Chapter 9

1 In *The Mind of the South*, W.J. Cash discussed the ideological effects upon poor whites of the southern plantation system, which compensated for poverty through "that other vastly ego-warming and ego-expanding distinction between the white man and the black. Robbing him and degrading him in so many ways, it yet, by singular irony, had simultaneously elevated this common white to a position comparable to that of, say, the Doric knight of ancient Sparta... Come what might, he would always be a white man" (1941, 38–9).

2 The challenge of terminology reflects in part the shifting nature of the phenomena being studied. Winter notes that the various players in her triangular relations have changing attributes and take up different positions: Québécois, in particular, are sometimes "others" sometimes "them" (2011, 6). As Winter recognizes: "The terms 'us,' 'them,' 'others' are proxies that operate interchangeably. Which category of 'others' is included conditionally within the pluralist we, and which is excluded ... is not fixed in time" (198).

3 The "speak white" insult is of long standing. In a 1945 debate, then-Independent MP Bona Arsenault depicted the fate of a "little Quebec farmer's son" who was conscripted, "and found himself lost, hundreds if

not thousands of miles away from his home, where he was often requested to speak 'white'" (Commons, 30 October 1945).
4 A Liberal MP offers an analogous claim, in support of trade with India: "We have much in common. Although India is a world away, literally, both countries are democracies with vibrant, multicultural societies" (Borys Wrzesnewskyj, 22 March 2018). India is certainly multicultural, and it could once boast a history of tolerance. But the MP's claim is deeply problematic under the reign of Modi, as it implies that the multiculturalism we supposedly share with India is *only* a matter of demographics and is compatible even with organized violence against religious minorities.
5 CPC MPs also offered the occasional intervention linking multiculturalism to problems such as services for newcomers (Dan Albas, 9 March 2017), intolerance (Sylvie Boucher, 30 January 2017), and hate crimes (Rachael Harder, 3 May 2017). (This last intervention also *opposed* a Liberal motion condemning Islamophobia, arguing that it "could take away the freedom of Canadians to debate the merits of religious ideas.")
6 The other two forms are "Relativism 1) All viewpoints have equal value," and "Relativism 2) All cultures are equally valid" (Ryan 2010b, 137).

Chapter 10

1 McAndrew and colleagues (2005) document the near-disappearance of multiculturalism funding for cultural activities in the 1980s and 1990s.
2 In chapter 6, I noted Thomas McCarthy's observation that much current-day racism rests less on biological notions than upon alleged "differences of culture and character" (2009, 11). This form of racism is ideally suited to be extended to the white working class, welfare recipients, and so on.

This does not mean that every claim of class superiority is a disguised form of racism. We might say that class becomes "race-like" when a set of traits is viewed as largely immutable and as transmitted from one generation to the next. Clifford Sifton's comment that the immigrants Canada needed were those "bred for generations to work from daylight to dark" (see chapter 6) is an example. When Adam Smith, on the other hand, argued that the modern division of labour reduced the majority of people to a state of imbecility – "as stupid and ignorant as it is possible for a human creature to become" (1937, 734) – he did not say that the condition was fixed, nor that it was hereditary.
3 X is a "permissive cause" of Y when it allows Y to happen without directly causing it. The concept of "permissive causes" rests on Weber's approach to causal analysis, according to which X can be said to cause Y *to the extent* that, in the absence of X, Y would not have occurred (1949, 164–73).

Homophobia within the Toronto police force, for example, was probably a "permissive cause" of the disappearance of gay men over many years, as it led the police to treat the disappearances with less seriousness than they might otherwise have done. X can be both a permissive cause of Y *and* an effect of it, if Y is an ongoing situation of domination and X is a set of beliefs that came about to justify it.

4 This is probably overstated: slavery most likely made use of, and reinforced, pre-existing prejudices. But the view that racism is at least in part an ideological reflex of material domination is sound.

Note that the passage cited in the previous chapter from W.J. Cash's *The Mind of the South* suggests that racism can function as a double mask, as it obscures the material exploitation of poor whites.

5 I will use "nation" in the minimal sense that the term is used in the label "United Nations": that is, with no assumption of any particular form of shared history, language, and so on. The *Oxford English Dictionary* entry for the term notes: "In early examples notions of race and common descent predominate. In later use notions of territory, political unity, and independence are more prominent, although some writers still make a pointed distinction between nation and state" (2000).

The restrictive understanding of the term, based on an alleged common descent, is naturally favoured by those who feel that the country somehow belongs to them. More relaxed understandings – such as Leopold Bloom's "A nation is the same people living in the same place" (Joyce rpt. 2000, 430) – have an obvious appeal for those trying to assert their membership within traditionally closed communities.

6 An irony of the proposal is that Nordhaus has long opposed serious climate action, yet his club idea may be our only hope in a world of sovereign states.

7 Compatibility with democratic consensus should be a vital *normative* constraint on many political decisions. With respect to international and environmental justice, things are more complicated. If one believes – as do Thobani, Benhabib, and I – that a significant portion of the wealth of the global North originates in past and present injustice towards citizens of the global South, then one must acknowledge that we are in possession of "ill-gotten gains." We are also in effect stealing from future generations, given our inaction on climate and other environmental challenges. Now, no one would say that it would be *wrong* to seize the ill-gotten gains of a drug cartel without the consent of its members: the normative constraint does not apply.

But the requirement of democratic consent remains a *practical* constraint on the path to global and environmental justice, unless one can imagine a radical and lasting restructuring of the rules and imperatives governing

the global economy coming about without the organized consent of the peoples of the global North.
8 Max Hastings writes of the "lasting revulsion" eventually provoked by the ubiquitous appeals to patriotism in the First World War, among many "who felt that they had been duped" (2013, 423).
9 This is not the only challenge. One can imagine a hypothetical society with a rich and inclusive sense of national identity, yet in which nationalist sentiment remains vulnerable to manipulation in the service of problematic goals such as military adventures. We will return to the problem of manipulation in a moment.
10 Slavoj Žižek rejects such attempts to distinguish the positive and negative elements of national pride:
> It is deeply wrong to assert that, when one throws out nationalist dirty water – "excessive" fanaticism – one should be careful not to lose the baby of "healthy" national identity, so that one should trace the line of separation between the proper degree of "healthy" nationalism which guarantees the necessary minimum of national identity, and "excessive" nationalism. Such a common sense distinction *reproduces the very nationalist reasoning which aims to get rid of "impure" excess*. (1997, 38)

Stripped of the obscurantism for which Žižek is (in)famous, this is a particularly nihilistic version of the "all limits are bad" thesis. Here, an exercise of moral and political discernment is dismissed as immoral, likened to nationalist xenophobia.
11 Today, the enthusiasts of overseas military adventures can be strikingly frank in stating the often tawdry objectives being pursued: "Canada's economy depends on trade with the United States, and this dependence cannot be changed. We are extremely vulnerable if the administration in Washington is unhappy with us, and we are in peril if border crossings are slowed for even a few minutes more for each truck or if passports are required to cross the border. The need to keep the economy strong ought to have determined the Iraq question for us" (Granatstein 2007, 151). The argument recalls Chesterton's observation that the reasons of *realpolitik* are "almost insanely unreal" for those who must die for them (1925, 158).
12 One of the virtues of Matt James's *Misrecognized Materialists* is that it makes an important contribution to that recovery (2006).
13 I am using one of the figurative senses of "textured": "as 'woven' of various qualities" (*Oxford English Dictionary* 2000).
14 It should be clear that in citing this particular point from Herder, I am not endorsing his overall view of culture and nationhood.
15 The following comments are based most immediately upon the body of parliamentary discourse studied in the previous chapter. But I believe

Chapter 11

1 For theologian Hans Küng, Hegel's dialectic was grounded in the insight that "I cannot state the truth absolutely clearly and distinctly merely in *one* sentence, but really need three, dialectically affirming, denying, surpassing: this is how it is, and yet not so, in fact there is more to it. And so on. In this sense truth lies in the totality, not in the individual steps, theses, propositions or elements of which it is made up" (1981, 30).

2 While the avoidance of mystery writing favours clear writing, it certainly does not guarantee it. Some dimensions of social reality are so tangled that one cannot offer even a basic description free of complexity. There are also articulations of specialized thought that will be too difficult for those outside a discipline to understand. Even in such cases, however, avoiding the imprecisions of mystery writing can make one's argument more amenable to a simplified rendering, which itself can provide a further test of intelligibility and political relevance.

3 Adolph Reed critiques "the 'whiteness' notion that has been fashionable within the academic left for roughly two decades: it reifies whiteness as a transhistorical social category. In effect, it treats 'whiteness' – and therefore 'race' – as existing prior to and above social context" (2013, 52). Analogously, as Gargi Bhattacharyya argues, if we try to understand patriarchy in isolation from capitalism, "we become stuck in ideas of culture or ideology which cannot be explained without 'the notion of some inborn aggressive or sadistic tendencies in men'" (2018, 45; the last words are from Maria Mies.)

4 Touré F. Reed's important *Toward Freedom: The Case against Race Reductionism* offers an analogous argument: "Given the disproportionate impact of deindustrialization, the decline of the union movement and public sector retrenchment on blacks," American Blacks can benefit disproportionately from "truly universal redistributive programs" (2020, 18, 120). The programs must, of course, be *truly* universal, without the racial exclusions that marred crucial New Deal policies.

5 For purposes of vividness, I have drawn here from two different versions. The first quote is Warner's translation (1954), the second is Crawley's (1874).

6 This is a key reason why slapping the label "terrorism" on a particular instance of political action is so decisive, as it can mobilize a "do whatever it takes to defeat this" sentiment among broad swaths of the public, silencing ethical qualms.

7 Pity for another, said Thomas Hobbes, is caused by "the imagination that the like calamity may befall himselfe." Contempt, on the other hand, is an "immobility of the heart," arising from "security of their own fortune" (rpt. 1968, 120, 126). This points to one of the effects of ideological masks such as racism, or concepts such as "culture of poverty": such masks attribute the suffering to qualities of the suffering person alone, and thus support the observer's sense of immunity.
8 In this light, we can also interpret many forms of information control and repression as attempts to *prevent* the conscience of significant parts of the public from being awoken.
9 Joppke's certainty that multiculturalism necessarily involves this would seem to require the fairly simple one-dimensional understanding of culture critiqued in chapter 3.
10 I make a Rawlsian assumption here that there would be *some* occupational inequality in a just society, but I would be happy to be proven wrong.

Works Cited

Abu-Laban, Yasmeen, and Christina Gabriel. 2011. *Selling Diversity*. Toronto: University of Toronto Press.
Akhtar, Ayad. 2020. *Homeland Elegies*. New York: Little, Brown.
Albert, Hans. 1985. *Treatise on Critical Reason*. Translated by Mary Varney Rorty. Princeton: Princeton University Press.
Allison, Graham. 1971. *Essence of Decision*. Boston: Little, Brown.
Almássy, Ferenc. 2018. "Kulturkampf in Hungary, goodbye 'gender studies' – and it's only the beginning." *Visegrad Post*, 25 August.
Alterman, Eric. 2004. *When Presidents Lie: A History of Official Deception and Its Consequences*. New York: Penguin.
Althusser, Louis. 1971. *Lenin and Philosophy and Other Essays*. New York: Monthly Review Press.
Amarasingam, Amarnath, Gayathri Naganathan, and Jennifer Hyndman. 2016. "Canadian Multiculturalism as Banal Nationalism: Understanding Everyday Meanings among Sri Lankan Tamils in Toronto." *Canadian Ethnic Studies* 48, no. 2: 119–41. https://doi.org/10.1353/ces.2016.0016.
Anderson, A.B. 1978. "Racism in Toronto." *Canadian Ethnic Studies* 10, no. 2: 141–8.
Anderson, Benedict. 1991. *Imagined Communities: Reflections on the Origin and Spread of Nationalism* [1983]. London: Verso.
Anderson, Bruce, and David Coletto. 2022. "Millions believe in conspiracy theories in Canada." *Abacus Data*, 12 June. https://abacusdata.ca/conspiracy-theories-canada.
APTN. 2020. "Remembering Joyce Echaquan: Frequently asked questions and the facts so far." *APTN National News*, 7 October.
Arbel, Efrat, and Alletta Brenner. 2013. *Bordering on Failure: Canada–US Border Policy and the Politics of Refugee Exclusion*. Harvard Immigration and Refugee Law Clinical Program (November).
Arendt, Hannah. 1958a. *The Human Condition*. Chicago: University of Chicago Press.

- 1958b. *The Origins of Totalitarianism* [1951], 2nd ed. New York: Meridian.
- 1972. *Crises of the Republic*. New York: Harcourt, Brace.
- 2003. *Responsibility and Judgment*. New York: Shocken.
- 2007. *The Jewish Writings*. New York: Shocken.

Aristotle. 1941. *The Basic Works of Aristotle*. Edited by Richard McKeon. New York: Random House.

Auden, W.H. 2007. *Collected Poems*. Edited by Edward Mendelson. New York: Modern Library.

Augustine. 1961. *Confessions*. Translated by R.S. Pine-Coffin. London: Penguin.

Austin, David. 2007. "All Roads Led to Montreal: Black Power, the Caribbean, and the Black Radical Tradition in Canada." *Journal of African American History* 92, no. 4 (Autumn): 516–39. https://doi.org/10.1086/JAAHv92n4p516

B&B Commission. 1969. *See* Royal Commission on Bilingualism and Biculturalism.

Bailey, Ian. 2020. "Six in 10 Chinese Canadians say they have adjusted routines to avoid racist run-ins during COVID-19." *Globe and Mail*, 22 June.

Bakht, Natasha. 2011. "Mere 'Song and Dance': Complicating the Multicultural Imperative in the Arts." In *Home and Native Land: Unsettling Multiculturalism in Canada*, edited by May Chazan, Lisa Helps, and Anna Stanley. Toronto: Between the Lines.

Balfour, Clair. 1969. "$1.4 million loss at Sir George Williams." *Globe and Mail*, 12 February.

Balint, Peter. 2017. *Respecting Toleration: Traditional Liberalism and Contemporary Diversity*. Oxford: Oxford University Press.

Bannerji, Himani. 1990. Interview by Arun Mukherjee. In *Other Solitudes: Canadian Multicultural Fictions*, edited by Linda Hutcheon and Marion Richmond. Toronto: Oxford University Press.

- 1996. "On the Dark Side of the Nation: Politics of Multiculturalism and the State of 'Canada.'" *Journal of Canadian Studies* 31, no. 3 (Fall): 103–28. https://doi.org/10.3138/jcs.31.3.103.
- 2000. *The Dark Side of the Nation: Essays on Multiculturalism, Nationalism, and Gender*. Toronto: Canadian Scholars' Press.

Banting, Keith, et al. 2006. "Do Multiculturalism Policies Erode the Welfare State? An Empirical Analysis." In *Multiculturalism and the Welfare State*, edited by Keith Banting and Will Kymlicka. Oxford: Oxford University Press.

Banting, Keith, and Will Kymlicka. 2006. "Introduction: Multiculturalism and the Welfare State: Setting the Context." In *Multiculturalism and the Welfare State*, edited by Keith Banting and Will Kymlicka. Oxford: Oxford University Press.

Barry, Brian. 2001. *Culture and Equality: An Egalitarian Critique of Multiculturalism*. Cambridge, MA: Harvard University Press.

Beaman, Lori. 2012. "The Missing Link: Tolerance, Accommodation and ... Equality." *Canadian Diversity* 9, no. 3 (Summer): 16–19.

Becker, Gary. 1976. *The Economic Approach to Human Behavior*. Chicago: University of Chicago Press.
Benhabib, Seyla. 2004. *The Rights of Others: Aliens, Residents, and Citizens*. Cambridge: Cambridge University Press.
Benjamin, Walter. 2006. *Selected Writings 1938–1940*, vol. 4. Cambridge, MA: Harvard University Press.
Benn, Tony. 1989. "Obstacles to Reform in Britain." *The Socialist Register 1989*.
Benson, Rodney. 2013. *Shaping Immigration News: A French–American Comparison*. Cambridge: Cambridge University Press.
Bercuson, David, J.L. Granatstein, and Nancy Pearson Mackie. 2011. "Lessons Learned? What Canada Should Learn from Afghanistan." Canadian Defence and Foreign Affairs Institute (October).
Bernier, Max. 2018. "Free speech and equal rights for all," 15 November. www.maximebernier.com/free_speech_and_equal_rights_for_all.
Berry, John, Rudolf Kalin, and Donald Taylor. 1977. *Multiculturalism and Ethnic Attitudes in Canada*. Ottawa: Ministry of Supply and Services.
Bhaskar, Roy. 1998. *The Possibility of Naturalism*, 3rd ed. London: Routledge.
– 2008. *A Realist Theory of Science*. London: Verso.
Bhattacharyya, Gargi. 2018. *Rethinking Racial Capitalism: Questions of Reproduction and Survival*. Lanham: Rowman and Littlefield.
Bird, Pat. 1975. *Of Dust and Time and Dreams and Agonies: A Short History of Canadian People*. Toronto: Canadian News Synthesis Project
Bissoondath, Neil. 1994. *Selling illusions: The Cult of Multiculturalism in Canada*. Toronto: Penguin Books.
Bloch, Marc. 1989. *La Société Féodale*. Paris: Albin Michel.
Block, Sheila, Grace-Edward Galabuzi, and Ricardo Tranjan. 2019. "Canada's Colour Coded Income Inequality." Canadian Centre for Policy Alternatives (December).
Blumenberg, Hans. 1987. "An Anthropological Approach to the Contemporary Significance of Rhetoric." In *After Philosophy*, edited by Kenneth Baynes, James Bohman, and Thomas McCarthy. Cambridge, MA: MIT Press.
Bolaria, B. Singh, and Peter S. Li. 1988. *Racial Oppression in Canada*, 2nd ed. Toronto: Garamond.
Bonelli, Laurent. 2020. "Les forces de l'ordre social." *Le Monde Diplomatique*, July.
Bonhoeffer, Dietrich. 1998. *Widerstand und Ergebung: Briefe und Aufzeichnungen aus der Haft. Munich: Gütersloher Verlagshaus*. [1951]. Munich: Gütersloher Verlagshaus.
Bourdieu, Pierre. 2000. *Esquisse d'une théorie de la pratique, précédé de Trois études d'ethnologie kabyle* [1972]. Paris: Éditions du Seuil.
– 2003. *Méditations Pascaliennes* [1997]. Paris: Éditions du Seuil.
– 2012. *Sur l'État: Cours au Collège de France, 1989–1992*. Paris: Éditions du Seuil.

Bramadat, Paul. 2001. "Shows, Selves, and Solidarity: Ethnic Identity and Cultural Spectacles in Canada." *Canadian Ethnic Studies* 33, no. 3: 78–98.

Brand, Dionne. 1990. Interview by Dagmar Novak. In *Other Solitudes: Canadian Multicultural Fictions*, edited by Linda Hutcheon and Marion Richmond. Toronto: Oxford University Press.

Breton, Raymond. 1986. "Multiculturalism and Canadian Nation-Building." In *Politics of Gender, Ethnicity, and Language in Canada*, edited by Alan C. Cairns and Cynthia Williams. Ottawa: Supply and Services Canada.

Bréville, Benoît. 2015. "Dix principes de la mécanique conspirationniste." *Le Monde Diplomatique*, June.

– 2020. "Quand les grandes villes font sécession." *Le Monde Diplomatique*, March.

Brown, Beth. 2020. "Man in violent Nunavut arrest video wants officer charged." *CBC News*, 5 June.

Bryce, P.H. 1910. "Report of Dr. P.H. Bryce, Chief Medical Officer." *Sessional Papers of the Dominion of Canada 1910*.

Buchanan, James M., and Gordon Tullock. 1962. *The Calculus of Consent*. Ann Arbor: University of Michigan Press.

Bulard, Martine. 2017. "Le Vietnam se rêve en atelier de la planète." *Le Monde Diplomatique*, February.

Bureau, Brigitte, and Sylvie Robillard. 2019. "'Distasteful alliances': The secret story of Canada's fight against migrants." *CBC News*, 21 May.

Burman, Jenny. 2016. "Multicultural Feeling, Feminist Rage, Indigenous Refusal." *Cultural Studies, Critical Methodologies* 16, no. 4: 361–72. https://doi.org/10.1177/1532708616638693.

Burnet, Jean. 1975. "Multiculturalism, Immigration, and Racism: A Comment on the Canadian Immigration and Population Study." *Canadian Ethnic Studies* 7, no. 1: 35–9.

– 1978. "The Policy of Multiculturalism within a Bilingual Framework: A Stock-Taking." *Canadian Ethnic Studies* 10, no. 2: 107–13.

Byfield, Ted. 2006. "We may be naive but we're not soft." *Calgary Sun*, 11 June.

C-Span. 2005. "Prime Minister news conference, 26 July." www.c-span.org/video/?187936-1/prime-minister-news-conference (24 April 2020).

Calhoun, Craig, ed. 1992. *Habermas and the Public Sphere*. Cambridge, MA.: MIT Press.

Cameron, David Robertson. 2007. "An Evolutionary Story." In *Uneasy Partners: Multiculturalism and Rights in Canada*, edited by Janice Gross Stein et al. Waterloo: Wilfrid Laurier University Press.

Camus, Albert. 1956. *La chute*. Paris: Gallimard.

Canada. 1984. *Response of the Government of Canada to: Equality Now! The Report of the Special Parliamentary Committee on Visible Minorities in Canadian Society*. Ottawa: Supply and Services Canada.

- House of Commons. 1890–2019. *Debates.* **Note**: Two sources were used – the official www.ourcommons.ca, and the more user-friendly www.lipad.ca, maintained at the University of Toronto.
- House of Commons. Select Standing Committee on Agriculture and Colonization. 1900. *Report.* Ottawa: Dominion Department of Agriculture.
- House of Commons. Special Committee on Participation of Visible Minorities in Canadian Society. 1984. *Equality Now!* Ottawa: Queen's Printer.
- Senate. 1964. *Debates.*
- Senate. Standing Senate Committee on Social Affairs, Science and Technology. 2011. *Proceedings.* Ottawa.
- Task Force on Government Information. 1969. *To Know and Be Known.* Ottawa: Queen's Printer.

Canadian Heritage. 2018. *Annual Report on the Operation of the Canadian Multiculturalism Act 2016–2017.* Ottawa. www.canada.ca/en/canadian-heritage/corporate/publications/plans-reports/annual-report-canadian-multiculturalism-act-2016-2017.html.

Canadian Press. 2018. "Conservative party pulls attack ad of black man walking over Trudeau tweet." *CBC*, 18 July.

Cannon, Margaret. 1995. *The Invisible Empire: Racism in Canada.* Toronto: Random House.

Caplan, Bryan. 2006. *The Myth of the Rational Voter.* Princeton: Princeton University Press.

Carastathis, Anna. 2014. "The Concept of Intersectionality in Feminist Theory." *Philosophy Compass* 9, no. 5: 304–14. https://doi.org/10.1111/phc3.12129.

Carranco, Shannon, and Jon Milton. 2019. "Canada's new far right: A trove of private chat room messages reveals an extremist subculture." *Globe and Mail*, 27 April.

Carty, Linda, and Dionne Brand. 1993. "'Visible Minority' Women: A Creation of the Canadian State." In *Returning the Gaze: Essays on Racism, Feminism, and Politics,* edited by Himani Bannerji. Toronto: Sister Vision.

Cash, W.J. 1941. *The Mind of the South.* New York: A.A. Knopf.

CBC. 2020a. "Black man beaten, stabbed by group of 5 in 'reprehensible' Brandon assault." *CBC News*, 4 September.
- 2020b. "Pembroke won't be 'defined by racism,' mayor vows." *CBC News*, 2 September.

CCF (Co-operative Commonwealth Federation). 1933. *The Regina Manifesto.* Regina. www.connexions.org/CxLibrary/Docs/CX5373-ReginaManifesto.htm.

Chambers, Lori, and Kristin Burnett. 2017. "Jordan's Principle: The Struggle to Access on Reserve Health Care for High-Needs Indigenous Children in Canada." *American Indian Quarterly* 41, no. 2: 101–24. https://doi.org/10.1353/aiq.2017.a663047.

Chambers, Simone. 1995. "Discourse and Democratic Practices. In *The Cambridge Companion to Habermas*, edited by Stephen K. White. Cambridge: Cambridge University Press.

Chazan, May, et al. 2011. "Introduction: Labours, Lands, Bodies." In *Home and Native Land: Unsettling Multiculturalism in Canada*, edited by May Chazan, Lisa Helps, and Anna Stanley. Toronto: Between the Lines.

Chesterton, G.K. 1925. *The Everlasting Man*. London: Hodder and Stoughton.

Chomsky, Noam, and Michel Foucault. 2006. "The Chomsky–Foucault Debate." New York: New Press. Note: In 1971, a Dutch TV network rather improbably carried a debate in French and English between Chomsky and Foucault. I have drawn on this source for Chomsky's contributions, and from the second volume of *Dits et écrits* (1994) for Foucault's.

CIC (Citizenship and Immigration Canada). 2009. *Discover Canada: The Rights and Responsibilities of Citizenship*. Ottawa: Minister of Public Works and Government Services.

Clarke, Douglass Burns. 1969. "Sir George Williams." *Globe and Mail*, 15 February.

Clarke, George Elliott. 2011. "For a Multicultural, Multi-Faith, Multiracial Canada: A Manifesto." In *Home and Native Land: Unsettling Multiculturalism in Canada*, edited by May Chazan, Lisa Helps, and Anna Stanley. Toronto: Between the Lines.

Cohen, Michael D., James G. March, and Johan P. Olsen. 1972. "A Garbage Can Model of Organizational Choice. *Administrative Science Quarterly* 17, no. 1 (March): 1–25. https://doi.org/10.2307/2392088.

Cohen-Almagor, Raphael. 2006. *The Scope of Tolerance: Studies on the Costs of Free Expression and Freedom of the Press*. London: Routledge.

Cole, Desmond. 2020. *The Skin We're In*. Toronto: Doubleday.

Coleman, James. 1990. *Foundations of Social Theory*. Cambridge, MA: Harvard University Press.

Collier, Andrew. 1994. *Critical Realism: An Introduction to Roy Bhaskar's Philosophy*. London: Verso.

Commission on Systemic Racism in the Ontario Criminal Justice System. 1995. *Report*. Toronto: Queen's Printer for Ontario.

Coulthard, Glen Sean. 2014. *Red Skin, White Masks: Rejecting the Colonial Politics of Recognition*. Minneapolis: University of Minnesota Press.

Coyne, Andrew. 2016. "'Liberals' commitment to diversity would be a lot more admirable if they were not so selective about it." *National Post*, 26 August.

Crepaz, Markus. 2006. "'If you are my brother, I may give you a dime!': Public Opinion on Multiculturalism, Trust, and the Welfare State." In *Multiculturalism and the Welfare State*, edited by Keith Banting and Will Kymlicka. Oxford: Oxford University Press.

Crick, Bernard. 2004. "All this talk of Britain is so ... English." *The Guardian*, 12 April.

Crozier, Michel, Samuel Huntington, and Joji Watanuki. 1975. *The Crisis of Democracy: Report on the Governability of Democracies to the Trilateral Commission.* New York: NYU Press.

CTV. 2020. "UCP founding member deletes tweet that criticized comment on racism." *CTV News*, 1 June.

Davey, Jacob, Cécile Guerin, and Mackenzie Hart. 2020. "An online environmental scan of right-wing extremism in Canada." Institute for Strategic Dialogue, 19 June. www.isdglobal.org/isd-publications/canada-online.

Day, Richard. 2000. *Multiculturalism and the History of Canadian Diversity.* Toronto: University of Toronto Press.

– 2014. "Never Coming Out to Be Met? Liberal Multiculturalism and Its Radical Others." In *The Multiculturalism Question: Debating Identity in 21st Century Canada*, edited by Jack Jedwab. Montreal and Kingston: McGill–Queen's University Press.

Day, Robert, and Robert Hamblin. 1964. "Some Effects of Close and Punitive Styles of Supervision." *American Journal of Sociology* 69 no. 5: 499–510. https://doi.org/10.1086/223653.

Dei, George J. Sefa. 2011. "In Defense of Official Multiculturalism and Recognition of the Necessity of Critical Anti-Racism." *Canadian Issues* (Spring): 15–19.

Derenoncourt, Ellora, and Claire Montialoux. 2020. "To reduce racial inequality, raise the minimum wage." *New York Times*, 25 October.

Derrida, Jacques. 1999. "Hospitality, Justice, and Responsibility" (interview by Brendan Purcell et al.). In *Questioning Ethics: Contemporary Debates in Philosophy*, edited by Richard Kearney and Mark Dooley. London: Routledge.

Dewing, Michael, and Marc Leman. 2006. *Canadian Multiculturalism.* Ottawa: Library of Parliament.

DiAngelo, Robin. 2018. *White Fragility: Why It's So Hard to Talk to White People about Racism.* Boston: Beacon Press.

Dickens, Charles. 1867. *Little Dorrit*, vol. 2. London: Chapman and Hall.

Doctorow, Cory. 2019. *Radicalized.* New York: Tor.

Dominion Bureau of Statistics. 1962. *Canada Year Book 1962.* Ottawa: Census and Statistics Office.

– 1968. *Canada Year Book 1968.* Ottawa: Census and Statistics Office.

Dormer, Dave. 2018. "Video of racially charged argument at Lethbridge restaurant sparks outrage on social media." *CBC News*, 9 May.

Downs, Anthony. 1957. *An Economic Theory of Democracy.* New York: Harper and Row.

Dubenko, Anna. 2017. "Right and left react to Trump's latest Charlottesville comments blaming 'both sides.'" *New York Times*, 16 August.

Eagleton, Terry. 1991. *Ideology: An Introduction.* London: Verso.

Edelman, Murray. 1988. *Constructing the Political Spectacle.* Chicago: University of Chicago Press.

Edsall, Thomas. 2020. "In God we divide." *New York Times*, 25 March.
Egan, Brian. 2011. "Recognition Politics and Reconciliation Fantasies: Liberal Multiculturalism and the 'Indian Land Question.'" In *Home and Native Land: Unsettling Multiculturalism in Canada*, edited by May Chazan, Lisa Helps, and Anna Stanley. Toronto: Between the Lines.
Elghawaby, Amira, and Bernie Farber. 2015. "Forget labels when we witness such dire human need." *Globe and Mail*, 5 September.
Eliot, T.S. 1963. "Four Quartets." In *Collected Poems: 1909–1962*. London: Faber and Faber.
Elkin, Stephen L. 1985. "Pluralism in Its Place: State and Regime in Liberal Democracy." In *The Democratic State*, edited by Roger Benjamin and Stephen L. Elkin. Lawrence: University Press of Kansas.
Elrick, Jennifer. 2022. *Making Middle-Class Multiculturalism: Immigration Bureaucrats and Policymaking in Postwar Canada*. Toronto: University of Toronto Press.
"Enoch Powell's 'Rivers of Blood' speech." 2007. *The Telegraph*, 6 November.
Environics Institute for Survey Research. 2022. "Canadian public opinion about immigration and refugees." https://www.environicsinstitute.org/docs/default-source/project-documents/focus-canada---fall-2022---immigration-refugees/focus-canada-fall-2022---canadian-public-opinion-about-immigration-refugees---final-report.pdf (21 November).
Fanon, Frantz. 1968. *Les Damnés de la Terre* [1961]. Paris: Maspero.
Fantino, Julian. 2018. "In support of our police: Recent upswing in violence fault of politicians, not cops." *Toronto Sun*, 8 July.
Fassin, Eric. 2009. "L'immigration, un 'problème' si commode." *Le Monde Diplomatique*, November.
Faulkner, William. 1953. *Requiem for a Nun*. London: Chatto and Windus
Fields, Karen E., and Barbara J. Fields. 2022. *Racecraft: The Soul of Inequality in American Life* [2012]. London: Verso.
Fish, Stanley. 1994. *There's No Such Thing as Free Speech: And It's a Good Things, Too*. New York: Oxford University Press.
– 1997. "Boutique Multiculturalism, or Why Liberals Are Incapable of Thinking about Hate Speech." *Critical Inquiry* 23, no. 2 (Winter): 378–95. https://doi.org/10.1086/448833.
Fitzpatrick, Meagan. 2013. "Harper on terror arrests: Not a time for 'sociology.'" *CBC News*, 25 April.
Fleras, Augie. 2015. "Beyond Multiculturalism." In *Revisiting Multiculturalism in Canada: Theories, Policies and Debates*, edited by Shibao Guo and Lloyd Wong. Rotterdam: Sense.
– 2021. "Fifty Years of Canadian Multiculturalism: A Riddle, a Mystery, an Enigma." *Canadian Issues* 18 no. 1: 18–21.
Fleras, Augie, and Jean Leonard Elliott. 2002. *Engaging Diversity: Multiculturalism in Canada*, 2nd ed. Toronto: Nelson Thomson Learning.

Forbes, Hugh Donald. 2019. *Multiculturalism in Canada: Constructing a Model Multiculture with Multicultural Values*. Cham: Palgrave Macmillan.
Ford, Henry, and Samuel Crowther. 1922. *My Life and Work*. Garden City: Garden City Publishing.
Forst, Rainer. 2012. *The Right to Justification*. New York: Columbia University Press.
Foucault, Michel. 1984. *Histoire de la sexualité III: Le souci de soi*. Paris: Gallimard.
– 1989. *Résumé des cours, 1970–1982*. Paris: Julliard.
– 1994. *Dits et écrits: 1954–1988*. Paris: Gallimard.
– 1997. "What Is Critique?" In *The Politics of Truth*, edited by Sylvère Lotringer and Lysa Hochroth. New York: Semiotext(e).
Frank, Thomas. 2004. "Lie Down for America." *Harper's*, April.
– 2016. "Tir groupé contre Bernie Sanders." *Le Monde Diplomatique*, December.
Fraser, Nancy. 1995. "From Redistribution to Recognition? Dilemmas of Justice in a 'Post-Socialist' Age. *New Left Review* 212 (July–August): 68–93.
Friedman, Milton. 1962. *Capitalism and Freedom*. Chicago: University of Chicago Press.
Frost, Catherine. 2011. "How Canada Killed Multiculturalism." *Canadian Ethnic Studies* 43, nos. 1–2: 253–64. https://doi.org/10.1353/ces.2011.0012.
Gadamer, Hans-Georg. 1989. *Truth and Method* [1960], 2nd ed. New York: Continuum.
Galabuzi, Grace-Edward. 2011. "Hegemonies, Continuities, and Discontinuities of Multiculturalism, and the Anglo-Franco Conformity Order." In *Home and Native Land: Unsettling Multiculturalism in Canada*, edited by May Chazan, Lisa Helps, and Anna Stanley. Toronto: Between the Lines.
Galeano, Eduardo. 1981. *Días y noches de amor y de guerra*. Barcelona: Editorial Laia.
Gallie, W.B. 1955–56. "Essentially Contested Concepts." *Proceedings of the Aristotelian Society*, new series 56: 167–98. https://doi.org/10.1093/aristotelian/56.1.167.
Gardiner, Stephen. 2011. *A Perfect Moral Storm: The Ethical Tragedy of Climate Change*. Oxford: Oxford University Press.
Gee, Marcus. 2016. "No, your kids shouldn't be exempted from music class on religious grounds." *Globe and Mail*, 6 September.
Gerson, Michael. 2010. "Gay Rights and Pro-Life: Two Divergent Movements." *Washington Post*, 12 March.
Giddens, Anthony. 1984. *The Constitution of Society*. Berkeley: University of California Press.
Gillis, Megan. 2018. "It's okay to be white" signs appear in Ottawa. *Ottawa Citizen*, 1 November.

Gilman, Sander L. 1999. "'Barbaric' rituals?" In *Is Multiculturalism Bad for Women?*, edited by Joshua Cohen, Matthew Howard, and Martha C. Nussbaum. Princeton: Princeton University Press.
Global Affairs Canada. 2016. "International Assistance Review: Discussion Paper." http://www.international.gc.ca/world-monde/assets/pdfs/iar-consultations-eai-eng.pdf (12 June).
Globe and Mail. 1963. "Yuzyk queries peace record of Pearson," 21 March.
– 1993. "A quota is a quota is a quota." 18 June.
– 1995. "Giving voice to the Canadian idea," 4 November.
– 1997. "Effort to boost nicotine in cigarettes linked to federal scientists," 17 March.
– 2010. "Editorial: Strike multiculturalism from the national vocabulary." 8 October.
Goethe, Johann Wolfgang von. 1893. *The Maxims and Reflections of Goethe*. Translated by Bailey Saunders. New York: Macmillan.
Goldberg, David Theo. 1993. Racist Culture: Philosophy and the Politics of Meaning. Oxford and Cambridge: Blackwell.
Gramsci, Antonio. 1971. *Selections from the Prison Notebooks*. New York: International.
Granatstein, J.L. 1998. Who Killed Canadian History? Toronto: HarperCollins.
– 2007. Whose War Is It? Toronto: HarperCollins.
Grant, Tavia. 2018. "Hate crimes in Canada rose by 47 per cent last year: Statscan." *Globe and Mail*, 29 November.
Greider, William. 1994. "Politics of Diversion: Blame It on the Blacks." In *Debating Affirmative Action*, edited by Nicolaus Mills. New York: Delta Trade.
Griffith, Andrew. 2013. Policy Arrogance or Innocent Bias. Ottawa: Anar Press.
The Guardian. 2017. "The counted: People killed by police in the U.S." 1 June. www.theguardian.com/us-news/ng-interactive/2015/jun/01/the-counted-police-killings-us-database.
Gutstein, Donald. 2014. *Harperism*. Toronto: James Lorimer.
Habermas, Jürgen. 1987. *The Philosophical Discourse of Modernity*. Translated by Frederick Lawrence. Cambridge, MA: MIT Press.
– 1989a. *The New Conservatism: Cultural Criticism and the Historians' Debate*. Translated Shierry Weber Nicholsen. Cambridge, MA: MIT Press.
– 1989b. *The Structural Transformation of the Public Sphere*. Cambridge, MA: MIT Press.
– 2006. "Religion in the Public Sphere." *European Journal of Philosophy* 14, no. 1: 1–25. https://doi.org/10.1111/j.1468-0378.2006.00241.x.
– 2008. *Between Naturalism and Religion: Philosophical Essays*. Translated by Ciaran Cronin. Cambridge, MA: Polity.
Hamilton, Graeme, and Stewart Bell. 2017. "'We never know how madness emerges': Friend of mosque shooting suspect speaks out." *National Post*, 2 February.

Hansen, James. 2012. "Game over for the climate." *New York Times*, 9 May.
Hansen, Randall. 2014. "Assimilation by Stealth: Why Canada's Multicultural Policy Is Really a Repackaged Integration Policy." In *The Multiculturalism Question: Debating Identity in 21st Century Canada*, edited by Jack Jedwab. Montreal and Kingston: McGill–Queen's University Press.
Haque, Eve. 2012. *Multiculturalism within a Bilingual Framework: Language, Race, and Belonging in Canada*. Toronto: University of Toronto Press.
Häring, Norbert, and Niall Douglas. 2012. *Economists and the Powerful*. London: Anthem Press.
Harris, Kathleen. 2020. "Conservatives blast MP who asked whether top pandemic doctor 'works for China' as Scheer steers clear." *CBC News*, 23 April.
Harvey, David. 1982. *The Limits to Capital*. Oxford: Basil Blackwell.
Hastings, Max. 2013. *Catastrophe: Europe Goes to War 1914*. London: William Collins.
Hayek, F.A. 2011. "Why I Am Not a Conservative." In *The Constitution of Liberty*. Chicago: University of Chicago Press.
Health Canada. 1999. "About Health Canada." http://www.hc-sc.gc.ca/english/about.htm (27 April 2000).
Hedges, Chris. 2002. *War Is a Force That Gives Us Meaning*. New York: Public Affairs.
Hegel, G.W.F. 1977. *Phenomenology of Spirit*. Translated by A.V. Miller. Oxford: Oxford University Press.
Herder, Johann Gottfried. 2004. *Herder: Philosophical Writings*. Cambridge: Cambridge University Press
Hinkelammert, Franz. 1981. *Las armas ideológicas de la muerte*, 2nd ed. San José: D.E.I.
Hobbes, Thomas. 1968. *Leviathan* [1651]. Harmondsworth: Penguin Books.
Hobsbawm, E.J. 1992. *Nations and Nationalism since 1780*, 2nd ed. Cambridge: Cambridge University Press.
– 1994. *The Age of Empire: 1875–1914*. London: Abacus.
Hochschild, Arlie Russell. 2018. *Strangers in Their Own Land: Anger and Mourning on the American Right*. Paperback edition. New York: The New Press.
Hodges, Donald C. 1974. *The Latin American Revolution: Politics and Strategy from Apro-Marxism to Guevarism*. New York: William Morrow.
Horowitz. Gad. 1968. *Canadian Labour in Politics*. Toronto: University of Toronto Press.
Hum, Derek, and Wayne Simpson. 1999. "Wage Opportunities for Visible Minorities in Canada." *Canadian Public Policy* 25, no. 3: 379–94. https://doi.org/10.2307/3551526.
Hume, Stephen. 1995. "Why evolution in our schools, but not creationism." *Vancouver Sun*, 5 April.

Hunter, James Davison. 1991. *Culture Wars: The Struggle to Define America*. New York: Basic Books.

Huntington, Samuel P. 1993. "The Clash of Civilizations?" *Foreign Affairs* (Summer).

Hutter, Kristy. 2018. "Three Percenters are Canada's 'most dangerous' extremist group, say some experts." *CBC News*, 10 May.

ICES. 2020. "New ICES report shows immigrants, refugees, and other newcomers account for nearly 44% of all COVID-19 cases in Ontario." 9 September. www.ices.on.ca/Newsroom/News-Releases/2020/New-ICES-report-shows-immigrants-refugees-and-other-newcomers-account-for-nearly-44-per-cent.

Ijaz, Nadine, and Heather Boon. 2018. "Chinese Medicine sans Chinese: The Unequal Impacts of Canada's 'Multiculturalism within a Bilingual Framework." *Law and Policy* 40, no. 4 (October): 371–97. https://doi.org/10.1111/lapo.12112.

Issa, Omayra. 2020. Dispatches from the Prairies. *Twitter*, 29 July. twitter.com/OmayraIssa/status/1288675104700821505.

James, Matt. 2006. *Misrecognized Materialists: Social Movements in Canadian Constitutional Politics*. Vancouver: UBC Press.

– 2012. "Neoliberal Heritage Redress." In *Reconciling Canada: Critical Perspectives on the Culture of Redress*, edited by Jennifer Henderson and Pauline Wakeham. Toronto: University of Toronto Press.

James, William. 1890. *The Principles of Psychology*, vol. 1. New York: Henry Holt.

– 1995. *Pragmatism*. New York: Dover.

Janis, Irving. 2016. "Groupthink: The Desperate Drive for Consensus at Any Cost. In *Classics of Organization Theory*, edited by Jay. M. Shafritz, J. Steven Ott, and Yong Suk Jang, 8th ed. Boston: Cengage.

Jaworsky, John S. 1979. "A Case Study of the Canadian Federal Government's Multiculturalism Policy." MA thesis, Carleton University.

Jedwab, Jack. 2014. "What keeps Canada together?" Association for Canadian Studies, 1 July. acs-aec.ca/old/img/nouvelles/ACS-CIIM-2014EN-R262.pdf.

– 2015a. "Assimilation of religious groups: Multiculturalism versus Republicanism." Association of Canadian Studies, 27 June. https://acs-metropolis.ca/wp-content/uploads/pdf_old/ACS-CIIM-2015EN-R284.pdf.

– 2015b. "Is Canada a land of equal opportunity for all?" Association of Canadian Studies, 29 June. https://acs-metropolis.ca/wp-content/uploads/pdf_old/ACS-CIIM-2015EN-R284.pdf.

Jedwab, Jack, and Vic Satzewich. 2015. "Introductory Essay: John Porter's *The Vertical Mosaic*, 50 years later." In *The Vertical Mosaic, 50th Anniversary Edition*. Toronto: University of Toronto Press.

Johnson, William. 1975. "Ottawa places emphasis on fight against discrimination in altering multicultural program." *Globe and Mail*, 26 November.

Jones, Ryan Patrick. 2020a. "Black boy's arm broken in racist attack." *CBC News*, 29 September.
- 2020b. "People of colour make up 66% of Ottawa's COVID-19 cases." *CBC News*, 21 September.
- 2021. "Paul Fromm donated $131 to leadership campaign of MP Derek Sloan." *CBC News*, 18 January.
Joppke, Christian. 2004. "The Retreat of Multiculturalism in the Liberal State: Theory and Policy." *British Journal of Sociology* 44, no. 2. https://doi.org/10.1111/j.1468-4446.2004.00017.x.
- 2014. "The Retreat Is Real – but What Is the Alternative? Multiculturalism, Muscular Liberalism, and Islam." *Constellations* 21, no. 2: 286–95. https://doi.org/10.1111/1467-8675.12090.
- 2017. *Is Multiculturalism Dead?* Cambridge: Polity.
Joyce, James. 1994. *A Portrait of the Artist as a Young Man* [1916]. New York: Dover.
- 2000. *Ulysses* [1922]. London: Penguin.
Kahneman, Daniel. 2011. *Thinking, Fast and Slow*. New York: Farrar, Straus and Giroux.
Kanji, Khadijah. 2020a. "Multiculturalism Can't Defeat Xenophobia." *Rabble*, 18 September. rabble.ca/blogs/bloggers/views-expressed/2020/09/multiculturalism-cant-defeat-xenophobia.
- 2020b. "Multiculturalism Is Not Anti-Racism." *Rabble*, 11 September. rabble.ca/blogs/bloggers/views-expressed/2020/09/multiculturalism-not-anti-racism.
Kant, Immanuel. 1964. *Groundwork of the Metaphysics of Morals* [1785]. Translated by H.J. Paton. New York: Harper Torchbooks.
- 1991. *Kant: Political Writings*, 2nd ed. Edited by Hans Reiss. Cambridge: Cambridge University Press.
- 2002. *Critique of Practical Reason* [1788]. Translated by Werner S. Pluhar. Indianapolis: Hackett.
- 2007. *Critique of Judgment* [1790]. Translated by James Creed Meredith. Oxford University Press.
Kashmeri, Zuhair. 1991. *The Gulf Within: Canadian Arabs, Racism, and the Gulf War*. Toronto: James Lorimer.
Kassam, Adam. 2020. "Ontario's lack of diversity data for COVID-19 is an embarrassment." *Globe and Mail*, 15 April.
Kearns, Erin, Allison Betus, and Anthony Lemieux. 2019. "Why Do Some Terrorist Attacks Receive More Media Attention than Others?" *Justice Quarterly* 36, no. 6: 985–1022. https://doi.org/10.1080/07418825.2018.1524507.
Keller, Anthony. 1997. "Free expression anti-smoke signals." *Globe and Mail*, 17 March.
Kelley, Ninette, and Michael Trebilcock. 2000. *The Making of the Mosaic: A History of Canadian Immigration Policy*. Toronto: University of Toronto Press.

Kent, Tom. 1988. *A Public Purpose*. Montreal and Kingston: McGill–Queen's University Press.

Kepel, Gilles. 2015. *Terreur dans l'hexagone: Genèse du djihad français*. Paris: Gallimard.

Keynes, John Maynard. 1963. *Essays in Persuasion* [1931]. New York: W.W. Norton.

– 2007. *The General Theory of Employment, Interest, and Money* [1936]. New York: Palgrave.

Khan, Sheema. 2017. "We must define Islamophobia by what it truly is." *Globe and Mail*, 7 October.

Kimball, Roger. 1992. "The Periphery vs. the Center: The MLA in Chicago." In *Debating P.C.: The Controversy over Political Correctness on College Campuses*, edited by Paul Berman. New York: Laurel.

King, Martin Luther. 1963. "The 'I Have a Dream' speech." www.usconstitution.net/dream.html.

King, Preston. 1998. *Toleration*. London: Frank Cass.

Kingsley, Patrick. 2019. "New Zealand massacre highlights global reach of white extremism." *New York Times*, 15 March.

Kirkup, Kristy, and Daniel Leblanc. 2020. "RCMP Commissioner faces grilling on systemic racism." *Globe and Mail*, 23 June.

Klein, Naomi. 2016. "It was the Democrats' embrace of neoliberalism that won it for Trump." *The Guardian*, 9 November.

Koestler, Arthur. 1969. *The Act of Creation*. London: Pan.

Kogawa, Joy. 1983. *Obasan*. Toronto: Penguin.

Krueger, Lesley. 1995. "Can't sneak creationism in by the back door." *Globe and Mail*, 30 June.

Küng, Hans. 1981. *Does God Exist? An Answer for Today*. Translated by Edward Quinn. New York: Vintage.

Kuppens, Toon, et al. 2018. "Educationism and the Irony of Meritocracy: Negative Attitudes of Higher Educated People towards the Less Educated." *Journal of Experimental Social Psychology* 76 (May): 429–47. https://doi.org/10.1016/j.jesp.2017.11.001.

Kymlicka, Will. 1998. *Finding Our Way: Rethinking Ethnocultural Relations in Canada*. Toronto: Oxford University Press.

– 2007a. "The Canadian Model of Diversity in a Comparative Perspective." In *Multiculturalism and the Canadian Constitution*, edited by Stephen Tierney. Vancouver: UBC Press.

– 2007b. "Disentangling the Debate." In *Uneasy Partners: Multiculturalism and Rights in Canada*, edited by Janice Gross Stein et al. Waterloo: Wilfrid Laurier University Press.

– 2007c. *Multicultural Odysseys*. Oxford: Oxford University Press.

– 2014. "The essentialist critique of multiculturalism: Theory, policies and ethos." Robert Schuman Centre for Advanced Studies, working paper

2014/59. http://cadmus.eui.eu/bitstream/handle/1814/31451/RSCAS_2014_59.pdf.
Lanchester, John. 2016. "How Economic Gobbledygook Divides Us." *New York Times Magazine*, 1 November.
Lane, Robert. 2000. *The Loss of Happiness in Market Democracies*. New Haven: Yale University Press.
LaPresse. 2018. "Quand on me demande d'où je viens, je sais que je n'aurai pas la job." *LaPresse*, 23 April.
Lawrence, Bonita, and Enakshi Dua. 2005. "Decolonizing Antiracism." *Social Justice* 32, no. 4: 120–43.
Lawrynuik, Sarah. 2019. "Poland's election features a confident right-wing ruling party despite abortion, LGBT debates." *CBC News*, 6 October.
Lebel, Ronald. 1969a. "The black and white case at Sir George Williams." *Globe and Mail*, 12 February.
– 1969b. "No injuries in either bombing: Blasts hit Loyola, St. Leonard deputy mayor's home." *Globe and Mail*, 21 November.
Leblanc, Daniel, and Kristy Kirkup. 2020. "RCMP commissioner 'struggles' with definition of systemic racism, but denies its presence in organization." *Globe and Mail*, 10 June.
Lenin, V.I. 1968. *Lenin on Politics and Revolution*. Edited by James E. Conner. Indianapolis: Bobbs-Merrill.
Léotard, Corentin, and Ludovic Lepeltier-Kutasi. 2018. "Un fonds de commerce pour les nationalistes hongrois." *Le Monde Diplomatique*, June.
Lepore, Jill. 2019. *This America: The Case for the Nation*. New York: Liveright.
Leskov, Nikolai. 2014. *The Enchanted Wanderer and Other Stories*. New York: Vintage Classics.
Leslie, Jacques. 2014. "Is Canada tarring itself?" *New York Times*, 30 March.
Lessig, Lawrence. 2011. *Republic Lost: How Money Corrupts Congress – and a Plan to Stop It*. New York: Twelve.
Levant, Ezra. 2009. *Shakedown: How Our Government Is Undermining Democracy in the Name of Human Rights*. Toronto: McClelland and Stewart.
Lippmann, Walter. 2004. *Public Opinion*. New York: Dover.
Lobel, Arnold. 1979. *Days with Frog and Toad*. New York: HarperCollins.
Logan, Nick. 2015. "The Canadian connection to the 'white supremacist' group that influenced Dylann Roof." *Global News*, 23 June.
Longfellow, Henry Wadsworth. 1882. *In the Harbor*. Boston: Houghton Mifflin.
Lovejoy, Arthur O. 1964. *The Great Chain of Being: A Study of the History of an Idea*. Cambridge, MA: Harvard University Press.
Lukács, Georg. 1971. *History and Class Consciousness: Studies in Marxist Dialectics* [1923]. Cambridge, MA: MIT Press.
Lupul, Manoly. 1982. "The Political Implementation of Multiculturalism." *Journal of Canadian Studies* 17, no. 1 (Spring): 93–102. https://doi.org/10.3138/jcs.17.1.93.

Lynch, Rene. 2012. "Florida lifeguard is fired for saving a life; uproar ensues." *Los Angeles Times*, 5 July.
Maalouf, Amin. 1998. *Les identités meurtrières*. Paris: Grasset.
Macdougall, Andrew. 2017. "Liberals waste no time playing the anti-Christian card." *Globe and Mail*, 29 May.
Maciel, Robert. 2014. "The Future of Liberal Multiculturalism." *Political Studies Review* 12: 383–94. https://doi.org/10.1111/1478-9302.12018.
Mackey, Eva. 2002. *The House of Difference*. Toronto: University of Toronto Press.
MacLean, Nancy. 2017. *Democracy in Chains: The Deep History of the Radical Right's Stealth Plan for America*. New York: Viking.
MacPherson, Don. 2006. "Mountie probe seems fishy." *Montreal Gazette*, 10 January.
Malik, Nesrine. 2020. "It seems black lives don't matter quite so much, now that we've got to the hard bit." *The Guardian*, 6 July.
Mangat, Palak. 2020. "Online tool tracks more than 100 pandemic-related racism incidents since February." *Hill Times*, 28 May.
Mann, Michael. 1970. "The Social Cohesion of Liberal Democracy." *American Sociological Review* 35, no. 3 (June): 423–39. https://doi.org/10.2307/2092986.
Mansur, Salim. 2010. *The Muddle of Multiculturalism: A Liberal Critique*. Halifax: Atlantic Institute for Market Studies.
– 2011. *Delectable Lie: A Liberal Repudiation of Multiculturalism*. Brantford: Mantua Books.
Marcoux, Jacques, and Katie Nicholson. 2018. "Deadly force: Fatal encounters with police in Canada: 2000–2017." *CBC News*.
Marcuse, Herbert. 1966. *One-Dimensional Man*. Boston: Beacon Press.
Marsden, William. 1999. "Tobacco company took advantage of smuggling: Chairman." *National Post*, 29 April.
Martin, Jeffery. 2020. "President Trump says 'something snapped' in police officers involved with George Floyd's death." *Newsweek*, 3 June.
Martineau, Richard. 2020. "Speak White Again!" *Journal de Montréal*, 9 June.
Marx, Karl. 1954. *Capital*, vol. 1 [1867]. Moscow: Progress.
– 1963. "Contribution to the Critique of Hegel's Philosophy of Right" [1844]. In *Early Writings*, edited by T.B. Bottomore. London: Watts.
– 1977. *The Poverty of Philosophy* [1847]. Peking: Foreign Language Press.
Marx, Karl, and Frederick Engels. 1969. *Selected Works in Three Volumes*. Moscow: Progress.
Massie, Alex. 2016. "A day of infamy." *The Spectator*, 16 June.
Mazurek, Kas. 1992. "Defusing a Radical Social Policy: The Undermining of Multiculturalism." In *Twenty Years of Multiculturalism: Success and Failures*, edited by Stella Hryniuk. Winnipeg: St. John's College Press.
McAndrew, Marie, et al. 2005. "Pour un débat éclairé sur la politique canadienne du multiculturalisme: une analyse de la nature des organismes

et des projets subventionnés (1983–2002)." *Politique et societés* 24, no. 1: 49–71. https://doi.org/10.7202/011495ar.
McCarthy, Michael. 2015. *The Moth Snowstorm: Nature and Joy*. London: John Murray.
McCarthy, Thomas. 2009. *Race, Empire, and the Idea of Human Development*. Cambridge: Cambridge University Press.
McDonald, Catherine. 2020. "Suspect in fatal stabbing at Toronto mosque connected to white supremacist group, expert says." *Global News*, 22 September.
Mcdonald, Norris. 1969. "Black students seize centre at Sir George, halt hearing on racism." *Globe and Mail*, 30 January.
McIlroy, Anne. 2001. "Racist remarks jeopardise Toronto Olympic bid." *The Guardian*, 25 June.
McNeilly, Gerry. 2018. "Broken Trust: Indigenous People and the Thunder Bay Police Service." Toronto: Office of the Independent Police Review Director.
McQuaig, Linda. 2007. *Holding the Bully's Coat: Canada and the U.S. Empire*. Toronto: Doubleday Canada.
McRoberts, Kenneth. 1997. *Misconceiving Canada: The Struggle for National Unity*. Toronto: Oxford University Press.
Melville, Herman. 1988. *Moby Dick* [1851]. Oxford: Oxford University Press.
Mendus, Susan. 1989. *Toleration and the Limits of Liberalism*. London: Macmillan.
Merrifield, Andy. 2020. "Mystified Consciousness." *Monthly Review* 71, no. 10 (March). https://doi.org/10.14452/MR-071-10-2020-03_2.
Michaels, Walter Benn. 2006. *The Trouble with Diversity: How We Learned to Love Identity and Ignore Inequality*. New York: Henry Holt.
Miliband, Ralph. 1969. *The State in Capitalist Society*. London: Quartet Books.
Mills, Charles W. 1997. *The Racial Contract*. Ithaca: Cornell University Press.
Mintzberg, Henry. 1987. "The Power Game and the Players." In *Classics of Organization Theory*, edited by Jay. M. Shafritz and J. Steven Ott, 2nd ed. Chicago: Dorsey Press.
Mishra, Pankaj. 2016. "The incendiary appeal of demagoguery in our time." *New York Times*, 13 November.
– 2017. *Age of Anger: A History of the Present*. New York: Farrar, Straus and Giroux.
Montpetit, Jonathan, and John MacFarlane. 2020. "Anti-mask protest in Montreal draws large crowd, propelled by U.S. conspiracy theories." *CBC News*, 12 September.
Moses, Wilson Jeremiah. 1978. *The Golden Age of Black Nationalism*. New York: Oxford University Press.
Mosleh, Omar. 2019. "Canada's yellow vest movement looks like it's here to stay – but what is it really about?" *Toronto Star*, 4 January.
Müller, Jan-Werner. 2018. "Homo Orbánicus." *New York Review of Books*, 5 April.
Murdoch, Iris. 1997. *Existentialists and Mystics*. Edited by Peter Conradi. New York: Penguin.

Nasser, Shanifa. 2018. 'Hate is alive here': Wife of beaten Mississauga man speaks out after attack." *CBC News*, 18 July.

Nerestant, Antoni. 2022. "Concordia University apologizes for mishandling 1969 Black student protests." *CBC News*, 28 October.

Nishiguchi, R.L. Gabrielle. 1997. "True north strong and hyphen-free." In *The Battle over Multiculturalism: Does It Help or Hinder Canadian Unity?*, edited by Andrew Cardozo and Louis Musto. Ottawa: Pearson-Shoyama Institute.

Nordhaus, William. 2015. "A new solution: The climate club." *New York Review of Books*, 4 June.

Nordlinger, Eric. 1981. *On the Autonomy of the Democratic State.*" Cambridge, MA: Harvard University Press.

Nussbaum, Martha. 2013. *Political Emotions: Why Love Matters for Justice*. Cambridge, MA: Belknap Press.

O'Connor, James. 1973. *The Fiscal Crisis of the State*. New York: St. Martin's Press.

OHRC (Ontario Human Rights Commission). 2018. *A Collective Impact: Interim Report on the Inquiry into Racial Profiling and Racial Discrimination of Black Persons by the Toronto Police Service*. Toronto: Government of Ontario.

Okin, Susan Moller. 1999a. "Is Multiculturalism Bad for Women?" In *Is Multiculturalism Bad for Women?*, edited by Joshua Cohen, Matthew Howard, and Martha C. Nussbaum. Princeton: Princeton University Press.

– 1999b. "Reply." In *Is Multiculturalism Bad for Women?*, edited by Joshua Cohen, Matthew Howard, and Martha C. Nussbaum. Princeton: Princeton University Press.

Ollman, Bertell. 1976. *Alienation: Marx's Conception of Man in Capitalist Society*, 2nd ed. Cambridge: Cambridge University Press.

Olson, Mancur. 1965. *The Logic of Collective Action*. Cambridge, MA: Harvard University Press.

Oreopoulos, Philip. 2009. "Why do skilled immigrants struggle in the labor market? A field experiment with six thousand résumés." Metropolis British Columbia. www.nber.org/papers/w15036.

Orwell, George. 2000. *Essays*. London: Penguin.

Oxford English Dictionary (Online). 2000. Oxford: Oxford University Press.

Pal, Leslie. 1992. *Public Policy Analysis*, 2nd ed. Scarborough: Nelson.

– 1993. *Interests of State: The Politics of Language, Multiculturalism, and Feminism in Canada*. Montreal and Kingston: McGill–Queen's University Press.

Pamuk, Orhan. 2005. *Snow*. New York: Vintage.

Parekh, Bhikhu. 1994. "Superior people: The narrowness of liberalism from Mill to Rawls." *Times Literary Supplement*, 25 February.

– 1999. "A Varied Moral World." In *Is Multiculturalism Bad for Women?*, edited by Joshua Cohen, Matthew Howard, and Martha C. Nussbaum. Princeton: Princeton University Press.

- 2000. *Rethinking Multiculturalism: Cultural Diversity and Political Theory.* Cambridge, MA: Harvard University Press.
Parker, Ashley, and John Wagner. 2017. "Trump retweets inflammatory and unverified anti-Muslim videos." *Washington Post,* 29 November.
Patriquin, Martin. 2019. "Quebec nationalism could once claim to be colour- and country-blind. Not anymore." *CBC News,* 29 January.
Perry, Barbara. 2015. "Disrupting the mantra of multiculturalism: Hate crime in Canada." *American Behavioral Scientist* 59, no. 13: 1637–54. https://doi.org/10.1177/0002764215588816.
Peters, Jeremy, et al. 2019. "How the El Paso killer echoed the incendiary words of conservative media stars." *New York Times,* 11 August.
Piketty, Thomas. 2019. *Capital et idéologie.* Paris: Éditions du Seuil.
Pinker, Steven. 2002. *The Blank Slate: The Modern Denial of Human Nature.* New York: Viking.
Plato. 1997. *The Republic.* In *Complete Works,* edited by John M. Cooper. Indianapolis: Hackett.
Polanyi, Karl. 1957. *The Great Transformation.* Boston: Beacon Press.
Polanyi, Michael. 1962. *Personal Knowledge.* Chicago: University of Chicago Press.
Pollitt, Katha. 1999. "Whose Culture?" In *Is Multiculturalism Bad for Women?,* edited by Joshua Cohen, Matthew Howard, and Martha C. Nussbaum. Princeton: Princeton University Press.
Porter, John. 1965. *The Vertical Mosaic.* Toronto: University of Toronto Press.
- 1969. "Bilingualism and the Myths of Culture." *Canadian Review of Sociology and Anthropology* 6, no. 2: 111–19. https://doi.org/10.1111/j.1755-618X.1969.tb02300.x.
- 1987. "Ethnic Pluralism in Canadian Perspective." In *The Measure of Canadian Society: Education, Equality, and Opportunity,* edited by Richard Helmes-Hayes. Ottawa: Carleton University Press.
Poulantzas, Nicos. 1978. *Political Power and Social Classes* [1968]. Translated by Timothy O'Hagan. London: Verso.
Presidential debate transcript: Trump and Clinton, verbatim. 2016. *Maclean's,* 26 September. www.macleans.ca/politics/washington/presidential-debate-transcript-trump-and-clinton-verbatim.
Proctor, Jason. 2020. "The Difficult History of Prosecuting Hate in Canada." *CBC News,* 13 June.
Proust, Marcel. 1988a. *Du côté de chez Swann* [1913]. *À la recherche du temps perdu,* vol. 1. Paris: Gallimard.
- 1988b. *À l'ombre des jeunes filles en fleur* [1919]. *À la recherche du temps perdu,* vol. 2. Paris: Gallimard.
Rana, Abbas. 2020. "Conservatives Party caucus split over Sloan's potential ouster, with lines drawn between Ontario and rural, Western Canada MPs." *Hill Times,* 14 May.

Rawls, John. 1996. *Political Liberalism*. New York: Columbia University Press.
- 2001. *Justice as Fairness: A Restatement*. Edited by Erin Kelly. Cambridge, MA: The Belknap Press.
Reed, Adolph, Jr. 2013. "Marx, Race, and Neoliberalism." *New Labor Forum* 22, no. 1: 49–57. https://doi.org/10.1177/1095796012471637.
Reed, Touré F. 2020. *Toward Freedom: The Case against Race Reductionism*. London: Verso.
Reitz, Jeffrey. 2011. "Pro-Immigration Canada: Social and Economic Roots of Popular Views." IRPP study no. 20 (October).
Ricento, Thomas. 2013. "The Consequences of Official Bilingualism on the Status and Perception of Non-Official Languages in Canada." *Journal of Multilingual and Multicultural Development* 34: 475–89. https://doi.org/10.1080/01434632.2013.783034.
Rieger, Sarah. 2018. "Calgary lawyer challenging gay-straight alliance bill compares pride flags to swastikas." *CBC News*, 11 November.
Riker, W.H. 1982. *Liberalism against Populism*. San Francisco: W.H. Freeman.
Rioux, Christian. 2019. "François Legault veut davantage d'immigrants français." *Le Devoir*, 21 January.
Rioux, Marcel. 1976. *La question du Québec*. Montreal: Partis Pris.
Robinson, Cedric J. 2000. *Black Marxism: The Making of the Black Radical Tradition* [1983], 3rd ed. Chapel Hill: University of North Carolina Press.
Rockmore, Ellen Bresler. 2015. "How Texas teaches history." *New York Times*, 21 October.
Royal Commission on Bilingualism and Biculturalism. 1969. *Cultural Contribution of the Other Ethnic Groups*. Ottawa: Queen's Printer.
Royal Commission on Canada's Economic Prospects. 1957. *Final Report*. Ottawa: Supply and Services Canada.
Rutenberg, Jim. 2020. "How President Trump's false claim of voter fraud is being used to disenfranchise Americans." *New York Times*, 30 September.
Ryan, Phil. 1988. *Compassion or Expediency: The Overseas Selection of Central American Refugees*. Ottawa: Office of Dan Heap M.P.
- 1995. *The Fall and Rise of the Market in Sandinista Nicaragua*. Montreal and Kingston: McGill–Queen's University Press.
- 1998. "Subverting Government Business." *Canadian Forum* 77, no. 871 (July–August): 14–19.
- 2001. "Stanley Fish's Case for Speech Regulation: A Critique." *Canadian Journal of Higher Education* 31, no. 2: 167–82. https://doi.org/10.47678/cjhe.v31i2.183392.
- 2003. "Pastoral Power in the Age of Partnership: Health Canada and the Jr. Jays Club." *Canadian Review of Social Policy*, no. 51: 87–102.
- 2004. "The Policy Sciences and the Unmasking Turn of Mind." *Review of Policy Research* 21, no. 5: 715–28. https://doi.org/10.1111/j.1541-1338.2004.00103.x.

- 2010a. "Beware Shared Memory." *Canadian Issues* (Winter): 28–31.
- 2010b. *Multicultiphobia*. Toronto: University of Toronto Press.
- 2014a. *After the New Atheist Debate*. Toronto: University of Toronto Press.
- 2014b. "The Multicultural State and the Religiously Neutral State: Comment on Cliteur." *International Journal of Constitutional Law* 12, no. 2: 457–63. https://doi.org/10.1093/icon/mou029.
- 2014c. "Our Multiculturalism: Reflections in the Key of Rawls." In *The Multiculturalism Question: Debating Identity in 21st Century Canada*, edited by Jack Jedwab. Montreal and Kingston: McGill–Queen's University Press.
- 2015. "Positivism: Paradigm or Culture?" *Policy Studies* 36, no. 4: 417–33. https://doi.org/10.1080/01442872.2015.1073246.
- 2018. "'Technocracy,' Democracy ... and Corruption and Trust." *Policy Sciences* 51, no. 1: 131–9. https://doi.org/10.1007/s11077-017-9305-1.
- 2019. "The Paradox of Hegemony and the 'Multiculturalism of the Individual.'" *Canadian Journal of Ethnic Studies* 51, no. 2: 153–68. https://doi.org/10.1353/ces.2019.0016.
- 2022. *Facts, Values, and the Policy World*. Bristol: Policy Press.

Sandel, Michael. 2009. *Justice: What's the Right Thing to Do?* New York: Farrar, Straus and Giroux.

- 2012. *What Money Can't Buy: The Moral Limits of Markets*. New York: Farrar, Straus and Giroux.

Santora, Marc. 2019. "Coke ad riles Hungary conservatives, part of larger gay rights battle." *New York Times*, 9 August.

Satzewich, Vic. 2018. "'Canadian Exceptionalism': Border Control Also Matters." *Canadian Diversity* 15, no. 2: 34–37.

Saunders, Doug. 2016. "The real reason Donald Trump got elected? We have a white extremism problem." *Globe and Mail*, 12 November.

Sayer, Andrew. 2011. *Why Things Matter to People*. Cambridge: Cambridge University Press.

Schedler, Andreas. 2011. "Concept Formation." In *International Encyclopedia of Political Science*, vol. 1, edited by Bertrand Badie, Dirk Berg-Schlosser, and Leonardo Morlino. Los Angeles: Sage.

Schutz, Alfred. 1970. *On Phenomenology and Social Relations: Selected Writings*. Edited by Helmut R. Wagner. Chicago: University of Chicago Press.

Scott, James C. 1998. *Seeing like a State: How Certain Schemes to Improve the Human Condition Have Failed*. New Haven: Yale University Press.

Seale, Lewis. 1968. "PM meets leaders of 2,000 demonstrators protesting language policies in St. Leonard." *Globe and Mail*, 13 September.

Sen, Amartya. 1977. "Rational Fools: A Critique of the Behavioral Foundations of Economic Theory." *Philosophy and Public Affairs* 6, no. 4: 317–44.

- 2006. *Identity and Violence*. New York: W.W. Norton.
- 2009. *The Idea of Justice*. Cambridge, MA: Harvard University Press.

Works Cited

Shakespeare, William. 1988. *The Annotated Shakespeare*. Edited by A.L. Rowse. New York: Greenwich House.

Shapiro, Ian. 2005. *The Flight from Reality in the Human Sciences*. Princeton: Princeton University Press.

Sharma, Nandita. 2011. "Canadian Multiculturalism and Its Nationalisms." In *Home and Native Land: Unsettling Multiculturalism in Canada*, edited by May Chazan, Lisa Helps, and Anna Stanley. Toronto: Between the Lines.

Shelley, Percy Bysshe. 1842. *The Masque of Anarchy*. London: J. Watson.

Shulman, Alix Kates. 1991. "Dances with Feminists." *Women's Review of Books* 9, no. 3 (December). https://doi.org/10.2307/4021093.

Sifton, Sir Clifford. 1922. "The Immigrants Canada Wants." *Maclean's*, 1 April. archive.macleans.ca/article/1922/4/1/the-immigrants-canada-wants.

Sinclair, Scott. 2018. *Canada's Track Record under NAFTA Chapter 11*. Canadian Centre for Policy Alternatives (January).

Singh, Inayat. 2020. "CBC's Deadly Force database looks at role of race, mental health in deaths." *CBC News*, 23 July.

Skidelsky, Robert. 2009. *Keynes: The Return of the Master*. New York: Public Affairs.

Sloan, Derek. 2020. "It's time to elect a government that puts the interests of Canadians first." *CBC News*, 20 August.

Smith, Adam. 1937. *The Wealth of Nations* [1776]. New York: Modern Library.

– 2009. *The Theory of Moral Sentiments* [1759]. London: Penguin.

Statistics Canada. 2010. *Projections of the Diversity of the Canadian Population, 2006 to 2031*. Ottawa.

– 2019. "Agricultural sector workers from the Temporary Foreign Workers Program, 2015." https://www150.statcan.gc.ca/n1/daily-quotidien/190708/dq190708a-eng.htm

– 2020. "Table 35-10-0067-01. Police-reported hate crime, by most serious violation, Canada (selected police services)." https://doi.org/10.25318/3510006701-eng.

– 2021. "Table 43-10-0002-01. Historical statistics, immigration to Canada, by country of last permanent residence." https://doi.org/10.25318/4310000201-eng.

Steele, Andrew. 2019. "Polarized politics could shatter Canada's fragile 'virtuous cycle' of immigration." *Globe and Mail*, 24 April.

Stokey, Edith, and Richard Zeckhauser. 1978. *A Primer for Policy Analysis*. New York: W.W. Norton.

Stone, Deborah. 1997. *Policy Paradox: The Art of Political Decision-Making*. New York: W.W. Norton.

Streeck, Wolfgang. 2016. *How Will Capitalism End?* London: Verso.

– 2017. *Buying Time: The Delayed Crisis of Democratic Capitalism*, 2nd ed. Translated by Patrick Camiller and David Fernbach. London: Verso.

Taub, Amanda. 2017. "Canada's secret to resisting the West's populist wave." *New York Times*, 27 June.
Tavris, Carol, and Elliot Aronson. 2007. *Mistakes Were Made (but Not by Me)*. Orlando: Harcourt.
Taylor, Charles. 1975. *Hegel*. Cambridge: Cambridge University Press.
– 1989. *Sources of the Self*. Cambridge: Harvard University Press.
– 1994. "The Politics of Recognition." In *Multiculturalism: Examining the Politics of Recognition*. Princeton: Princeton University Press.
– 2007. *A Secular Age*. Cambridge: Belknap Press.
Taylor, Scott. 2020. "CAF still has far to go to address racism in its ranks." *Hill Times*, 16 September.
Thatcher, Margaret. 1987. Interview by Douglas Keay. *Woman's Own*, 23 September.
Therborn, Goran. 1977. "The Rule of Capital and the Rise of Democracy." *New Left Review* 103: 3–41.
Thobani, Sunera. 2007. *Exalted Subjects: Studies in the Making of Race and Nation in Canada*. Toronto: University of Toronto Press.
– 2010. "Multiculturalism displaces anti-racism, upholds white supremacy." *Restructure!*, 15 March. restructure.wordpress.com/2010/03/15/canadian-multiculturalism-displaces-antiracism-upholds-white-supremacy.
Thompson, Allan. 1993. "Most think immigrants must adapt." *Toronto Star*, 14 December.
Thucydides. 1874. *The History of the Peloponnesian War*. Translated by Richard Crawley. London: Longmans, Green.
– 1954. *The Peloponnesian War*. Translated by R. Warner. Harmondsworth: Penguin.
Times of London. 1819. "Our accounts from Manchester are full of the agitation excited amongst the timid and industrious." 17 August.
Tocqueville, Alexis de. 1986. *De la démocratie en Amérique* [1835]. Paris: Gallimard.
Triadafilopoulos, Triadafilos. 2012. *Becoming Multicultural: Immigration and the Politics of Membership in Canada and Germany*. Vancouver: UBC Press.
Trinh, Judy, and Nazim Baksh. 2020. "Human rights complaint is among 38 ongoing complaints of sexual misconduct by colleagues on Toronto force." *CBC News*, 26 November.
Trudeau, Justin. 2017. PM speaking notes for the annual international gathering of energy industry leaders, 9 March. https://pm.gc.ca/en/news/speeches/2017/03/09/pm-speaking-notes-annual-international-gathering-energy-industry-leaders.
– 2018. PM speaking notes for NYU Commencement Address, 16 May. pm.gc.ca/eng/news/2018/05/16/pm-speaking-notes-nyu-commencement-address.

Trudeau, Pierre Elliott. 1968. *Federalism and the French Canadians*. Toronto: Macmillan.
– 1972. *Conversation with Canadians*. Toronto: University of Toronto Press.
Truth and Reconciliation Commission. 2015. *Honouring the Truth, Reconciling for the Future*. Ottawa.
United Nations, Department of Economic and Social Affairs, Population Division. 2015. *World Population Prospects: The 2015 Revision*. DVD Edition.
Veblen, Thorstein. 1994. *The Theory of the Leisure Class* [1899]. New York: Dover.
Waal, Frans de. 2016. *Are We Smart Enough to Know How Smart Animals Are?* New York: W.W. Norton.
Wacquant, Loïc. 2022. *The Invention of the "Underclass."* Cambridge: Polity.
Walcott, Rinaldo. 2011. "Disgraceful: Intellectual Dishonesty, White Anxieties, and Multicultural Critique Thirty-Six Years Later." In *Home and Native Land: Unsettling Multiculturalism in Canada*, edited by May Chazan, Lisa Helps, and Anna Stanley. Toronto: Between the Lines.
Walker, Julian. 2018. "Hate Speech and Freedom of Expression: Legal Boundaries in Canada." Ottawa: Library of Parliament. lop.parl.ca/staticfiles/PublicWebsite/Home/ResearchPublications/BackgroundPapers/PDF/2018-25-E.pdf.
Wallace-Wells, David. 2019. *The Uninhabitable Earth: Life after Warming*. New York: Tim Duggan Books.
Walton-Roberts, Margaret. 2011. "Multiculturalism Already Unbound." In *Home and Native Land: Unsettling Multiculturalism in Canada*, edited by May Chazan, Lisa Helps, and Anna Stanley. Toronto: Between the Lines.
Weber, Max. 1949. *The Methodology of the Social Sciences*. Edited by Edward A. Shils and Henry A. Finch. New York: Free Press of Glencoe.
– 1958. *From Max Weber: Essays in Sociology*. Translated by H.H. Gerth and C. Wright Mills. New York: Oxford University Press.
– 1978. *Economy and Society* [1922]. Edited by Guenther Roth and Claus Wittich. Berkeley: University of California Press.
– 2003. *The Protestant Ethic and the Spirit of Capitalism* [1904]. New York: Dover.
Wherry, Aaron. 2018. "Two MPs are locked in a Twitter brawl over race and identity. Time to talk?" *CBC News*, 31 May.
Wildavsky, Aaron. 1979. *Speaking Truth to Power*. Boston: Little Press.
Williams, Eric. 1964. *Capitalism and Slavery*. London: A. Deutsch.
Winter, Elke. 2011. *Us, Them, and Others: Pluralism and National Identities in Diverse Societies*. Toronto: University of Toronto Press.
– 2015. "Rethinking Multiculturalism after Its 'Retreat': Lessons from Canada." *American Behavioral Scientist* 59, no. 6: 637–57. https://doi.org/10.1177/0002764214566495.
Wohlstetter, Roberta. 1962. *Pearl Harbor: Warning and Decision*. Stanford: Stanford University Press.

Wolf, Martin. 2015. *The Shifts and the Shocks*. New York: Penguin.
Wollstonecraft, Mary. 1993. *A Vindication of the Rights of Men* [1790]; *A Vindication of the Rights of Woman* [1792]; *An Historical and Moral View of the French Revolution* [1794]. Edited by Janet Todd. Oxford: Oxford University Press.
Wolterstorff, Nicholas. 2008. *Justice: Rights and Wrongs*. Princeton: Princeton University Press.
Wong, Joseph. 1997. "The Only Way to Go: Why Multiculturalism Can Help Unity." In *The Battle over Multiculturalism: Does It Help or Hinder Canadian Unity?*, edited by Andrew Cardozo and Louis Musto. Ottawa: Pearson-Shoyama Institute.
World Bank. 2019a. "Data release: Remittances to low- and middle-income countries on track to reach $551 billion in 2019 and $597 billion by 2021" (16 October). blogs.worldbank.org/peoplemove/data-release-remittances-low-and-middle-income-countries-track-reach-551-billion-2019.
– 2019b. Population, total – European Union. https://data.worldbank.org/indicator/SP.POP.TOTL?locations=EU.
Wortley, Scot. 2019. "Halifax, Nova Scotia: Street checks report." Nova Scotia Human Rights Commission. humanrights.novascotia.ca/sites/default/files/editor-uploads/halifax_street_checks_report_march_2019_0.pdf.
Wright, Lawrence. 2011. *The Looming Tower*. New York: Vintage.
Yaffe, Barbara. 1995. "A B.C. minority spells referendum f-r-u-s-t-r-a-t-i-o-n." *Vancouver Sun*, 21 September.
Younge, Gary. 2020. "What Black America means to Europe." *New York Review of Books*, 6 June.
Zaputovich, Maria. 1973. "Assimilation among Ukrainian-Canadian students at the University of Toronto." *Student*. Toronto: Ukrainian Canadian University Students' Union.
Ziadah, Rafeef. 2017. "Disciplining Dissent: Multicultural Policy and the Silencing of Arab-Canadians." *Race and Class* 58, no. 4: 7–22. https://doi.org/10.1177/0306396816686272
Zimonjic, Peter. 2020. "Stockwell Day exits CBC commentary role, corporate posts after comments about racism in Canada." *CBC News*, 3 June.
Žižek, Slavoj. 1997. "Multiculturalism, or, the Cultural Logic of Multinational Capitalism." *New Left Review* 225 (September–October).

Index

4chan, 30, 32

Abdi, Abdoul, attempted deportation, 238
Abu-Laban, Yasmeen: diversity as sales pitch, 57, 60; employment equity, 258n16
age of anger, political challenge, 34
agency, menu of choices, 88, 240
Akhtar, Ayad, so-called conservatism, 246n4
Alexander, Lincoln, 123, 192
Allison, Graham: governmental politics model, 44; organizational process model, 42; unitary genie model, 37, 46
Anderson, Benedict: imagined communities, 221; progressive role of nationalism, 222
Arendt, Hannah, 90, 153, 254n8; critique of uniformity assumptions, 114; danger of statelessness, 219; praise of America's openness, 245n2
Aristotle, 262n5; essence and accident, 193; wealth and dignity, 196
Association Coopérative d'Économie Familiale, 254n7

Auden, W.H.: climate of opinion, 57; language and truth, 230
Augustine of Hippo, 195
Austin, David, 131
authoritarianism, 17–19; elected authoritarians, 18; obsession with sexuality, 247n2

Bakht, Natasha, 97, 101, 108
Balint, Peter, on tolerance, 183, 190
Bannerji, Himani, 102, 246n5, 257n11; eternal and deliberate oppression, 141; false consciousness claim, 102; multiculturalism as distraction, 127; reproduction of "under classes," 162
Banting, Keith, 67; multiculturalism more than basic liberal rights, 211; multiculturalism policy index, 73
Barry, Brian: against identity politics, 236; fourth-hand certainty, 69
Beaman, Lori, 191; critique of tolerance, 180, 181, 191
Bengal famine, 65
Benhabib, Seyla, 220, 222, 266n7; on anti-refugee policies, 247n4; self-governance dilemma, 220

Benjamin, Walter, 187; revolution as emergency brake, 7
Benson, Rodney, media preference for simplicity, 246n9
Bernier, Maxime, 21, 106, 185; failure of xenophobia, 26
Bhaskar, Roy, 124, 252n26
Bhattacharyya, Gargi, 219, 268n4
bilingualism: coast-to-coast model, 173, 261n6; territorial, 173
Bilingualism and Biculturalism Commission, 13, 85, 121, 123, 158, 164–76, 251n16, 255n2; commitment to cultural duality, 167; contradiction on language and culture, 168; language hierarchy, 169, 170; relation to multiculturalism policy, 168; submissions on language of education, 166, 174; terms of reference, 120, 165, 169
bin Laden, Osama, 43
binary interpretation, critique of, 9, 246n8
Bird, Pat, 223–7
Bissoondath, Neil: critique of multiculturalism, 4; critique of tolerance, 181; denial of contemporary racism, 29, 58; media influence, 246n5
Black Lives Matter, 139
Blair, Tony, gutsy discourse, 251n17
Bloc Québécois: critique of tolerance, 194; opposition to multiculturalism, 21, 203; two founding nations rhetoric, 261n5
Bloch, Marc, 261n4
Blumenberg, Hans, rhetoric as policy, 54
Bolaria, B. Singh, multiculturalism a support for racism, 129
Bolsonaro, Jair, 18, 247n1

Bonhoeffer, Dietrich, 229
Bourdieu, Pierre, 38, 41, 44, 80, 126; against binary reading, 9; everyday theology of the state, 36; linear vision of power, 45; reification of concepts, 75; scholasticism, 85
Bramadat, Paul, 262n1
Brand, Dionne, 100; co-optation of civil society, 127; multicultural smugness, 197
Breton, Raymond, 121
Buchanan, James, undermining of democracy, 95, 187
Burnet, Jean, 123, 168

Caesar-Chavannes, Celina, 185
Cameron, David Robertson, 57
Camus, Albert, 195
Canadian Advisory Council on Multiculturalism, 132
Canadian Anti-Hate Network, 31
Canadian Arab Federation, 189
Canadian Centre for Policy Alternatives, 27
Canadian Consultative Council on Multiculturalism, 157
Cannon, Margaret, 128
capitalism, as cosmos, 235
Caravaggio, 244
Carmichael, Stokely, 131
Carty, Linda, 100; co-optation of civil society, 127
Cash, W.J., racism and class mystification, 264n1, 266n4
Charter of Rights, 124
Chesterton, G.K., 39; critique of realpolitik, 267n11
Chomsky, Noam: danger of fascist US, 254n9
Churchill, Winston, and Bengal famine, 65

citizen identification, 25, 224
civil service: demographic profile, 261n6; language policy, 174
Clarke, George Elliott, 101, 254n3
climate emergency, 7, 103, 109; and capitalism, 235; climate club proposal, 219; climate refugees, 19; impact of tar sands development, 260n30; implications for capitalism, 52; Kyoto accord, 52; political effects, 136; time-lag challenge, 237
Clinton, Hillary, 150; support for globalization, 247n3
Co-operative Commonwealth Federation, 53; Regina Manifesto, 54
Cole, Desmond, 238, 239
Commission on Systemic Racism (1992), 145–9
concepts: as blinkers, 231; collective, 75; essentially contested, 251n22; familiar vs. meaningful, 232; and fast thinking errors, 35; gross, 13, 184–6, 193, 231; as intellectual tools, 36, 231; as shorthand, 75; reification, 35, 75; thinking with vs. thinking about, 36
conservatism, ersatz, 6, 246n4
conservative critiques, definition, 6
Conservative Party of Canada: use of multiculturalism, 206; xenophobic advertising, 24
conspiracy theories, 37; great replacement, 18, 24, 66, 103
constrained normativity, 41, 240
Cools, Anne, 131
Coulthard, Glen Sean, 80, 251n18
COVID: anti–public health protests, 24, 128, 218; uneven distribution of cases, 29
Cox, Jo, murder of, 18, 24

Cuban Missile Crisis, 37, 42, 43
cultural Fordism, 3, 155, 192
culture: container view, 62–9, 251n18; multidimensional view, 63, 66

Day, Richard, 88, 110, 125, 180, 252n23, 253n3; alternative to multiculturalism, 111; anthropomorphized multiculturalism, 83; canonical Canadians, 92; conflation of person and actions, 262n4; conflation of person and culture, 67; constructionist ontology, 156, 259n25; DNA discourse, 93; essentialist view of multiculturalism, 71; false consciousness claim, 103; influence of, 80; multiculturalism an instrument of racial hierarchy, 129; multiculturalism as active agent, 83; mysterious power claims, 85, 87; night-watchman state, 6; passive voice formulations, 81; rejection of limits to tolerance, 182; tolerance as assimilation tactic, 182; trivialization of concentration camps, 87; undialectical split, 102
Day, Stockwell, childhood trauma, 30
Dei, George J. Sefa, 100
democracy, minimalist definition, 249n10
democratic self-governance: and global injustice, 220; normative and practical constraint, 266n7; progressive value, 220
demography: Canadian projections, 24; global immigration flows, 19; population decline in post-Soviet Europe, 19

Department of Canadian Heritage, 56
Derrida, Jacques, unconditional hospitality, 112–13
dialectical approach: definition, 98; Hegel, 268n2; limits, 100. *See also* undialectical analyses
DiAngelo, Robin, analytical weaknesses, 9
Dickens, Charles, Circumlocution Office, 250n14
Diefenbaker, John, 120
discernment, need for, 223, 233
DNA discourse, 93
Doctorow, Cory, 241
Douglas, Rosie, 131
Dua, Enakshi, 246n10
Duterte, Rodrigo, 18, 247n1

Eagleton, Terry, 215
Echaquan, Joyce, death of, 29
economic inequality, colour coded, 27
economics, neoclassical, 251n19
Edelman, Murray, 54
Egan, Brian, 102, 125
Eliot, T.S., 225
Elliott, Jean Leonard, 61, 132, 182, 183
Elrick, Jennifer, 163, 259n22, 260n32, 270
employment equity, 143
Engels, Frederick, 51; definition of dialectics, 253n2; second thoughts, 251n20; state-bourgeoisie relation, 39
Equality Now!, 1984 report, 61, 124, 158, 258n19
Erdoğan, Recep Tayyip, 18
ethnic majority, homogeneous, 92–7; political effects of assumption, 113

Fairclough, Ellen, 159
false consciousness, 86, 92, 101–6; of the ethnic majority?, 106; partial defence of concept, 103
Fanon, Frantz, recognition as manipulation, 5
Fantino, Julian, defence of police carding, 32
Farage, Nigel, xenophobic rhetoric, 18, 24
Farooq, Mustafa, 29
Faulkner, William, 197
FGM, 57, 62, 63
Fish, Stanley, 263n6; critique of Kymlicka, 185; critique of tolerance, 180, 182
Fleras, Augie, 132, 182; multiculturalism as deceptive agent, 83; multiculturalism as shackles, 86, 231; mysterious power statement, 86; postnational world, 218
Floyd, George, murder of, 139, 145
Forbes, Hugh Donald, 184, 186
Ford, Henry, 3
Forst, Rainer, permission conception of tolerance, 188
Foucault, Michel, 45, 88, 187, 223, 233, 243; disavowal of claims, 253n4; enthusiasm for unmasking, 254n9; obscurity as despotism, 79; Panopticism, 249n6; refusal to offer alternatives, 109; state tolerance of the intolerable, 190; understanding of power, 100, 241
Fox News, 18; promotion of xenophobia, 66
Frank, Thomas, 51, 68, 103
Fraser, Nancy, 255n11; recognition and redistribution, 231
Friedman, Milton, 40, 248n3

Fromm, Paul, inspiration for Charleston terrorist, 263n7

Gabriel, Christina: diversity as sales pitch, 57, 60; employment equity, 258n16
Gadamer, Hans-Georg: sense-making, 232
Galabuzi, Grace-Edward, 129, 132, 138; critique of state funding, 88; mysterious power statement, 86; roots of multiculturalism, 126
Galeano, Eduardo, 50
garbage can model, 172
Gardiner, Stephen, 237
Genuis, Garnett, 102
Giddens, Anthony, 40
Gilman, Sander L., 62, 63, 84, 250n15
globalization, 19
Goethe, Johann Wolfgang von, critique of tolerance, 180
Goldberg, David Theo, 180, 183
Goldman, Emma, 252n27
Gramsci, Antonio, 39, 67, 107, 125, 129, 140, 234, 249n9; good sense, 115; learning from enemies, 234; transformism, 144
Granatstein, Jack: prickly national pride, 225; support of Iraq invasion, 267n11
Griffith, Andrew, 47, 107

Habermas, Jürgen, 188, 255n11; authority of the better argument, 238; civic solidarity, 224; deliberative tolerance, 194; on the welfare state, 99; self-conscious multiculturalism, 253n2
Haidasz, Stanley, 122
Hansen, James, climate impact of tar sands development, 260n30

Haque, Eve, 13, 260n1; alternative to multiculturalism, 111; contradiction on language and culture in B&B Commission, 168; discomfort with limits, 182; manufactured crisis claim, 172; multiculturalism and bilingualism, 164–76; mysterious effects claim, 89; mysterious power statement, 85; unconditional hospitality, 112–13
Harper, Stephen: exclusion of Muslim refugees, 23; measures to intercept irregular migrants, 22; on committing sociology, 146
Harvey, David, spatially fixed capital, 218, 260n33
hate crime, 26–7, 56, 97, 210–12; official definitions, 27
Hayek, F.A.: liberal, not conservative, 245n4
Health Canada, 44, 55; Jr. Jays program, 45, 46
Hedges, Chris, 65, 66, 251n18
Hegel, G.W.F., 99, 268n2
hegemony, 115, 234, 236; capitalist, 136, 141; paradox of, 59
Henry, Frances, study of Toronto racism, 259n26
Herder, Johann Gottfried, 227, 267n14
Hérouxville, Quebec, 25
Hinkelammert, Franz, critique of Friedman, 248n3
Hobbes, Thomas: pity and contempt, 269n8
Hobsbawm, E.J., 153, 221
Hochschild, Arlie Russell, 68, 138, 216
Hum, Derek, 248n6; labour market analysis, 27

Huntington, Samuel, 243; clash of civilizations claim, 66
Hussen, Ahmed, 30, 238

ideal interests, 195; imagined superiority, 95, 197; in academia, 236; smugness, 197
ideology, 215–17; definition, 215; fog-producing, 240; meritocratic, 216; racism as mask, 217; universal phenomenon, 215
Ijaz, Nadine, 175
immigration: Conservative–Liberal public opinion split, 24; public support for, 20
immigration policy: history of racial exclusion, 133; international competition, 155–6; labour force needs, 151; points system, 23, 154; seasonal workers, 259n23, 260n31; shift in source countries, 154, 160; skilled vs. "cheap" labour strategy, 163, 260n33
Indigenous Canadians: condominium of oppression, 135; multiculturalism and memory, 208–9
interpellation, 68, 234
Iraq, invasion of, 94

James, Matt, 101, 126, 255n10, 267n12; caution on postmaterialism, 255n1
James, William, 42; network of beliefs, 81
Janis, Irving: groupthink, 45
jargon, 80
Jaworsky, John, 121, 158, 168
Jedwab, Jack, 33, 216, 224, 248n2
Joppke, Christian, 71, 192, 243, 269n10
Joyce, James, 262n7, 266n5

Kahneman, Daniel, fast thinking, 35, 63
Kanji, Khadijah, 79, 94
Kant, Immanuel, 41, 112, 262n5; communication and thought, 8; maxims of understanding, 233; obscurity of happiness, 104
Kashmeri, Zuhair, 249n7
Kelley, Ninette, 154, 157, 162, 259n23; alternative to skills-based immigration policy, 23; history of discriminatory immigration policy, 133, 151; international pressure on Canadian immigration policy, 138
Kenney, Jason, 47, 114, 189
Kent, Tom, 162
Keynes, John Maynard: business climate, 48; state fallibility, 49, 51
Khalid, Iqra, 205; anti-Islamophobia motion, 33
King, Martin Luther, 61, 99; aspirational national pride, 226
King, William Lyon Mackenzie: 1944 Throne Speech, 53; opposition to immigration from Asia, 133, 142
Koestler, Arthur: incubation, 108
Kogawa, Joy, 95, 119
Küng, Hans, 268n2
Kwan, Jenny, 206, 209
Kymlicka, Will, 4, 22, 67, 82, 120, 133, 162, 251n16, 252n25; bilingual education, 262n8; *Brown v Board of Education*, 137; critiqued by Fish, 185; liberal expectancy, 185; multiculturalism and pacification, 132; multiculturalism more than basic liberal rights, 211, 243–4; multiculturalism policy index, 73; points system-labour market mismatch, 162; really existing multiculturalism, 72

Lastman, Mel, diplomatic tact, 57
Latulippe, Henri, 131; social-nativism, 257n10
Laurendeau, André, 120, 172
Lawrence, Bonita, 246n10
Legault, François, quest for white immigrants, 31
Lenin, V.I., democracy as mask, 106
LePen, Marine, 257n10
Lepore, Jill, nationalism and patriotism, 221, 224
Lesage, Jean, 120
Leskov, Nikolai, 42, 249n4
Levant, Ezra, 33, 215
Li, Peter S., multiculturalism a support for racism, 129
Lippmann, Walter, 3, 253n1, 262n1
Loku, Andrew, killing of, 139
Longfellow, Henry Wadsworth, 79, 81
Lucki, Brenda, 145–7; understanding of systemic racism, 30
Lukács, Georg, 196, 239
Lupul, Manoly, 121, 123

Maalouf, Amin, 65, 182
Macdonald, John A., 169
Mackey, Eva, 55, 94, 127, 187, 220; asymmetrical tolerance, 187; critique of tolerance, 180, 181; discomfort with limits, 182; mysterious effects claim, 89; unmarked core culture, 94, 98
MacLean, Nancy, 95, 153, 155, 253n1
Mansur, Salim, 71; inflammatory rhetoric, 245n1
Marcuse, Herbert, 47
Martin, Trayvon, killing of, 139
Marx, Karl, 51, 61, 234, 236; collective agents, 252n29; conservative aspect of revolution, 7; fetishism, 75; illusions and social conditions, 228; original accumulation, 88; second thoughts, 251n20; state–bourgeoisie relation, 39; struggle between and within classes, 49; unidimensional model of actors, 67
mask hypothesis, 33, 99, 214
McAndrew, Marie, evolution of multiculturalism spending, 265n1
McCarthy, Thomas, evolution of racism, 258n17, 265n2
McRoberts, Kenneth, 168
Melville, Herman, 262n2
Mendus, Susan, 180, 183
methodological individualism, 40, 248n3
Michaels, Walter Benn, 145, 211
Miliband, Ralph, ideological controls within state, 48
Miller, Marc, 30
Mills, Charles W., 134; race solidarity claim, 138
Mintzberg, Henry, 45
Mishra, Pankaj, 17, 18, 146; compulsory modernization, 49
Modi, Narendra, 18, 247n1, 265n4
moral economy, 58
multiculturalism: abolition of?, 106–8; alternatives to?, 108–13; and bilingualism, 164–76; and historical memory, 197, 207–9; anthropomorphized, 83; anti-backlash policy, 140; anti-Ford vision, 3–5, 88; as climate of opinion, 71; as ideological tool, 215; as mask, 33; conservative critiques, 4; conservative media coverage, 21; contested meaning, 71–2; history, 119–63; multiculturalism hypothesis, 157;

multiculturalism policy index, 73; multiculturalism-J, 73–4, 243–4; neoliberal multiculturalism, 74; really existing multiculturalism, 72; song and dance, 252n27; support for racism?, 129
Multiculturalism Act (1988), 55
Munro, John, 157
Murdoch, Iris, 184, 185
mystery writing, 8, 234; costs, 12; multiculturalism as subject of sentence, 82; mysterious effects, 89–90; mysterious power, 85–8; mysterious subjects, 81–5; passive voice formulations, 81; political effects, 90, 113–15; relation to thought, 8

nation: continued relevance, 218, 220; working definition, 266n5
National Council for Canadian Muslims, 29
national imaginary claims, 93
National Post: coverage of BLM, 139; multiculturalism coverage, 21
national pride, 221–8; and liberation movements, 221; as shield, 221; definition, 215; dimensions of differentiation, 223, 227; nationalism and patriotism, 221
Nehru, Jawaharlal, 226
Netanyahu, Benjamin, 18, 247n1
Nicaraguan revolution, 254n4
Nishiguchi, R.L. Gabrielle, 222
Nordhaus, William, 266n6; climate club proposal, 219
Nordlinger, Eric, 50
Nova Scotia Human Rights Commission, 31
Nussbaum, Martha, 217, 224–6; essential role of nation, 219, 220; law and sentiments, 193; love and justice, 70; political emotions, 57; progressive role of nationalism, 222

Ockham, William of, 250n15
Okin, Susan Moller, 62, 63
Ollman, Bertell, 253n2
Ontario Human Rights Commission, 32
Orbán, Viktor, 18, 19, 66, 247n1, 257n10
Oreopoulos, Philip, 69, 147
Orwell, George, 214

Pal, Leslie: anaemic multiculturalism, 132; anatomy of policy, 53; state elite monitoring US events, 130; state funding of civil society, 100, 127, 128; symbolic policy impact, 123
Pamuk, Orhan, 196
paradigms: as tools, 85; not self-validating, 85
Parekh, Bhikhu, 70, 181
Parizeau, Jacques: referendum meltdown, 199
parliamentary multiculturalism discourse, 202–11; celebratory statements, 203; critical resource statements, 205; over-the-line statements, 203, 227
Parti Québécois, 173
passive voice, political effects, 82, 253n1
patriotism, shallow, 25. *See also* national pride
Pearl Harbor, 43
Pearson, Lester, 120, 123
permissive causes, 217, 265n3
Perry, Barbara, 97, 212
Peterloo Massacre, 236, 256n6
Piketty, Thomas, 201, 219, 257n10

Pinker, Steven, 250n11
Plato, on persuasion, 240
Plutarch, need for discernment, 223, 233
Poilievre, Pierre, analytical prowess, 146
Polanyi, Karl, 103; countermovement, 230; skittishness of capital, 128
Polanyi, Michael, 230; paradigms as tools, 85; subsidiary awareness, 36
police: Arar inquiry, 150; mental illness and killing by, 248n7; Montreal police strike, 149; Ottawa occupation, 190, 258n20; police violence at Toronto G20 summit, 259n20; power of job action threat, 149; racial disparities in killing by, 30, 32, 148; racial disparities in street checks, 31; racism in Thunder Bay Police Service, 32; RCMP intervention in 2005–6 election, 150; systemic racism in RCMP, 30
policy: anatomy, 53–7; can be pushed further, 60; imperfect permeation of society, 58, 97–8; rhetorical uses, 59
political correctness, 185, 263n6
Porter, John, 122, 167; Canada a demographic railway station, 259n21; critique of concept of culture, 64; disappearance of non-official languages, 175; global South brain drain, 23; role of immigration in post-war economy, 151
Poulantzas, Nicos, 50
Powell, Enoch, 155
progressive critics: affinities with conservatives, 5, 98, 102; contrast with conservatives, 90; essential role, 217, 242

progressive critiques, definition, 6
progressive thought, maxims, 233–7
progressivism, conservative dimension of, 6
Proust, Marcel, 192; verbal overshadowing, 231
public–private partnerships, 46
Putin, Vladimir, 18

QAnon, 24; influence in Canada, 218
Quebec, exit option, 171
Quiet Revolution, 120
Qutb, Sayyid, 137

race: class as race, 153, 265n2; founding races discourse, 121, 165; race solidarity?, 138, 257n13
racism: anti-allophonic, 32; anti-Asian, 29, 30; anti-Black, 28, 29; anti-Chinese, 31; anti-indigenous, 29, 30, 32; anti-Muslim, 32; anti-Semitic, 31; and class mystification, 264n1, 266n4; as mask, 217
racism, systemic, 145–50, 258n20; definition, 145; sustained by individual agents, 52
rational actor model, 40, 41, 248n3
rational choice theory, 95, 237
Rawls, John, 41, 185, 193, 269n11; coercive transactions, 253n5; critique of rational actor model, 248n3; need for cultures to bend, 244; original position, 73; reasonable vs. rational, 249n3; veil of ignorance, 220
recognition, as gross concept, 231
Reed, Adolph, 216; critique of neoliberal diversity, 74; against reification of "whiteness," 268n4
Reed, Touré F., 268n5
relativism, 212, 265n6

remittances, 23
Ricento, Thomas, 94
Robinson, Cedric, race as justification of domination, 217
Rousseau, Jean-Jacques: civic love, 224

Saint-Léonard, Quebec, school controversy, 172
Sandel, Michael, 58; coercive transactions, 253n5
Sanders, Bernie, 139
Sandinistas, 254n4
Sarkozy, Nicolas, 22
Satzewich, Vic, 248n2; Canadian fears of irregular immigration, 22; contingency of Canadian support for immigration, 23
Scheer, Andrew, 193; rhetoric on immigration, 24
Schutz, Alfred, 105, 230
Scott, James C., 43
Sen, Amartya, 64–6, 107, 251n20; rational fools, 248n3
settler-colonialism, 165, 260n1
Shakespeare, William, 130, 258n18
Shapiro, Ian, gross concepts, 184
Sharma, Nandita, 83, 101, 102; Indigenous claims as neo-racism, 246n10
Shelley, Percy Bysshe, 236
Sifton, Clifford, 155, 265n2; economic criteria trump "race" ones, 153; policy proposals rejected, 153; racial understanding of class, 153; understanding of "quality" immigration, 152
Simpson, Wayne, 248n6; labour market analysis, 27
Sir George Williams affair, 130–2, 156, 256n7–257n10; 2022 Concordia apology, 256n7; masterminded by Mao?, 131

Sloan, Derek: anti-Chinese xenophobia, 31; white supremacist support, 263n7
Smith, Adam, 265n2; critique of colonialism, 51; insolence of human wretchedness, 241
social constructionism, 90
social-nativism, 257n10
Special Committee on Hate Propaganda in Canada, 155
Spicer, Keith, 122
Stanfield, Robert, 122
state: capitalist, 47–52, 135–7; conflicts between state organizations, 43–4; democratic constraints, 50; fallible, 49, 51; funding of civil society, 88, 127; individual interests within, 44–5; inter-state competition, 49; need for relative autonomy, 50; set of organizations, 41–4; spectrum of responses to pressure, 126; staffed by individuals, 39–40; white supremacist?, 134–50, 162
Statistics Canada, 260n28; demographic projections, 24; hate crime data and definition, 26–7
Stone, Deborah, 26
Streeck, Wolfgang, 50, 58, 135, 250n12; conflicting state imperatives, 51
structures and individuals, 52, 229

Task Force on Government Information (1969), 46, 130
Taylor, Charles, 67; ontology, 156; politics of recognition, 71, 252n24; subtraction stories, 222
terrorism: Charleston S.C., 263n7; Charlie Hebdo attack, 37; Christchurch, 18; disparities in media coverage, 254n5; El Paso,

18, 66; London, ON, 28; lone wolf theory, 146; Oslo, 71, 245n1; Quebec City, 24; 11 September attacks, 97
Thatcher, Margaret, 40
Therborn, Goran, 250n10
Thobani, Sunera, 97, 107, 137, 266n7; analytical path not taken, 96; condominium of oppression, 257n12; co-optation of civil society, 127; DNA discourse, 93; false consciousness claims, 86, 102, 104; homogeneous ethnic majority, 13, 94, 95, 114; imputed state goal, 141, 258n14; influence of, 80; law as violence, 187; multicultural erasure of history, 197; multicultural smugness, 197; multiculturalism and class prejudice, 201, 216; multiculturalism as active agent, 82; multiculturalism as mask, 33; multiculturalism supports white supremacy, 102, 129; mysterious effects claim, 89; mysterious power statement, 86; mystery writing, 80; national imaginary claims, 93; national subjects, 92; origin of multiculturalism, 126; passive voice formulations, 82; problematic reading of official texts, 142; self-governance dilemma, 220; unidimensional vision of human identity, 96
thoughtlessness, 187, 233
Three Percenters, 218
Thucydides, debate at Melos, 237
Tocqueville, Alexis de: culpable tolerance, 190; racial understanding of class, 153, 216; unenlightened egoism, 222
tolerance, 179–94; agent of assimilation?, 182; asymmetrical tolerance, 187–8; culpable tolerance, 190; definitions, 179; deliberative tolerance, 194; forbearance tolerance, 183; as gateway, 191–3; as obstacle, 191; permission conception, 188; religious practices and forbearance tolerance, 190–1; and repugnance, 180
traditional Chinese medicine, 175
Trebilcock, Michael, 154, 157, 162, 259n23; alternative to skills-based immigration policy, 23; history of discriminatory immigration policy, 133, 151; international pressure on Canadian immigration policy, 138
Triadafilopoulos, Triadafilos, 159, 160, 260n27–9
Trilateral Commission, crisis of democracy claim, 50
Trudeau, Justin, 24, 238; attack on BDS movement, 263n11; critique of tolerance, 181; measures to intercept irregular migrants, 22; symbolic gestures, 20; tar sands support, 161
Trudeau, Pierre Elliott, 13, 121, 122, 132, 168; 1971 policy declaration, 85, 123, 157, 163, 164, 255n4; justification of language hierarchy, 170, 171; multiculturalism and national identity, 198
Trump, Donald, 18, 24, 90; anti-globalization rhetoric, 247n3; appeal to American workers, 19; Islamophobic tweets, 18; on murder of George Floyd, 146; praise of neo-Nazis, 18; support from small communities, 25
Truth and Reconciliation Commission, 209, 260n1

Ukrainian-Canadian Congress, 170
Ukranian Canadian Committee, 122
undialectical analyses, 101, 236; political effects, 113
United Conservative Party, 30; homophobia, 247n2
Universal Declaration of Human Rights, 133, 143

Veblen, Thorstein, 195
verbal overshadowing, 230
Vimy Ridge, marketing of, 223
Visegrád group, 25
visible minority: criticism of concept, 248n2; justification of concept, 259n24

Waal, Frans de, 227
Wacquant, Loïc, 148
Walcott, Rinaldo, 83, 84, 90, 125; undialectical split, 83
Wallace-Wells, David, 19, 52
Walton-Roberts, Margaret, 154; mysterious effects claim, 89
Weber, Max, 35, 44, 65, 198; against binary reading, 9; causality, 265n3; domination and legitimacy, 215; material and ideal interests, 195; transient role of Protestant ethic, 234; "damned duty," 48, 234

Williams, Eric, racism born of slavery, 217
Winter, Elke, 101, 108, 114, 243; shift in Canadian identity, 20, 22, 198, 210, 252n25; triangular relations, 196–8, 201, 209, 264n2
Wohlstetter, Roberta, 43
Wollstonecraft, Mary, 60
Wolterstorff, Nicholas, 194
World Bank, 19, 23

Yegenoglu, Meyda, 112
Yellow Vest Canada, 31
Yuzyk, Paul, 169; acceptance of language hierarchy, 174; critique of biculturalism, 166, 260n2; Senate speech on multiculturalism, 166; settler-colonial language, 260n1

Zaccardelli, Giuliano, intervention in 2005-6 election, 150
Zafis, Mohamed-Aslim: murder of, 29
Ziadah, Rafeef, 189, 263n11
Žižek, Slavoj, 108, 187; critique of tolerance, 182; multicultural smugness, 197; multiculturalism is racism, 94; nihilistic opposition to limits, 267n10

www.ingramcontent.com/pod-product-compliance
Ingram Content Group UK Ltd.
Pitfield, Milton Keynes, MK11 3LW, UK
UKHW041847020425
457001UK00002B/186